UNIVERSITY OF LAUSANNE
Faculty of Theology

FREEDOM IN MISSION:
THE PERSPECTIVE
OF THE KINGDOM OF GOD

AN ECUMENICAL INQUIRY

THESIS
submitted to the Faculty of Theology of the University of Lausanne
to obtain the degree of Doctor of Theology

by
EMILIO CASTRO

WCC Publications, Geneva
1985

Imprimatur

The Council of the Theological Faculty, University of Lausanne, on the basis of a report by a commission composed of professors Claude Geffré, O.P., Paris, Ion Bria (WCC, Geneva) and Klauspeter Blaser, supervisor, authorizes publication of the thesis of the Rev. Emilio Castro entitled "Freedom in Mission: the Perspective of the Kingdom of God — an Ecumenical Inquiry", defended in public on 12 November 1984. The opinions expressed by the author are not necessarily those of the Council.

Dean of the Faculty of Theology
Pierre Gisel

Cover design: Michael Dominguez
ISBN 2-8254-0824-7
© 1985 Emilio Castro
This thesis has been published by the Publications Office of the World Council of Churches, 150, route de Ferney, 1211 Geneva 20, Switzerland.

TABLE OF CONTENTS

FOREWORD

It is impossible for me even to attempt to name all the many
friends who have helped in shaping and formulating my thoughts,
but I would like to mention a few:

Prof. Klauspeter Blaser, my tutor, whose critical remarks and
suggestions were essential to the formation of my work;

The Iliff School of Theology in Denver, Colorado, its President,
Dr Donald Messer, and the staff and students who provided an
excellent occasion to organize and test my ideas;

Ms Jean Stromberg, my co-worker over many years in the editing
of the International Review of Mission, for her untiring work in
editing my "Spanglish";

Mr T.K. Thomas for his cooperation in preparing the manuscript for
publication.

Special recognition goes to Ms Ursula Zierl, my colleague in the
World Council of Churches' Commission on World Mission and
Evangelism, who faithfully and indefatigably worked on the
ordering of the bibliography and typed the manuscript many times.

My thanks go also to my daughter Ruth for her cooperation in
typing the first draft of the original project, and last but not
least to my wife Gladys whose patience and inspiration is behind
each chapter.

Emilio Castro

INTRODUCTION

The central thesis of this book is given in its title: mission, understood in the perspective of the kingdom of God, allows -- even demands -- total freedom to serve that kingdom, to partici- pate in its announcement and in its manifestation. A recognition of this Christian freedom could generate untapped resources of imagination and energies in the churches; it could save us from frustrating discussions around secondary issues and provide unity for the most diverse forms of the church missionary vocations in the service of Jesus, the Servant King.[1]

This book is in two distinct parts. The first part, a biblical, theological discussion of the kingdom of God and its missionary implications, begins with a reference to several situations where churches are confronting difficult choices as they make missionary decisions. This is followed by an analysis of the world ecumenical discussion on missionary priorities during the last twelve years, highlighting the values that are at stake, both in local situations and in ecumenical dialogue. The biblical symbol of the kingdom of God, seen as the focal point of Jesus' ministry, is presented as the basic theological category in consideration of the mission of the church. The first part concludes with the affirmation that the nature of the kingdom of God invites and expects free and imaginative responses, from Christians and churches, which point towards the King, Jesus the Christ, and the coming kingdom, the new earth and the new heaven.

The second part introduces a series of articles, written ap- proximately during the same period as is covered in the survey of international discussion, where the basic hypothesis of this book has been explored and discussed.

The articles are organized under the following titles:

1. Mission in the Perspective of the Kingdom

2. Latin American Kairos

3. The Church and its Agenda in the Mission of the Kingdom

4. Mission Yesterday - Today - Tomorrow

While it has been my privilege to be in close relationship with churches in mission in many parts of the world, the dominant perspective here is Latin American. We have learned that it is impossible to do theology in a neutral context, and I hope my own personal perspective does not distort the main argument of the book -- that the kingdom framework should enable us to develop many different forms of missionary obedience which, through creative dialogue, complement and enrich one another.

PART 1

A Biblical, Theological Discussion
of the Kingdom of God
and its Missionary Implications

Chapter I

A LOOK AT THE SITUATION

For several years an American missionary had shared the gospel
with the local animistic people in a West African country. He
is a committed Christian with an evangelistic orientation. He
is back in the United States now. His present mission, he says,
is to give whatever help he can to families whose gas supply is
cut, in the middle of winter, because of their inability to pay
the gas bills.

Any assembly of the World Council of Churches is seen to cover
the most diverse human concerns; from genetics to the problems
of Afghanistan, from nuclear power to monastic life, from worship
to the condemnation of racism. No wonder some people have
commented ironically: "They seem to be the U.N. at prayer!"

How do Christians and churches find and define their missionary
obedience? Do we have some canonical laws, some discipline book,
that establishes our missionary tasks and responsibilities? What
is the specific vocation of Christians and churches? What makes
a church different from other human communities involved in
service to humankind?

These are vital questions for the churches everywhere.[1] They
are questions of life and death for Christians in many parts of
the world. Churches and Christians trace their missionary
vocation to Jesus' commandment "to make disciples of all nations,
baptizing them in the name of the Father, the Son and of the
Holy Spirit, teaching them to observe all that I have commanded
you" (Mt 28:18-20), but they are divided in their assessment of
what needs to be done as *mission* in particular places and times.
There are even critical voices which question the very relevance
of world mission, especially the possibility of its implementation through cross-cultural missions.[2]

Such differences and reservations are basically expressions of
different missionary options and priorities. But they are
generally taken as conflicting options and irreconcilable
approaches. Is it not possible, however, that these are complementary and not contradictory? That is not to suggest that
everybody is right and there are no special ecclesial understandings of situations which call for particular options and
common action of a distinctive nature.

They are nevertheless complementary in the sense that each one
of our priorities could, or should, become an entry point to the
total project of God's love. Our affirmation of freedom in mission
refers specifically to the unlimited possibilities which churches
and Christians have to join in the struggle of the kingdom of God.

Let us take a look at some of the situations in the world
today where churches try to define their mission as they face
diverse circumstances and respond to different challenges.

LATIN AMERICA - THE BURDEN OF HISTORY

Latin America is the so-called Christian continent. We have
almost five centuries of Christian presence and evangelization.
The priest came with the soldiers, the church with the conquerors.
The strange mixture of the cross and the sword led to the
Christianization of Latin America. It is, perhaps, the best
example of the total conversion of a continent to the Christian
faith. Statistically speaking, more than ninety per cent of the
people in Latin America would consider themselves Christian,
most of them Roman Catholic. So, if our fundamental criteria
were the planting of the church, the growth of the church and
the baptism of all people, we could indeed be very pleased with
the situation in Latin America.[3]

But with almost five centuries of domination, and of the
oppression of the native, black, and poor populations of Latin
America behind us, can we feel satisfied because almost everybody is Christian? With what yardstick of the kingdom do we
measure the situation in Latin America?[4]

Today we are acutely aware of this ambiguous and sinful situation.
Through data provided by the social sciences on the relations of
power in Latin American society, we now understand how the economy
works against poor people.[5] We cannot any longer plead ignorance;
we know how people are oppressed, and the political and economic
forces working against them.

We do not only know the facts. We also see the awakening of
people. Themselves conscientized the poor people expect the
churches to take a clear stand. The poor are discovering that
their plight is not a matter of fate or providence. It is not
God's will.[6] It is the consequence of relations of power, of
the prevailing structures in society, and so the poor are
now organizing themselves to challenge those structures.
These very same poor people, who are aware of their predicament,
are members of churches and faithful participants in the life of
congregations. The people of Latin America are poor, and they
are believers![7] How will the churches respond to a faith that
refuses to accept poverty as ordained by God?

The churches in Latin America have gone through a great biblical
renewal. Since the Second Vatican Council, the whole attitude of
the Roman Catholic Church to the Bible has changed dramatically;
today in almost every country in Latin America it cooperates
with the United Bible Society in the publication and distribution
of the Bible.[8] Thousands of Basic Ecclesial Communities meet to

4

read the Bible, to pray, and to face practical questions. How do we work for God's justice, they ask: how do we change our situation?(9) The theology of liberation has developed and it has promoted an historical reading of the Bible which seeks to recover the socio-political and economic context in which the Bible was written, and tries to come to grips with the biblical message in relation to the social, political, cultural, and economic realities of our day.(10)

The knowledge we have acquired of our past and our present, the growing historical awareness of the poor, the biblical renewal: all these have dramatically posed the question to the Latin American churches: What is our Christian vocation? What is our Christian identity? If the kingdom of God has to do with God's will in all realms of life, searching questions inevitably pose themselves to the Christian church.

And the answer was heard all over the continent: We are the church of the powerless Christ who made his own the fate of the poor and the least. Nothing short of the affirmation of *God's preferential option for the poor* and a programme evolved in the light of that affirmation could do justice to our present mission-ary calling.

In 1968 in Medellín, Colombia, and 1979 in Puebla, Mexico, the Conference of Roman Catholic Bishops affirmed such solidarity with the poor.(11) The pronouncements of both gatherings were preceded and followed by intense controversy. Traditionalists and progressivists clashed. Ideological differences were evident all along. But a clear emphasis had emerged. Within the Catholic Church there was a radical change of priorities and of pastoral emphasis. Now they are in the middle of the turmoil produced in the social, political and economic life of these nations through this radical change. The alliance between the sword and the cross has given place to a solidarity with the downtrodden and con-frontation with the powerful.(12)

We have so far referred primarily to the four or five hundred years of Christian *Catholic* presence in Latin America. The Prot-estants came to Latin America in the second half of the nine-teenth century. Most of them came invited by the more liberal-minded people, Free Masons, who were interested in fighting the cultural and political control of the Roman Catholic Church.(13) Protestants could say: "We have rejected the traditional Christianity that is dominant in Latin America and we represent a more liberal outlook, a more progressive perspective."

But we must take such claims with a pinch of salt, because Protestantism brought its own neo-colonialism. The expansion of U.S. Protestant churches abroad took place in a way that was suspiciously parallel or coincided with the colonial and commercial expansion of the United States.(14) Thus, while it is true that simply because we are small in number we cannot, as

Protestants, be accused of the same complicity that the Catholic
Church had with the dominant establishment in Latin America, we
cannot naively pretend to be innocent of the *de facto* complicity
with the *actual* forces of domination in the life of our nations.
Protestant missions also include new sects and groups, especially in Central America, who proclaim a gospel that defends the
"values of western civilization". In the name of fighting communism, they work actively against all forces for change in Latin
American society.*(15)*

The Protestant churches, however, have gone through the same
process of conversion as the Roman Catholic Church. They too have
become aware of the situation of the poor and the socio-political
forces behind such poverty. This awareness came to an institutional manifestation in the Conference in 1981, in Huampaní,
Peru, of the Latin American Council of Churches (CLAI) which represents more than a hundred Protestant churches. CLAI has taken
a clear stand, and has called upon the churches to become involved
in the struggle to overcome all dependence and oppression.
"Wherever a single human being is prevented from living humanly,
there we have a situation of sin. Love and justice must become
manifest in all aspects of life."

Through a "Pastoral (ministry) of Consolation", CLAI has made the
churches increasingly aware of the repeated violations of human
rights and of the plight of displaced populations and political
refugees. For Protestant churches in Latin America, evangelism
understood as church growth has been the non-negotiable priority.
Now they are obliged to see that priority against the background
of a new understanding of their past history and of the total
human reality.*(16)*

Our ecumenical challenge today, whether we are Catholic or
Protestant, is to face the question: What is the missionary
obedience that corresponds to our past history, to our present
awareness and to the demands of the kingdom, as we read the Bible
today? In this ecumenical era we face together the question of
the future.

Let me illustrate this with a few concrete situations.

Pope John Paul II visited Nicaragua in 1983. He spent only eight
or nine hours in the country. He celebrated mass, when his
message focused on the authority of the church.*(17)*

The Pope called the Nicaraguan people, and especially the
Nicaraguan priests, to recognize the central authority of the
bishops. He saw that the unity of the church was jeopardized
by the participation of priests in the Sandinist government!

One particular episode during the visit dramatically illustrated
the situation. On the Pope's arrival, Father Ernesto Cardenal,
Minister of Culture, knelt before the Pope, who rebuked him and

said: "You must put your relation with the church in order." In the Pope's understanding, the option of working at the political level, in this moment of the country's history, was the wrong option for a priest.(18)

Of course, this could be interpreted simply as a political, ideological difference of opinion. The Pope, or his advisers, do not feel convinced that the Sandinist government can deliver the goods; the priests think it can. That is a matter of political judgement. But the discussion is not at that level, it relates to what is the *central* vocation or *priority* of the church.(19)

What are the arguments for going beyond the traditional observance of priestly functions in local parishes to assume responsibilities in the government of a nation? The Pope seems to be saying: "The kingdom of God must become manifest through the work of the parish." The priests are saying: "The kingdom of God must also become manifest through the building up of a new social organization in our country."

Or take a similar dilemma, now from a Protestant angle.

In 1981, a military coup took place in Guatemala and a new general, Efraim Rios Montt, came into power.(20) He announced that he was a "born again" Christian who belonged to a small church, Verbo, from California, USA. He supported a whole range of Protestant activities in the country. Several groups in the United States put to young people the challenge of a missionary vocation; their goal was to send one thousand American missionaries to Guatemala to take advantage of this God-given chance to evangelize a country with four or five hundred years of Christian history! While many new missionaries were going to Guatemala, and many evangelistic campaigns were under way, the genocide of the Indians in the mountains continued and those who were calling for justice continued to be eliminated!(21)

For some Christians the kingdom of God in Guatemala demanded the defiance of the powerful; they opted to suffer with the little ones, even at the risk of death.(22) For others the priority was to "save" as many souls as possible. Behind this dilemma is the same old question: What is the goal of Christian mission? Are we in the business of saving individuals who will receive a passport to go to certain bliss in heaven or are we called to announce the rule of God, calling for justice and the defense of the "little ones"? Are we in the business of "converting" individuals or are we called as Christians to serve the cause of the kingdom of God which implies the transformation of the whole reality?

Or are we posing the wrong questions? Do we need to accept this either/or? What is the interplay between a religious experience and a Christian participation in the total human struggle?

Church Growth and Social Justice

In South Korea, traditionally a Buddhist country, the church is
growing very fast. Today about twenty-two or twenty-three per
cent of the population confess the Christian faith. Church growth
in Korea is a recent phenomenon, and the rate of growth shows no
sign of slowing down.(23) But the central concern of the churches
there is not evangelism. Evangelism simply happens!

The military government is interested in promoting and supporting
church work insofar as it gives the masses of people a sense of
achievement, and of success and happiness. Through belonging to
successful church movements, people could become alienated from
the problems of a society that is growing too fast economically
along neo-capitalist lines. Christians are confronted with the
question: Should we be satisfied with growth at this pace, making
of it our only goal, or should we also face the situation of the
little ones, the poor people, who are the victims of minimal
salaries and demanding work schedules, and are sacrificed to
promote the economic development of the society?

On the one hand, there are successful stories of church growth(24)
and, on the other, stories of persons related to urban industrial
mission who are paying the price for organizing the poor to
struggle for their rights.(25) But church growth and social
justice concerns do not contradict each other. Some of those who
went to jail are pastors of growing congregations!

Church growth is a very useful social tool; it makes the churches
all the more useful as they live in solidarity with the poor.
We cannot say no to evangelism and to church growth because all
people have the right to a personal knowledge of Jesus Christ.
Who am I to decide who should be converted and who should not?

No, theologically there is no contradiction. But it is a
situation where we are confronted with the temptation to be
content with the fact of rapid church growth and the temptation
to sidestep questions of where the kingdom of God is suffering
violence.(26)

For the churches in Korea the challenge is to put all the gifts
of the church, including its growth, at the service of the poor.
It is to see the growth of the churches not as a process which
alienates people from the real dilemmas of society, but as an
invitation to participate in the total endeavour to shape society
more in accordance with God's will and the pattern of God's
kingdom.(27)

Conversion or Renewal?

With the exception of the Philippines, Christianity in Asia
is a minority religion, and it lives side by side with highly
developed religious systems. It could be said that from a purely numerical point of view Christian mission in Asia has been
a failure! But, important as numbers are, they do not tell the
whole story. The kingdom values have been shared and the gospel
has had its impact on Asian cultures.

We must, however, face the reality of missionary history. We
cannot ignore the widespread revival of ancient religions. Nor
can we ignore the need to assure a decent possibility of life
for the masses of poor people in the Asian countries. No wonder
Christians and churches are raising crucial questions, and re-
thinking the nature and the future of the missionary endeavour.

C.S. Song, a theologian from Taiwan, writes about the calling of
Christians and churches to participate in the renewal and the
re-animation of Asian cultures. They cannot be ambassadors of
the western cultures. They are called to share the gospel from
within these Asian cultures, participate fully in the renewal
of the cultural life of the Asian nations -- even in the renewal
and re-animation of Asian religions. (28)

Theologians in India have been working with similar realities.
Should we baptize people into the Christian community? Often
baptism symbolizes the breaking of family and communal ties, so
should the "converts" be urged to remain in their families and
communities, and try to discover the meaning of Christ from the
centre of the cultural and religious values of the nation? Is
there any chance that a marriage similar to the one between the
gospel and the Hellenistic culture could happen between the Indian
culture shaped by religion and the Christian gospel? M.M. Thomas
thus talks about a Christ-centred syncretism! (29)

Tissa Balasuriya, a Roman Catholic theologian from Sri Lanka,
conveyed some of the indignation present in this passionate
search for Asian Christian authenticity: "As an Asian I cannot
accept as divine and true any teaching which begins with the
presupposition that all my ancestors for innumerable generations
are eternally damned by God unless they had been baptized in or
were related to one of the Christian institutional churches.
Theology must honestly respect these millions upon millions of
my ancestors and future human beings, before I can accept
theology as a true interpretation of revelation from a loving
God, Father of all." And again. "We have to rethink basically
our 'conversion mentality'. We have to rid ourselves of a
competitive mentality with regard to other religions; suspicions
need to be replaced by warmth and a desire for understanding." (30)

In January 1979 the EATWOT Asian Theological Conference met in Sri
Lanka on the theme "Asia's Struggle for Full Humanity: Towards a

9

Relevant Theology". There conflict and tension surfaced as new and old perspectives met in open confrontation. With much difficulty the Conference agreed upon a final statement. It said:

To be authentically Asian, theology must be immersed in our historical-cultural situation and grow out of it. A theology that emerged from the people's struggle for liberation would spontaneously formulate itself in the religio-cultural idioms of the people.

In many parts of Asia, we must integrate into our theology the insights and values of the major religions, but this integration must take place at the level of action and commitment to the people's struggle and not to be merely intellectual or elitist. These traditions of Asia's great religions seem to understand liberation in two senses: liberation from selfishness both within each person and in society. These religious traditions also contain a strong motivation for personal conversion in life. These religions, together with our indigenous cultures, can provide the Asian sense in our task of generating the new person and the new community. We view them as a potential source of a permanent critique of any established order and a pointer towards the building of a truly human society. We are conscious, however, of the domesticating role religions have often played in the past, so we need to subject both our religion and our culture to sustained self-criticism. In this context, we question the academic preoccupation to work toward the so-called "indigenization" or "inculturation" of theology divorced from participation in the liberational struggle in history. In our countries today there can be no truly indigenized theology that is not liberational. Involvement in the history and struggle of the oppressed is the guarantee that our theology is both liberating and indigenous.(31)

To some Christians outside Asia, all this will sound like very dangerous language.(32) We must listen, however, to what Christian people who are in daily contact with people of other religious persuasions are saying. They invite us to enter into a necessary dialogue with people of other faiths, and not to assume that a western aggressive understanding of the missionary activity of the church is the only understanding that could correspond to faithfulness to the gospel.(33) We need to raise with them basic questions: For example, what are the kingdom values that one promotes when calling the Christian communities in Asia to participate in the renewal of society? What are the biblical criteria that are basic to one's option there?(34) We could have different ways of expressing our Christian obedience but we need to be able to justify these to each other in terms of a basic common Christian conviction that is articulated in a way that will provide reciprocal inspiration and correction.(35)

AFRICA

Struggle for Authenticity

Where is the Christian missionary priority at this given moment in Africa? Let me quote Desmond Tutu, the General Secretary of the South African Council of Churches. Writing about Christian churches and Christian theology in Africa, he says:

> *African theology has failed to produce a sufficiently sharp cutting edge. It has seemed to advocate disengagement from the hectic business of life because very little has been offered that is pertinent, say, about the theology of power in the face of the epidemics of coups and military rule, about development, poverty, disease, and other equally urgent present-day issues. I believe this is where the abrasive black theology from America may have a few lessons for African theology. It may help to recall African theology to its vocation to be concerned for the poor and the oppressed, about (people's) needs for liberation from all kinds of bondage to enter into an authentic personhood which is constantly undermined by pathological religiosity and by political authority that has whittled away much personal freedom without too much opposition from the church. (36)*

Look at his list of priorities of missionary options for the church: a consideration of the question of power from the Christian perspective confronting all the military coups that take place in Africa; a clear position on poverty, disease; the liberation from all kinds of bondage. Desmond Tutu is a bishop of the Anglican Church. Of course he is interested in all aspects of the life of the church, but he affirms that in the particular situation of South Africa or Africa in general they cannot go on with business as usual. They cannot be uninvolved; they are obliged to confront all these missionary frontiers where Christian presence and witness is necessary.

Many Christians in Africa are with Bishop Tutu in his passionate plea for Christian participation in liberation struggles. On this they are one with Christians from all regions of the world who realize the historical nature of the Christian gospel and the challenge to God's loving will posed by the prevailing injustices of today. But African churches and African theologians do face specific problems and they are raising concrete theological questions that are relevant for our missiological research. Fundamentally they try to recover an African identity, a sense of authenticity in their response to the gospel. They do this by affirming values of the traditional culture and religion of Africa, not simply as a way to facilitate the penetration of the gospel, but to contribute to the total spiritual richness of the Christian church. So M. Oduyoye:

> *We must note that since "traditional" life was permeated in all its aspects by religion, any appeal we make to traditional values and practices is ultimately religious. Also we must bear in mind that the basic element in religion does not consist of practices of cultic places and persons but the beliefs that are manifested through them. So that even when modernization has modified ceremonies and other cultic practices, human beings will continue to depend on the beliefs as a rock on which to build. So, for example, the belief in the living-dead, in the existence of spirits, and in magic and witchcraft are a*

11

*part of the African's recognition that life is not entirely materialistic.
These beliefs are an expression of the yearning for life after life.
Since the Supreme Being is believed to be the Source of Life, the search
after the life-force is itself a groping for a closer and more personal
relationship with Being Itself.*

*To contribute more effectively to the religious development of people,
African Christian theologians have a duty to theologize from this
context and incorporate the authentic African idiom to Christian theology.
Utilizing African religious beliefs in Christian theology is not an
attempt to assist Christianity to capture and domesticate the African
spirit; rather it is an attempt to ensure that the African spirit
revolutionizes Christianity to the benefit of all who adhere to it.(37)*

They also explore the many links existing between the biblical
story and Africa.

Professor Kwesi A. Dickson elaborates on the continuity between
the Old Testament and African life and thought.*(38)* Everywhere
in Africa preachers point to the Exodus story, to the Queen of
Sheba and King Solomon, and very specially to the refuge provided
by Egypt to the infant Jesus and his parents. African independent
churches emphasize this linkage as an affirmation of their belonging to the biblical tradition without any western mediation.
Perhaps the most important illustration of this search for roots
and identity is provided by the "Confession of Alexandria",
drafted by the General Committee of the All Africa Conference
of Churches in Cairo in 1976.

*We have become conscious of the fact that we are inheritors of a rich
tradition. Our current concern with issues related to economic justice,
the total liberation of men and women from every form of oppression
and exploitation, and peace in Africa, as well as our contemporary
search for authentic responses to Christ as Lord over the whole of our
lives has led us to a deeper understanding of the heritage delivered to
us by the Fathers of the early church in North Africa. ... It is this
heritage which inspires us to confess that it is the same incarnate
Christ who is calling us to respond to him in terms that are authentic,
faithful and relevant to the men and women in Africa today.(39)*

We must also remember that the missiological debate about moratorium developed in Africa, first through Dr John Gatu from Kenya,
and later in the Assembly of the AACC, in Lusaka 1974. "The call
to moratorium enabled Africans to ask if it was God's design to
make their continent a mission field for Europeans and people of
European descent. The moratorium closes the door on ideas tested
elsewhere and opens the way for God's self-disclosure to people
of every nation, race and tribe, and the development of programmes tuned to the real needs of people.*(40)*

The misunderstandings, fears and anxieties provoked by the debate
on moratorium should not blind us to the central intention of the
proposal, to open a space, an area of freedom, for the African
churches where they could discover their own identity.

The examples we have given from Africa, Asia and Latin America illustrate the diversity of the missionary dilemmas confronting the churches today. But because these examples are about the experience of what were called "younger churches" and relate to areas that the churches in Europe and America have considered as "mission fields", we are likely to be misunderstood.

We take for granted mission in six continents. We affirm that the very being of the church is missionary and that everywhere churches are sent to proclaim God's salvation to all people and to all areas of life. Very old churches are also confronted with old and new problems. The affirmation of freedom as our central missiological principle, and the vision of the kingdom as the frame and aim of Christian mission should provide for them also old and new possibilities to affirm their vocation and their faithfulness.

Take, for example, the Orthodox churches in northern Africa or the Middle East, surrounded by powerful Islamic communities which control the political power of their nations - like Iran, Syria, Iraq, Lebanon and Egypt. For over one thousand years they have not been allowed to develop any evangelistic work. Conversion to Christianity was legally prohibited and any attempt to convert people was discouraged -- even invited punishment. They have been limited to the transmission of faith from parents to children generation after generation. (41) They developed an understanding of the Christian mission that is not so much geographical, not in terms of the expansion of the church, but chronological, and sacramental. (42)

Are the preservation of the church for the coming generations and the priestly intercessory prayer for the whole community mission in the model of Abraham? Is this concentration on the chronological and sacerdotal vocation a betrayal of the missionary command of the gospel or the faithful and relevant manifestation of it under peculiar circumstances?

Today these churches are facing a new situation. Many of their members have migrated to other continents and established churches there which serve their ethnic groups. The great challenge to them is to discover their new missionary potential in situations where the historical constraints are no more operative. The whole issue of the mission of the Orthodox diaspora demands ecumenical consideration.

In western Europe, we are passing from the situation of a "people's church" (Volkskirche), a situation where everybody was supposed to belong to the church, to a very rapid de-Christianization process, at least a "de-churchification" process. (43) Erstwhile majority churches are now obliged to rethink their mission in the light of new circumstances which have made them minorities in society.

13

What should be the mission of the faithful remnant in such situations? In the last two centuries it was very easy to equate mission with overseas mission. Now we not only talk about mission in six continents, we know that mission is at home, right in our neighbourhood.

W. Visser't Hooft describes the situation in Europe as "neo-pagan".(44) Lesslie Newbigin traces the rise of the modern *Welt-anschauung* and describes its failure to provide an adequate frame of reference within which the contemporary challenges facing a technological society could be tackled.(45) Both of them invite the churches to recover the biblical message in living interplay with new historical situations.

In North America the churches continue to be full, but more and more people are sceptical about "civil religion" and question the easy identification of the American way of life with the gospel of Jesus Christ. What is the relation between church growth and faithfulness to the gospel, between success and the cross of Jesus Christ?

The American churches send more missionaries abroad than any other church. A passionate debate goes on in the United Methodist Church, between those who want to send more missionaries -- and more evangelistic-minded missionaries -- and those who affirm the national leadership of sister churches and the obligation to assume a political advocacy role on behalf of the third world. The debate is by no means limited to the United Methodist Church. It raises fundamental questions concerning our missionary priorities.(46)

Eastern Europe faces its own missionary challenges. Here politi-cal, ideological and cultural life is organized around the communist party. The churches which were traditionally the focus of culture and national identity have now -- officially -- been marginalized. In such circumstances the churches must look for different theological perspectives and missiological options. J. Hromadka and his theology of diakonia continue to influence churches in Czechoslovakia and Hungary. The search for the people and the expression of the national soul seem to be the answer of the Roman Catholic Church in Poland and of the Orthodox churches in Bulgaria, Romania and the Soviet Union. Personal evangelization oblivious of the social system, seems to be the answer of Pente-costal and free churches.(47)

THEOLOGICAL AND PRACTICAL MANIFESTATIONS

The churches in our day face a variety of missionary options. These options give rise to controversy and conflict. They have also inspired a number of different theological systems and organizational schemes.(48)

Even a few decades ago, the North Atlantic churches were the arbiters of Christian theology. Today the situation is totally different. Feminist theology, black theology, liberation theology, dialogue theology, minjung or people's theology -- each one of these theologies attempts to see the missionary vocation of the church in a particular setting. They are basically missiologies. They are not explanations of God's being but represent a passionate search for new options for the mission of the churches. *(49)*

Behind each of those theologies -- liberation, African, black, feminist, minjung -- there is a situation of conflict. No new theological system has emerged in the last twenty years that does not condemn some kind of oppression and affirm some specific perspective of the gospel which emerges out of the problems of the groups doing the theological work. In fact, most of these theologians say that their theology is an elaboration, *a posteriori*, of a stand taken in conflict situations. They are trying to explain themselves as Christians and to find guidelines for action. *(50)*

These theologies also reflect the richness of the church in our day, the interplay of culturally linked manifestations of the Christian faith. We must try to understand how far these theological attempts are responsible uses of our missionary freedom.

The programmatic division of labour within the structure of our churches is another dimension of this problem. We have, in most of our western churches, departments for social action and departments for evangelism, each trying to be faithful to its particular mandate. *(51)* This is useful up to a point, but it could also lead to an abdication of our total Christian responsibilities. There are indeed different gifts in the life of the church. They call for a logical division of callings and of tasks. But if these charisms -- whether considered individually or organized structurally in the life of the church -- limit or distort the total witness to the kingdom, then they become a stumbling block for the mission of the church. *(52)*

The problem becomes serious when the organizations created in western churches to relate to churches in the third world evolve bylaws and guidelines external to the churches themselves. For example, the fact that one can get substantial help for whatever goes under the magic term "development" but that it is much more difficult to get help for church growth, theological education, evangelism, etc., constitutes a true distortion. *(53)*

That a church or council of churches in a given country in Africa or in Asia devotes the major part of its energies in the area of development, does not necessarily mean that Christian people have become convinced that it is through development that they must witness to the kingdom at this particular moment. It simply means that foreign funds are available for that particular work

and are not available for other kinds of work. The question
being asked is: How can each one of our particular concerns
or gifts become an entry point to the total dynamic of the kingdom and not become departmentally isolated and stratified?

THE KINGDOM AND ITS FREEDOM

Two fears seem to haunt theologians. One is the fear of being
unfaithful to the demands of today's world, the fear of being
irrelevant, the fear of being out of touch. In the sixties in
ecumenical discussions it was often heard that the "world set
the agenda". The church was thought of as responding to the
priorities set in the world's agenda.(54) The church is indeed
sent into the world to respond to situations where human beings
suffer, hope, live and die. But that does not mean that it has
no mission of its own except to respond, no internal compulsion,
no given convictions, no values that it must share with the world.

The other fear is that in being busy over the affairs of the
world Christians might forget their essential vocation of proclaiming the gospel. It is the fear that in responding to the
need to fight oppression, racism, sexism and similar evils, we
might neglect our calling to preach "the Word".(55) If the
proclamation of the gospel of the kingdom were possible without
reference to the concrete human situations of the kingdoms in
which we live, then of course our problem would be easy! But the
gospel happens in the encounter between the word of God and
concrete human beings and situations.(56)

It is our basic conviction that the kingdom of God is the central
biblical category which gives content and direction to our
missionary vocation. Our goal is the kingdom. The church is called
to serve the kingdom, to be a privileged instrument of that kingdom, called in fact to exist for the sake of the kingdom.

We follow the living Christ, led by the Holy Spirit. Within the
horizon of the kingdom of God, we have total freedom and total
responsibility -- a total freedom to discern, to plan and to
act.(57)

Given the nature of the kingdom, the freedom of the Spirit, the
churches are free to respond to that freedom of God.(58) Nothing
can be *a priori* proscribed, among the action possibilities of the
church. We refer to the freedom of the Spirit, calling Christians
to different responses. We call this presence of the Risen Christ
and this action of the Holy Spirit missionary freedom, because it
invites us to respond and persuades us to act. We could substitute
"responsibility" for freedom, but I rather prefer the word freedom
because it opens up our imagination and provides space much more
than the word responsibility. It is, however, by being free that
we are responsible.

We shall look to the ministry of Jesus and to the history of the early church to find there examples of freedom that could serve as inspiration and guideline to our own freedom.

When we use the word freedom theologically we mean the gift of the Holy Spirit that enables us to respond; but we need to look at that freedom possibility in sociological and political terms as well. I could claim that I am freed, but in fact I might be a victim of my own biases, social prejudices and class advantages. As when the rich white people in South Africa find support for apartheid in the Bible and claim that they are using their Christian freedom!

After the great teachers of suspicion -- Marx, Freud, or Nietzsche -- we are only too aware of the constraints that work against real freedom. We cannot ignore those constraints even in the life of the church. But the Bible, the findings of human scientific disciplines, the community of faith, especially in its ecumenical dimensions, and the praxis of love -- all provide reference points that will help us, if not to escape from these historical constraints, at least to struggle to transform them in the perspective of the coming kingdom. *(59)*

Chapter II

THE PROBLEM IN PERSPECTIVE:
THE THEOLOGICAL DEBATE 1972-1984

BANGKOK 1973

Through a series of international encounters we have pursued
the search for missionary clarity in our century.*(1)* Edinburgh
1910, to which we trace the beginnings of the modern ecumenical
movement, was the first in the series. It was followed by periodic
meetings. The World Mission Conference convened by the Commission
on World Mission and Evangelism of the World Council of Churches
in Bangkok was the eighth in the series.*(2)*

There were, however, significant differences between Edinburgh
and Bangkok. In 1910, the participants represented western
Protestant missionary agencies. There were only a handful of
participants from the "younger churches". At Bangkok, the majority
of delegates were from the younger churches; there were also
delegates from Orthodox churches, and a fraternal delegation of
the Roman Catholic Church.

There were also differences in content. Edinburgh had agreed not
to consider "doctrinal" matters -- to avoid polemics. Bangkok is
perhaps the first missionary conference to take as theme a central
faith affirmation: "Salvation Today".*(3)* In general, missionary
gatherings discuss how to reach people and how to develop the
missionary task; they are concerned with methodologies, approaches,
practices. Bangkok focused rather on the salvation we are proclaiming. It addressed itself to the question: What is the
meaning today of the central affirmation of our Christian faith
that there is salvation in Jesus Christ?

In preparation for the conference, a fascinating book on the
theme was published with stories from every part of the world,
telling how people are experiencing salvation and showing the
relationship of this theological concept to diverse areas of
human life.*(4)* Bangkok examined the heart of our conviction that
God is a saving God, and asked how this conviction could come
alive and become real in the missionary task of the church.

Bangkok is the capital of Thailand, a Buddhist country where only
one out of a thousand people is Christian.*(5)* The location influenced the conference at two very different levels. First, the
whole question of Christian attitude towards other religions, in
this situation, Buddhism, inevitably came up for discussion. Two
attitudes were evident at the assembly. One of them was expressed
by the General Secretary of the Church of Christ in Thailand,

Rev. Wichean Watakeecharoen, who preached the opening sermon on Isaiah 53 and Romans 5. He emphasized salvation by grace through faith in Christ. He explained that the main concern of the Church of Christ in Thailand was church growth; their goal was to double the membership of the church in four years. So they preached to people and invited them to become Christians and to join the church. (6)

Another attitude towards Buddhism was evident when a few Buddhist monks were invited to a plenary session. A dialogue took place between religious leaders in Thailand and a selected group of assembly delegates. It illustrated an approach that pointed to the need to respect other religions and to learn from them.

The official report of the conference makes only a passing reference to this encounter with Buddhists. (7) But the exposure to a Buddhist culture and the experience of a minority church left a lasting impression upon all participants. It is significant that an ecumenical consultation was organized in Chiang Mai, Thailand, four years later to discuss the whole issue of dialogue with different faiths. That encounter resulted in a document called "Guidelines for Dialogue with People of Living Faiths and Ideologies", where the witnessing and listening dimensions of Christian mission are brought together. (8)

When the delegates at Bangkok talked about salvation, they were well aware that they were surrounded by millions of people who too were seeking salvation, though their lives were centred in a totally different set of values. The challenge of other religions remains an open question in the missionary task of the church. What is the place of other religions in God's kingdom? (9)

The second important consequence of meeting in Thailand was that the delegates were made acutely aware of American military presence. From an American air base in the neighbourhood bombers were taking off at regular intervals to deliver their lethal load over the city of Hanoi and its surroundings. A delegate from the Netherlands proposed that we go to Hanoi and demonstrate our solidarity with the people. It was a dramatic moment. The international press promptly reported that a conference of Christians wanted to go to Hanoi. We did not go to Hanoi, but the word salvation took on a new meaning. And it helped us to understand the passion, the tensions, that pervaded the conference. Here were we, Christians, talking about salvation, while twenty miles away the messenger of death was taking off to kill and destroy. (10) It was impossible to speak of salvation without relating it to this historical reality. History, the political reality, was very much present in the minds of the delegates; they were forced to consider the relation of salvation to these world events.

Bangkok described salvation in terms that indicate its global, holistic nature. Salvation is seen at work in the struggle for economic justice and for human dignity, in the struggle against

the alienation of person from person; and in the struggle of
hope against despair in personal life. "The salvation which
Christ brought and in which we participate offers a comprehensive
wholeness in this divided life. We understand salvation as newness of life, the unfolding of true humanity in the fullness of
God (Col 2:9-10). It is salvation of the soul and the body of
the individual and society, humankind and the 'groaning creation'
(Rom 8:19)." *(11)*

The salvation Christ brings offers comprehensive wholeness, and
this wholeness is newness of life. It is true humanity, the
salvation of the total person's soul and body -- and person means
individual and society. The salvation of humankind embraces the
whole of creation. This global and total understanding of salvation
was accompanied by a recognition that we cannot always be totally
inclusive. We have a global understanding of salvation that has to
do with all aspects of the person, with all aspects of the person's
relation to society, with all aspects of humankind's relation to
nature. But we cannot always be totally inclusive. We are obliged
to enter into this total salvation through particular doors.

*There are historical priorities according to which salvation is
anticipated in one dimension first, be it the personal, the political,
or the economic dimension. This point of entry differs from situation
to situation in which we work and suffer. We should know that such
anticipations, such entry points, are not the whole of salvation, and
we must keep in mind the other dimensions while we work. Forgetting
this denies the wholeness of salvation. Nobody can do in any particular
situation everything at the same time. There are various gifts and tasks,
but there is one Spirit and one goal.(12)*

There are certain priorities, and we must use our freedom to
discern them. There are various gifts and tasks -- personal gifts,
personal tasks, personal vocations -- but there is one Spirit and
one goal. And now comes the most polemic phrase in the report of
the conference. "In this sense" -- this sense of historical
priorities, anticipations -- "it can be said, for example, that
salvation is the peace of the people in Vietnam, independence in
Angola, justice and reconciliation in Northern Ireland, and
release from the captivity of power in the North Atlantic community,
or personal conversion in the release of a submerged society into
hope, or of new lifestyles amidst corporate self-interest and
lovelessness." *(13)*

There are historical priorities, dimensions, particular gifts
that are entry points into the total dynamic of the kingdom, and
the total reality of salvation. In a given moment, the conference
says, "peace in Vietnam is salvation". Those who are working for
peace in Vietnam are fulfilling a missionary duty. Those who are
looking for reconciliation in Northern Ireland are fulfilling a
missionary duty. Those who are inviting people to conversion
among societies which deprive people of their humanity are working
for the kingdom. But each one of those are entry points, historical

20

priorities, anticipations of salvation in response to one particular gift or to one particular task.

This is central to our work in the setting of historical or contextual priorities as points of entry into the total struggle of the kingdom of God. This statement was much misunderstood and misinterpreted. People concentrated on the second part: "Salvation is peace in Vietnam". Of course we cannot forget the dimensions of reconciliation with God and our neighbours, and eternal life. But the statement does not say the *whole* salvation is peace in Vietnam, but rather that this is one historical priority. It is one dimension. It is one anticipation. It is an entry point. We should not forget the other dimensions that will complete the picture, but we need to enter by a particular door if we want to be concrete in our missionary obedience. Our freedom in mission is so that we may be relevant in mission.

This understanding should help reconcile certain Christian positions that seem contradictory. If peace in Vietnam is the entry point into the kingdom or the missionary priority for Christians concerned with that nation, could it not be that building the church, calling to conversion, should also be recognized as the entry point, as the dimension to be emphasized in certain other parts of Asia and of the world?

The Bangkok assembly had heard of the "growing questioning among people in Bangkok about the meaninglessness of life for many, and their search for something deeper, indeed for a new identity."*(14)* If there is this meaninglessness, then sharing the story of the gospel might become one of the best answers in that situation. But as the concern for peace in Vietnam is not the whole of salvation, so also, telling the story of Jesus is not the whole of salvation unless in both cases we point with our words and our deeds beyond those particular emphases, to the total dynamics of the kingdom of God. The theological approach of Bangkok, while providing examples of priorities in terms of political and social situations, did not fail to recognize other priorities that have traditionally held sway, like the preaching of the word and the building of the church. We should see all of them as legitimate entry points into the total mission of the church, and into the total meaning of salvation.

After Bangkok -- Critical Voices

After Bangkok, the debate centred on the implications of statements like the ones we have quoted. Some of the evangelical friends considered them as a confirmation of certain emphases that they trace to the Uppsala Assembly of the World Council in 1968. They protested against the reduction of theology to some kind of anthropology and of Christian faith to some kind of humanism. Hal Lindsell, the former editor of Christianity Today, said that the emphasis in Uppsala that came to fruition in Bangkok was on "humanization, secularization, socio-political involvement,

economic development of third world nations, the elimination
of racism, revolution, and a virulent anti-American feeling that
centred on the war in Vietnam. The gospel of personal salvation
through the substitutionary atonement of Christ on Calvary was
supplanted by a secularized this-worldly version of social
action as the mission of the church."(15)

He was not the only one who interpreted Bangkok that way; persons
more friendly to the World Council offered also similar criticism.
Arthur Glasser from Fuller Theological Seminary said that in
Bangkok "the cultural mandate was central rather than the evangelistic mandate". He said, describing the evangelistic and cultural
mandates, that "salvation really has implications for both.
According to the cultural mandate, God decides to involve men in
accepting responsibility for the world. He is concerned about the
poor, the oppressed, the weak. He is concerned about government,
injustice, oppression, and so on." But, Glasser says, this is one
dimension of the Christian calling. The other dimension, the
evangelistic dimension, he does not see very clearly in Bangkok.(16)

Towards the end of the conference the official representative of
the Vatican, Father Jerome Hamer, greeted the delegates in the
name of the Roman Catholic fraternal delegation; he said very
frankly: "I am appalled that you people can discuss salvation
today, day after day, in all of its ramifications, but not listen
to what the Apostle Paul said about it. I have not heard anyone
speak of justification by faith. I have not heard anyone speaking
of everlasting life. What about God's righteous wrath against
sin?"(17)

We must also note the criticism that came from the Russian
Orthodox Church, voiced in a letter addressed to the WCC Moderator,
M.M. Thomas from India:

> Perplexity and great regret are aroused by the fact that in the letter
> to the churches from Bangkok, there is no significant reference about
> eternal life, in God, nor does anything point to the moral improvement
> and perfection as an indispensable condition for the achievement of this
> goal -- eternal life. The examination of the other documents of the
> conference only increases this perplexity and regret. For instance, though
> there is a stipulation in the introduction, namely, "Our concentration
> upon the social, economic, and political implications of the gospel does
> not in any way deny the personal and eternal dimensions of salvation",
> nevertheless, the deviation from positively indicating these dimensions
> as integral to the true understanding of salvation in the part of the
> report that is especially devoted to theological reflection can easily
> be assumed as a deliberate trend towards one-sided and detrimental under-
> standing of salvation in the spirit of boundless horizontalism. Or, simply
> put ... there is no room left for the main vertical dimensions that could
> have indicated that salvation requires personal perfection as a part of
> the social organism called upon to fight against the sin that is both in
> and out, in order to achieve the fullness of life in the life of communion
> with God in both the temporal and eternal worlds.(18)

Values at Stake

These three critical responses -- the evangelical, the Roman
Catholic, and the Orthodox, each point to a value to be considered
and preserved. Evangelicals and Roman Catholics demand a more
clear message addressed to individuals, in terms of their personal
relation to God, their need for forgiveness, faith, to receive
eternal life. They could not hear in the heated debates in
Bangkok this invitation to faith and personal conversion. The
Russian Orthodox Church did not hear a clear reference to eternal
life in God, as the consummation of all Christian expectation of
salvation. Personal conversion, evangelism in terms of an invitation to a personal faith, eschatological hope in God -- all
those are central Christian affirmations which the people gathered
in Bangkok would never deny. Their concern was to correct the
deviations of the past and read the *kairos* of God, where the Spirit
was calling the church to act obediently today.

Bangkok was breaking new ground; in some ways it was even talking
a new language which was somewhat difficult to understand. What
were the values at stake for the people gathered in Bangkok? They
wanted to keep in mind the interplay, even the unity, between
religious and secular history, between salvation history and
human history. For Arthur Glasser, there is a cultural mandate
and an evangelistic mandate; both are necessary, but they are
different. Bangkok attempted to see the evangelistic dimension
within the cultural mandate; and within the evangelistic dimension,
the need to call for the recognition of the lordship of Christ,
the cultural dimension.

Thus in Bangkok, there was the attempt to take seriously the
cultural history given to us, to root our church, our theology,
the gospel, in the past of our nation, and, within that history,
to participate in the liberation of our people and the building
of our culture, in the creation of new human relations in an
eschatological perspective -- with the hope of contributing to
the richness of the final banquet of the kingdom of God.

What Bangkok said is not very different, in fact, from what
Orthodox theologians were saying. Christians should become the
ferment within history which could save that history. The transfiguration of the world is the goal toward which our Christian
mission should work. The Holy Spirit is at work in the totality
of creation.[19] And that was what Bangkok attempted to express:
to bring these theological affirmations down to earth and put
them in the language of social, political and historical realities.
We discerned in Bangkok that the theological schizophrenia that
separates relations with God from relations with our neighbours
disappears in the wonderful knowledge of a God whose Spirit works
through different agents of liberation but who, fundamentally
through the church, conveys to humankind the secret of God's love
and offers the possibility of a conscious decision to incorporate
our service into the divine mission of salvation and liberation.

This understanding of salvation redeems the historical task of humankind and provides the basis for all evangelistic concerns. Nothing human is foreign to the Christian community. In the birth of a child, in its development as a person, in the person's integration into the human community, in the fight for freedom of the whole community, in the search for more human forms of life -- in all these we see the manifestation of God's care and love. The God who was active in the exodus, providing freedom for the people of Israel, and the God who acted through the death and resurrection of Jesus Christ and offers new life to all humankind, is the same God who has called us to work for total human salvation.

THE EVANGELICAL DEBATE

A second important element in the discussion was the evangelical concentration on the evangelization of the world. A Congress on World Evangelism, called by the Billy Graham organization and the magazine Christianity Today, met in Berlin in 1966.[20] It was followed in 1974 by a second congress, attended by 4,000 participants, in Lausanne, Switzerland, around the theme: "Let the Earth Hear His Voice".[21] The Lausanne Covenant, a document that, although it was not an official document of the congress itself, was prepared and signed during that congress, is a good summary of the convictions of the Lausanne congress.[22] According to it "more than 2,700 million people, which is more than two thirds of humankind, had yet to be evangelized. We are ashamed that so many have been neglected. It is a standing rebuke to us and to the whole church." The congress coined the phrase "reaching the unreached" as the main slogan to mobilize the church. While this slogan provides a good indication of the numerical and geographical dimension of the problem, the word "unreached" does not quite explain the situation. That slogan seems to imply that there are people who have not been reached even by God, and that, of course, belongs to a dimension of reality that is hidden from us. God alone knows where the Spirit has reached and in what form. That is not to deny the tragic fact that the vast majority of the population of the world has not embraced the Christian faith and that Christians are commanded to share the gospel of Jesus Christ with everybody, because it is God's will that everybody should come to the knowledge of the truth and be saved (1 Tim 2:4).

Lausanne was not a response to Bangkok. The organizers of the congress did not think of it as such. Their concern was the evangelization of the world, understood as the telling of the story of Christ to people so that they might be converted; they were discussing the ways and means to reach that goal.[23] Implicit in the discussions was a criticism of the World Council of Churches and the Commission on World Mission and Evangelism -- which were considering issues of culture and justice in a missionary conference. But, unavoidably, most of the participants were under the influence of the same historical events as the delegates in

Bangkok. They came from the same world at war; they were reading the same Bible; most them came from the same churches. Sixty-five per cent of the 4,000 people in Lausanne were from member churches of the World Council of Churches. They too were trying to be faithful to the Holy Spirit. The net result was that the Lausanne Covenant incorporated some of the key concepts of Bangkok -- dialogue, moratorium, justice, culture -- but gave to those concepts a more precise definition in order to make sure that they did not obscure basic tasks of the missionary vocation.

Distinctions are made; priorities established. Evangelism is defended as an independent category, related to but independent of the demands of social justice. "Social justice is not evangelization," it was said very clearly. But "...social justice belongs to our mandate." Bangkok raised moratorium as a possibility to stop the sending of missionaries and funds to a particular church, for a given period, to give that church a chance to discover its own self and to know its own identity in relation to the surrounding community.(24) The Covenant indicates that moratorium if it could liberate funds for other regions not yet reached by the gospel, might not be a bad idea! Dialogue is needed -- provided it facilitates evangelization!

Lausanne marks the beginning of a coming together of different theological positions concerned with the mission of the church.

Within the evangelical family, there has been a growing demand for an evangelical commitment to the cause of historical change, to participation in human struggles for justice. In fact, in Lausanne itself a sizeable number of delegates signed a complementary statement to the Covenant called "A Response to Lausanne".(25) It is a more radical paper but it does not contradict the Covenant. It affirms the Covenant, but highlights the dimension of social justice and of social involvement by Christians.

A world consultation was organized by the Lausanne Committee for World Evangelization in June 1980 in Pattaya, Thailand. Its purpose was to study at greater depth the question of techniques and methodologies for reaching specific groups. The original intention was to confine the discussion to practical considerations of how to undertake the evangelization of Moslems, Hindus, nominal Catholics, nominal Protestants, and similar identifiable sections of people. But a number of participants, especially coming from the third world, under the leadership of Bishop David Gitari from Kenya, asked the organizing committee to include the consideration of questions of justice in the world and the responsibility of Christians in relation to such questions.(26) They argued that the Lausanne Covenant recognized the importance of justice in relation to evangelism, and they were afraid that the Lausanne Committee for World Evangelization was now following a one-sided interpretation of the Covenant by keeping the concerns of evangelism unrelated to the total concern of God for the whole human situation. They demanded the calling of a world conference

on Christian social responsibility to consider issues of
justice, especially their relationship with evangelization.
That gave rise to an internal discussion in the committee. The
fear was expressed, particularly by the church growth school in
America, that such a conference could distort the perspectives
and betray the original vocation of the Lausanne movement.(27)
In the view of the church growth school, the Lausanne Committee
should be concerned basically with the expansion and growth of
the church, with reaching the unreached, while others could
feel free to express their concern for social justice.

We must mention the efforts of other groups which are even more
committed to a calling for reaching those who are totally out
of touch. For example, Ralph Winter from Pasadena, California
(USA), would say that the real challenge today is to reach those
who are beyond our cultural borders and that cannot be attempted
at the level of local congregations. For such a task one needs
more specialized organizations as well as people who have a
particular vocation to cross cultural frontiers and evangelize
those of other cultures.

This was the rationale behind a conference which was held in
Edinburgh in 1980. The conference did not produce a covenant
or a statement. It did, however, produce a pledge, which
participants were urged to sign. It read:

> *"A CHURCH FOR EVERY PEOPLE BY THE YEAR 2000"*
> *By the grace of God and for His glory*
> *I commit my entire life*
> *to obeying His commission of Mt 28:18-20*
> *wherever and however He leads me*
> *giving priority to the peoples*
> *currently beyond the reach of the Gospel (Rom 15:20-21)*
> *I will also endeavour to impart this vision to others.*

There were strict doctrinal requirements for participation in
this conference, which meant that its impact was limited to a
small sector of the Christian community.(28)

Meanwhile, an increasing number of evangelicals, especially from
the third world, claim that the concern for human justice has
always belonged to their tradition. The best evangelists never
made a clear-cut separation between the two. They might have made
distinctions; they might have prescribed one direction for today
and another for tomorrow, but they were convinced that the task
of evangelism should point towards the total mission of God,
including the concern for justice.(29)

To respond to this concern and to face squarely the internal
differences two complementary meetings were called. The one
organized by the Lausanne Committee for World Evangelization
and the World Evangelical Fellowship brought 50 evangelical
leaders to Grand Rapids, USA, in June 1982, to consider the

relation between evangelism and social responsibility. "Many
fear," they said, "that the more we evangelicals are committed
to the one, the less we shall be committed to the other." The
consultation affirmed that "evangelism and social responsibility,
while distinct from one another, are integrally related in our
proclamation of and obedience to the gospel. The partnership is
in reality a marriage."(30)

The World Evangelical Fellowship organized in Wheaton, Illinois,
in 1983 a series of three simultaneous consultations on "The
Church in Local Settings", "The Church in New Frontiers of
Mission", and "The Church in Response to Human Need".(31) The
concern for a clear relation between evangelism and social
justice, voiced in Lausanne, raised in Pattaya, alive in communities like the Sojourners' community in the USA and in movements
like the Fellowship of Evangelical Theologians in Latin America
and among many groups in Asia -- all these came clearly to
fruition in this meeting in Wheaton in 1983.

> *The reality of the presence of the kingdom gives us the courage to
> begin here and now to erect signs of the coming kingdom by working
> prayerfully and consistently for more justice and peace and toward
> transformation of individuals and societies. Since one day God will
> wipe away all tears, it grieves us to see people suffer now. Since
> one day there will be perfect peace, we are called to be peacemakers
> now. We humbly yet urgently call upon you, the churches, to stand with
> us in this ministry of practising love and seeking to restore the
> dignity of human beings created in the image of God.(32)*

There is an eschatological vision: the kingdom will bring the
shalom (peace) of God, and God will wipe away our tears, bringing
perfect peace, whole salvation. That vision urges us to be active
in history, helping those who suffer now, working for peace,
opposing all injustice. Because we are on our way to the kingdom,
we are called to plant signs of the kingdom in this place and at
this moment. We may well have theological differences, but we are
convinced that God's calling to the church is a holistic calling.
That is a living reality, and here we have a truly ecumenical
meeting point.

Nor can we forget that the evangelical movement is primarily
concerned with the evangelization of the whole world, especially
of the billions of people who have not yet heard of Jesus Christ.
We may or may not agree with some methodologies advocated; we may
disagree with talk of people outside the Christian church as
"lost".(33)

But the gospel needs to be shared. It cannot be the private
property of Christians. We do not have the right to prevent anyone from coming to the knowledge of Jesus Christ. In this particular concern for individuals, there is a valid reminder of the
question of faith in our world today. The missiological discussion
in ecumenical circles, however, has been more concerned with the

27

question of faithfulness in mission, of integrity, of the
necessary correspondence between word and action; it recognizes
that the lack of faithfulness on the part of Christian people
is the main stumbling block in all evangelistic enterprises.*(34)*
Our evangelical friends have been more concerned with the actual
attempt to provide an opportunity for people to come to faith
in Christ. Both concerns belong inseparably together. Without
a faithful community that in itself is a sign of the kingdom it
will be difficult to convince the world of the radical novelty
of the gospel of Jesus Christ. But every attempt to be faithful
involves the desire to share the gospel with others. Evangelism
belongs to our faithfulness towards God. Without a commitment to
evangelism our Christian commitment is incomplete. At the same
time we need to bring together these dimensions of faithfulness
and faith because becoming a Christian, being invited to accept
Jesus Christ, means to be invited also to participate in his
kingdom, in his own movement of love in history. By becoming
Christians we cannot escape from history.

THE ROMAN CATHOLIC POSITION

In 1974 a Synod of Bishops of the Roman Catholic Church took place
in Rome around the theme "The Evangelization of the World". Synods
of Bishops in the Catholic Church assist the Pope in his pastoral
and teaching function. In general, they reflect the collective
wisdom of the bishops; their findings are then shared with the
Pope, who later incorporates them in whatever he wants to say on
his own authority.

On 8 December 1975, the Pope published an apostolic exhortation
under the title *Evangelii Nuntiandi* (Evangelization of the Modern
World).*(35)* He recognized the work of the bishops and then went
on to elaborate on his own thinking. Paul VI began with the
reminder that the presentation of the gospel message is not
optional for the church. It is a duty laid on her by the command
of the Lord Jesus so that people can believe and be saved. [5]
Christ is the supreme evangelist. He proclaims the kingdom and
in the kingdom a liberating salvation [8]; he accompanies his
evangelistic mission with evangelical signs, and especially one
sign to which Christ gives great importance -- it is that the
humble and the poor are evangelized. [12] The disciples of John
the Baptist asked Jesus: "Are you the one that we were expecting
or do we need to wait for somebody else?" Jesus did not answer
yes or no. He said: "Tell John what signs are being manifested --
the healing of the sick, and the poor have good news preached to
them" (Lk 7:18-23). The announcing of the gospel to the poor was
one sign of the kingdom, one clear sign of the messianic vocation
of Jesus. For the Pope, the task of evangelizing all people
constituted the essential mission of the church. [14]

In this he agrees with the General Secretary of the WCC, Dr Philip
Potter, who, addressing the Synod, declared that "evangelization

is the test of the ecumenical vocation".(36) He also agrees
with the Lausanne emphasis that evangelization is the central,
essential mission. The church evangelizes when it "seeks to
convert solely through the divine power of the message she
proclaims both the personal and collective consciences of
people, the activites in which they engage, and the lives and
concrete milieu which are theirs". [18]

There is a tension here. The Pope wants to make it clear that
evangelization, in the sense of calling people to faith in
Christ, is the central vocation of the church. At the same time,
he recognizes that it is impossible to fulfil that mission without relating it to all aspects of people's lives.

The salvation that is promised by Christ is transcendent and
eschatological, but it has its beginning in this life. Therefore
the message is also "about the rights and duties of every human
being, about family life, life in society, about international
life, peace, justice, and development". It is "a message
especially energetic today about liberation". [29]

It is clear that the Pope wants to affirm two things -- keeping
them in constructive tension. First, salvation has to do with
eternal life; it is something that depends on our relation to
God in Christ with consequences far beyond our daily historical
life. At the same time, it also has consequences for human life
here and now, and there "it is impossible to accept that in
evangelization one could or should ignore the importance of the
problems so much discussed today concerning justice, liberation,
development and peace in the world. This would be to forget the
lesson which comes to us from the gospel concerning love of our
neighbour who is suffering and in need." [31]

But the Pope says, talking about the church that "she reaffirms
the primacy of her spiritual vocation and refuses to replace
the proclamation of the kingdom by the proclamation of forms of
human liberation. She even states that her contribution to
liberation is incomplete if she neglects to proclaim salvation
in Jesus Christ." [34] There would not be many people in the
Catholic Church who would like it to replace the proclamation
of the kingdom of God by the proclamation of human liberation
of one kind or another. Many people would like, however, to see
the manifestation of the kingdom of God in forms of human
liberation as a pre-taste, as *avant-garde* of the kingdom. The Pope
himself indicates that Christ carried out his proclamation through
innumerable signs which amazed the crowds, and that the most
important sign was that the poor were evangelized. [12] So, words
and deeds, signs and miracles, are all components of our proclamation, anticipation and living out of the kingdom of God.

As far as methodology is concerned, the Pope recognizes freedom
to respond to the most diverse contexts. [40] His concern is to
make sure that the right concern for liberation should not be

conceived as taking the place of the announcement of salvation in Christ. It is the same concern expressed in the letter from the Russian Orthodox Church to the World Council of Churches which urged that we should not forget the eschatological nature of salvation and the reality of eternal life.

The positive side of the *Evangelii Nuntiandi* is its affirmation of the need to name the name of Christ, to point to him, his life, his teaching, his death, his resurrection, in our evangelization and the simultaneous recognition that mission and evangelism involve responsibility for all realms of life. The dialogue on evangelism both inside the Roman Catholic Church and in the ecumenical movement could profit from a new reading of "The Constitution of the Church in the Modern World" and from the work of theologians of liberation who attempt to overcome the dualism between eschatological salvation and actions in history.*(37)*

Is it possible to preserve this dimension of eternal life, the eschatological consummation of our salvation, and at the same time to see the operation of this salvation in our day-to-day history?

TOWARDS A CONVERGENCE - NAIROBI 1975

In Nairobi, Kenya, in 1975, the Fifth Assembly of the World Council of Churches met under the theme "Jesus Christ Frees and Unites".*(38)* One of the six sections concentrated on "Confessing Christ Today". This assembly, and in particular this section, had the benefit of the participation of people who had been in Bangkok and in Lausanne, as well as Roman Catholic advisers. Nairobi, therefore, was the first ecumenical gathering that could attempt to bring together the different positions.*(39)*

The Lausanne Covenant on World Evangelization, the Pope's Encyclical and "Confessing Christ Today" -- all of them wish to preserve a clear doctrinal content, a central core of evangelization and, at the same time, make a serious commitment to the cause of human justice. Nairobi, responding to that concern, said: "The gospel always includes the announcement of God's kingdom and love through Jesus Christ, the offer of grace and forgiveness of sins, the invitation to repentance and faith in him, the summons to fellowship in God's church, the command to witness to God's saving words and deeds, the responsibility to participate in the struggle for justice and human dignity. The obligation to denounce all that hinders human wholeness and a commitment to risk life itself."*(40)*

Bangkok has affirmed the value of entry points; because we cannot do everything everywhere at every moment, we must, through particular obedience to one particular aspect of the gospel, enter into the whole of the gospel.

30

Nairobi affirmed that the gospel *always* includes "the participation in the struggle for justice, the obligation to denounce all that hinders human wholeness". *(41)* Having learned from the critical responses to Bangkok, Nairobi used some safeguards to avoid misunderstanding: "We regret that some reduce liberation from sin and evil to social and political dimensions, just as we regret that others limit liberation to the private and eternal dimensions." *(42)* But participants were conscious of the reality of the millions of people who have not had a chance to hear the gospel, and in that awareness they confessed the failure of the churches to be faithful to their mandate, their vocation to share the gospel with every person and with every creature. *(43)*

Nairobi was a friendly assembly. In a reconciling mood it reminded Christians that to be engaged in mission and evangelization meant a costly discipleship. "Confessing Christ and being converted to his discipleship belong inseparably together. Those who confess Jesus Christ, deny themselves, their selfishness and slavery to the godless 'principalities and powers', take up their crosses and follow him." Then the assembly spelt out the cost of discipleship, the price that many people are paying today for being faithful to the gospel. We know that the acceptance of the suffering Christ is the only way to overcome our feelings of powerlessness over against evil.... "We deplore cheap conversions without consequences. We deplore a superficial gospel, preaching an empty gospel without a call into personal and communal discipleship." *(44)*

MELBOURNE 1980 - THE POOR

In 1980 the Commission on World Mission and Evangelism of the World Council of Churches called another missionary conference, this time in Melbourne, Australia. The main theme was the prayer of Jesus, "Your Kingdom Come". *(45)* The selection of the theme was in itself a spiritual exercise, an attempt to read the situation of humankind today, in the light of the biblical message. There was the awareness of the seriousness of human suffering in the world and the conviction that there were no ready-made human solutions. The best thing would be to concentrate on the prayer of Jesus. The increasing polarization in the world of big power politics; the threat of nuclear annihilation; the growing gap between the rich and the poor, among the nations and within each nation; the continuing marginalization of millions of people -- all these influenced the choice of the theme. *(46)*

There was the general conviction at the conference that we could not speak or think about God's kingdom without concentrating our thought and our prayer on the situation of the poor of the earth today. *(47)* The Bible studies reinforced that conviction. They led the participants to rediscover God's special concern for the poor, the downtrodden and the marginal. Jesus' own ministry could not be understood outside of his powerlessness and his identification with the poorer sectors of his society. He went to die outside the gates to express his belonging to the periphery, to those who were nothing in the eyes of the powerful. *(48)* This spiritual awareness of Melbourne was undergirded by social, economic and political analyses which indicated that the phenomenon of poverty today has nothing to do with God's will. Poverty is not a matter of fate; it is the consequence of the organization of national and international relations. It has to do with the relations of state, trade, dominion, dependence, class and the exploitation that prevail in the world of nations and within every nation. Christians are called to tackle this issue from the perspective of the kingdom of God. Once we recognize the identification of Jesus with the poor, we cannot any longer consider our own relation to the poor as a social ethics question; it is a gospel question. Our love for our neighbours becomes concrete in our transactions with the poor. *(49)* For many of us this implies a recognition of our participation in the collective guilt, whether it is on the part of our country, or of our social class which benefits from the situation prevailing today.

The poor of the earth were seen as the "sinned against". *(50)* We are all sinners, the rich and the poor alike; that is one dimension of the gospel. But Jesus looked at the multitudes with compassion because he recognized them as "sinned against", as people who were victims of the sins of others, of the oppression of others. Often in the Old Testament the references to poverty or to the poor are also statements on exploitation and oppression. *(51)* This concentration on the poor resulted in a spiritual dynamic; the meeting called on the churches to identify with the poor and to become churches in solidarity with the poor. There was also a recognition that the poor, as objects of God's love, should become subjects of their own history, and that the mission of the church should facilitate the organization of the poor and their participation in God's kingdom and in the mission of the church. *(52)*

In the past twenty years it has been said again and again that the church should be the "voice of those who are voiceless". We now realize that this was a necessary function, but it is a paternalistic role. What is more important is to help the poor to organize themselves so they can make their own voice heard. God's call to conversion is a personalizing call; it is a call to play a protagonist role. To take this seriously in the life of the church is to suggest that the poor should become the real evangelizers. It envisions a movement of the Spirit of God among masses of poor people in the world who are able to evangelize the poor. *(53)* Through the evangelization of the poor, a calling to repentance, a calling to solidarity, a calling to new life comes for all persons and for all sectors of society.

Jesus established a clear link between the coming of the kingdom in him and the proclamation of the good news to the poor (Lk 4:18; 7:22). The churches cannot neglect this evangelistic task. The

world's poor, who form the majority of people, are waiting
for that witness of the gospel which will really be good news
for them.

At the Melbourne conference we began to discern something that
is of vital importance to all those concerned with the world
mission of the church: When we talk about the poor and when our
evangelical friends talk about the "unreached", we are talking
of the same people, because the majority of the poor people of
the world are not Christians. (54) So our approach to our neighbours
is not so much in terms of their religious convictions but in terms
of their total human condition. We address them as persons who are
victims of the world's division of power and the world's division
of labour, and we address them as persons for whom God has a
preferential option, and engage with them in actions which will
make that a reality in history. If we believe that Jesus brings
good news to the poor, we must faithfully follow up its consequences for the mission of the church. Might it not be that the
poor have the "clearest vision, the closest fellowship with the
crucified Christ who suffers in them, as with them, and it may
be that today they are the *avant-garde* of the mission of the
church?" (55)

But for all of us, poor or not poor, the calling to be in
solidarity with the poor raises the question of the structures
that create poverty. There is a Christian responsibility to
mediate love in the form of justice. If we care for the poor
but only as victims of poverty and if we avoid addressing the
root causes of that poverty, we betray our calling. This indeed
is the new discovery -- that we cannot limit ourselves to the
"direct proclamation of the gospel" unless we take with the utmost seriousness the situation of the people to whom the gospel
is proclaimed. (56)

Our evangelical friends are also struck by the fact that the unreached are the poor. I quote from the consultation on "The Church
in Response to Human Need", to which we have already referred
before.

> *As we reflect on the nearly three million people who still have to*
> *hear of Christ and his gospel, we were struck by the awesome aware-*
> *ness that most of them are poor and that many are getting even poorer.*
> *Millions of these people live in situations where they suffer exploi-*
> *tation and oppression and where their dignity as people created in*
> *God's image is being assaulted in many ways. We must be deeply moved*
> *by their plight. Our Lord Jesus Christ redeems us from eternal lostness*
> *and establishes his Lordship over all of our lives. Let us not limit*
> *our gospel then to a message about life after death. Our mission is far*
> *more comprehensive. God called us to proclaim Christ to the lost and to*
> *reach out to people in the name of Christ with compassion and concern*
> *for justice and equity.* (57)

The language is different, but the concern, the awareness is
the same. We face a human reality that challenges the whole of
our Christian commitment. It is impossible to say that one can
limit oneself to a spiritual or to a material gospel because in
Jesus Christ and in the actual experience of our missionary work,
the material and the spiritual gospel are one gospel: the gospel
of God incarnate in Jesus Christ, calling us to participate with
God in that invasion of love.(58)

MISSION AND EVANGELISM - AN ECUMENICAL AFFIRMATION

The Ecumenical Affirmation on Mission and Evangelism is the result
of a long process of consultation with member churches, specialized
organizations, and theologians of many persuasions.(59) The
Affirmation opens with the eschatological vision of a new
earth and a new heaven -- as the inspiration behind all Christian
activity in history. It passes on to a recognition of the monstro-
sity of human sin. The two together provide a framework to understand the urgency of the mission of the church -- to call people
and nations to repentance, to announce forgiveness of sins and a
new beginning in relations with God and with neighbours, through
Jesus Christ. Evangelization is affirmed as a central dimension
of the life of the World Council of Churches, which is described
as a pilgrimage towards unity under the missionary vision of John
17:21: "so that the world may believe that thou has sent me". [1]

The freedom of the church in the fulfilment of its mission derives
from the freedom we see in Jesus and in the New Testament church.
Through participation in God's love, the church is enabled to
respond in love to every situation. [4-5] The church is invited
to an identification with humankind in loving service and joyful
proclamation, in order that it may fulfil its priestly role of
offering intercessory prayer and eucharistic worship. [6]

The starting point of our proclamation is Christ and Christ
crucified. Christ is recognized as the one who took upon himself
all suffering, sin, and death, making available through
his resurrection possibilities of new and full life. "Evangelism
calls people to look towards that Jesus and commit their life
to him, to enter into the kingdom whose King has come in the
powerless child of Bethlehem, in the murdered one on the cross." [7]
The document ends with a series of affirmations: these relate to
conversion, the gospel to all realms of life, the church and its
unity in God's mission, mission in Christ's way, good news to the
poor, mission to six continents, witness among people of living
faiths and a vision of the future.

THE LOCAL AND THE UNIVERSAL IN MISSION

It is often said that the world has become a global village. The
inter-relationship between the local and the universal is easy to

34

see in our day.*(60)* Every small village in Sri Lanka is affected
by the fluctuations of the markets in New York or London. What
happens to black people in southern Africa is an issue in internal
political discussions in western Europe and in the United States.

World mission cannot be blind to these realities. A church which
supports apartheid in South Africa or is indifferent to it cannot
claim Christian credentials to carry on missionary work in other
countries. What Christians are doing in a particular geographical
area at a particular time affects events in other areas and at
other times.*(61)* This is a lesson we have learned dramatically
in the World Council of Churches with the Programme to Combat
Racism.*(62)* When this programme supported African liberation movements struggling for racial justice, it provoked protest and
criticism in churches in the northern hemisphere.

From a Christian or missionary perspective, however, we cannot be
faithful to the gospel of Jesus Christ unless we are with the
downtrodden and the marginalized. Boycotting the products of
transnational corporations, withdrawing our accounts from banks
which support apartheid, lobbying in parliaments or with political
parties -- all these do not appear like mission. But in the modern
world, with all its interrelations, we cannot be effective unless
we express our solidarity at local and global levels.*(63)*

Of course, when we open the understanding of the mission of the
church to practically every human activity -- boycott, support
of workers on strike, voluntary farm work in the fields, jail
reforms, the rights of the Indians, etc. -- the question is posed
as to where then is our specific Christian vocation. What is it
that the church could contribute which no one else is able to
contribute to the human community? What is it that distinguishes
the particular participation of the church in this collective
struggle, in this international solidarity, in this very secular
frontier? How can it be justified as Christian vocation?*(64)*

The concern for our neighbour, especially for the poor neighbour,
needs to be expressed in terms of historical relevancy and of
historical efficiency. We do not love our neighbour to save ourselves. We do not love in order to feel better. We want to express
our love in such a way that the situation of our neighbour can be
changed. But our solidarity and our identification with the poor
is in the name of Christ; our actions come out of a Christian
community, and they are rooted in the discipline of worship and
prayer. There these "secular" actions are a kind of testimony.
They must be relevant, but they should also point to the source
of our participation; they should point toward Jesus Christ. This
is integral to a theological understanding of our missionary freedom today. We are free to engage in all kinds of human activities
provided that those human activities become entry points to the
kingdom, that from there we point in the direction of Jesus.*(65)*

Let me close this chapter with a reference to a discussion at
the Sixth Assembly of the WCC in Vancouver. The very first
question that was raised at the plenary meeting was from a
Swedish delegate who asked why there was no mention of the
word "evangelism" in the report of the General Secretary of
the World Council of Churches. Dr Philip Potter's response was
brief. He said that every single paragraph of his report had
implicitly referred to evangelism; more explicitly there was a
call to the churches to become confessing churches. *(66)*

This brief exchange in the plenary hall of the assembly illustrates the question as to whether evangelism is a dimension of
the whole life of the church or a specific, intentional activity.
Is evangelism something that is incorporated in all aspects of
the church's life, or is it something that we do consciously?
If the mission of the church is concerned with the whole human
situation, where is the specific evangelistic vocation of the
church? *(67)*

How do we plan for the preaching of the gospel? Do we organize
home or foreign missionary activities in such a way that they
are considered *opera ad extra*? Or do they belong to the evangelistic
vocation, to the evangelistic significance of everything the
churches are doing daily? If the whole of what the churches are
doing are entry points into the kingdom, all those actions have
a missionary reality and an evangelistic potential. But if the
church has become a self-centred, self-caring community, if the
concern of the church is not for the kingdom but for itself, at
that moment, of course, the whole dimension of evangelism is lost.
Most of the foreign missionary enterprises of the last two or
three centuries were organized outside the official church
structures because the churches did not respond to that particular
call. *(68)* But biblically, the call to mission comes to the whole
church. The whole Christian community is called to assume the
responsibility of the body of Christ, to manifest the person of
Christ in the world.

The actual realization of this vocation could be through all our
activities or through an intentional organization of concrete
activities. In both cases, the question should be asked: Do these
activities serve the kingdom? Are they entry points into the
whole dynamic of the kingdom of God?

The theological symbol of the kingdom will help us to overcome
all dichotomies, separations and divisions, and do justice to
the particular emphasis represented in each one of the positions
we have described. Professor Verkuyl from Holland has said that
the purpose of God's mission and ours is the kingdom of God. *(69)*
The entire Bible speaks of the purpose of God's words and deeds
as being the revelation of his kingdom and the restoration of his
liberating rule. *(70)*

36

Because it is the all-embracing kingdom, because the Spirit opens our eyes to the presence of the King in concrete situations and circumstances, we are invited to follow, using our God-given freedom. We are empowered to assume our particular missionary vocations. All of them should contribute to the total economy of the kingdom. Silence or proclamation, action or contemplation, resistance or endurance -- many other seemingly contradictory terms could be used to focus attention on the manifold possibilities open to Christians and churches in the fulfilment of their mission. What we need is a clear vision of what that mission is all about; and then we must discern how our particular entry into the service of the kingdom of God could relate to other entry points and to the participation of others in the same dynamics of the kingdom.

Chapter III

THE MISSION OF THE KINGDOM OF GOD: BIBLICAL PERSPECTIVES

WHY THE KINGDOM?

The symbol of the kingdom of God is central to the synoptic gospels. John the Baptist and Jesus announce the kingdom of God and declare that it is "at hand". It is true that the kingdom symbol does not receive the same attention in most of the other books of the New Testament. We shall come back to this surprising difference between the synoptic gospels and the other New Testament books.

The fact that the synoptic gospels, written about the same time or soon after the epistles, emphasize the teaching of Jesus on the kingdom of God must point to the centrality of this symbol for Jesus himself. The early church concentrated its teaching and proclamation on the expectation of the *parousia* -- the second coming. It worshipped the risen Lord, retelling the stories of the cross of Jesus Christ and his resurrection. Stories of his earthly life and extracts from his teaching were at the same time circulating in a parallel or complementary tradition. The gospels were produced through the organization of independent pericopes that were told and retold again and again to preserve the memory of Jesus.

While the early church, whether of Jewish or Hellenistic origin, interpreted both the acts and sayings of Jesus in the light of its own experience, it is evident that the core of the basic affirmations concerning the kingdom came from Jesus himself. Mortimer Arias calls this teaching of the kingdom the "subversive memory of Jesus"[1] that has remained alive and comes, from time to time, to the central attention of the church.

We select the kingdom as the central theme around which to organize our understanding of mission because that memory has come back forcefully today. It would be difficult to find a more inspiring biblical theme when we face the challenges of the contemporary situation.[2]

Nor is the selection of the symbol of the kingdom of God an arbitrary one. First, because -- as we shall see -- it is the central concern of Jesus Christ himself. Second, because we believe that it responds to the inspiration of the Holy Spirit that is calling our attention once again to that ongoing memory of the kingdom, to provide the intellectual and inspirational categories that will help the church in its missionary obedience today.

Jesus came announcing the kingdom of God to a people living in anticipation of radical events. Leonardo Boff puts it this way:

The Messiah is he who will install the kingdom of God. All the people prepared for his coming. The Pharisees thought that they could speed up the coming of the transformation of this world by the minute observance of all the laws. The Essenes and monks of the Qumran community retired to the desert so that in absolute purification, legal observance, and an ideal life, they could await and accelerate the breakthrough of the new order. The Zealots (the fervent ones) were of the opinion that they ought to provoke the salvific intervention of God by means of guerrilla tactics and violence. Their motto was: "Only Yahwe is King and Him only will we serve." They thus contested the Caesars, the census, the taxes, and especially the head tax, which at that time was the equivalent of recognizing the emperor as lord and god. The coming of the Messiah would transform all and would also realize the end of this world by beginning the eternal reign of God. The apocalyptic writers studied and tried especially to decipher the signs of messianic times; they made calculations of the weeks and years in an attempt to determine in terms of space and time the occasion of salvific events. (3)

Luke and Matthew develop their stories of Christmas in the light of these expectations. Luke describes Simeon (Lk 2:25-32) as "righteous and devout, looking for the consolation of Israel, waiting for the kingdom to come". When he saw the child Jesus, he was convinced the moment had come: "My eyes have seen thy salvation." Matthew tells of the wise men coming from the Orient looking for a new-born king in Herod's palace. The massacre of children indicates how seriously rumours of the coming king were taken by the authorities (Mt 2:1-18). The whole atmosphere was pregnant with expectation. Inside this world of expectation, and into it, came Jesus. He confirmed and corrected those expectations.

For the three synoptic gospels the centre of the preaching and teaching of Jesus was clearly the kingdom of God (of "heaven" in Matthew, but with no difference in meaning). John's gospel replaces the kingdom with "life eternal", an example of a dynamic translation of a Hebrew concept for Hellenistic readers. (4) Whatever the terms used, the concentration in Jesus' teaching on the symbol of the kingdom is clear; and the kingdom language figured conspicuously in his trial and sentence. Both Matthew and Luke organized their material carefully; they begin with the expectation and arrival of the king and conclude with the risen Christ assuming the authority of the kingdom and pointing to future culmination. "All authority in heaven and on earth has been given to me ... to the close of the age" (Mt 28:18-20). In Luke, the disciples ask Jesus: "Lord, would you at this time restore the kingdom to Israel?" The response of Jesus provides a corrective to their understanding of the kingdom, limiting it to Israel. It is a promise rather than a description: "You shall receive power when the Holy Spirit has come upon you; and you shall be my witnesses in Jerusalem and in all Judea and Samaria and to the end of the earth" (Acts 1:6-8).

In the Lord's Prayer Jesus taught his disciples to pray for the kingdom (Mt 6:10), putting this expectation at the core of the religious practice of his disciples. Prayer is an anticipation of the reality for which we pray. The interplay between the present and the future, which is a central dimension of the notion of the kingdom, is completely at home with the life of prayer. The prayer for the kingdom is completed in a Hebrew parallelism: "Your will be done on earth as it is in heaven." The kingdom for which the disciples are taught to pray is the rule of God over all historical happenings.(5)

In the teaching of Jesus the kingdom of God embraces all the longings and anguished cries of the people of Israel, responds to the basic message of the Old Testament, reveals the purpose, character and power of the coming rule of God, and invites people to respond in radical obedience. The proclamation of the kingdom is always accompanied by a call to decision, to follow Jesus, to participate in the mission of God. For Jesus, the coming kingdom is the transforming rule of a compassionate God.

Jesus does not give a conceptual definition of the kingdom of God. As D. Senior says:

At no point in the Gospels or in the New Testament as a whole does Jesus offer his definition of the kingdom of God. The phrase is explicitly cited in some of the important summaries of his ministry in the Synoptic Gospels (cf., for example, Mk 1:14-15 and parallels) and is a refrain for many of his parables and sayings (cf., for example, Mk 4:26.30; Mt 13:44,45,47), but its meaning is not spelled out. What Jesus meant by this metaphor must be deduced from the overall message of his preaching, his lifestyle, his commitments. That is why we have to keep in mind the comprehensive scope of the kingdom theme. Jesus' parables about a gracious God, his fellowship with outcasts and women, his healing and exorcisms, his conflicts over interpretations of law -- all of these become a cumulative definition of what the kingdom of God meant.(6)

We do not propose to make any detailed study of the biblical teachings about the kingdom of God. Our purpose is to see how the kingdom perspective helps us to answer some of the urgent, down-to-earth missiological questions, and we hope that this will not violate the total testimony of the Bible.

Our reading of the Bible and our consideration of the symbol of the kingdom of God need to be tested and checked both through the practice of love and through exegetical consideration of the texts. There is a hermeneutical process: as Christians we have the texts; attempting to be obedient we enter into the human situation as Jesus did; we make our own the fate of the needy, the marginalized, the exploited, the sinners. From this perspective we recover the memory of the kingdom of God. The Bible sheds new light and we are sent once again to test the insights in new historical manifestations of faithfulness. *(7)*

Jesus began with the prevalent expectations among his people. When he preached the kingdom of God, he could build on the idea of the kingdom in the minds of his listeners. *(8)* He elaborates; he confirms; but he also corrects. Let us first concentrate on the Old Testament, indicating those basic affirmations concerning the reign of God that were assumed in Jesus' teaching, and then explore how he leads us to a new understanding of the kingdom.

THE KINGDOM OF GOD IN THE OLD TESTAMENT

In the Old Testament the hope of the kingdom has two main historical sources. One is the experience of liberation; the exodus as the central event. *(9)* The other is the experience of powerlessness, of despair. *(10)* If God does not save us, who can?

Liberation is followed by celebration and worship, and the establishment of the Covenant. God establishes a covenant with the liberated people. It entails a vocation, a calling, and it provides the ground rules for the future relationship between God and God's people.

To liberation and the covenant belongs the prophetic tradition. *(11)* The prophets denounce the present reality both in terms of the experience of liberation in the past and of the coming day of the Lord. That day would be a day of judgement; but there is always the promise of rebuilding, of re-establishing the people. The prophets reminded Israel of its missionary calling. It is to be faithful to Yahwe, to assure justice, to care for the weak, to be the people of the promise and of the kingdom. Israel has been established as God's partner in the covenant; through that calling, Israel will be a light to the nations, showing forth God's final purpose of redemption for all. *(12)*

The other source for the hope of the kingdom is the awareness of God's silence, the experience of the total powerlessness of the people. *(13)* During the period of the Greek and Roman occupation of Palestine, the odds were heavily loaded against the expectation of the people. They could only wait for God's judgement on history. The apocalyptic literature sees the rule of God as practically absent in present history, but it will be fully manifested in the future. There is what amounts to a negation of historical action; living the present evil situation, the people look forward to the final triumphs of God. *(14)*

In both perspectives, there is a final future that belongs to God. The difference lies in the response to the present situation, in

whether one works for approximations to God's rule in the
actual conditions of history or acquiesces in the present
depending on the promise of final judgement.

The two lines meet in the Messiah, conceived by the prophets
of Babylon as the Suffering Servant.(15) There is a chronological problem; apocalyptic literature comes after Second
Isaiah; but by New Testament times all the traditions had merged,
and they were no longer concerned over historical sequence. Jesus'
selection of Isaiah 61 to describe his own vocation and his
acceptance of the road to the cross provide sufficient theological authority to suggest that the reconciliation between the
apocalyptic and prophetic line is to be found in the symbol and
reality of the Suffering Servant.(16)

Here we have a full recognition of the evil of the human
situation. There is no easy solution for the problems of the
world. In his missionary freedom Jesus converted the path of
suffering and defeat into God's instrument to transform all
human history and to attain real victory. He puts himself in the
prophetic line announcing liberation to the people, the year of
freedom granted by God. His awareness of the power of the devil
and his own imminent death could be interpreted as the Suffering
Servant accepting even the silence of God, which is at the very
heart of the apocalyptic perspective. He goes to his death in
order to liberate new historical forces to carry out his universal
mission.(17)

Historical and Eschatological -- Present and Future

The reign of God, the kingdom of God in the Old Testament, is to
be realized in human history. God is a living God whose will is
to be recognized and implemented in the life of the nation.(18)
Israel's faith is a historical faith.

An excellent example of this historical understanding of the
kingdom of God comes from the period of the Judges. Professor
George Pixley, in his book God's Kingdom,(19) calls attention
to the faith of Israel in Yahwe as King and to its political
consequences. The tribes that came from Egypt into Canaan could
not conquer the promised land at a single stroke. They first
occupied the hills; they were not strong enough to take
possession of the valleys. Soon they were joined by people who
had escaped from the villages in the valley to find refuge among
the Hebrew people in the mountains. The tribes of Israel constituted a loose association of villages kept together by their
faith in the lordship of Yahwe expressed through the covenant.
They rejected all central authority; their only authority was
Yahwe himself, and the only law was the law that had taken shape
in the difficult years of the exodus.(20) In political language,
this was Israel's revolutionary project: to realize Yahwe's kingdom in the land of Canaan. In moments of danger, the villages
sought a measure of military unity and looked for a "judge" who

42

would lead them into battle. It was under much pressure that they went to Gideon to ask him to become king over Israel. He would not; he said to them: "Yahwe rules over you" (Judg 8:22-23). Later on, when the elders of the people asked the prophet Samuel to anoint a king for them he warned them of the sad consequences that would follow (1 Sam 8:4,5,10,17). A similar example of that historical faith in Yahwe as king is provided by Joshua 24:14,18. Joshua calls the people to make up their mind: If they want to serve Yahwe, they cannot serve other lords. He and his house know what they will do. The unique loyalty to Yahwe involves a clear rejection of all kings from outside or from within. The attitude of the early Christians towards the cult of the emperor and their affirmation that Jesus alone is Lord have their parallels in the Old Testament.

There is more than the rejection of authority here; there is also the recognition that the protection and justice Israel enjoyed should be extended to the strangers and to the weak (Ex 22:20-23). The jubilee year proclamation (Lev 25) was the built-in legal provision to ensure that justice prevailed -- especially in the ownership of land by every family.(21) These laws and the kind of injunctions included in Joshua 24 are important in understanding the ministry of Jesus and Paul's message of justification, new beginning and personal faith. They do not constitute a "spiritualization" of the Old Testament; they attempt to translate these basic perspectives into new historical situations.

There is no complete coincidence between the facts of history and the rule of God, but God actively participates in the shaping of human history, calling, rebuking, correcting, inspiring.(22) The prophets do not provide an interpretation of history as an intellectual exercise but as a calling to the obedience that God expects and demands. They announce the coming judgement of God. They demand repentance to be manifested in historical actions of reparation. It is in history where anticipations of the kingdom are experienced and where the calling toward a new day of Yahwe is heard.

The kingdom of God is an invitation to see, beyond the present realities, the power of the age to come, and to find in that power the inspiration to confront the actual historical ambiguities.(23) God calls people to go forward, to look for the new land, for the new justice. The vision of the kingdom, even if based on an historical experience of the past -- the oppression in Egypt and liberation from it -- is always related to the future. Even historical experiences of failure did not militate against the messianic hope.

The prophetic tradition is sometimes utopian in describing the new reality that God promises, but precisely for that reason, the new reality becomes the people's historical task. The prophets speak of a future that is coming as judgement and promise, but

in the light of that future, there is also the call to
repentance, new faithfulness and new justice.(24)

History is the scene of conflict with evil, sin, oppression and
injustice. It is also where anticipation of the kingdom is
experienced and the summons to live in a new day, the day of
Yahwe, are heard. God's final purpose is the establishment of
God's peace, shalom.(25) It is the full implementation of God's
justice, the establishment of right relations with one another,
with God and with nature. The jubilee year provided for periodic
correction of prevailing injustices. The kingdom of God looks to
the consummation of history, in and through a dynamic historical
process in which God is the final and deciding protagonist. John
Bright says, commenting on the teaching of the kingdom of God in
Isaiah:

> *History is moving onward to its consummation. The great eschatological
> drama is about to commence. It is as if the prophet were witnessing in
> the present suffering the birth pangs of a new creation (66:7-9). In
> almost shocking language he depicts Almighty God, Himself in the agony
> of travail (42:14-16), impatient to bring forth the new thing that he
> has prepared. Through the prophecy from end to end, run two parallel
> motifs. There is on the one hand the imagery of the judgement, the Day
> of Yahwe. It is seen in the awful picture of chapter 34: ruin, blood,
> fire, smoke, stench, and desolation. And we are left at the end with
> the worm that dieth not and the fire that is not quenched (66:34 c.f.;
> 63:1-6; 49:26; 50;2-3; 51:6). Opposite this, is the imagery of the new
> creation, of nature rejuvenated (35;1-2; 41:19; 55:13; 60:13). There
> will be long life and peace (65:20-23). The warfare in nature would
> be ended (65:25), fellowship with God restored (65:24). The primitive
> Eden peace (51:3) will once more come to earth and the rule of God,
> long disrupted by sin, will be re-established. In this coming triumph
> of God toward which all history moves, the people of God will find
> redemption. Indeed the prophet sings so eloquently of a new heaven and
> a new earth (65:17-19) that the author of the great New Testament
> apocalypse, when he wished to speak of the ultimate triumph of God
> over all the powers of evil, could do no better than borrow the same
> language (Rev. 21:1-4).(26)*

The intervention of God is absolutely necessary to bring to an end
the ambiguities of history and the contradiction of human disobedience, and to incorporate nature in the new reality. But the vision
of the prophet is always historical, concrete, calling the people
to move from Babylon back into Palestine. The shalom of God will
be the culmination and the purification of all human exodus.(27)

The Kingdom as Rule and Realm

The symbol of the kingdom of God has a double reference all through
the Bible. It is the rule of Yahwe and reminds us of our relation
to God as king. Kingship in the Old Testament indicates the
authority of Yahwe, and that is not limited by geography. It points
to the dignitiy of the king more than to any particular province

44

over which the king has dominion. But by extension of that first meaning, it is also the kingdom of God as a communal concept. The people as a whole are called to proclaim their loyalty to the Lord, and, consequently, to organize their collective life within the framework of the law given by Yahwe, the covenant, the decalogue, the jubilee. The first -- the affirmation of God's sovereignty -- is basic. To be chosen by God, to accept God as Lord, is to accept God's exclusive claim on us.(28)

The prophets rebuke the people of Israel because they have betrayed their covenant relation with their God. Hosea describes it rightly as a violation of human faithfulness. Perhaps this sense of the absolute sovereignty of Yahwe was the distinctive feature of Hebrew religion. God's power was no⁺ limited to a particular region or to a specific aspect of the life of the community. The God of history was the God of Abraham, Isaac and Jacob, the God who liberated them from oppression, marched with them through those difficult years in the desert, and helped them at every stage in the conquest of Canaan. With this understanding the concept of Yahwe as King assumed a dynamic quality. While the anonymous poet of Psalm 137 could not sing "one of the songs of Zion" in a foreign land, Jeremiah could write to exiles: "You will seek me and find me, when you seek me with all your heart" (Jer 29:13). And Deutero Isaiah could proclaim: "In the wilderness prepare the way of the Lord, make straight in the desert a highway for our God...and the glory of the Lord shall be revealed..." (Is 40:3-5). To bring out the dynamism of the kingdom symbol, many translators render "God reigns", "God rules", or "God will save his people".

The calling and promise of God is to Abraham *and* his people (Gen 12:1-3). Israel is meant to be a light for the *nations*. Peace and justice would kiss each other in the historical shalom of God (Ps 85). This dialectic of the relation to Yahwe the King and the anticipation of a historical destiny -- the working and the waiting for the new city coming from God -- is *cantus firmus* of the kingdom in the whole Bible. Personal and communal, historical and eschatological at the same time, it is a vision of the creator God who wants to recreate the people even from dry bones (Ezek 37:1-14)! This dialectic determines the whole Old Testament eschatological hope. The loyalty to God challenges the status quo. The building of the nation is the test of all religious practices in Israel. The justice visible in inter-human relations will be the evidence of their faithfulness to Yahwe. This double focus of the kingdom in the Old Testament is very helpful in understanding the transition from the proclamation of the kingdom in the gospels to the proclamation of Jesus in the epistles.(29)

Israel and Nations

Israel has a universal mission. Israel also has this concrete sense of God's particular relationship with her. Looking back on her history and looking forward to the culmination of God's rule over all creation, Israel was able to discern in Adam and Eve (Gen 1:26-31), in Noah (Gen 9:13-17) and later in Abraham (Gen 12:2-3), the concern of God for all people, all humanity. God is the creator, the sustainer, the judge and the redeemer of all.*(30)*

The notion of "election" plays a central role in the Old Testament.*(31)* Yahwe is a personal God, calling a particular people to a specific course of action. Election does not happen because of their merit, but because of the mercy of God who hears the "cry of his people" (Ex 3:7-10). Israel was invited and expected to organize her life in response to that grace. It was -- and it is -- very easy to confuse election with a sense of ownership. The calling of Israel was to organize a nation where justice would prevail, where the poor, the orphans, the widows, the foreigners would be specially protected (Is 1:1-20). The prophets' constantly reminded them of their vocation in response to God's election. They referred to God's dealings with other nations and peoples (Amos 1,2) and God's using them for the correction of Israel (Hab 1). While Israelite nationalism was often reinforced and political manipulations justified by the notion of election, the vision of the prophets was that of a world of nations, all under the loving rule of God.

While the Bible as a whole concentrates on the history of God's relationship with Israel and on the formation of the church, it indicates clearly God's deep concern for the nations. God is the Lord of all nations (Amos 9:7). All nations belong to God (Ps 82:8). Israel has a vocation to be a blessing to all nations (Is 42:6; Jer 4:2; Is 2:3; Mic 4:2). Chapters 45 and 56 of Second Isaiah make a clear connection between God being the only God and all the nations being called to kneel before him. The promise is that "his house will be a house of prayer for all people" (Is 56:7). God rules over Israel and his action in history is for the good of the people of Israel at all times. God blesses, judges, acts through promise and fulfilment, in the concrete events of the people. But the meaning of these extend beyond Israel; they are also to become paradigmatic, sacramental, representative.*(32)* God's concern for Israel is the concern for a people he has chosen for a specific purpose; but this very concern -- expressed in Israel, through Israel and even outside Israel -- embodies God's concern for all other people. Two Indian leaders of the evangelical movement point out that:

> *The eschatological vision in the Old Testament looks forward to Egypt and Assyria being God's people along with Israel (Is 19:24-25). "In that day Israel will be the third with Egypt and Assyria, a blessing in the midst of the earth, whom the Lord of hosts has blessed, saying, Blessed be Egypt my people, and Assyria the work of my hands, and Israel my heritage." Egypt will not have to join Israel to become "my people". Egypt will attain the status of God's people and at the same time retain her identity. The people of other nations will be gathered to God not as*

46

subsidiaries of Israel, but as themselves under the lordship of the Messiah. Thus the Old Testament shows that while Israel is distinct from other nations, and is already God's people, others will be His people. (33)

What belongs to Israel is the vocation of being a light to the Gentiles and the nations (Is 49:6). God's particularism is rooted in God's universal love. Old Testament history remains for all nations a central point of reference for their own national history.*(34)* While Israel needs to be reminded that the fact of being children of Abraham does not give them a place in the kingdom, all the other nations are invited to look toward the history of Israel in order to discover clues for their own histories. Miguez Bonino puts it this way:

To confess the kingdom is not for us, Gentile Christians, only to enter into the heritage of our own history but at the same time to take distance from it and to become engrafted into this other one. It is to confess the exodus, the exile, Bethel and Nazareth, Golgotha and the tomb of Joseph of Arimathea as our own -- and this not merely in their significance or in their exemplariness but in their particular and un-repeatable historicity. Consequently, an inevitable duality of history appears. We Gentiles, in distinction to Israel, cannot believe without this double historical reference and, therefore, without asking ourselves how to relate God's action to this double historical reference in which the gospel involves us. (35)

To summarize, the commanding vision of the Old Testament is the rule of God over the life of Israel and over all creation. Yahwe brought liberation to people in the terrible circumstances of yesterday; Yahwe will bring liberation even in situations that seem to be hopeless. He commands history. To believe in God is to respond in obedience, building the community in justice. In fact, Jeremiah goes so far as to affirm that "to do justice is to know God" (Jer 22:15-16).

This response is made in history. Even when a day of judgement, of God's own intervention is envisaged or resurrection is promised, it is within history. All of creation will be included in the total transformation that is poetically anticipated. The kingdom demands a personal loyalty to Yahwe and the community Yahwe wills, the vision of a transformed society. While the Old Testament concentrates on Israel, it recognizes the place and vocation of all nations under God's sovereign rule. The historical experience and the theological understanding of Israel thus were meant to provide a perspective for all. The memory of liberation and the reality and frustration of prevailing oppression together led to the anxious expectation of the coming of the day of the Lord, the arrival of the Messiah. The prophets pointed to the coming of the Messiah, the anointed one, sent by God to initiate the new age. In the apocalyptic literature the image of the Son of Man represented the final action of God, God's intervention in the human drama.*(36)* Into that world, charged with hope and fear,

Jesus came announcing: "The time is fulfilled, and the kingdom of God is near at hand. Repent and believe in the Gospel" (Mk 1:14-15).

THE KINGDOM OF GOD IN THE NEW TESTAMENT

The Kingdom is Here

Jesus joined John the Baptist and the prophets of old announcing the arrival of the kingdom of God and calling all people to repentance. The new element is the affirmation that the time is fulfilled (Mk 1:15) and that *in his own person the kingdom is present and at work.(37)* When Jesus read the Scriptures in the synagogue of Nazareth he amazed the people with his bold affirmation: "Today this Scripture has been fulfilled in your hearing" (Lk 4:21). The messianic promises of Isaiah 61 and 58, woven by Luke into the reading, were manifested in Jesus' actions. His compassion for the powerless represented Yahwe's royal concern for the poor of Israel. The acts of healing and exorcism were powerful manifestations of the kingdom of God challenging the power of the devil.(38) The demons flee, signifying the dawn of the kingdom of God (Mt 12:28). Jesus forgives sins, and promises a new beginning, as in jubilee year.(39)

When Jesus sends out his disciples on a missionary journey, he gives them powers related to the kingdom: they are to proclaim the good news to the poor, heal the sick, cast out demons. And when they come back and report to him, Jesus interprets what they experienced as a radical defeat of the forces of evil. "I saw Satan fall like lightning from heaven" (Lk 10:18). He tells the Pharisees: "The kingdom of God is not coming with signs to be observed; nor will they say, 'Lo, here it is!' or 'There!' for behold the kingdom of God is in the midst of you" (Lk 17:20-21).

But such direct references to the breaking in of the kingdom of God in his person and through his acts are not very numerous. The synoptic gospels recognize a certain secret, a mystery in the person of Jesus and in the manifestation of God's kingdom. It is like inviting people to make up their minds, to come to their own conclusions. When John the Baptist sent his disciples to ask Jesus: "Are you he who is to come, or shall we look for another?" Jesus answered: "Go and tell John what you hear and see: the blind receive their sight and the lame walk, lepers are cleansed and the deaf hear, and the dead are raised up, and the poor have good news preached to them" (Mt 11:2-5). John should form his own judgement. Many people were drawing their own conclusions; some decided to follow him, "for he taught them as one who had authority, and not as their scribes" (Mt 7:28-8:1). Others were scandalized, and ascribed his power "to Beelzebul" (Mt 10:25) or went so far as to conspire to kill him (Mt 21:46; 26:3). There are hints in the gospels of the faith of common people; they trust in the authority of Jesus, some leaving every-

48

thing to follow him. Many of them are foreigners. The exclamation of the Roman centurion by the cross can be taken as a good summary of the response of faith hoped for in the gospels: "Truly this was the Son of God" (Mt 27:54). The parables are a teaching aid to help people to understand the mysteries of the kingdom. At the same time they are an invitation to discover by faith in the humble beginning of Jesus' life the hidden potential of the kingdom yet to be manifested.(40)

We can feel in the pages of the New Testament the excitement prevailing in the early Christian communities. No wonder that many took them for drunkards! (Acts 2:13) After the resurrection their faith was confirmed: the authority manifested in the Rabbi of Nazareth could not be set aside by the power of the cross. They did not yet have the conceptual categories to explain all those events, but one thing was clear: in this Jesus a radical action of God had taken place, a new age had dawned, and their personal destiny and the destiny of all humankind was now linked for ever to those events.

The kingdom has dawned. The king has visited the people and "will come again". It is amazing that the expectation of the *parousia*, the affirmation of the coming of Jesus in glory, provides the perspective to interpret the actual life of the Christian community and to read back into the life of Jesus the manifestation of his kingship. For the New Testament as a whole, the life, death and resurrection of Jesus are powerful manifestations of the kingly rule of God in action. A definitive battle has taken place, and it has changed the human situation; a new period has opened. Christ will come again; but the kingdom has already been made manifest in history, and from that moment on the whole human situation has been already transformed. Meanwhile he has been exalted, and every tongue should confess that "Jesus Christ is Lord, to the glory of God the Father" (Phil 2:5-11).

A new, radical dimension has been added to the kingdom perspective of the Old Testament. A particular person in a concrete historical period becomes the embodiment of God's final purpose for all creation. Through the coming of the Holy Spirit the Christian community is empowered to remember him, to experience his presence here and now, and to look forward to his coming in judgement and glory. In order to proclaim this faith, they are ready to confront the Jewish authorities and to challenge the imperial pretensions of Caesar.(41) The lordship of Christ is at the very centre of the New Testament vision of the kingdom of God. In him, "once for all" (Heb 9:26) the foundation stone of the kingdom has been laid.

The Battle for the Kingdom

From the first attempt at killing Jesus in Nazareth (Lk 4:29) to the actual execution on the cross, the life and ministry of Jesus was a continuing confrontation with the powerful of his days. It is not strange that Matthew has Roman soldiers looking for the

49

child born to be king and murdering all the children under two in that region (Mt 2:16-18). In Luke's story Simeon describes the conflictual nature of Jesus' vocation: "Behold this child is set for the fall and rising of many in Israel, and for a sign that is spoken against (and a sword will pierce through your own soul also) that thoughts out of many hearts may be revealed (Lk 2:34-35). Jesus puts himself in the prophetic tradition, and suffering and persecution belong to his vocation. He also incorporates in himself the apocalyptic tradition that describes end-time calamities; he goes through those calamities by submitting himself to the trial and the cross. Even if we take the anticipations of the death of Jesus Christ in the gospels as resulting from the reflections of the early church, it is clear that Jesus did not try to avoid confrontation. In fact he took the initiative in exposing the hypocrisy of the powerful, in denouncing the exploitation of the poor, in calling them to the promise of the kingdom.

A great debate divides the interpretations of the gospel with regard to the political character of Jesus' ministry. Behind the different positions in this debate it is possible to read the different ideological presuppositions of the interpreters. Porfirio Miranda writes:

The thesis that Christ did not engage in politics is a denial of precisely those historical facts which we know with the greatest certitude. I refer not only to the testimony of Suetonius, who, in his Vita Claudii (25:4) describes the Christians as "impulsore Chresto assidue tumultuantes" ("ever in frantic tumult at the instigation of someone called Chrest"), although this document would suffice. No, the most incontrovertible of all scientifically certain historical facts is that Jesus died by crucifixion and that crucifixion was the death reserved for political transgressors. No serious researcher omits this, but we shall cite only two. Johannes Schneider, in the article on the word staurós in Theologisches Wörterbuch zum Neuen Testament (8:573) says:

"In the Roman provinces the punishment of crucifixion was one of the most powerful means for the conservation of order and security. The government inflicted the death of the cross, proper to slaves, especially upon the freedom fighters who strove to gain their peoples' independence from the Roman authority."

As for a Catholic scholar, let us consult Heinrich Schlier: "The death of Jesus on the cross ... is the death which the Roman authority inflicted on 'rebels and bandits'" (Die Zeit der Kirche, p. 59).

For more confirmation: the sign that Pilate ordered attached to the head of the cross of Jesus (INRI) specifies political delict as the motive of the punishment of this particular crucified criminal. Raymond E. Brown, a Catholic, comments: "All the Gospels agree that the charge of being a royal pretender was inscribed against Jesus" (The Gospel According to John, 2:919). Further, as Schlier observes, "from the words

50

of Jesus about his kingdom Pilate could only infer that he was a king,
and that accordingly his action concerned the political sphere. And
what is remarkable is that Jesus admits it: 'You have said it'" (Die
Zeit der Kirche, p. 63). Jesus was executed for political sedition.
This is a fact that no serious person, Catholic, Protestant, or
agnostic, can call into question.

Moreover, Matthew and Mark inform us that Jesus was crucified between
two "robbers" (Mt 27:38, Mk 15:27). Now, this was the depreciatory
denomination applied by the authorities to rebels and insurgents,
as can be seen by comparing "Barabbas was a robber"(John 18:40) with
"who had been incarcerated for an uprising and homicide occurring in
the city" (Lk 23:19). Consequently, Jesus was crucified side by side
with two other rebels -- only, he was more deserving than they, so
he was put in between them, with a placard stating his crime: that
of being a royal pretender.

No single historical fact about Jesus of Nazareth is more demonstrable
than this one: that he engaged in revolutionary political activity.
In his study on the parables (The Jesus of the Parables, p. 17), C.W.F.
Smith comments very aptly, "No one would crucify a teacher who told
pleasant stories to enforce a prudential morality." (42)

He continues affirming the public character of Jesus' ministry,
and, commenting on Lk 13:31-33, he adds:

Three things are evident in this little pericope. First, the absolute
lack of respect with which Jesus speaks of the ruler. This is the
language of a rebel, not of an obedient subject. Second, that Jesus
himself realized that his activity and teaching were of a kind that
would bring upon him the death penalty. And third, that not only
the government of Judea sought to kill Jesus, but that of Galilee as
well -- which is understandable only if both saw in him a political
danger.

John H. Yoder, who makes a clear non-violent option, illustrates
the involvement of Jesus in all aspects of the life of his people,
including the political line. He says that the real debate should
be on the "how" of Jesus' participation and the implications of it
for our own participation.(43) The story of the temptations seems
to indicate different methodologies for influencing public opinion
and securing political power. "The kingdom of this world" is the
final bribe offered by the devil! No, Jesus will not follow the
political options preferred by the powerful of this world. His
prophetic and messianic vocation leads him to a confrontation with
the historical forces of oppression and the powers and principalities that manipulate all human existence.

For Leonardo Boff, politics as a limited, partial, particular
field of human activity cannot describe the total richness of
Jesus' life.

He is indeed the Messiah-Christ, but not one of a political nature.
His kingdom cannot be particularized and reduced to a part of reality,

51

*such as politics. He came to heal all reality in all its dimensions,
cosmic, human, social. The great drama of the life of Christ was to
try to take the ideological content out of the word "kingdom of God"
and make the people and his disciples comprehend that he signified
something much more profound, namely, that he demands a conversion
of persons and a radical transformation of the human world; that he
demands a love of friends and enemies alike and the overcoming of
all elements inimical to God and humankind. (44)*

The kingdom of God, God's power, was active in Jesus for the
benefit of his fellow citizens. Jesus took seriously the
historical predicament of his nation and, at the same time,
in his life, God was working out God's purposes for the whole
of humanity. There are not two different histories, one secular
and the other religious.(45) Jesus' was a very down-to-earth
ministry. This ministry was for the blessing of Israel; it was
at the same time for the benefit of the whole of humankind and
to reveal to all nations God's saving will. In Jesus we have
the kingdom in action. He takes as his main vocation the jubilee
year proclamation and its implementation in the person of the
Suffering Servant. His whole life, till his death on the cross,
is the final and complete manifestation of God's kingdom of
love.(46) In Jesus, as in the Old Testament, God is the defender
of the forgotten and marginalized of society. By receiving sinners
and outcasts, caring for Samaritans and Gentiles, he comes into
conflict with the prevailing forces of society. His strictures
on the observance of the Sabbath and his attitude to the temple,
the symbol and centre of the internal oppression of the Jewish
people, angered the religious leaders.(47)

The International Ecumenical Congress of Theology held in
February 1980 in Brazil says in its final document:

*Jesus proclaims the new presence of God's kingdom to this same people.
The kingdom that Jesus points to with his messianic practice is the
efficacious will of the Father who desires life for all his children
(Lk 4, 7:18-23). The meaning of Jesus' existence is to give his life
so that we all might have life, and abundantly. He did this in
solidarity with the poor, becoming poor himself (2 Cor 8:9; Phil 2:7)
and in that poverty announced the kingdom of liberation and life. The
religious elite and political leaders that controlled Jesus' people
rejected this gospel: they "took from their midst" the Witness to the
Father's love, and "they killed the Author of life". Thus the "sin of
the world" reached its limit (Acts 2:23; 3:14-15; Rom 1:18-3:2; John
1:5,10-11; 3:17-19).*

*But God's love is greater than human sin. The Father carries his work
forward, for the Jewish people and for all the peoples of the world,
through Jesus' resurrection from the dead. In the risen Christ we have
the definitive triumph over death and the first fruits of "the new
heaven and the new earth", the city of God among humankind (Rev 21:1-4). (48)*

The followers of the king are called to carry the message of his
victory into every nook and corner. As Professor Käsemann said

at the World Missionary Conference in Melbourne in 1980:

> *Of course, Jesus was not a revolutionary. Nevertheless his*
> *appearance on the scene has revolutionary consequences which*
> *were inescapable. For when someone is called King of kings and*
> *Lord of lords (as Jesus is in 1 Timothy 6:15), and announces his*
> *claim to his creation, when truth and falsehood contend together*
> *for every individual human being, when the crucified snatches his*
> *kingdom out of the hands of tyrants and usurpers and destroys the*
> *works of the devil on earth, a universal conflict breaks out. When,*
> *therefore, the demons appear in the New Testament as the real*
> *enemies of Christ and every Christian service in its deepest sense*
> *must consequently be regarded as a kind of exorcism, as the ex-*
> *pulsion of evil spirits, it is this universal conflict which is*
> *being described. The rule of the Spirit of God on earth in the*
> *realm of the demons always takes the form of the exorcism of these*
> *demons and victory over them.*
>
> *Any version of Christianity is incredible which, while professing*
> *belief in the Holy Spirit, fails to carry his power and victory*
> *into every deepest hole and corner. What our world needs everywhere*
> *today is this exorcism of its demons. For it is only when the heavens*
> *open and the Spirit descends that God's good creation comes into being*
> *and continues in being. (49)*

The whole world, even the whole of creation, is the battlefield
of the kingdom. Politics has no privileged position, but it is
not excluded either. The affirmation of the love and justice of
the kingdom led Jesus, and will lead Christians, to conflictual
situations. How did Jesus go into that battle?

The Suffering Lord

The evangelists give what appears disproportionate space for the
story of the crucifixion. Paul says, summing up his own mission:
"I decided to know nothing among you, except Jesus Christ and
him crucified" (1 Cor 2:2). There, in the cross, history and
eschatology, the present and the future meet. The cross marks
the climax of a historical conflict. If we forget this historical
dimension, we fall into docetism. But the cross is also the focal
point of the divine-human drama. The New Testament confesses that
through his death and resurrection Jesus confronted all forces of
evil, oppression and death and, vindicated by God in the
resurrection, is now proclaimed victorious over all powers and
principalities.

The cross was the consequence of the social and political struggle
in which Jesus was engaged. His love for the outcasts, his
preference for the poor, his proclamation of God's kingdom as
manifested in him could not go unchallenged. He could perhaps
have avoided the cross by making concessions to the authorities,
but he would not. The non-resistance that he preached was lived
to the end. All this is very historical, very political; but at
the same time, through the same events, the drama of God's saving

53

and liberating will for all people was being enacted and disclosed.(50)

Whether we use historical and political language or apocalyptic
language, we are describing the same reality. The morning of
the resurrection confirms that both the hidden negative forces
and their historical manifestations in Israel have been defeated.
Evil at its worst could not extract from the crucified one a
word of hate, a word of condemnation. Evil has been dethroned
by the suffering of the innocent one.(51) Of course, there still
are tragic manifestations of evil in human history, but evil has
been defeated. The followers of Jesus know that there is no
completely hopeless situation because hope has triumphed in the
cross.(52)

This applies also to the manifestation of evil that we know as
oppression with its consequences of poverty. The Apostle Paul
could say that Jesus became poor so that out of his poverty we
all could become rich (2 Cor 8:9). No situation of poverty is
now definitive; it does not correspond to God's will. It is
condemned. It needs to be challenged. And the final enemy, death,
is also defeated. This is the revolutionary affirmation of the
Christian faith. In Jesus Christ, the power of the kingdom was
at work, transforming the whole of human history. The rule of
God has been vindicated over death, misery, and evil. The new
people of God are called to proclaim these events and to give
hope to all humankind.

It is in this context that we should understand the differences
between the preaching of the kingdom of God in the gospels and
the announcement of Jesus as Lord and Saviour in the book of
Acts and in the epistles.(53) Attempts have been made to explain
the difference as a result of the post-Pauline spiritualization
of the message and its transformation into a non-historical
"salvation of souls", but they do not carry conviction.

What we have here, in this transfer of emphasis, is a double
process: (1) an interpretation of the meaning of the life of
Jesus in the light of the resurrection and the coming of the
Holy Spirit; and (2) a translation of symbols belonging to the
Palestinian culture and religious background into categories belonging to the Greek culture and Mediterranean religions. For
Luke (in Acts 8:12; 28:23) the theme of the kingdom is linked
to the recognition of Jesus as the Christ. Paul mentions the
word "kingdom" only twelve times, but his use of the word is
in total harmony with the affirmations of the synoptic gospels.
He sees the kingdom in concrete actions; he recognizes Jesus as
the foundation of the kingdom; he is aware of the conflict that
belongs to the kingdom; he is convinced about the future
vindication of the kingdom (Rom 14:17; 1 Cor 4:20; Col 1:13;
1 Cor 15:25,50, etc.). The reality of God's reign, manifest in
the exaltation of Jesus Christ, is pervasive in Paul's letters,
even when the word "reign" or "kingdom" is not used. Jesus stands

in clear opposition to demonic forces. Paul sees precisely this
cosmic struggle against principalities and powers reaching its
climax in the cross and resurrection (1 Cor 2:8; Eph 1:21;
Col 2:15). Here we have both the post-resurrection interpretation
of the cross and the rendering of the forces which oppose the
kingdom in Hellenistic language. The kingdom becomes present in
Jesus as Lord, as the *autobasileia*. Ronald Sider says:

> *It is central to the biblical word that precisely the One whom the
> principalities and powers crucified (1 Corinthians 2:8) is now their
> Lord and Master. The risen Jesus is Lord of the world as well as the
> church. Every strand of New Testament literature boldly proclaims this
> message. "All authority in heaven and on earth has been given to me,"
> the risen Jesus told his disciples (Matthew 28:18). In Colossians 2:10,
> Paul declares that Christ is the head of the principalities and powers.
> The resurrected Christ is "far above all rule and authority and power
> and dominion, and above every name that is named, not only in this age
> [i.e., certainly in this age!] but also in that which is to come"
> (Ephesians 1:21). First Peter also reminds us that angels, authorities
> and powers are now subject to Christ (3:22). Likewise the author of
> Hebrews declares that everything is put in subjection under Christ
> (2:8,9). Nowhere is this stated more powerfully than in the book of
> Revelation where it is repeatedly affirmed that the risen Jesus is now
> "ruler of kings on earth" (1:5). Even now He is King of kings and Lord
> of lords (19:16; 17:14).*

> *To announce Christ's lordship to the principalities and powers is to
> tell governments that they are not sovereign. It is to tell them that
> whether or not they know or acknowledge it, they are subject to the
> risen Lord Jesus who summons them to do justice, to seek peace, to pro-
> mote shalom on the earth. It is to tell governments that Jesus Christ,
> who is one with the Father, is on the side of the poor and that He is
> at work in history pulling down the rich because of their oppression and
> neglect of the poor and exalting the lowly. Again, it is clear that merely
> to witness in a biblical way to the principalities and powers is to en-
> gage in dangerous, subversive political activity. (54)*

But it is also when faith proclaims Jesus as Lord (Phil 2:5-11;
1 Cor 12:3) that we need to call to our mind the relation between
the kingdom and suffering as God's chosen methodology
to express his redeeming love and the inclusiveness of
his kingship. How far the song of the servant, especially Isaiah 53,
influence Jesus is still being debated by scholars.(55) But it
cannot be denied that through the centuries the church has seen
this connection, and that the actual text of the gospel supports
it.

It is in Isaiah 53 that we find the highest perception in the
Old Testament of liberation through vicarious suffering.

To us this connection is very important because the liberation
proclaimed in Isaiah 53 is an integral salvation that involves
justification, healing, liberation from oppression, prosperity,

peace and koinonia, even eternal life! Tomas Hanks, for
example, underlines that

> *Isaiah 53 gives us, on the one hand, the basis to understand that
> the work of the servant is presented as a "penal substitution" and
> also proposes very clearly the political sense of the cross as option
> and "identification of the servant with the oppressed". The gospels
> describe Jesus' option to become poor. Isaiah 53 underlines that
> the servant suffers the oppression that is characteristic of the
> life of the poor. In the resurrection and exaltation of the servant,
> God universalized the original revolution that the Exodus was for
> Israel. In this way we must understand that the preaching of Peter
> on the day of Pentecost represents a prophetic denunciation against
> the oppression and institutionalized violence expressed in the
> crucifixion of Jesus (Acts 2:23-24). And his call to repentance is
> above all a call to the people to repent of the oppression against
> God's poor, Jesus (Acts 2:36-38), whose gift of the Holy Spirit at
> Pentecost indicates the democratization of the gifts of God (Acts 2:
> 17-18) and the end of all oppressive oligarchy (Mt 20:20-28). ...
> As St Peter indicates, the message of the cross has three inseparable
> and unavoidable dimensions: "He himself bore our sins in his body on
> the tree, that we might die to sin and live to righteousness. By his
> wounds you have been healed, for you were straying like sheep, but
> have now returned to the Shepherd and Guardian of your souls" (1 Pet
> 2:24). "He took our sins" so that we might "live for justice" and with
> his wounds we have been "healed". In Isaiah 53, like everywhere in the
> Scriptures, these three dimensions (took our sins -- Catholic-evangelical;
> to live for justice -- liberation; and to be healed -- Pentecostal)
> clarify and strengthen one another, and "a three-fold cord is not
> quickly broken" (Eccles 4:12).* (56)

The obedience of Jesus unto death, his participation in the
poverty and in the oppression of humankind reveals the magnitude
of his love, the all-embracing scope of his mission and the power
of redeeming suffering in history.

The Kingdom to Come

"In the preaching of Jesus the reign of God is an eschatological
concept, without prejudice to the sayings about its imminent
outbreak or its present realization, and it stands within the
framework of a transcendental expectation of salvation; in other
words, it is moulded by apocalyptic."(57) We have referred
earlier to the new fact introduced by Jesus -- the time is
fulfilled, the kingdom is at hand. We have also considered the
dynamic historical character of the struggle of the kingdom. Now
we further realize that the early Christians were full of the
expectation of the kingdom to come, the second coming, the judgement, and the transformation of all reality. The prevailing
spiritual and theological atmosphere of the early Christian
communities was one of praying and waiting for the return of
Jesus. The synoptic gospels provide evidence that this expectation was shared by Jesus himself. At the same time that he was

acting in the power of the kingdom -- being himself the kingdom -- he called the people to prepare themselves for the
radical novelty of its final coming. He used the apocalyptic
image of the Son of Man, poor and powerless, coming with divine
power to judge all people and to inaugurate the kingdom. Most
of the parables of the kingdom point to this future coming.
The mystery of the kingdom is its inconspicuousness; small
like mustard seed (Mt 13:31 ff. and par.) but it is pregnant
with explosive potential.

> From this standpoint, the kingdom of God is a cosmic catastrophe
> depicted in certain events which constitute the eschatological drama
> of Jewish apocalyptic. Jesus is at one with those of his Jewish
> contemporaries whose hope is not set on a visionary political kingdom
> but who look for the Son of Man coming on the clouds of heaven (Dan 7:13).
> Even though the community, in its intoxication with apocalyptic visions,
> might have made some addition, esp. in the so-called Synoptic Apocalypse
> in Mk 13 and par., there can be no doubt that Jesus spoke of eating and
> drinking in the kingdom of God (Mk 14:25 and par.). (58)

The prayer of Jesus maintains the dialectic between the kingdom
we pray for and the will of God that is to be implemented on
earth. God's kingdom is future, it will come, we are called to
enter it; but the kingdom is also at work. Günther Bornkamm
explains this dialectic as follows:

> We must not separate the statements about future and present, as is
> already apparent from the fact that in Jesus' preaching they are re-
> lated in the closest fashion. The present dawn of the kingdom of God
> is always spoken of so as to show that the present reveals the future
> as salvation and judgement, and therefore does not anticipate it.
> Again, the future is always spoken of as unlocking and lighting up
> the present, and therefore revealing today as the day of decision.
> It is therefore more than a superficial difference, more than one of
> degree, concerned, so to speak, only with the quantitiy of colour
> employed by the apocalyptic painter, when one notes that Jesus'
> eschatological sayings do not describe the future as a state of
> heavenly bliss nor indulge in broad descriptions of the terrors of
> the judgement. Hence in Jesus' preaching, speaking of the present means
> speaking of the future, and vice versa.

> The future of God is salvation to the man who apprehends the present
> as God's present, and as the hour of salvation. The future of God is
> judgement for the man who does not accept the "now" of God but clings
> to his own present, his own past and also to his own dreams of the
> future. We might say with Schiller: "What we have denied the moment,
> eternity will never give back." Only here it applies in a new and
> fulfilled sense. In this acceptance of the present as the present of
> God, as we have tried to make clear, pardon and conversion are one in
> the works of Jesus.

> God's future is God's call to the present, and the present is the time
> of decision in the light of God's future. This is the direction of

Jesus' message. Over and over again, therefore, we hear the
exhortation: "Take heed, watch" (Mk 13:33-37; cf. 5, 9, 23, etc.).
This "take heed to yourselves" (Mk 13:9) stands in marked contrast
to all curious questioning. Therefore, those very words of Jesus
which refer to the future are not meant to be understood as
apocalyptic instruction, but rather as eschatological promise, as
W.G. Kümmel has pertinently observed. (59)

Many of the sayings of Jesus concerning the future kingdom come
to us in apocalyptic language and it is not possible to consider
here all the difficulties that scholars face in interpreting
them. However, in comparison with the apocalyptic writers of
his time, Jesus himself had exercised tremendous restraint. He
refused to provide dates, he refused to speculate. And the
intention of his teaching through the parables is clear.

1. The kingdom is a gift of God. The ethical demands made and
   the blessings offered by Jesus derive from the assurance that
   God has decided to bring God's kingdom. God's coming does not
   depend on human strategies. The tragedy of the present
   situation is not the whole reality; the kingdom is coming --
   and that is an invitation to trust.

2. The invitation does not kill human initiatives; in fact it
   invites people to prepare themselves for the kingdom: watch,
   be ready (Mt 24:44; 25:10-13; Lk 12:35-37). We must be alert,
   especially because when the king comes in his glory, he will
   judge us in terms of our previous, unexpected and even un-
   recognized encounters with him in history in "these little
   ones" (Mt 25:31-46).

3. The servants of the kingdom should persevere notwithstanding
   failures and difficulties. The final harvest is guaranteed
   (Mt 13:3-8). "My word shall not return empty" (Is 55:11).

4. The kingdom is the highest value to which all others should
   surrender (Mt 6:33; 13:44-46).

5. Opposition is to be expected. There can be no elimination of
   ambiguity in history. This is the time of God's patience, the
   time to repent. The day is coming when all truth will be
   revealed and it will be a great surprise for all (Mt 7:21-23;
   13:24-30).

In Jewish expectations, the coming of the Messiah means the breaking
in of the shalom of God, the arrival of God's kingdom.(60) With
the resurrection of Jesus we have a different understanding of the
end of time. The resurrection opened a new age; it marked the
beginning of the eschatological missionary era.(61) There is a
period between the arrival of the Messiah in suffering and the
coming of the Messiah in triumph. The final arrival of God's
kingdom will take place after the completion of the missionary
period. From now on the kingdom will have a double reference:

(1) Something radically new has already happened in Jesus; the world has been reconciled to God. All people are called to recognize themselves in this event. (2) Living in the present historical period, we are called to look forward to the fulfilment of all the hopes of Israel in the culmination of history, the judgement and redemption of history that will take place in God's own time.

This expectation of the kingdom that permeates the life of the early church, rooted in the experience of the lordship of Christ, enlarges the horizon of faith to embrace the whole of human history and its final destiny. In Paul and the other writers of the New Testament, we have the final expectation of a total transformation of creation -- a new heaven and a new earth. The prophetic utopia of universal shalom is thus re-affirmed in the wider context of a universal mission.

The Mission of the Kingdom

There is a certain consensus that Jesus conceived his mission and the mission of his disciples as being confined to Israel (Mt 10:5). Perhaps he shared the Old Testament expectation that the nations will come to worship in Jerusalem. The cleaning of the temple courts reserved for worship by foreign pilgrims and the parables of the banquet of the kingdom (Mt 8:11; Lk 14:16-24) support this view.

However, the whole ministry of Jesus was geared to the overcoming of all human barriers. He clearly rejected the prevailing notion that the promise of God's salvation was limited to the Jewish people. John the Baptist had declared that God could raise children of Abraham from stones (Mt 3:9). The hero of one of Jesus' central parables is a despised Samaritan. The most impressive testimonies of faith are given by foreigners, e.g. the centurion (Mt 8:10), the Syrophenician woman (Mk 7:25), the soldier who saw him die (Mt 27:54). In the great parables of the judgement (Mt 25:31-46) "*all people* will be assembled before the Son of Man"; at the very beginning of his ministry he provoked the wrath of the people in Nazareth by reminding them of God's blessing to the foreigners (Lk 4:24-27).

The Gentiles also belong to the redeemed as is clear from Matthew 8:11 = Luke 13:24 seq. (see section 9) and also from Matthew 25:32 seq. and the universal character of the banquet parable. If Jesus repudiated the current picture of the future community, he never destroyed the basic ideas on which it was built. The people of God will stream into the kingdom of God, once it has been purified in the great judgement from all the unworthy and from evildoers (Mt 13:30,48; 22:11-13; 25:32 seq.). The "elect" will be assembled from all quarters of the heavens and brought into the perfect kingdom (Lk 17:34 seq. = Mt 24:40 seq.; Mk 13:27 par.). In God's plan the atoning death of Jesus has a decisive significance for the redemption of the "many" (Mk 10:45; 14:24) and for the gathering of God's scattered flock (Mk 14:27 seq.), to which the

early Christians were convinced that the Gentiles belong (see
John 11:51 seq.; 10:16 seq.; 12;24,32). The success of its
mission to the Gentiles brought home more strikingly to the
early church what was in principle contained in Jesus' description
of the Gentiles at table with the Jewish patriarchs (Mt 8:11 par.).
We must insist that Jesus never abandoned the notion of a community
of the redeemed, particularly in the context of the proclamation of
the eschatological kingdom. (62)

We must conclude that for Jesus the kingdom involves the nations
of the world, though he understood his own historical mission
and the immediate mission of his followers as centred in Israel.
Nor can we dispute Jesus' special preference, among his own
people, for the poor and the marginalized.

The people who receive help from Jesus are therefore throughout,
as the gospels show, people on the fringe of society, men who because
of fate, guilt or prevailing prejudice are looked upon as marked men,
as outcasts: sick people who, according to the current doctrine of
retribution, must bear their disease as a punishment for some sin
committed; demoniacs, that is to say, those possessed of demons; those
attacked by leprosy, "the first-born of death", to whom life in
companionship with others is denied; Gentiles, who have no share in
the privileges of Israel; women and children who do not count for any-
thing in the community; and really bad people, the guilty, whom the
good man assiduously holds at a distance. (63)

In the Acts the church is described as learning the implications,
for its life in the world, of Jesus' coming. It took many
disturbing events to convince the early church of its cross-
cultural vocation. When the Holy Spirit came upon them at Pentecost, the disciples were able to communicate with the pilgrims
and worshippers in Jerusalem. Persecution scattered the
Christians; it also gave them an opportunity to explain the
happenings in Jerusalem to more inclusive groups. A special
revelation turned Saul, the hated persecutor, into Paul the
Apostle to the Gentiles. The visions which Peter and Cornelius
had meant a real breakthrough in the understanding of the inclusiveness of the kingdom of God. As their understanding of the meaning
and expectation of the *parousia* changed and as they grew in their
sense of the true significance of the cross and the resurrection,
they were able to articulate a vision of the kingdom as embracing
the whole oikoumene. It marked the great leap from centripetal to
centrifugal mission.

The great commission summarizes the experience of the early
church in relation to the risen and exalted Christ. "All authority
in heaven and on earth has been given to me. Go therefore and make
disciples of all nations, baptizing them in the name of the
Father and of the Son and of the Holy Spirit, teaching them to
observe all I have commanded you; and lo, I am with you always,
to the close of the age" (Mt 28:18-20).

Their horizon expands. Its centre is the faith that Jesus
Christ is King of kings and Lord of lords (1 Tim 6:15), that
he fills all things (Eph 1:23; 4:10), and in him "all things
will be united" (Eph 1:10). The mighty acts of God will result
in a "new heaven and a new earth". And to the new Jerusalem
the "kings of the earth shall bring their glory, the glory and
the honour of the nations" (Rev 21).

The Church and the Kingdom

The easy and frequent remark that Jesus preached the kingdom and
the result was the church could be taken as a useful rhetorical
challenge to the faithfulness of the Christians, but in no case
as an historical or theological truth.

Jesus gathered around him disciples, in different numbers and
categories, in order to continue the proclamation of the coming
kingdom -- the twelve, the seventy, the many. These disciples
later became witnesses of the resurrection and developed an
awareness of their mission as followers of Jesus and in the
expectation of his second coming.

Jesus called the whole people of Israel to repentance and to a
new lifestyle which will be in keeping with the coming kingdom.

> *The invitation to the kingdom of God must be accepted in metanoia;*
> *for its sake all the other things of this world -- riches and fame --*
> *must be abandoned. We are not to be like those invited to the wedding*
> *who pleaded all kinds of obstacles (Mt 22:1-14 par. Lk 14:16-24).*
> *Again there are various parables which emphasize this with particular*
> *sharpness. For the sake of the kingdom of God, which is like the*
> *treasure hid in a field or the goodly pearl for which all else will*
> *be exchanged (Mt 13:44-46), we must pluck out the treacherous eye or*
> *cut off the treacherous hand (Mt 5:29 ff.). The most startling is*
> *that we must reflect that many have made themselves eunuchs for the*
> *sake of the kingdom of God (Mt 19:12). At any rate, true regard for*
> *the kingdom of God requires the most serious decision, the most*
> *serious weeding out of the few from the many (Mt 22:14). A sharp*
> *alternative demands a pitiless decision. "No man, having put his*
> *hands to the plough, and looking back, is fit for the kingdom of*
> *God" (Lk 9:62). (64)*

The disciples responded to this call and were ready to sacrifice
everything in order to follow Jesus. Of course they were afraid,
especially during the days after the crucifixion of their master.
Nor could they understand the full meaning of the resurrection.
They experienced both the joy of his presence and the fear of
persecution.

In the book of Acts, we have a description of the early Christian
community. They experienced the presence of the Holy Spirit which
produced in them an abiding sense of joy. They lived in fear of
those who were determined to obliterate even the memory of Jesus.

61

In joy and fear they constituted a community of reciprocal support. There were no needy people among them. Little by little they were led to discover the wider dimensions of their being at the service of the kingdom and their life was marked by loving care of others (Acts 3:1-7); fearless witness to the lordship of Jesus when confronting the authorities (Acts 4:19-20), and the proclamation of the "word of God with boldness" (Acts 4:31). As Christians continued to grow in numbers and spread beyond Jerusalem, and their expectation of the kingdom deepened, the self-identity of the church became more and more evident. There was a process of institutionalization at work, but there was also a growth in self-awareness and in response to new challenges. Thus Paul developed the image of the body (1 Cor 12), first in instrumental terms, showing how the different members could work harmoniously together for the fulfilment of the total ministry; later, in the letter to the Ephesians and Colossians, the church becomes the body of which Christ is the head, in a dialectical relation of sharing in the glory of God's plan and being the precious instrument to fulfil a servant role for the benefit of the whole creation. As Markus Barth puts it:

> In Ephesians and Colossians fullness and filling denote a dynamic unilateral relationship: the revelation of God's glory to the world through Jesus Christ; the power exerted by God in Christ and in the church for the subjection of the powers and the salvation of all mankind; the life, growth, and salvation given by Christ to his body; or, in brief, the presence of the living God and his Messiah among his chosen people for the benefit of all creation. If there is a cosmic role ascribed to the church in Ephesians then it is as servant (cf. 2:7; 3:10; 6:10-20; 4:12). She is to manifest the presence of the loving and powerful God. Not God, Christ, or the Head, but solely the body of Christ, that is, the house of God, the church, is "to grow" (2:21-22; 4:15-16; 4:13). Any notion of world dominion by the church is missing, but the church is equipped to do a "work of service" and to "stand against" and "resist" the attacks of evil powers (4:12; 6:13-14). The idea is lacking that one day the church will fill or replace the world. Assurance is given that Christ is filling all things (1:23; 4:10) and that the saints will attain or will be filled with all of God's and the Messiah's fullness (3:19; 4:13). (65)

In the perspective of the kingdom the church is called to be and to go. To be an anticipation of the kingdom; to show in its internal life the values of justice and supportive love; to develop a priestly servant vocation in interceding in Abrahamic tradition for the whole human community; to celebrate liturgically, in anticipation, the coming of the kingdom; to watch like the virgins of the parable for the coming of the Lord; and then to be the missionary people of God, called and sent all over the world to proclaim and serve, announcing and manifesting the coming of the kingdom of God.(66)

Meanwhile, in the process of Christian living and working towards the kingdom, waiting for the kingdom, the power of the kingdom

begins to manifest itself through the Holy Spirit in the transfiguration that takes place in the lives of Christians.(67)
They are invited to participate in the transformation of the
whole creation through the guidance of the Holy Spirit. Peter
writes of Christians as partaking in the divine nature (2 Pet
1:4), and writes of the new life in Christ. The kingdom becomes
a process of conversion and sanctification. It manifests itself
in the change of allegiance, in passing from the kingdom of
darkness to the kingdom of light, and consequently in the
shaping of all things, both in individual and communal life
towards the plenitude of the kingdom to come.(68)

To sum up, the New Testament continues to live in one history:
in Jesus, in the history of occupied Israel; in the early church,
in the history of a scattered community of believers in the
wider Roman Empire. But in every case, Jesus is proclaimed as
Lord; the kingdom is manifested in the power of the Spirit
calling Christians to a kingdom-oriented lifestyle, to live in
expectancy of the total redemption, transformation and glorification of this world in God's coming kingdom. Between Jesus'
ascension and his second coming, his *parousia*, a new people, the
Israel of God, the church, is called into being. In one sense,
it replaces the old Israel. It is now up to this community to
show God's universal care for all nations, to testify to the
breaking through of the kingdom of God in the life and death of
Jesus Christ.(69) This community should not repeat the mistake
of Israel and take its calling as a private privilege. The
calling is to a mission. It is to engage in the announcement
of the King, Lord Jesus; to challenge in his name all powers
that afflict and oppress; to be a priestly people interceding
for others, Christ's servant people, projecting Jesus' spirit
of love in the world, a waiting people pointing towards the
promises of God.(70) The churches are sent to love God and neighbour, to follow the path and model of Jesus, and with the
assurance of the actual power of his kingship to proclaim,
teach, disciple and baptize all nations. The church is sent as
a servant to all people, with a priestly, missionary and evangelistic vocation. The gospel of Jesus Christ belongs to all
people. The kingdom is the hidden meaning of their history. The
church witnesses to the kingdom of God until the end of the
earth and until the end of time.(71)

Chapter IV

THE MISSION OF THE KINGDOM OF GOD:
THE KINGDOM THEME AS A THEOLOGICAL CONCERN

In 1968 Wolfhart Pannenberg could complain that the kingdom of God was a theme that did not figure in contemporary theology;[1] today it would be difficult to come across a theological search for missionary clarity that is not conducted from the perspective of a kingdom theology. Practically all contextual theologies of the third world attempt to interpret their reality -- historical, cultural and political -- in terms of visions of the future within a kingdom perspective.[2]

It is possible in our present time to cherish a common hope for our world. Because of that, we cannot be satisfied with a theological perspective that would interpret our situation -- the situation of our nation or our religious group -- without reference to the destiny of other people and other cultures. Because the world has become smaller, the vision of God has become bigger.[3] We are convinced that God's concern is for the whole of reality and not just for the particular group to which we belong. The growing pluralism in the world is posing questions that demand a frame of interpretation for both the secular and the religious aspects of reality.

There is a common hope; there is also widespread despair. The new concern with the kingdom theme is also a result of a certain apocalyptism, this growing despair over the possibilities of humankind today.[4] Only with the vision of the kingdom as a prayer that centres on the promises of a new day in God could one find strength and power to continue in hope.[5]

To take an example, Christians in El Salvador live under the constant threat of institutionalized violence; they are also subject to the random violence which challenges the institutional violence. Simple Christians, facing death or imprisonment, are in this situation inspired by the hope not born of an appraisal of the power factors in the situation, but arising out of the conviction that the present reality does not correspond to God's will, cannot be permanent, and that a new day must come.[6] The vision of the kingdom of God is not the product of their despair; it comes from the Bible they read. It is the response of grace to their despair.

The full manifestation of the kingdom is in the person of
Jesus Christ. In him, the powers of the kingdom are at work.
He acts with the authority of the King, forgiving sins and
casting out demons. He breaks into the domain of the forces of
evil. His death reveals the kingdom's dynamics of love. He
takes upon himself the sin, the oppression, the mortality of
humankind and his resurrection marks the victory over evil,
suffering and death. (7)

He assumed human flesh, was made sin, became poor, and through
his death and resurrection brought new life and the promise and
anticipation of the coming kingdom. Because we see the powers of
the kingdom in operation in the life of Jesus Christ, we realize
that he points, beyond its limited manifestation on earth, towards
the deeper mystery of God. Jesus is the revealer of God. Jesus is
not self-contained; he faces life and meets death in obedience to
the Father and filled with the Spirit. The doctrine of the
Trinity is the conceptual formulation of a reality lived by
Jesus, experienced by Christians, and affirmed by the church. (8)
The doctrine appears in the history of Christian thought to express the experience of the apostles and the early Christians
who have seen in and through Christ the reality of a creator God
and a sustainer Spirit. Jürgen Moltmann writes:

> The history of Christ is interpreted in the light of its origin. The
> gospels relate the story of Jesus as the story of the Messiah sent
> from God into the world for the purpose of salvation and anointed with
> the Spirit of the new creation. They present the history of Jesus in
> the light of his sending, his mission. ... The relation between the
> Jesus of history and the God whom he called Father corresponds to the
> relation of the Son to the Father in all eternity. The missio ad extra
> reveals the missio ad intra. The missio ad intra is the foundation for
> the missio ad extra. (9)

The suffering and death of Jesus resulted both from the historical
controversy in which he was involved and of the saving will of God.
Those who were actors in that history were acting in terms of
their understanding of the situation and responding to factors of
power in society. The events that took place in Jerusalem did
really take place. They were historical events. At the same time
they were a revelation of the suffering, saving will of the
Father. (10) Through the suffering of Christ in history we also
see that the God who sent him participates in his suffering. The
cry on the cross, "My God, my God, why hast thou forsaken me?"
(Mt 27:46) reveals the suffering of the Son in the silence of
the Father; it also reveals the suffering of the Father in the
fulfilment of his deepest manifestation of missionary love in
order to recover the fallen creation. God is a passionate lover,
and whoever loves, suffers. (11) The only way out of suffering is
through reconciliation and rehabilitation. The Holy Spirit works

65

in mysterious ways to call humankind to reconciliation, pointing
to the goal of the kingdom which is life in all its fullness. In
Jesus we discern God as a missionary God, reaching out to rescue
and save, creating in freedom a relationship of love.*(12)* The
historical kingdom of God takes shape as the Spirit of God calls
humankind to a new relationship. Christ represents the expression
of God's missionary love reaching out to recover the loyalty, the
love, the covenant relationship that was granted in freedom and
lost in sin.*(13)*

The faith in the triune God corresponds to our experience of
Jesus Christ and of the coming of the Spirit. Christian reflection
on this historical reality led the church to the conviction that
it is the manifestation *ad extra* of an internal reality in God.
Jesus is sent by the Father and constituted, confirmed, anointed
by the Holy Spirit. He points towards the creative purposes of
God, and towards the redemptive action of the Holy Spirit, calling
the whole creation to reconciliation. When we talk of the mission
of Jesus Christ we are talking of the eternal mission of God. We
understand our own mission in the light of the mission of Jesus
Christ who was sent by the Father in the power of the Spirit.*(14)*

The cross tells us that in history the kingdom suffers violence.
Because of the cross we cannot live in facile optimism about
history. The forces of evil are real. To defeat them God's Son
had to be sent. The cross signifies God's recognition of the
power of evil. It also shows how God deals with evil. Jesus'
encounter with evil leads to the cross, and to the vindication
of love in the resurrection.*(15)* Our mission is the same. The
mission of the church is indeed the continuation of the incarnation. God the Father sends the Son in the power of the Spirit;
Jesus calls the church to enter into this missionary movement of
God.

The sin which resulted in the cross is however present in all
human beings, and does not spare the churches. We can only put
our faith in God's calling, in the indwelling of the Spirit, on
Jesus' promises to be present wherever two or three meet in his
name -- and not in a particular quality or merit of the Christian
churches! But the frailty of our condition or the sad reality
of our sin should not blind us to our vocation to become ambassadors for Christ calling everybody to reconciliation with
God (2 Cor 5:16-21)! We are called to share in God's redemptive
passion.

EXTRAORDINARY AND ORDINARY MISSION?

Because the kingdom is the mission of the triune God, creator,
redeemer, sanctifier, it is concerned with the whole of reality.
Nothing, especially nothing human, is outside this loving
concern. God's rule is seen in the preservation of nature, in
the movement of the stars, in the changing seasons, and in God's

care for people. God's care for people must happen through
people. God calls us to love and to justice, but God is not
an agent outside history intervening always in miraculous ways.
The miracle of God's love happens through free human beings who
are called to be co-workers in the working out of God's purposes.(16)

In the words of a Danish theologian, Johannes Aagaard, God
works through one extraordinary mission and many ordinary
missions.(17) The extraordinary mission is the mission of Jesus
Christ, the mission of the church -- manifested in the sending
of Jesus Christ and in the calling of the church to its particular
vocation of witnessing to the kingdom of God. The ordinary
missions are the missions of the nations, the missions of all
historical agents that cooperate in the building up of the human
community. Through all aspects of human history -- political,
economic, cultural and social -- human beings are called, as
communities and individuals, to participate in God's providential
care -- which includes the building up of caring, protective
communities.(18)

This distinction is useful, but it cannot be absolutized because
Christians and churches are also necessarily involved in the so-
called ordinary missions through diaconial ministries. The fact
that the church is a social institution has in itself socio-
political consequences. The church is called into existence to
serve the extraordinary mission, God's own revelation in Christ,
but through its very existence it becomes involved in all aspects
of God's caring mission for humankind. The distinction is useful
insofar as it points to the special responsibility of the church
for the extraordinary mission. The recognition of histories
other than the history of Israel and of agents other than
the church of Jesus Christ as agents of the kingdom of
God is itself possible only because of the ministry of Jesus
Christ. It is the vocation of the church to proclaim the King
and to declare the values, the perspectives, the goals and the
signs of the kingdom in such a way that both missions of the
kingdom could one day be one -- as they already are in God.(19)

The church is the bearer of the secret of God's purpose revealed
in Christ. Therefore it has a missionary responsibility to share
that knowledge with other agents, who are also serving the kingdom, though they are unaware of it and cannot through their
service meet the ultimate demands and goals of the kingdom.(20)
It is not that the mission of the church sacralizes secular
reality by claiming it for the kingdom. The mission of the church
introduces, from the revelation perspective, an element of
renewal, of repentance, that will enable these agents to become
part of the total mission of God -- extraordinary and ordinary.
We must also recognize that the so-called ordinary mission, the
mission of preservation of life, is bound up with the extraordinary
mission; it is fundamental for the mission of the church. Secular
factors and political forces help or hinder the ministry of the

church. Roads were constructed in the Roman Empire purely for military or for economic purposes; but it facilitated the spread of the gospel in the first century. A law that provides for religious freedom is not unrelated to the extraordinary mission of God; it creates the frame within which the extraordinary mission can take place. The preservation of life is never just "secular or ordinary", it is visibly extraordinary when those lives enter into living relationship with the God of Jesus Christ through the church. The Persian King Cyrus was an instrument of God, as Second Isaiah saw so clearly. (21)

We could, and should, distinguish between the mission of God through the church, the people who have responded to the call of God in Jesus Christ, and the mission of God through other agents who are promoting aspects of that mission. But from the kingdom's perspective there is a continuum of love between the preservation of life and the new birth to a life of faith. (22) Once again in trinitarian categories: The creator Father is not absent from the work of the Son or from the action of the Spirit; the Spirit is present in creation and in redemption; the Son is present in creation and in sanctification. It is in the total movement -- action -- of the life of the Trinity that the kingdom reaches every community and every person. (23)

CONVERSION TO THE KING, PERSONAL AND COLLECTIVE

Because the kingdom is God's mission, fully manifested in the total self-emptying of Jesus Christ, those who listen to the message of the kingdom are invited to respond in radical discipleship. (24) Conversion is not an option for the pastoral work of the church. It is the only possible answer to the dramatic disclosure of God's passionate love. To proclaim the kingdom is always an invitation to join the forces of the kingdom and to enter into the kingdom. (25) Repentance is the first act of response. Sins are confessed, allegiances changed and attitudes transformed. If the kingdom is God's plan in action, and if what the Christians experience is the anticipation of that kingdom that is coming into the actual life of today, then we move in a world of wonder and excitement, a world of final decisions. No other word than conversion would serve here. Of course, the word conversion has been misused; it has been reduced to mean a psychological experience. But we need to recover the meaning of that word for the act of response to the call of the Servant King, Jesus Christ, that will send us, as the Father sent Jesus, sustained by the Spirit, on the same path of suffering and hope. (26)

In our response to the kingdom we are integrated into the process of life in God. The movement of love from the Father, Son, and the Holy Spirit continues through the church, calling us to be servants and to show the first-fruits of the Spirit. Jesus put the poor and the children at the centre of the concern of the disciples to symbolize the radical demand of love made by God. The prophets, John the Baptist and Jesus held up the poor as the final challenge to test our response to the kingdom.(27) Response to the kingdom could mean abandoning wealth, family and social relations, but never as an end in itself. Renunciations are necessary in order to integrate ourselves into the movement of love which works for the poor and the outcasts. Justice is the response demanded from those who listen to the call of the kingdom; it is a penultimate goal, paving the way for the actualization of the kingdom of love in *history*.(28) Justice in its biblical sense is rehabilitating justice. It is not to give to each one what he or she deserves; it is to provide everyone what he or she needs to enter into the dynamics of the kingdom.(29)

Very often in the Bible, people are spoken of or addressed as a collective entity. Israel is conceived as a whole.(30) Even in the theological treatise on Israel that Paul presents in the letter to the Romans (9-11), Israel is seen as a collective body that has had its existence through generations, and at the end of time, when God will have mercy on everybody Israel will also receive salvation.

Even today, there is a conflict among Christians concerning mission to the Jews. Are we entitled to call individual Jews to be converted to faith in Jesus Christ or do we need to pray and wait for the conversion of Israel as a body, because that conversion will be the sign that the end is near and the kingdom is coming?(31) In any case, collective language is applied to Israel, as it is applied to the Assyrians or the Egyptians. There is a vocation in the kingdom of God for these collective entities. They are called to repentance, conversion, obedience. Perhaps Jesus' "death for many" could also be understood along these lines; it is also for the collective realities of cultures and nations.

We speak of the church as one such entity. The church is not a club of individuals who pool their private religious experiences in a common body. The church is the body of Christ. It is a corporate reality preserved through the centuries into which we are integrated.(32) This aspect of a collective identity is not easy to appreciate in our day because we put so much stress on individualism. To contemporary consciousness it appears not unlike a narrow nationalism. But the family and the nation and all the collective fruits of culture should be considered as the offerings that the kings of the nations bring to the kingdom: "The kings of the earth shall bring their glory into it" (Rev. 21:24). The kings of the earth here are not individual kings who come personally; they stand for their nations, with all their heritage of cultures and values. That corporate reality is also the object of the concern of God.(33) All our sacrifices offered in love for friends, family, humanity are not lost. To spend ourselves in the struggles for justice and peace is not a waste of time and energy. These are all the collective offerings that will

69

be presented to the King of kings. It is important to labour this point because we often tend to forget this collective dimension in our emphasis on personal salvation.

There is of course a personal call.(34) The parables of the kingdom make that very clear. To follow Jesus is to become a new creature in him; it is to taste something of what the gospel of John calls eternal life, life in all its abundance. It is indeed important that we preserve this individual, personal dimension.(35) Even to work for the corporate good of humankind we need a faith commitment and personal conviction.

THE PRIZE OF THE KINGDOM

We need to recover in our Christian preaching and teaching the belief in resurrection and life after death.(36) Our civilization tends to forget the reality of death. It is true that an undue preoccupation with life after death could be, in fact, has been, a way to evade historical responsibilities. But we cannot deny the testimony of the Scriptures concerning the resurrection of Jesus Christ and the promise of eternal life in him and the kingdom through God's final triumph over death. We need to affirm this conviction that life overcomes death in our daily life, and especially in moments of conflict. Julia Esquivel has said:

Thus the reign of God is the ability to believe until death, and even beyond death, that God is our father and that we are brothers and sisters. It means living so as to break down all divisions, all injustices, to dry every tear, to love in such a way that we may share our lives, because we believe that death no longer has any power over us.

He who believes that on the throne of God the lamb reigns who was slain for love does not dare kneel down before any god made of gold or stone. He dares to oppose any political project that produces injustice or death for the people. Although he may die, he has already been resurrected. The kingdom cannot be taken away from him because he carries it within himself with the violence and strength of God in the people, and he shall never die. That is the light of the everlasting fire.

For that kingdom Moses renounced the throne of Egypt and preferred to share the ills of the people of God. Others die after being beaten, without accepting the transactions that would have rescued them, because they preferred resurrection. Others suffered the trials of mockery, beatings, and even the chains of prisons. They were stoned; others were tortured, burned, persecuted and discredited. Others are marked so that their movement can be controlled. Others are left without food and land. Others are shot while they bury their martyrs. Others flee to the mountains and find refuge in caves. But all of them, even though they continue to be oppressed and mistreated in the factories, the fields and the cities, march onward, lifting their eyes to the future, towards Jesus from whom they derive their faith and who shall give them their prize. For his sake

*and for their sake we must resist until death, knowing that he has
conquered the world.*

*"Therefore, be careful not to refuse God when he speaks to us. When
God spoke to us in those days, the earth shook; this time I shall
make not only the earth to tremble, but also the heavens...says the
Lord." (37)*

That text comes from an experience of confronting death. The sense
of fear and trembling, of trust and joy, comes to us because our
life has already been taken up by God. The maximum that a human
ideology can promise is that the sacrifice of people through the
centuries will find its fulfilment in the classless society. It
does inspire people to acts of heroic self-sacrifice. But in the
Christian eschatological perspective, everyone is invited to
give up life in the service of neighbours and in working for love
and justice, simply because God cares for history and our service
is part of that caring.(38) We do not sacralize history; we
surrender our life to God in the knowledge that our personal
and collective life will find their fulfilment in the kingdom.

The invitation to the kingdom is addressed to each one because
God is a caring personal God. We respond to it because we know
that our being now and forever is in God. We engage ourselves in
historical action in the trust and the ambiguity of our involvement and the risk of death cannot defeat God's creative and
liberating purpose and that in the power of the Spirit even our
death could serve God's purposes. This, perhaps, is the wisdom
of the pietistic movement that demands a personal experience of
God in order to be able to enter fully, joyfully, into the risk
of missionary obedience.(39) But when we become content to bask
in personal piety and do not involve ourselves in the struggle
of the kingdom with all its risks, then faith becomes a sedative
and missionary engagement loses its edge.

OFFERING THE PENULTIMATE

The kingdom is coming. We are asked to pray for it. The assurance
of that future already conditions our present.(40) The kingdom
is the power of the future operating in the present reality.

The kingdom is a present reality. Jesus sends the disciples, and
tells them: "All authority, all power, the reign in heaven and on
earth has been given to me" (Mt 28:18-20). As a consequence the
disciples go into all regions of the world knowing *a priori* that
those regions are already being shaped by the kingdom that has
been given to Christ and that is surely coming.(41) Hope becomes
a motivation, and the life of the Christian community becomes an
anticipation of the power of the kingdom. The Holy Spirit is
active, producing the fruits of love that belong to the final
manifestation of the kingdom.

71

The teaching of Orthodox theologians on the transformation of the whole reality on the model of the transfiguration can help us in our understanding of the relation between history and eschatology.

The liturgical celebration is the moment of awareness, of experiencing the beauty of the kingdom to come. It is the anticipation of the kingdom, the moment when we offer to God the whole cosmos, society, nature and life, which needs to be transformed.(42) In Jesus' ascension, human nature has been taken up to God. Paul is able to say (Col 3:3) that "our life is hidden with Christ in God".

This transformation is not an automatic process; it is a continuous search. It is an exposure of ourselves in worship to the action of God. Because we find ourselves, after Jesus' resurrection, in the new aeon, we do not seek merit; our works now are expressions, tainted with sin surely, but nevertheless an offering brought to the altar to be burned, purified, and accepted.(43)

What we do today for the sake of the kingdom, what past generations have done, what coming generations will do are all preserved in God's own being. God's faithfulness was the guarantee of the covenant in the Old Testament; it is also the guarantee of the new covenant. The kingdom is the goal towards which God wants to take all history. In this God of the future our *present* is received, purified, and preserved.(44)

There are many failures in history. We know of a few heroes here and there who paid with their lives in an attempt to change situations of human oppression. But there are many more who have spent themselves in acts of love and whose names are totally absent from books of history and the memory of people.(45) In God, however, there is memory. Everything that is of value to the kingdom belongs and remains because the kingdom is God's plan and promise, from the beginning of time; its reality is in the missionary being of God.(46)

Karl Barth affirmed that there is no point of contact built into us that would give us access to God. The reality of sinfulness as described in the Bible, especially in the letter to the Romans, is such that there is nothing in us that could enable us to have access to God. It is only in the God-man Jesus Christ that God established the point of contact with humanity.(47) It is in Christ that we are related to God, *in Christ* and not in ourselves. Therefore I cannot trust in my own experience of conversion and in my own experience of forgiveness. I can only trust in God's grace manifested fully in Jesus Christ and in his promises. By living in Christ in this relationship I am able to say that I have the assurance of my salvation in Christ.(48) But the only *guarantee* is God's love for me and not my love of God. That is the fundamental message of Paul in the letter to the Romans:

"For I am sure that neither death, nor life, nor angels, nor
principalities, nor things present or things to come, nor power,
nor height, nor depth, nor anything else in creation will be
able to separate us from the love of God in Christ Jesus our
Lord" (8:38-39). Often we quote this in a spirit of boastfulness,
to suggest that there is no power in the world that could destroy
our love for Christ. But Paul is not saying that we would not
fail, but that there is no power that can make God fail us! Our
life in Christ is guaranteed in God's faithfulness towards us
(Col 3:3).

That faithfulness must extend to our communities as well. What
is true for our individual lives should also be true for our
collective life. We cannot of course claim that the families we
build, the communities we organize and the culture we develop
belong to the economy of the kingdom.(49) We enter into these
activities in the hope that they will be taken as our offering
to the kingdom of God, but finally our trust is in God whose
wisdom rejects, accepts and perfects.(50) Precisely because there
is this continuity of faithfulness in God, we can engage in many
different kinds of activities, knowing that God will apply the
criteria of selective love to all we do. As the Apostle Paul
writes (1 Cor 15:58): "Therefore, my beloved brethren, be steadfast, immovable, always abounding in the work of the Lord, knowing
that in the Lord your labour is not in vain."

The judgement of God will cleanse and transform the offerings we
make so that they become worthy of the kingdom. We do not build
the kingdom, but we build the human community in the light of the
kingdom that is coming.(51) We offer whatever we can produce
under the inspiration of the Holy Spirit to be burned on God's
altar. Because it is an offering to God, we want to offer the
best that we have. Expressions like "building" the kingdom are
best understood in terms of our intention to offer to God the
best, knowing that God is the one who brings the final shalom,
the consummation of all things.

*The utter realism of the biblical literature is evident in its
proclamation of the kingdom of God as the coming reality. No matter
how well things were going, no matter how intimately the communion
with God was felt, the kingdom of God was announced as the future,
the coming kingdom. In the light of the futurity of God's kingdom, it
is obvious that no present form of life and society is ultimate.*

*This insight does not paralyze political activity. The future kingdom
of God -- because it is God (for God's being cannot be separated from
his rule) -- demands obedience already in the present. The future of
the kingdom releases a dynamic in the present that again and again
kindles the vision of man and gives meaning to his fervent quest for
the political forms of justice and love. The new forms that are
achieved will, in contrast with the ultimacy of God's kingdom, turn
out to be provisional and preliminary. They will in turn be called upon
to give way to succeeding new forms. Superficial minds might think that
the political quest is therefore futile. They fail to recognize that the*

*satisfaction is not in the perfection of that with which we begin
but in the glory of that toward which we tend. We possess no perfect
programme, but are possessed by an inspiration that will not be
realized perfectly by us. It is realized provisionally in the ever-
renewed emergence of our striving in devotion of history's destiny. (52)*

Of course this adapting of the present to the promised future
will call for informed action, based on sociological research and
scientific analysis.*(53)* The approximations we achieve will be
marked by the sinfulness of our situation and the mistakes arising
out of human limitations. We can only offer the fruit of our
labours as an offering that needs to be purified, and integrated
into God's plan, in the wisdom of God's own will.

We can also say that the penultimate is a preparation of the way
of the Lord. That is the prophetic expression that John the
Baptist applied to himself; he came to prepare the way of the
Lord. To apply it to ourselves will appear pretentious. But seen
from the perspective of the kingdom that is coming, it is the
path of obedience and discipleship.

No human situation is ultimate; every human situation is penultimate. On this all Christians agree. What we are saying here
is that the penultimate human situations assume ultimate significance because God is interested in this penultimate.*(54)* God is
active in word and sacraments and is present in the poor waiting
for our response to God. They are indeed relative, ambiguous and
penultimate, but they become ultimate because of the hidden and
yet revealed presence of Christ. And within that reality the
judgement on each situation is a final, ultimate judgement! We
cannot pretend that anything that we do corresponds to the final
reality of the kingdom of God. But we engage ourselves in action
with all seriousness because the God of the kingdom seeks our
response and our obedience. This is what takes all religions in
general, and Christianity in particular, to the verge of
fanaticism and intolerance; a relative situation becomes an
ultimate situation in the perspective of God's presence! We
need to recognize the relativeness of each situation; we need
to be reminded of its penultimate character. The kingdom that
is coming is the final critique of all our historical reality. But
we offer in trust the fruit of our labours!*(55)*

"YOUR KINGDOM COME"

The New Testament links the kingdom to the realm of prayer. There
are two prayers that need to be kept in constructive tension:
"Your kingdom come" and "Maranatha, come Lord Jesus" -- the
prayer of Jesus and his disciples and the prayer of the early
church.*(56)* Our understanding of the kingdom as God's plan from
the beginning of time and part and parcel of God's own missionary
being, expressed in creation, liberation and redemption, culmi-
nating in the ministry of Jesus, fills us with wonder, and we can

74

respond only in worship. We are transported into a reality
that permeates all creation. Prayer is the only language to
express such mystery; even our theological reflection on the
kingdom needs to be done in prayerful conversation with God.[57]
In this sense, the kingdom is a spiritual reality. But the word
"spiritual" does not mean "separated from reality". It points
to the presence of God and the freedom of the kingdom, and gives
meaning to the whole of reality. The kingdom that we pray for is
the kingdom that incorporates the promises of the final shalom
of God in historical situations.

The second prayer, Maranatha, is a necessary reminder that we
are waiting for the kingdom of *God* and that we cannot be satisfied with the tentative mediations that we offer for the
implementation of the kingdom in history. Our prayer is for the
coming of the *King* whose presence, fully manifested, is the mark
of the kingdom. Bishop Lesslie Newbigin says that it is easier
for Christians to pray "Your kingdom come" than to pray
"Maranatha".[58] In the kingdom concept, we rightly include
most of the basic aspirations of humankind for peace and justice
which exist even independently of the Christian revelation. But
we are praying for the kingdom of God, for the kingdom manifested
historically in Christ and coming in all its fullness in the
return of Jesus Christ. Ideologies can be offerings to the kingdom, but never a substitute for it.

Finally, the new in the Christian vision of the kingdom is the
King, Jesus of Nazareth. He is the Servant King. The centre of
our Christian hope is Jesus Christ.[59] This becomes evident as
we turn to the mission of the church in the serving of the kingdom and the freedom that belongs to that mission. The King who
is coming will be the commanding reference for all our options
and priorities, and for the whole of our Christian vocation.

Chapter V

FREEDOM IN THE MISSION OF THE KINGDOM

We have seen, biblically and theologically, that the kingdom of God embraces the whole of reality. Nothing historical is foreign to God's creative and redeeming love. Nothing is outside the authority given to Christ as Lord, and no events are outside of the work of the Holy Spirit. We have also discerned in Jesus Christ the full historical manifestation of the kingdom, the kingdom in action. By calling him Lord, the early church recognized in him the authority that in the Old Testament belonged to Yahwe, the King.(1)

THE INVASION OF LOVE IN HISTORY

Jesus is, according to Revelation 1:5, the true witness to God. In his life, his teachings, his death and resurrection, he reveals God's purpose, God's plan which we call the kingdom. He manifests the powers of the kingdom and engages in the final struggle with the powers of the anti-kingdom on the cross. He is the one who witnesses, finally and fundamentally, to God's liberating purposes.(2) He calls the church to assume the vocation of witness.(3) The church's witness is derived from Jesus' own commission, "as the Father has sent me, so I send you" (John 20:21). As he was the witness in the power of the Spirit, so the disciples will receive the Spirit to become witnesses (Acts 1:8). The disciples, and the church they helped build up, are witnesses to God's powerful invasion of love into history in the person of Jesus Christ.

If we want to sum up in a few words the meaning of Jesus, it will be difficult to find a better expression than this -- an invasion of love, the outpouring of love, from the incarnation, through his whole ministry, to the cross.(4) His own definition of his mission is found in the passage in Luke 4:18-21; in him is manifested the rehabilitating justice which is one of the biblical definitions of love. He looked on the multitudes with compassion (Mt 9:36). And the gospel of John summarizes Jesus' mission; of his decision to go to Jerusalem and to the cross it says that "Having loved his own who were in the world, he loved them to the end" (John 13:1).

Jesus said that he came to serve, to give his life as a ransom for many (Mk 10:45). The vocation to be the witness of the kingdom meant a total manifestation of self-surrendering love. In manifesting that love, in witnessing to the kingdom, he exercised a total freedom to respond, to act, to be love unrestricted.(5)

76

A dramatic example of his love and his freedom is seen in the event of the woman who had hemorrhage (Mk 5:24B-34): "A great crowd followed him and thronged about him. And there was a woman who had a flow of blood for twelve years and she came up behind him in the crowd and touched his garment. And immediately the hemorrhage ceased, and Jesus, perceiving in himself that power had gone forth from him, immediately turned about in the crowd, and said, 'Who touched my garment'?" Then he tells the woman, "Daughter, your faith has made you well; go in peace, and be healed of your disease."

Here is the bearer of God's revelation for all time. Here is the prophet who for the multitude was the hope of the coming kingdom. And he stops to pay attention to a woman in distress. The story reveals in a dramatic way the normal attitude of freedom that Jesus had at all times. When he was on the cross, involved in the internal drama of God's own being, he was able to care for the robber at his side and the woman at the foot of the cross. That is missionary freedom -- the capacity to respond to the cry, to the need of all, in love because finally love is the ultimate manifestation of the kingdom.(6)

JESUS' MINISTRY TO THE KINGDOM -- SIGN OF FREEDOM

According to Matthew (4:23ff.), "He went about all Galilee, teaching in the synagogues, and preaching the gospel of the kingdom and healing every disease and every infirmity among the people." It is very difficult to make a distinction between the teaching and preaching of Jesus; the teaching nature of the healing, or the proclamation around the casting out of demons. There is no priority; there is no distinction. This description of Matthew is not normative, but helps us understand Jesus' vocation.

According to Matthew, Jesus teaches, preaches, heals. Perhaps we need to start with preaching because that is what he did, coming after John the Baptist, proclaiming that the "kingdom of God is at hand". His proclamation centres around the kingdom, announcing good news to the poor (Lk 6:20) and denouncing the rich (Lk 6:24), the scribes and Pharisees (Mt 23:23-36). He rebukes the political powers (Lk 13:31-35; Mk 10:42). The proclamation of Jesus has a double function; it announces the inbreaking of the kingdom of God that brings the good news of redemption, of liberation for the poor and the outcast; it also contains a warning of judgement on all those who are powerful in society and reject the call to repentance.

Jesus heals. It is very interesting that in this passage from Matthew there is no mention of the fact that Jesus forgives. We give today more importance to the forgiveness of sins than to the healing of the bodies and minds of people. But in the gospel these distinctions do not have much significance. The word "salvation", as used in the gospels, implies both.(7)

In this relationship between healing and forgiveness we see again the freedom of Jesus. The friends of the paralytic, who go through a great deal of trouble on behalf of the patient, are looking for healing. The man's real problem, from the perspective of his friends, was his ill-health. Jesus, looking at the man, speaks a word of forgiveness. That is a scandal to the Pharisees (Mk 2;1-12) and a disappointment to the friends. Some of the scribes questioned in their hearts, "Why does this man speak thus, it is blasphemy. Who can forgive sins but God alone?" The healing that follows is for Jesus a sign to authenticate the forgiveness. Here is an illustration of the dynamic, creative relationship between forgiveness and healing. We see in the gospels many who come to Jesus in search of healing, and they receive only healing! Jesus is free in his love to respond to what he sees as the need of the person, and of the situation that the person is facing.*(8)*

Whether he heals or forgives, Jesus manifests his love in response to the concrete situations of people. This is the freedom of love. Jesus feels free, after proclaiming the gospel to the poor, to enter the house of rich people. But the fruits of that encounter with rich people are related to his concern for the poor, as is clear in the story of Zacchaeus (Lk 19).

Jesus teaches, and his teaching is about the kingdom. It is about the quality of life that belongs to the citizens of the kingdom. But his teaching is also contained in actions that must oblige people to rethink their interpretations of the law and the prophets. For example, he breaks the law by healing people on the Sabbath. He feels free to break the law in order to save, to heal, to help. He sympathizes with his disciples when they break the religious law which prescribes they should rest on the Sabbath, and the religious ethical law concerning property. In the freedom of love, he sees the law of need or the law of life as being more important.*(9)*

Jesus casts out demons; that is to say, he fights the spiritual forces which oppress people and lie behind individuals and structures of society, so that he may liberate people and society from their power. The all-embracing kingdom of love is the basic guideline. The concrete occasion, the invitation to a kingdom action or a kingdom proclamation, is provided in Jesus' ministry by the needs of the outcast, the powerless, the marginalized.

It is his vocation, his assumption of the burden of the world that provides unity to his freedom. Each action of Jesus responds to a situation, an opportunity, a need, a challenge. He sees a need and he responds to that. But always it is love in action; it is freedom in action. While each action represents a response to a situation, a need, a challenge, each one achieves a fuller meaning because of Jesus' own Messianic vocation.*(10)* In the feeding of the multitude, a particular need of the people was met. At the same time, it achieves a richer meaning when it is interpreted as an anticipation of the Holy Communion, and even of the Messianic banquet in the coming kingdom.(11)

Each one of these independent actions points to the whole, which is the revelation of God's love and the inauguration of God's kingdom. For the lame people who were brought to Jesus a discourse on the kingdom could not be an entry point to the kingdom. There were occasions to make long discourses on the kingdom, and Jesus used them. He preached regularly in the synagogue; that was part of his normal, ongoing work. Every one of these actions was necessary to point to an understanding of shalom, and all the actions together provided a vision of the promise of God. They enabled people to understand salvation as forgiveness, as healing, as the invitation to follow Jesus, as love of one's neighbour, as the struggle against all powers and principalities, as the affirmation of freedom of love as against the bondage of law.(12)

Some of the actions of Jesus acquire their full meaning only after the resurrection, because it is only in the light of the whole that the parts can be understood. As a church today, we have the advantage that we know the total story of Jesus; that enables us to apply all parts of the story to the different and particular actions of love which the church is called to develop in specific situations.

THE CHURCH'S WITNESS TO THE KINGDOM

The church is constituted to give witness to the breaking in of the kingdom of God in Jesus. By the indwelling power of the Holy Spirit, it is called to be the mirror of the mystery, to be the revelation of the kingdom of God. Christians are servants of the whole kingdom; but within the world-embracing dynamics of the kingdom, the special vocation of the church is to announce the kingdom, to invite people to the kingdom.(13) In the Great Commission (Mt 28:18-20) Jesus first refers to the authority that he has been given, and says to his disciples: "...go therefore and make disciples of all nations, baptizing them in the name of the Father and of the Son and of the Holy Spirit, teaching them to observe all that I have commanded you; lo, I am with you always, to the close of the age." Several other biblical passages deal with this particular responsibility of the church within the total economy of the kingdom of God. The vocation of the church is to announce the kingdom, and to invite people to the kingdom.(14)

Both the nature of the kingdom that we proclaim and the personality of the King who commissions us make it impossible for us to be satisfied with a purely conceptual, intellectual proclamation. Because the kingdom is life, Jesus is the living Lord, and the Spirit is empowering reality, the proclamation needs to be acted upon, manifested, and incarnated.(15) It is impossible to speak of the kingdom of God in a convincing way unless we manifest the powers of the kingdom. Paul said that the "kingdom does not consist in words but in power" (1 Cor 4:20).

79

Proclamation is a central dimension of the work of the church;
the word of God needs to be shared through the words of the
church. The story of Jesus Christ and the story of God's covenant
with the people of Israel need to be told and retold time and
time again. (16) But the church not only announces God's plan of
salvation; it is also called to an active role. As a social
community, the church must act in history. Its existence must
facilitate the wider manifestation of the kingdom in history.

Do we organize competitive activities so that our members cannot
participate in the meetings of neighbourhood groups, trade unions,
cooperatives, etc.? Do we include in the intercessory prayers of
the congregation those dynamics of the human search for justice
that also embody God's care for humanity?(17) Even in the internal
life of the church, in the celebration of the sacraments, the
actions of the church have secular consequences. Baptism and Holy
Communion, a wedding or a funeral service are all religious events;
but they address serious human moments of our life, and they have
an inevitable impact on the surrounding community. The church
prays on those occasions with the belief and in the hope that its
prayers will have wider consequences.(18)

In a normative sense, the sacramental, inspirational functions of
the church cannot be isolated from its total witness to the whole
community and the way it will further God's total plan. The
baptism of a child reminds the family and the community that the
child is called to be a co-worker with God in the shaping of
creation and the building of community. The celebration of a
wedding is not the consecration of a family made up of two people;
it is a commissioning of the couple to contribute to the life of
the whole community from their privileged coming together in mutual
love. Every activity of the church should be seen in terms of its
calling to proclaim the kingdom. It should be seen as an action
that helps spread the knowledge of the kingdom; but it also should
be seen as manifesting the reality of the kingdom of God. The
church is a protagonist of the kingdom. As servant, its work
results in signs of love -- in healing, in community building,
in acts of service. As a prophet, the church announces the good
news to the poor, denounces the forces that work against the
kingdom, and encourages whoever and whatever manifests the kingdom in concrete ways.(19) As priest, the church intercedes for
all people. In its worship life it must incorporate the hopes and
needs of the surrounding community.(20)

As the community that announces the kingdom, the church becomes
the first-fruit of the kingdom and a pre-taste of its final
reality; it becomes a sacrament of the kingdom, a manifestation
to the world of God's final goal, a sign in itself pointing towards
the kingdom. The eucharist is the fullest manifestation of this
dimension of anticipation of the kingdom. Through bread and wine,
we anticipate the banquet of the kingdom, the final communion with
God, and "we announce the death of the Lord until he comes" (1 Cor
11:26).(21)

80

The church is thus called to witness to God's powerful acts in history. It is the carrier of the secret to all history in Christ. Its vocation is to bear Christ, and it is implemented through proclamation. But given the nature of the reality that is proclaimed, this proclamation can take place only through participation, service, intercession, suffering, love that is lived.

As Jesus Christ is the free invasion of love, so the church is sent in the same freedom to witness to that love. We must be clear about the difference between a clerical and an ecclesial reality. The church is the people with a particular task in the service of the kingdom of God, but it is not that kingdom and it has no monopoly on it. It is not the only agent of the kingdom. We betray the freedom of the kingdom if we insist that all people should be under the authority of the church. We can no longer accept Christendom as a model. That was an attempt to create a monolithic community subject to the authority of the church. The vocation of the church is to witness to the kingdom in the midst of history, to point toward the King, to make known to the world what has been revealed to it in the life and ministry of Jesus Christ.(22)

THE FREEDOM OF THE CHURCH IN ITS MISSION

Having recognized the specific vocation of the church, we must now affirm that the church is free to select the appropriate means and ways to fulfil its vocation.(23) We can illustrate this freedom of the church by looking at the first Christian community in Jerusalem as described in the book of Acts.

a) The coming of the Holy Spirit in Acts 2 is a profound collective and personal experience that generated enthusiasm and enabled people to speak in tongues -- and to communicate. The reference to speaking in tongues is evidently a reference to the tower of Babel (Gen 11:1-9). The Holy Spirit is launching the church as a missionary community of reconciliation, symbolically, dramatically and historically. This new community is sent into the whole world to call all of humanity, scattered as a consequence of its proud attempt in Babel, to become united with Christ, the real and final link between human beings and God.

b) But what happened provoked the comment: "They are drunk." The action of the Spirit gives rise to surprise and scorn. Peter explains: "They are not drunk, it is too early in the morning for that!" And without realizing it, he finds himself preaching! He goes on to explain and interpret, but that interpretation cannot be complete until he addresses the people saying, "Repent and be baptized...in the name of Jesus Christ" (Acts 2:38-39).

c) The community was together, having all things in common,
    caring for one another according to need, manifesting love
in all relationships and celebrating the communion (Acts 2:43-
47; 4:32-37). This was a powerful attraction. The fact of being
the community and its very style of life were the mission and
"God was adding to the church those who were being saved".

d) Peter and John go to the temple to pray. They see a lame man
    begging at the door. Love takes hold of the apostles, and be-
fore going to pray, they stop to heal. This produces amazement,
and Peter is obliged to explain what happened. He proclaims Jesus
as the Christ and invites people to repent. He acts in freedom
and that freedom opens the door to the proclamation of the gospel.

e) Then follows a series of circumstances that lands the apostles
    in prison. From prison to the temple and back to prison! Con-
fronted with the questioning of the authority (Acts 4:5) they give
testimony to the power under which they find themselves and the
vocation that is given to them. They cannot stop giving testimony
to Jesus because they must obey God rather than men (4:19-20).

They were clear about their vocation. Their service to the kingdom is to give witness to Jesus Christ. Obliged to explain the
events of Pentecost, the healing, the disobedience of authorities,
they do so by pointing to the source of their calling. They engage
in all kinds of activities, some on their own will as they respond
in love to a situation and others as they are called to account,
through the persecution they face. But all of them become entry
points to bear testimony to the total care of God for the people
and to the calling they have received.(24)

The early church, following the example of Jesus Christ, felt
free to respond spontaneously or in organized ways. There was the
time when they had to organize a division of labour between the
apostles and the deacons (Acts 6:1-7) in order to correct an
injustice. What we come across is not anarchy, but it is not a
rigid organization either. Stephen is a deacon, but we see him
preaching -- very soon after the division of labour was made!
There must be divisions of labour, but not an oppressive law which
would prevent any member of the community from pointing towards
the kingdom and inviting others to Jesus Christ.(25)

f) They are all scattered under persecution (Acts 8:1-4). It is
    not a planned outreach programme, but it provides an opportunity
for the disciples to explain why they are where they are and what
is happening in Jerusalem. Implicit in that explanation is an
evangelistic invitation: this has meaning for you, too, and not
only for the people in Jerusalem!

g) Acts could be called the book of the Spirit. We have a series
    of Spirit surprises: Philip being led to the encounter with the
Ethiopian eunuch (Acts 8:26-38); Christ unexpectedly confronting

Paul on the road to Damascus (9:1-19); Cornelius and Peter both being led by visions to an encounter (10:1-11:18) which brings home to the church God's missionary concern for the Gentiles. During the first missionary journeys of Paul and Barnabas (13:1-4), time and time again the church is surprised by God's calling it to face entirely new missionary situations (10:17; 16:9-10).

Paul is passionately convinced that his vocation is to proclaim the gospel and to get as many as he can to accept the new faith (1 Cor 9:19-23). But when he is asked not to forget the poor, he gladly takes on the new task. That was the main recommendation made by the Council of Jerusalem, to take care of the poor (Gal. 2:10; 2 Cor 9). Paul does not hesitate to interrupt his missionary journeys and take to Jerusalem the funds he had collected for the victims of famine (Rom 15:25-26). In freedom he responds to the challenges which new situations bring up.*(26)*

THE FREEDOM OF OBEDIENCE

Following on the example of the early church, the church is free to make options, to fulfil its missionary calling in the most diverse ways and in the most different circumstances. There is only one priority for the church -- to reflect and mediate the love manifested in Jesus Christ. There is only one goal -- the kingdom. There is only one central reference -- Jesus the King. And there is one concrete, historical concentration point -- the poor and the powerless.*(27)*

A document produced in 1959 by the World Council of Churches refers to this freedom of the church in these terms:

> *There is no single way to witness to Jesus Christ. The church has borne witness in different times and places in different ways. This is important. There are occasions when dynamic action in society is called for; there are others when a word must be spoken; others when the behaviour of Christians one to another is the telling witness. On still other occasions the simple presence of a worshipping community or man is the witness. These different dimensions of witness to the one Lord are always a matter of concrete obedience. To take them in isolation from one another is to distort the gospel. They are inextricably bound together, and together give the true dimensions of evangelism. The important thing is that God's redeeming Word be proclaimed and heard. (28)*

Of course, we recognize that there are gifts, vocations, divisions of labour. Such gifts can be personal or collective. A religious order or a missionary organization working in the inner city or involved in a cross-cultural mission to proclaim the gospel to people who are far away from any Christian church makes its own witness. But we must recognize all such enterprises as contingent answers, actions to be taken here and today that are not necessarily to be repeated tomorrow, there or here. The vocations and the contingencies stand in a reciprocal relation of freedom and not of law.

83

The evangelist who is confronted with a situation of human need cannot argue that his or her gift lies in another direction. We are all called to serve this total invasion of love in the kingdom of God. The division of labour, the recognition of different gifts and the creation of specialized organizations are all necessary, but they should not undermine the freedom which obedience demands or take away from the plenitude of the kingdom of God.(29) The vocation of the church is indeed the proclamation of the kingdom but the nature of the kingdom makes it impossible for proclamation to remain conceptual or verbal.

What are the priorities prescribed for the church in our day? Three points of concentration are generally proposed. They arise from God's particular care for the poor, God's sending of the church to proclaim the gospel to all nations (the unreached), and God's promise of a new day of peace and justice. My thesis is that these are intimately inter-related aspects of one and the same call to Christian obedience in the service of the kingdom, which is basically a call to freedom.(30)

RISKS OF FREEDOM

This freedom is not something new; it belongs to the being of the church and the service of the kingdom. It has been manifested in the history of the church, and is manifest today.(31) A rapid selective historical survey will reveal how such freedom has been exercised, sometimes with positive and at other times negative consequences.

First, even today Orthodox theology would like to preserve a certain harmony between the church and the civil authorities.(32) This is based on the conviction that both are meant to work for the common and total good of the people and that, working together, they would be a blessing for all the people. For us, from a western church perspective, it is reminiscent of the unhappy history of the alliance between church and state from Constantine on. In our books of history and theology, and even in current discussions of the situation of the church, we often regret the fact that the Christian church became the official church of the Roman Empire.(33)

But we need to raise the question as to whether the prevailing conditions of the Roman Empire offered any other responsible alternative. I am not a church historian, and I can only raise the question. Are we not too quick in condemning a particular event because of the consequences that it brought about? In this case those consequences were not apparent when the option was made. It was made so that the witness of the church and the values of the civilization symbolized by the Roman Empire could be preserved.(34) Later the church became a prisoner to the logic of power, and from a persecuted church turned into a persecuting church. That was a tragedy, and it proves that no solution, no manifestation of the freedom of the church, is a final one, but needs to be submitted continuously to the question: How do we testify today, anew, to the Servant King of the kingdom of God?(35)

At the present time, in the dynamics of the culture of eastern Europe, the state seeks to be an entirely autonomous centre of culture and values in terms of Marxist philosophy. The church is making an effort to keep close to the people, to the national history, to the language, affirming as part of its vocation the preservation of that tradition.(36) The most striking example of this is the church in Romania, though the most popular one, as far as the press is concerned, is the Roman Catholic Church in Poland. Where traditionally there had been a close relationship between the church and the state, the church now is no longer involved in the state; instead, it comes closer to the people and upholds the national values. The freedom of the church takes account of the factors of power in the given society, and chooses not to be identified with the state. It is related to but also critical of the state; it does not become civil religion, but in freedom follows its vocation.(37)

A second historical example, also polemic in nature, is monasticism. Nothing in Jesus' ministry indicated that this would be a normal phenomenon in the life of the church. The early church did not, as far as we know, commend it as a style of life. Monasticism represented an attempt to preserve the integrity of the Christian faith when there was the possibility that it would be compromised through the alliance of church and state. It was also an attempt to escape from the corrupt world and preserve personal spirituality.(38) But soon, the monasteries developed into centres which offered hospitality to foreigners and refuge to those in need. They developed into hospitals, and, later on, into schools and centres of intercessory prayer. From the monasteries came the missionary impulse which led to the conversion of the whole of central and northern Europe.(39) The church freely assumed an institutional form that already existed in other religious systems. The monastic style of life corresponded to Qumran, to various gnostic sects, etc.; even to centres of Hindu spirituality. What began as a retreat, an escape from the world, became transformed into a powerful missionary instrument. The reformers were critical of monasticism; there was no place for it in the churches they founded. They denounced the degradation of the monastic ideal in the sixteenth century. Once again we find that we cannot absolutize any instrumentality that the church has made use of in the past, in responsibility and freedom, to cope with a particular need at a historical moment. Nor can we dismiss such movements; they are all possible methodologies in the work of the church.(40)

Let us look at two contemporary models of concentration adopted on the basis of perceived priorities. One is the concentration on church growth as the main goal of Christian mission, in terms of cross-cultural evangelism and of planting and developing numerically growing churches.(41) This has always been a priority for the church.

85

During the last two centuries it has been the dominant model
of western mission. From a kingdom perspective it cannot be
challenged. We need to fulfil the Great Commission. We must
reveal God's purpose for the whole of humankind in all cultures.
We need to call people to become co-workers, participants, in
the active, historical struggles of the kingdom of God. (42) But
if it becomes an end in itself, and church growth does not obtain within a concern for the totality of the kingdom, it
becomes irresponsible. Church growth, when it degenerates into
mere recruitment of members in a club, becomes a betrayal of
the kingdom. But the possibility of abuse is not an excuse to
evade the missionary challenge that it contains. (43)

The other example has to do with the present concern for Christian
participation in liberation struggles. We could use the example
of Nicaragua or South Africa, or the priority for mission which
Desmond Tutu recommends for the churches in that region. We
cannot evade the call to witness to God's saving and liberating
news. (44) If the church of Jesus Christ does not tackle the
question of the oppression of billions of people, especially the
question of racism as institutionalized and practised in South
Africa, the whole credibility of the gospel will suffer. (45) So
this particular vocation is a privileged one, absolutely necessary,
if we want to proclaim in a convincing manner the message of the
kingdom. But if this same emphasis on Christian participation in
liberation struggles does not include the dimensions of celebration,
of worship, and of discerning the eschatological pointers to the
kingdom that is coming and the Christ who is the King, then that
too becomes a betrayal of the gospel. (46)

The fact that, in the struggle for liberation in Latin America,
people are taking time to develop a theology, is itself an
indication of their awareness that they are not in a "secular"
struggle, but that the shaping of new societies is a matter of
Christian obedience, and an important means of proclaiming the
gospel.

Gustavo Gutierrez said:

> In Jesus Christ we encounter God. In the human word we read God's word.
> In the historical events, we recognize the fulfilment of the promise.
> This is the hermeneutical fundamental circle: from human being to God
> and from God to human being, from history to faith and from faith to
> history, from fraternal love to the love of the Father and from the love
> of the Father to the love of the brothers and sisters, from the human
> justice to the holiness of God and from the holiness of God to the
> human justice, from the poor to God and from God to the poor. (47)

There is no guarantee that missionary freedom will not be misused. In the ecumenical dialogue we have the possibility of ongoing reciprocal challenge, correction and inspiration. (48)

But are there not axioms or "logical" priorities in mission? We
need to face this question. The consultation on evangelism and
social responsibility held in June 1982 in Grand Rapids, Michigan,
stated that the two concerns of justice and evangelism belong
intimately together, and while they can be distinguished, they
cannot and should not be separated. The participants affirmed,
however:

> *Evangelism relates to people's eternal destiny; in bringing them the*
> *good news of salvation, Christians are doing what nobody else can do.*
> *Seldom, if ever, should we have to choose between satisfying spiritual*
> *and physical hunger, or between helping bodies and saving souls. An*
> *authentic love for our neighbour will lead us to serve him or her*
> *as a whole person. Nevertheless, if we must choose, then we have to say*
> *that the supreme and ultimate need of all humankind is the saving grace*
> *of Jesus Christ, and that therefore a person's eternal and spiritual*
> *salvation is of greater importance than his or her temporal and*
> *material well-being. (49)*

There are others who feel that the priority should be given to
acts of mercy; they do not want to proclaim the gospel in words,
and they are even willing to suppress their very identity as
Christians.(50) In the sixties, in Europe, a theology of Christian
presence in the world was developed which went to the extreme of
demanding total silence on the part of Christians. It prescribed
a moratorium on words in order first to earn the right to be
heard. But it cannot be a permanent solution or recommendation,
for there is a story to be told.

We must say no to any attempt to permanently prioritize the ways
and means of obedience in the service of the kingdom.(51) The
only priority is the kingdom, the King and his invasion of love.
And the word spoken and a glass of cold water given in Jesus'
name are both, depending on the circumstances, correct entry
points into the total dynamic of the kingdom. There can be no
gospel of individual salvation without reference to the justice
of the kingdom. There is no love of God unrelated to my neighbour.
The encounter between church members and persons outside the
Christian community is, *de facto*, a total encounter where words
receive meaning from the entire behaviour of the Christian
community. We cannot decide whether our neighbour is saved; that
needs to wait for the final surprise of the Last Judgement (Mt 7:
21-23; 25:31-46). We proclaim salvation *in* Christ. That means
salvation in his body, salvation in his kingdom, salvation in his
plan to transform all reality. So any word that announces the
gospel is an entry point into the total kingdom or it is not an
authentic proclamation of the gospel. And no Christian solidarity
with the poor can exist which does not point to the totality of
the kingdom promises which include the invitation to personal
faith and witness.(52) Gustavo Gutierrez says:

> *The liberating praxis, inasmuch as it is part of an authentic solidarity*
> *with the poor and oppressed, is finally a praxis of love, of real love,*
> *efficient, historical, love for concrete people, love to the neighbour,*

*and in that love, love to Christ who identified himself with the most
little one of our brethren, the human beings. All attempts to separate
love to God and neighbour, gives place to attitudes that make poorer
our gospel. It is easy to oppose a praxis of heaven to a praxis of
earth and vice versa. It is easy, but it is not faithful to a gospel
of God-made-man. More authentic and more profound seems to us to talk
of a praxis of love that has its roots in a free, gratuitous love of
the Father as it becomes history in solidarity with the poor and
dispossessed, and through them, in solidarity with all human beings.* (53)

There is, after Jesus Christ, such an incarnation of God in human
beings that our roots in Christ bring us to love our neighbour,
and our love of our neighbour brings us to Jesus Christ.(54)

There is a double injustice to which the poor are subjected. They
are the oppressed who have been deprived of the good things of
the earth. Most of them are also oppressed because they are denied
the knowledge of him who promised to them the kingdom of God
(Lk 6:20).(55)

CONCLUSION

The kingdom of God is an eternal reality in God; it is the
historical manifestation of his trinitarian love. God is in
command; he speaks; he preserves; he purifies; he will judge;
he will complete. He will gather up our tentative, partial,
ambiguous manifestations of obedience. Because we trust in God
and believe in his plan for us today and in eternity, and we
pray "Your kingdom come"; because we look to the future with
expectation and eagerness; we can, in faith, offer a cup of water,
a word of love, the open hand of communion, all in his name.
Preaching the word, interceding in prayer, living in solidarity
with the poor -- these are all ways to affirm and fulfil our
vocation as the church. As a priestly people fulfilling our
vocation, we obey our calling by pointing to Jesus the King in
whose life every life can find a new beginning.(56)

The biblical model for the vocation of the church is provided by
John the Baptist, who points to Jesus Christ: "Behold the lamb of
God, who takes away the sin of the world." The mission of the
church is to point to him through whose life, death and
resurrection has been revealed the plenitude of God's forgiving
and redeeming love. We are haunted by the example of Mary, the
mother of Jesus. At the wedding in Cana, she instructs the
servants, "Do whatever he tells you." Mary has become a source of
inspiration in both Roman Catholic and Orthodox piety; she can
also be such for Protestants. She calls our attention to him,
on whose authority alone we can rely.

Paul, on the road to Damascus, is given the vision of the risen
Christ. His response gives us the final paradigm for the mission
of the church: "What shall I do, Lord?" (Acts 22:10) Missionary
freedom means asking what we shall do, and being perpetually
prepared to do what he asks of us.

NOTES

INTRODUCTION

1 I make mine the following explanation offered by Mortimer Arias, *Announcing the Reign of God - Evangelization and the Subversive Memory of Jesus*. Philadelphia: Fortress Press, 1984, p. 16.

> *The term "kingdom" is an unfortunate one in today's world: it is seriously questioned by many because of its monarchical political connotations and its associations with patriarchal structures and language. It is a particularly sensitive expression for those who are challenging the implications of sexist language and trying to translate the Scriptures in a way that expresses their faith in nonsexist language. "Reign of God" has been suggested as a better alternative, and it is already in circulation. In my original language -- Spanish -- we use the word reino, which includes the meanings of kingdom, reign, and realm. Because I speak another language, I do not pretend to understand all of the nuances of the English language nor would I attempt to solve this sensitive issue. I would like, however, to share in this concern and to express my solidarity with those who feel discriminated against or oppressed by language. I accept the fact, however, that "kingdom of God" has become a technical term in theology and religious language and a symbol so intimately related to Jesus' message that we cannot avoid it. I hope that our study of the meaning Jesus gave to this special term will show precisely that the reign of God puts under judgement not only old monarchies and patriarchal values but any system that denies God's given freedom and dignity to any human being. I will use the term "reign of God" whenever I refer to the general concept myself. Otherwise, quoting from Scripture or from others or with reference to "the kingdom", I will use the traditional English translation for the Hebrew malkuth shamayim or the Greek basileia.*

CHAPTER I

1 VERKUYL, Johannes. *Contemporary Missiology*. Grand Rapids: Eerdmans, 1978, pp. 3-4.

2 BOSCH, David. *Witness to the World*. London: Marshall, Morgan and Scott, 1980, pp. 6-7.

3 According to the *World Christian Encyclopedia*, edited by David Barrett, Oxford University Press, 1982, p. 4, there were 348,658,273 Christians in Latin America -- practically the whole population!

4 GALEANO, Eduardo. *Open Veins of Latin America*. New York: Monthly Review Press, 1974.
See also DUSSEL, Enrique. *History and the Theology of Liberation*. Maryknoll, N.Y.: Orbis, 1976, pp. 75-86.

5   GOROSTIAGA, Xabier. Notas sobre Metodología para un Diagnóstico Económico del Capitalismo, en *Encuentro Latinoamericano de Científicos Sociales y Teólogos*. San José, Costa Rica: Educa, Tomo I, pp. 39-61.

6   CASTRO, Emilio. *Amidst Revolution*. Belfast: Christian Journals Ltd., 1975, pp. 20-21.
    GUTIERREZ, Gustavo. *A Theology of Liberation*. London: SCM, 1975, pp. 88-92.

7   GUTIERREZ, Gustavo. The Poor and the Christian Communities, in *The Challenge of Basic Christian Communities*, ed. by Sergio Torres and John Eagleson. Maryknoll, N.Y.: Orbis, 1981.

8   CELAM. *Puebla and Beyond*. Official translation of the final document: Evangelization in Latin America's Present and Future. Washington, D.C.: National Conference of Catholic Bishops, 1979, paras. 150, 210, 905, 981, 1107.

9   BARREIRO, Alvaro. *The Basic Ecclesial Communities*. Maryknoll, N.Y.: Orbis, 1982.

10 MESTERS, Carlos. The Use of the Bible in Christian Communities of the Common People, in *The Challenge of Basic Christian Communities*, pp. 197-210. See also KIRK, Andrew. *Liberation Theology*. Atlanta: John Knox Press, 1979.

11 CELAM. Latin American Episcopal Council. *The Church in the Present-Day Transformation of Latin America in the Light of the Council*. Medellín, 1968. Bogotá: CELAM, 1970.
    Puebla and Beyond, op.cit.

12 PRIEN, Hans Jürgen, hrg. *Lateinamerika: Gesellschaft, Kirche, Theologie*. Band 2. Göttingen: Vandenhoeck und Ruprecht, 1981, pp. 82-83.
    GUTIERREZ, Gustavo. *A Theology of Liberation*, p. 139.

13 *Protestantismo y Liberalismo en América Latina*. San José, Costa Rica: DEI, 1983.
    MIGUEZ BONINO, José. Análisis de las Relaciones del Protestantismo con el Catolicismo Romano hasta 1960, en *Lectura Teológica del Tiempo Latino-americano*. San José, Costa Rica: Seminario Bíblico Latinoamericano, 1979, pp. 195-206.

14 LORES, Ruben. El Destino Manifiesto y la Empresa Misionera, ibid., pp. 207-227.

15 NACLA. *The Salvation Brokers: Conservative Evangelicals in Central America*, Vol. XVIII, No. 1, 1984, pp. 26, 32 and 33.
    TORRES, Sergio. *Latin America and the Puebla Conference*. New York: Theology in the Americas, 1979, p. 5.

16 ALTMANN, Walter, RITCHIE, Nelida y ZORRILLA, Hugo. *Jesucristo: Vocación Comprometida con el Reino*. San José, Costa Rica: CLAI, 1982.

17 *Time Magazine*, USA, March 14, 1983, pp. 34-39.

18 ibid., p. 39

19 See *Osservatore Romano*, August 11, 1984; the official warning of the
    Holy See to the priest in government functions.

20 *Newsweek*, USA, December 13, 1982, pp. 56-58.
    See also *Amnesty International Report on Guatemala*, 1982.
    Christianity Today, USA, July 15, 1983, pp. 12-13.

21 ibid., September 2, 1983, p. 46.

22 *Les droits de l'homme à Guatemala*. Résumé. Comité pro Justicia y Paz
    de Guatemala, février 1984.

23 *World Christian Encyclopedia*, p. 441.

24 *Religions in Korea Today*. Seoul: Korean Religious Research Institute,
    June 1984.

25 *Documents on the Struggle for Democracy in Korea*, ed. by Emergency
    Christian Conference on Korean Problems. Tokyo: Shinkyo Shuppansha, 1975,
    pp. 36-43.

26 NA, Won Jong. *Church Growth and Evangelism in Korea*, and PARK, Keun Won.
    *Evangelism and Mission in Korea: a Reflection from an Ecumenical
    Perspective*. Papers from a consultation on evangelism, October 1983,
    NCC Korea, Seoul. Geneva: CWME.

27 SONG, Choan Seng. *Third-Eye Theology*. Maryknoll, N.Y.: Orbis, 1979,
    pp. 197-198.

28 SONG, Choan Seng. *Christian Mission in Reconstruction*. Maryknoll, N.Y.:
    Orbis, 1977, pp. 57, 66.

29 WCC. *Breaking Barriers: Nairobi 1975*, ed. by David M. Paton. Geneva: WCC,
    1976, pp. 236.

30 BALASURIYA, Tissa. Liberation of Theology in Asia, in *Asia's Struggle
    for Full Humanity*. Maryknoll, N.Y.: Orbis, 1980. pp. 19-20.

31 Final Statement of the Conference on Asia's Struggle for Full Humanity,
    ibid., p. 157.

32 WCC. *Breaking Barriers*, pp. 70-72.

33 LABAYEN, Julio Xabier. The Gospel in Asian Context, in *Toward a New Age
    in Mission*. Book 3. Manila: International Congress on Mission, 2-7 December,
    1979, pp. 132-133.
    AMALADOSS, Michael. Inculturation and Mission, ibid., p. 38.
    "Just as the church may find an ally in various secular movements in its
    pursuit of justice, it will find help and collaboration in the various
    spiritual traditions of Asia, their methods of prayer and psycho-physio-

logical techniques (e.g. Yoga, Zen) and their symbols and rituals that give expression to popular religiosity in its pursuit of self-realization."

34 SONG, Choan Seng. *The Compassionate God*. Maryknoll, N.Y.: Orbis, 1982, pp. 77-83.

35 WCC/Faith and Order. *Confessing our Faith around the World*. Geneva, 1980, a common statement of our faith, pp. 81-84.

36 TUTU, Desmond, quoted by James Cone in *African Theology en Route*, ed. by Kofi Appiah-Kubi and Sergio Torres. Maryknoll, N.Y.: Orbis, 1979, p. 182.

37 ODUYOYE, Mercy, ibid., p. 116.

38 DICKSON, Kwesi, ibid., pp. 95-107.

39 AACC. *Confession of Alexandria: Comments and Reactions*. Nairobi, 1981.

40 CHIPENDA, Joseph, in *African Theology en Route*, p. 70.

41 Catholicos KAREKIN II. Life in Christ through Suffering and Endurance, in *Jesus Christ, the Life of the World: An Orthodox Contribution*, ed. by Ion Bria. Geneva: WCC, 1982, pp. 25-28.

42 Patriarch IGNATIUS IV. The Patriarchate of Antioch, in *Martyria – Mission*, ed. by Ion Bria. Geneva: WCC, 1980, pp. 78-80.
    KESHISHIAN, Very Rev. Aram. The Armenian Church in Diaspora. ibid., pp. 209-217.

43 DIAS, Zwinglio. Evangelism among Europe's Masses, in *International Review of Mission*, Geneva, Vol. LXVI, No. 264, October 1977, pp. 360ff.

44 VISSER'T HOOFT, Willem A. Evangelism Among Europe's Neo-Pagans, ibid., pp. 349ff.

45 NEWBIGIN, Lesslie. *The Other Side of 1984*. Geneva: WCC, 1983.

46 A polemic presentation of the case for the foundation of "The Mission Society for United Methodists" is given by Gerald H. Anderson in his address "Theology and Practice of Contemporary Mission in the United Methodist Church", given to the World Division, General Board of Global Ministries, New York, March 14, 1984, Mimeographic.

47 KUZMIC, Peter. Evangelical Witness in Eastern Europe, in *Serving our Generation*, ed. by Waldron Scott. Colorado Springs: World Evangelical Fellowship, 1980, pp. 77-85.
    BRIA, Ion, ed. *Martyria – Mission*. Articles on Orthodox Churches in Socialist Countries.
    Metropolitan ANTONIE of Ardeal. Church and State in Romania, in *Faith and Order Paper*, No. 85. Geneva: WCC, 1978, pp. 90ff.
    also Comment on Church-State Relations in Eastern Europe, ibid., pp. 106ff.

48 See especially the publications of the conferences organized by the
    Ecumenical Association of Third World Theologians:
    The Emergent Gospel. Maryknoll, N.Y.: Orbis, 1977.
    African Theology en Route. Maryknoll, N.Y.: Orbis, 1979.
    Asia's Struggle for Full Humanity. Maryknoll, N.Y.: Orbis, 1980.
    The Challenge of Basic Christian Communities. Maryknoll, N.Y.: Orbis,
    1981.
    Irruption of the Third World. Maryknoll, N.Y.: Orbis, 1983.

49 COSTAS, Orlando E. *The Church and Its Mission: A Shattering Critique from
    the Third World*. Wheaton, Illinois: Tyndale House, 1974, pp. 240ff.

50 MIGUEZ BONINO, José. *Doing Theology in a Revolutionary Situation*. Phila-
    delphia: Fortress Press, 1975, pp. 61ff.

51 WCC. *International Review of Mission*, Geneva, Vol, LXXIII, No. 290,
    April 1984, pp. 223-236.

52 Let me illustrate with one very well known example. During the Vietnam
    War, when some people were criticizing Dr Billy Graham because he was
    not taking a stand on the war, he defended himself saying that his
    calling was to be an evangelist, not to be a prophet. I am sure Dr Graham
    would explain himself differently today. The stand he has taken on the
    peace question is the stand that would normally belong to a prophet!

    Christianity Today. Billy Graham's Statement, January 19, 1973, Vol. XVII,
    No. 8, p. 36.
    ibid., The Christian Faith and Peace in a Nuclear Age. Address given in
    Moscow, URSS, May 11, published June 18, 1982, Vol. XXVI, No. 11, pp. 20-23.

53 GENSICHEN, Hans-Werner. Missionarisches Zeugnis und kirchlicher Entwick-
    lungsdienst - Stationen in einem Lernprozess, in *Ökumene: Gemeinschaft
    einer dienenden Kirche*, Oct.-Nov. 1983, p. 41:

    *This - it appears to the observer - is a turning upside-down of the
    South Indian experience which, at the time, was expressed by the
    English Bishop F. Whittaker with the famous words: "We thought we
    were bringing them Christ; they thought we were bringing them a
    school." In Africa 1983 one could rather say: "We thought you were
    in solidarity with our missionary-evangelistic task; they, the Germans,
    thought that material and economic help for self-help was the highest
    priority." And how was that twelve years ago - even then the African
    partner in the person of the Evangelical Church Mekane Yesus questioned
    precisely this "imbalance" of German inter-church development aid which
    was seen to be based on an illegitimate "separation of service and
    witness". Was it a false hope on the part of the Ethiopians, "that our
    sister churches would not measure our needs exclusively by their
    own criteria and by the conditions they formulate?" Or do the problems
    appear differently today?*

    WCC. The Theological Basis for Ecumenical Sharing. Report of the
    Consultation on the Resource Sharing System, Glion, Switzerland, 1982,
    in *International Review of Mission*, Geneva, Vol. LXXIII, No. 290,
    April 1984, pp. 210ff.

54 WCC/DWME. *The Church for Others*. Geneva, 1967, pp. 20-23.

55 For a critical review of this discussion around Uppsala, see
    BEYERHAUS, Peter. *Missions: Which Way? Humanization or Redemption*.
    Grand Rapids: Zondervan Publishing House, 1971.

56 BOSCH, David, op.cit., p. 19.

57 WCC/CWME. *Bangkok Assembly 1973*. Official Report, p. 88.
    MIGUEZ BONINO, José. Reino de Dios e Historia, en *El Reino de Dios*,
    ed. by René Padilla, Buenos Aires: Certeza, 1975, pp. 11-16.

58 MOLTMANN, Jürgen. *The Trinity and the Kingdom of God*. London: SCM Press,
    1981, pp. 213-222.

59 MIGUEZ BONINO, José. *Toward a Christian Political Ethics*. Philadelphia:
    Fortress Press, 1983, pp. 42-44.

CHAPTER II

1   For a thorough presentation of the World Missionary Conference, see
    International Review of Mission, Edinburgh to Melbourne, Vol. LXVII,
    No. 267, July 1979.
    See also BASSHAM, Rodger C. *Mission Theology*. Pasadena, California:
    William Carey Library, 1979.

2   WCC/CWME. *Bangkok Assembly 1973*.
    SOVIK, Arne. *Salvation Today*. Minneapolis: Augsburg Publ. House, 1983.

3   BLASER, Klauspeter. *Gottes Heil in heutiger Wirklichkeit*. Frankfurt/
    Main: Verlag Otto Lembeck, 1978, p. 23, note 30.

4   CWME. *Salvation Today and Contemporary Experience*. WCC: Geneva, 1972.

5   *World Christian Encyclopedia*, Article on Thailand, pp. 664-667.

6   WATAKEECHAROEN, Wichean. Sermon. CWME Archives. Geneva: WCC, Box 272.008,
    Document No. 59.

7   WCC/CWME. *Bangkok Assembly 1973*, pp. 78-80.

8   WCC/DFI. *Guidelines on Dialogue with People of Living Faiths and
    Ideologies*. Geneva: WCC, 1979.

9   WCC. *Gathered for Life*. Official Report, VI Assembly, Vancouver, Canada,
    24 July-10 August, 1983, ed. by David Gill. Grand Rapids: Eerdmans and
    Geneva: WCC, 1983, pp. 39-42.

10 VEEN, Rein Jan van der, ed. "Waar blijft God? - De Roep om Bevrijding
    in Deze Wereld en Het Getuigenis van Het Evangelie". Baarn: Ten Have,
    1973, pp. 107-109.

11 WCC/CWME. *Bangkok Assembly 1973*, p. 88.

12 ibid., p. 90.

13 ibid.

14 ibid., p. 78.

15 WINTER, Ralph, ed. *The Evangelical Response to Bangkok*. Pasadena,
    California: William Carey Library, 1973, p. 125.

16 ibid., pp. 90-91.

17 HAMER, Jerome. Bangkok 1973. Audio-tape. Geneva: WCC.

18 PIMEN Patriarch of Moscow and All Russia. Letter to the Central
    Committee of August 7, 1973, in *International Review of Mission*, Geneva,
    Vol. LXIII, No. 249, January 1974, pp. 125ff.

19 NISSIOTIS, Nikos. Introduction to a Christological Phenomenology, in
    Technology and Social Justice, ed. by Ronald H. Preston. London: SCM
    Press, 1971, pp. 148-155:

    *Two remarks are to be made here. First, sacred and profane are not
    two opposed or separated realms. The sacred is the secular under-
    stood at a deep level. Secondly, the vision of salvation extended
    into the secular is based on the particular intervention of God in
    Christ, whose salvation reveals that every historical event contains
    a possibility of becoming an agent of this salvation if it acquires
    the broad dimension given to it by Christ's incarnation, death and
    resurrection. A historical event acquires its deeper significance in
    the eyes of a Christian only when it really assists in the restoration
    of humanity to all men according to the cosmic understanding of the
    reality of Christ's salvation. This is not automatically given to
    every historical event. A service to humanity as a whole is a highly
    complicated affair which cannot be reduced only to the limits of a
    welfare programme of economic and social change. There is always
    something missing in the eyes of a Christian phenomenologist. This
    can be captured only if the event is transformed into a service to
    man, i.e. if the event extends the salvation of Christ understood
    as a vehicle for the regeneration of history.*

    See also Bishop ANASTASIOS (Yannoulatos). Sermon on "The Ascent of Human
    Nature", in *Your Kingdom Come - Mission Perspectives*. Report on the
    World Conference on Mission and Evangelism, Melbourne, Australia, 12-25
    May, 1980. Geneva: WCC/CWME, 1981 (second edition), pp. 237-241.

    FOUCAULD, Théologue de, in *L'Orthodoxie Hier, Demain*. Paris: Buchet/
    Chastel, 1979, pp. 67-68.

    BRIA, Ion, ed. *Jesus Christ, the Life of the World: An Orthodox
    Contribution*, pp. 5, 12.

20 HENRY, Carl F.H. and MOONEYHAM, W. Stanley, eds. *One Race, One Gospel,
    One Task*. Minneapolis: World Wide Publications, 1967.

21 Lausanne Committee for World Evangelization. *Let the Earth Hear His Voice*, ed. by J.D. Douglas. Minneapolis: World Wide Publications, 1975.

22 ibid., pp. 3ff.

23 ibid., pp. 32.
Dr Billy Graham states: "This congress convenes to consider honestly and carefully the unevangelized world and the churches' resources to evangelize this world."

24 WCC/CWME. *Bangkok Assembly 1973*, p. 106.
Lausanne Covenant, para. 9.
See also *The Willowbank Report - Gospel and Culture*. Lausanne Occasional Papers, No. 2. Wheaton, Illinois: Lausanne Committee for World Evangelization, 1978, chapter 8 on Church and Culture, especially (c) on the freedom of the church.

25 *A Response to Lausanne*. Mimeographic document distributed at the end of the congress.

26 GITARI, David, SAMUEL, Vinay, COSTAS, Orlando, KIRK, Andrew, SIDER, Ronald, HILLIARD, Clarence, KUZMIC, Peter, et.al. *A Statement of Concern on the Future of the Lausanne Committee for World Evangelization*. Pattaya, Thailand, June 16-27, 1980, mimeographic document.

27 COSTAS, Orlando E. *Christ Outside the Gate*. Maryknoll, N.Y.: Orbis, 1982, p. 158.

28 STARLING, Allan, ed. *Seeds of Promise*. World Consultation on Frontier Missions, Edinburgh 1980. Pasadena, California: William Carey Library, 1981.
For a critical consideration, see COSTAS, Orlando E., op.cit., pp. 64-67.

29 DAYTON, Donald W. *Discovering an Evangelical Heritage*. New York: Harper & Row, 1976.

30 *Evangelism and Social Responsibility*. The Grand Rapids Report. Exeter, U.K.: Paternoster Press, 1982, p. 24.

31 SINE, Tom, ed. *The Church in Response to Human Need*. Monrovia, California: Missions Advanced Research & Communication Center, 1983.

32 Wheaton '83 Conference. Letter to the Churches, in *Mission Notes*, Newsletter of LWF Geneva, No. 3, December 1983, p. 15.

33 STOTT, John. Response to Bishop Mortimer Arias, in *International Review of Mission*, Geneva, Vol. LXV, No. 257, January 1976, pp. 30-33.
I think that we could consider Dr Stott's address as the friendly and firm challenge that the evangelical brethren and sisters gathered in Lausanne wanted to put before the member churches of the WCC:
Bishop Arias headed his paper with a quotation from the original aims of the IMC, namely the proclamation of the gospel of Jesus Christ "to the end that all may believe in him and be saved." This

statement presupposes that until men hear and believe the gospel they are lost. This Assembly is listening with great sensitivity to the cry of the oppressed, and rightly so; but are we also listening to the cry of the lost?

The only references to the judgement of God in pre-Assembly literature concern his judgement of oppressors and of the structures of injustice. God's judgement certainly rests on these. Yet the same Bible which teaches this, teaches also that all men (the oppressed as well as the oppressors) are sinners under the judgement of God and are on the broad road which leads to destruction (Mt 7:13). This is what Bishop Arias rightly calls "the horror of a world without Christ". It is simply not true that all men and women are "anonymous Christians", and need only to have their true identity disclosed to them. Nor are they already "in Christ" and simply need to be told so. No, according to the New Testament they are "dead in their trespasses and sins", "separated from Christ" and "perishing". Our Christian responsibility in the face of this terrible human condition is not to deny it but to weep over it and to take action, like the Apostle Paul, "by all means to save some".

Universalism, fashionable as it is, is incompatible with the teaching of Christ and his apostles, and is a deadly enemy of evangelism. The true universalism of the Bible is the call to universal evangelism in obedience to Christ's universal commission. It is the conviction not that all men will be saved in the end, but that all men must hear the gospel [of salvation] before the end, as Jesus said (Mt 24:14), in order that they may have a chance to believe and to be saved (Rom 10: 13-15).

34 POTTER, Philip. Address to the Synod of Bishops of the Roman Catholic Church, October 11, 1974, in *International Review of Mission*, Geneva, Vol. LXIV, No. 255, July 1975, p. 318.
    The crisis we are going through today is not so much a crisis of faith as a crisis of faithfulness of the whole people of God to what he has offered us of his grace in the crucified and risen Lord and in what he demands in the wisdom and power of his Holy Spirit.

35 Pope PAUL VI. *Evangelii Nuntiandi*. Osservatore Romano, Weekly English Edition, December 25, 1975 (the numbers in [] refer to paragraphs of the Encyclical).

36 POTTER, Philip, op.cit.

37 II Vatican Council. *Constitution of the Church in the Modern World*. U.S. National Catholic Conference, 1966, Chapter III, para. 39. Document of the First Bishops' Institute for Missionary Apostolate of the Federation of Asian Bishops' Conferences, in *Toward a New Age in Mission*, p. 18.
    Reflecting on these key issues of our mission to Asia we found ourselves at the very centre of the polarity that characterizes the mission of the church today: the church as a sacrament of Christ and the church as sacrament of mankind. Lumen Gentium emphasized the former, with focus on institutional hierarchy,

universality of the church's mission and a strong emphasis on the uniqueness of the Christian revelation and the role of the church. It understands evangelization more as divinization of man. Gaudium et Spes emphasized the latter, with focus on the particular church, community, laity, cultural diversity, "diakonia" for the suffering, oppressed mankind. It conceives humanization as an integral part of evangelization, without excluding man's divinization, and grants other religions an important role in this process. Evangelii Nuntiandi has tried to focus both problems correctly, but we still face the hiatus between church and culture, evangelization and liberation, humanization and divinization. The document makes it clear that we cannot discuss evangelization in the context of present-day realities without also discussing liberation. And yet Evangelii Nuntiandi, with all the emphasis on liberation, basic communities and inculturation, still remains ecclesiocentric, with its stress on liturgy, sacraments, hierarchy, priests, while passing over lightly the salvific value of non-Christian religions.

38 WCC. *Breaking Barriers.*

39 Dr John Stott wrote a paper for the National Initiative on Evangelism in Great Britain: "World Evangelization: Signs of Convergence and Divergence in Christian Understanding". I take from the document the ten common affirmations on evangelism:
    1. The church is sent into the world.
    2. The church's mission in the world includes evangelism and social action.
    3. The content of the gospel is derived from the Bible.
    4. The gospel centres on Christ crucified and risen.
    5. Salvation is offered to sinners in the gospel through Jesus Christ.
    6. Conversion is demanded by the gospel.
    7. True conversion invariably leads to costly discipleship.
    8. The whole church needs to be mobilized and trained for evangelism.
    9. The church can evangelize only when it is renewed.
    10. The power of the Holy Spirit is indispensable to evangelism.

40 WCC. *Breaking Barriers,* p. 52, para. 57.

41 ibid.

42 ibid., p. 45, para. 19.

43 ibid., p. 45, para. 15.

44 ibid., p. 44, para. 14.

45 WCC/CWME. *Your Kingdom Come - Mission Perspectives.*

46 CWME. Letter to the Churches, Geneva, April 1978. CWME Archives, Box 273.005, Document AD.I.

47 WCC/CWME. *Your Kingdom Come - Mission Perspectives,* p. 235. The message to the churches says:

*The poor and the hungry cry to God. Our prayer "Your kingdom
come" must be prayed in solidarity with the cry of millions
who are living in poverty and injustice. Peoples suffer the pain
of silent torment; their faces reveal their suffering. The church
cannot live distant from these faces because she sees the face of
Jesus in them (Mt 25).*

*In such a world the announcement of the kingdom of God comes to
all. It comes to the poor and in them generates the power to affirm
their human dignity, liberation and hope. To the oppressor it comes
as judgement, challenge and a call for repentance. To the insensitive
it comes as a call to awareness of responsibility. The church itself
has often failed its Lord by hindering the coming of his kingdom. We
admit this sin and our need for repentance, forgiveness and cleansing.*

48 ibid., p. 219, Section IV, para. 20.

49 ibid., p. 171, Section I, para. 1.

50 FUNG, Raymond. Good News to the Poor: A Case for a Missionary Movement,
    ibid., p. 85.

51 HANKS, Tomas. *Opresión, Pobreza y Liberación*. San José, Costa Rica:
    Ed. Caribe, 1982.
    See also TAMEZ, Elsa. *La Biblia de los Oprimidos*. San José, Costa Rica:
    DEI, 1979.

52 WCC/CWME. *Your Kingdom Come - Mission Perspectives*, pp. 177-178.

53 ibid., pp. 220-221.

54 ibid., pp. 175-176, Section I, para. 16.
    See also WCC. *Mission and Evangelism: An Ecumenical Affirmation*, para. 32.

55 WCC/CWME. *Your Kingdom Come - Mission Perspectives*, Section IV, para. 21,
    p. 219.

56 COSTAS, Orlando E. *Christ Outside the Gate*, pp. 13-16.

57 Wheaton Letter to the Churches, p. 15.

58 WCC. *Mission and Evangelism: An Ecumenical Affirmation*, para. 34.

59 ibid., A Study Guide for Congregations. New York: NCCCUSA, 1983. p. 3
    (the numbers in [] refer to paragraphs in the Ecumenical Affirmation).
    *In 1976, immediately after the Fifth Assembly of the World Council
    of Churches (WCC) in Nairobi, the Central Committee of the World
    Council of Churches asked the Commission on World Mission and
    Evangelism (CWME) to prepare a document containing the basic
    convictions of the ecumenical movement on the topic of mission and
    evangelism. The Central Committee itself began to work in that
    direction by preparing in 1976 a letter to the churches, calling
    their attention to the confessing character of every local commu-
    nity (see Ecumenical Review, Oct. 1977). During the preparation of
    the world mission conference held in Melbourne in 1980 on the theme*

"Your Kingdom Come", CWME engaged in a long and fruitful con-
versation with churches of all confessions and regions, assessing
the priorities for our missionary obedience today.

In 1981, the Central Committee received this document, "Mission
and Evangelism: An Ecumenical Affirmation", for a first reading;
in July 1982, this affirmation was approved by the Central
Committee and sent to the churches for their consideration,
inspiration and implementation.

60 *Bearing Witness to the World.* Board of Global Ministries, United Methodist
    Church, U.S. Education and Cultivation Division, June 1978, LE 45 M.

61 BRAATEN, Carl E. *The Flaming Center.* Philadelphia: Fortress Press, 1977,
    p. 90.

62 ROGERS, Barbara. *Race: No Peace without Justice.* Geneva: WCC/Programme
    to Combat Racism, 1980.
    ADLER, Elisabeth. *A Small Beginning - An Assessment of the First Five*
    Years of the Programme to Combat Racism. Geneva: WCC, 1974.
    KARNER, Peter, hrg. *Antirassismus-Programm 1969-1979 - Eine Dokumentation*
    von Erika Fuchs. Aktuelle Reihe Nr. 16, 1979.

63 WCC. *Mission and Evangelism: An Ecumenical Affirmation*, para. 33.

64 WCC. *International Review of Mission*, Geneva, Vol. LXXIII, No. 290,
    April 1984, pp. 223-236.

65 WCC. *Mission and Evangelism: An Ecumenical Affirmation*, para. 34.

66 WCC. *Gathered for Life*, pp. 198-199.

67 This is not a new problem, but it is still alive! See BOSCH, David,
    op.cit., pp. 17, 18, 199-201.
    GENSICHEN, H.-W. *Glaube für die Welt.* Gütersloh: Verlagshaus Gerd Mohn,
    1971, pp. 80-96, 168-186.

68 VERKUYL, Johannes, op.cit., pp. 18-25.

69 ibid., pp. 197-204.

70 WCC. *Mission and Evangelism: An Ecumenical Affirmation.* See Preface.

CHAPTER III

1   ARIAS, Mortimer, op.cit., pp. 66-67.

2   ARAYA, Victorio. *El Dios de los Pobres.* San José, Costa Rica: DEI, 1983,
    p. 187.
    Each epoch has its own questions and problems and from them reads
    and re-reads the Scripture. The theological vision of the theology

of liberation has given more attention to certain biblical
perspectives because they respond better to our specific situation.
It is so then that since the beginning some points have become
revealers: the identification of Christ with the poor (Mt 25),
the theme of the Exodus - liberation; the unity of history
(creation, salvation and eschatological promises); faith that
acts through love; the option of Jesus for the marginals of his
time; the announcement of the kingdom.

See also STENDAHL, Krister, in *Your Kingdom Come - Mission Perspectives*,
p. 76.

The simplest answer is this: it was a good term for expressing the
full range of God's redemption. Contrary to the views of many modern
exegetes, it does not point only to a "relationship" between the be-
liever and God, but also to the whole of creation. Thus the gospels
see the miracles of Jesus as means of redeeming the creation from
the destructive forces of illness, demonic possession, and even
death. The miracles are not just illustration-stories about faith,
they are acts of redeeming the creation, pushing back the frontiers
of Satan. And the distinctive mark of the kingdom is justice (a word
that should not easily be replaced by the more spiritual-sounding
word "righteousness").

In praying for the coming of that kingdom we pray for a redeemed, a
healed, a mended creation.

3 BOFF, Leonardo. *Jesus Christ Liberator*. Maryknoll, N.Y.: Orbis, 1978, p. 58.

4 BORNKAMM, Günther. *Jesus of Nazareth*. New York: Harper & Row, 1960, p. 200.
ROTTENBERG, Isaac. *The Promise and the Presence: Toward a Theology of the
Kingdom of God*. Grand Rapids: Eerdmans, 1980, p. 10.

5 STENDAHL, Krister, op.cit., pp. 76-77.

6 SENIOR, Donald and STUHLMUELLER, Carroll. *The Biblical Foundation for
Mission*. Maryknoll, N.Y.: Orbis, 1983, pp. 145-146.

7 This hermeneutical circulation concentrates on the interplay between text,
context and practice and, of course, is fully aware of the scientific
problems facing biblical interpretation today, be it of a linguistic,
structural or historical nature. We assume theologically that the whole
process of the writing, editing and collecting of the Bible has taken
place under the inspiration of the Holy Spirit, and also that the believing
community that inquires today about the practice that belongs to their
specific situation reads the Bible in prayer and under the same
inspiration of the Spirit. In no way do we want to suggest a re-opening
of the old and false dichotomy between the inspiration of the Bible and
its direct interpretation, and its scientific study through the mediation
of the biblical sciences. That would mean to forget that we are called
to love God also with *all our mind*. We should bring to our Bible reading
all the honesty of our intellectual knowledge. In fact, our hermeneutical
circulation demands not only a consideration of the historical situation
and the ways in which the text came into being, but also the use of human
sciences today to understand our context, to discover our ideological pre-

suppositions in such a way that an encounter between the text and the situation could happen responsibly. Of course, we need to ask the scientific scholars of the Bible about their own ideological pre-suppositions. We cannot assume that there is anything called neutral or objective biblical study, but it is precisely through the reciprocal recognition and challenging of our presuppositions that the Bible has a chance to be fully the authoritative word of God for our situation.

See especially SEGUNDO, Juan Luis. *The Liberation of Theology*. Maryknoll, N.Y.: Orbis, 1976, Chapter 1.

8 SCHMIDT, K.L. Article on Basileia, in *Theological Dictionary of the New Testament*, ed. by G. Kittel. Grand Rapids: Eerdmans, 1964, p. 584.

9 SCOTT, Waldron. *Bring Forth Justice*. Grand Rapids: Eerdmans, 1980, pp. 67-69.

10 LADD, George E. *The Presence of the Future*. Grand Rapids: Eerdmans, 1974, pp. 51-54.

11 MOLTMANN, Jürgen. *The Church in the Power of the Spirit*. New York: Harper & Row, 1977, pp. 76-78.

12 ANDERSON, Bernhard W. *The Living World of the Old Testament*. London: Longman Group Ltd., 1975, pp. 411ff.

13 ibid., pp. 536-550.

14 BOFF, Leonardo, op.cit., p. 58.

15 SONG, Choan Seng. *Third-Eye Theology*, p. 54.

16 See Note 55.

17 BOFF, Leonardo. *Way of the Cross - Way of Justice*. Maryknoll, N.Y.: Orbis, 1980, pp. 10-17.
    YODER, John H. *The Politics of Jesus*. Grand Rapids: Eerdmans, 1972, pp. 115-131.

18 We use two expressions: *reign*, to underline the active, dynamic mani-
    festation of God's royal authority; *kingdom*, to affirm the same but adding
    the social, communal dimension, the changed reality of nation, even nature
    in the perspective of the kingdom.

    See also LADD, George E., op.cit., p. 123.

19 PIXLEY, George. *God's Kingdom*. London: SCM Press, 1981.

20 GOTTWALD, Norman K. *The Tribes of Jahwe*. Maryknoll, N.Y.: Orbis, 1979, especially pp. 584-587.

21 YODER, John H., op.cit., pp. 64-77.

22 BRIGHT, John. *The Kingdom of God*. Cokesbury, N.Y.: Abingdon, 1953, p. 87.

23 LADD, George E., op.cit., p. 66.

24 ROTTENBERG, Isaac, op.cit., pp. 3-6.

25 NEWBIGIN, Lesslie. *The Open Secret*. Grand Rapids: Eerdmans, 1977,
    p. 36.

26 BRIGHT, John, op.cit., p. 143.

27 LADD, George E., op.cit., pp. 51-52.
    See also Amos 9:7.

28 NEWBIGIN, Lesslie. *Your Kingdom Come*. Leeds: John Paul the Preacher Press,
    1980, pp. 21-22.

29 See Chapter III, page 58.

30 BRIGHT, John, op.cit., pp. 144-145.

31 SENIOR, Donald and STUHLMUELLER, Carroll, op.cit., pp. 83-109.

32 VOGEL, Walter. *God's Universal Covenant*. Ottawa, Canada: Saint Paul
    University, 1979, pp. 39-72.

33 SAMUEL, Vinay and SUGDEN, Chris. Tensions between Eschatology and History,
    in *The Church in Response to Human Need*, ed. by Tom Sine, p. 183.

34 CAMPS, Arnulf. *Partners in Dialogue*. Maryknoll, N.Y.: Orbis, 1983,
    pp. 30-36.
    C.S. Song, in *The Compassionate God*, takes a strong position against any
    kind of *Heilsgeschichte*. He writes (pp. 38-39).

> *This has been an all too brief discussion that does not quite do
> justice to the long and complex history of Israel, but it at least
> shows us that the growth of the faith of Israel has to be seen in
> the light of the dynamic of disruption and dispersion that moves
> history. We have identified three great cycles of disruption and
> dispersion, with each cycle giving rise to a theology reflecting
> how the people of Israel apprehended their God and their relations
> with the surrounding world.*
>
> *The first of these cycles begins with Abraham's response to God's
> call to leave his home and set out on a journey to the promised
> land. This is the framework within which theology of migration comes
> into being. The next cycle comes from the complex of the exodus and
> and the conquest. Here it is the theology of the covenant that be-
> comes fundamental to the alliance of the Hebrew tribes trying to
> establish themselves in the midst of hostile nations. As we have
> seen, this theology of the covenant later becomes a state ideology
> serving as the religious foundation for the construction of the
> Israelite kingdom. The third cycle is that of the exile that carries
> the people of Israel and Judah to Assyria and Babylon, to the region
> where Abraham's migration originated. This is perhaps more than just
> a coincidence, for it is in the land of their origin that they have
> to realize that they share their roots with other nations. In the*

*territory of foreign nations they must wrestle with the theology
of the nations.*

*Through the experience of the exile and captivity, the Jews must
have learned that there is no such thing as theology of history by
proxy. The Assyrians and the Babylonians are not related to God
through them. These foreign nations seem to have a direct access
to God. They are not absent after all before the court of God's
counsel. They are not represented by the Jewish people as their
proxy. They can speak for themselves before God; they can even be
sent by God as an instrument in the punishment of Israel and Judah.
What an upsetting thought this is! To think of these other nations
in terms of proxy will no longer do.*

*Christian theology of history has, to a large extent, been a proxy
theology. The church has inherited the mantle of representation
from Israel and takes upon itself the task of representing other
people before God. It seldom occurs to it that people outside it
may be quite capable of speaking for themselves and giving account
of themselves before God. In its theology it leaves little room for
them to come directly to the throne of God's grace. In its systems
of beliefs and theology they gain salvation only through the proxy
of the church.*

*Why has the Christian church come to acquire this proxy character?
Why has Christian theology taken upon itself to speak on behalf of
all humanity almost totally from the religious and cultural stand-
points of Christianity? One of the reasons seems to be the concept
of "uniqueness" that Christians freely use to describe the faith and
life of the Christian church. The history of Israel is a unique
history. The history of Christianity is also a unique history. Being
unique, the history of the Judeo-Christian traditions is a history
set apart from all other histories. The history represented by Israel
and the Christian church becomes "sacred" history. It is a unique
history that illuminates other histories but is in no need of
illumination by them.*

*In this way, Christian theology has created a vacuum between the
history of Israel-church and the history of other nations and peoples.
This has led to the concept of Heilsgeschichte in which those outside
the sacred history of Israel and the church have only marginal
importance. Obviously this kind of theology hardly enables us to see
how a nation not included in the Judeo-Christian tradition fares in
God's creating and redeeming work for the world.*

The debate is just beginning. However, in a rapid historical survey of
Old Testament convictions on the kingdom of God, I think we must
recognize that Israel considered herself as a people with a specific --
unique? -- vocation. It is against this background of Jerusalem-centrism
that we can understand Jesus' novelty in history.

35 MIGUEZ BONINO, José. *Doing Theology in a Revolutionary Situation*, p. 136.
SAMUEL, Vinay and SUGDEN, Chris, op.cit., p. 191.
   *For example, traditionally in Protestant missionary thought, the
   history of mission in Africa, Asia and Latin America has been
   essentially written as the history of the expansion of the*

Protestant churches of Europe and America. Thus African churches have to perceive their histories as part of the history of western Christianity. Their relationship to their own African histories is submerged. This biblical perspective would encourage us to relate the history of Africa to the history of Israel, and draw the continuity between God's action in Israelite history and African history. This process is crucial for the discovery of African or Asian or Latin American Christian identity as the recent conference of Evangelical Mission Theologians from the Two Thirds World affirmed. It is also crucial, as we shall note later, for taking into account the difference which our contexts make to the way we perceive God at work in history.

36 HAHN, Ferdinand. *The Titles of Jesus in Christology*. London: Lutterworth Library, 1969, Chapter 1, especially p. 25.

37 ARIAS, Mortimer, op.cit., pp. 14-16.
    NEWBIGIN, Lesslie. *The Open Secret*, p. 23.
    BRIGHT, John, op.cit., pp. 196-197.

38 BURCHARD, Christoph. Jesus für die Welt, in *Fides Pro Mundi Vita*, ed. by Theo Sundermeier. Gütersloh: Verlagshaus Gerd Mohn, 1980, pp. 15-16:
    For Jesus I base myself on Lk 11:20 par. Mt 12:28. "If it is by the finger (Mt: Spirit) of God that I cast out demons, then the kingdom of God has come upon you." The expression may originally have been passed independently. It is taken for granted, as is the genuineness of the contents. The word illustrates an event, the exorcisms of Jesus. I assume that the "if" sentence does not want to list which ones they were, but puts into words experiences made by the audience. There is no doubt that Jesus exorcized. It is not certain what is meant by "by the finger of God", but at any rate it means: commanded by God, with his strength, not because of his own power. In the framework of the exorcisms, the healings of Jesus are pertinent and in addition all acts which we call miracles. Again, there is no doubt that Jesus did this. Therefore, Lk 11:20 par. may be understood to read: "If it is by the finger of God that I perform miracles...".

    The main clause relates the kingdom of God to these things: "then it has come upon you." That must mean: it is here, not: it is imminent. The opinion is that the miracles are not just outward signs of the kingdom, but pertain to it. The sentence thus describes what the kingdom of God means for Jesus, though not necessarily exhaustively: casting out of demons, healing of the sick, if need be also on the Sabbath (Mk 3:1-6), saving from drowning in a storm and from hunger. A kingdom, therefore, which manifests itself not so much in dominion over human beings but rather as protection from the pressures to which human beings are exposed, in a subsidiary way and in the framework of creation.

    BORNKAMM, Günther, op.cit., pp. 63-69.

39 SOBRINO, Jon. *Christology at the Crossroads*. Maryknoll, N.Y.: Orbis, 1978, pp.46-50.
    YODER, John H., op.cit., pp. 66-74.
    ARIAS, Mortimer, op.cit., p. 21.

40   HAHN, Ferdinand, op.cit., p. 102.

The gospels come to us through the mediation of the first church which developed the description of Jesus as Lord not only in view of his earthly activity, but above all to express the exalted rank and authority of the One who was to return. The sayings material and the tradition of parables in the early church use the address "Lord" in reference to the judge of the world. Further, he whose return is expected is invoked by the church in its cult as "our Lord", as is shown especially by the prayer "Maranatha" stemming from the most ancient Palestinian tradition. The latter has its secure place in the eucharistic liturgy and at times carries in this context eschatological overtones. "Maranatha" can therefore be understood only as an imperative, the linguistically possible interpretation of it as a perfect or historic present must be excluded. Further, the imperative sense is to be regarded as strictly eschatological and not as a prayer for the presence of Jesus at the eucharist. The most ancient church lived not in a time of fulfilment but in a time of trustful waiting for the final coming of its Lord. No doubt the Spirit had been granted to it as a pledge of the ultimate aeon, and it was able to some extent to anticipate the final consummation, but it was not yet familiar with the concept of the exaltation and the present reality of Jesus. In liturgical usage, "our Lord" was long maintained and even later the description as Lord was preferred in connection with the parousia and the eucharist. With this description the early church forged a christological conception quite independently of any traditional concept of a saviour, and was able to include in it both the earthly and the ultimate activity of Jesus.

41   ibid., pp. 111-113.
See also Acts chapters 3, 4, 5, 16, 24, 25, 26; 1 Cor 12:1-3, etc.

42   MIRANDA, José Porfirio. *Communism in the Bible.* Maryknoll, N.Y.: Orbis, 1982, pp. 69-70.

43   YODER, John H., op.cit., Chapter 2, especially pp. 62-63.
FOUCAULD, Théologue de, op.cit., p. 17.

44   BOFF, Leonardo. *Jesus Christ Liberator*, p. 60.
ECHEGARAY, Hugo. *La Práctica de Jesus.* Lima, Peru: Centro de Estudios y Publicaciones, 1981, p. 88.

Jesus is not an ethereal being floating at equal distance from all groups, demands and conflicts. He participates and takes positions, and does so from within a distinct social context taking into account opposing interest, discerning authentic quests and, above all, making clear his position on the vital question of his time, for another society, a people free of domination and a pure Israel. An ideal attacked from contradictory quarters, on the one hand by Zealots and Essenes; by Pharisees and scribes on the other. From that it follows that the centre of Jesus' preaching and of his initiatives, is none other than the demanding and challenging proclamation of the regenerating kingdom of God.

45   ELLACURIA, Ignacio. *Freedom Made Flesh.* Maryknoll, N.Y.: Orbis, 1976, pp. 15-18.

106

46 WEBER, Hans-Ruedi. The Claim Made for Jesus, in *The Lord of Life*, ed. by William Lazareth. Geneva: WCC, 1983, pp. 81-91.

47 ECHEGARAY, Hugo, op.cit., pp. 85-87.
ARIAS, Mortimer, op.cit., pp. 50-51.

48 TORRES, Sergio and EAGLESON, John, eds. *The Challenge of Basic Christian Communities*. Final document, p. 236.

49 KÄSEMANN, Ernst. The Eschatological Royal Reign of God, in *Your Kingdom Come - Mission Perspectives*, p. 66.
BURCHARD, Christoph, op.cit., p. 19.
It is true that Jesus does not call for a rebellion against Rome. Maybe the explanation given by Christoph Burchard could help us:
> *The fact that Jesus does not show us anything of a great political horizon (sentences like Mk 10:42 par. or Mt 11:8 par. are common places) may be due to a certain provincialism. Where there is no history being made, there is nothing promising in trying to improve it. On the other hand, the kingdom of God indeed strongly intervenes in the social sphere when it has come in the form of exorcisms and healings of lepers or the granting of civil rights to women, children, heathens, prostitutes and publicans and will come in the exaltation of the poor. What is missing with Jesus is an analysis of the really existing circumstances. But it is not missing like a cripple is missing a leg. It is overcome by the kingdom of God and with it any justification of these circumstances.*

50 SOBRINO, Jon, op.cit., pp. 217-229.

51 BLASER, Klauspeter. *La mission: dialogues et défis*. Geneva: Editions du Soc, Labor et Fides, 1983, pp. 40-41.

52 WCC. *Mission and Evangelism: An Ecumenical Affirmation*, paras. 7, 8, 9.
SOBRINO, Jon, op.cit., pp. 222-235.

53 FOULKES, Irene W. de. El Reino de Dios y Pablo, en *Vida y Pensamiento*, Vol. 1, No. 2, Julio 1981. San José, Costa Rica: Seminario Bíblico Latinoamericano, pp. 9-24.

54 SIDER, Ronald. *Christ and Violence*. Scottdale: Herald Press, 1979, pp. 56-57.

55 According to Günther Bornkamm, op.cit., Chapter VIII, almost every one of the Messianic titles claimed for Jesus is the expression of the devotion of the post-Easter Christian community. "There is in fact not one single certain proof of Jesus' claiming for himself one of the Messianic titles which tradition has ascribed to him" (172). And this is as it should be, because "no customary or current conception, no title or office which Jewish tradition and expectation held in readiness, serves to authenticate his mission, or exhausts the secret of his being" (178). According to Ferdinand Hahn, op.cit. (Excursus I, p. 54) it is very difficult if not impossible to prove a direct influence of Isaiah 53 on the life of Jesus, or in the stories of the gospels. "The exegetical

basis is extremely small and by far the main point of the argument
is to explain the lack of actually recognizable references to
Isaiah 53" (63). Hahn discusses contradictory opinions of Hans Walter
Wolf, Joachim Jeremias and Oscar Cullmann. Waldron Scott, op.cit.
(pp. 89-90) takes for granted Jesus' self-understanding as Isaiah's
Suffering Servant. "St Matthew understood this clearly" (Mt 12:17-21).
That is a quotation from Isaiah 42:1-4.

John Bright, op.cit. (p. 208) affirms that "Jesus took his stand
squarely in what was properly a Messianic tradition -- specifically
in that of the Suffering Servant. In fact, it would seem that he
consciously adopted the pattern of the servant and suffered all the
other Messianic patterns with it." He goes on to elaborate on the
"striking parallels between the figure of the servant and the Christ
whom we know from the gospels".

Without ignoring the data provided by Bornkamm and Hahn, we would like
to affirm the following:
1. Something objectively real in Jesus' life gave the "hook", the
   linking possibilities to the Messianic titles ascribed to him by
the early church. As Bornkamm himself says: "In the light of the coming
reign, and in the presence of God with his claims, each of his words
and deeds has a decisive significance for the presence and the future"
(169-170).
2. The gospels are full of references -- implicit or explicit -- to the
   book of Isaiah. It seems to have been a certain permeation of the
spiritual life of Christ and his disciples with the message of this book.
3. While the whole question of the Messianic secret, or the Messianic
   vocation of Jesus, remains open, it seems to be clear from the
gospels' data that Jesus has a sense of direction, of vocation, and that
he sees even the final confrontation with the authorities -- perhaps in
the prophetic tradition -- as essential component of his role.

All these considerations, it seems to me, point to the legitimate right
of the early church, and of us today, to interpret Jesus' life and
death in the perspective of the Suffering Servant; of course, recognizing
that the uniqueness of Jesus reveals the limitations of all Old Testament
images, but we can only recognize that uniqueness against the background
of the Old Testament! With Tomas Hanks, an Old Testament scholar from
Costa Rica, we detect in Isaiah 53 perspectives that help us to see more
inclusive meanings in Jesus' suffering than those which our divided
Christian traditions have been able to appropriate.

56 HANKS, Tomas, op.cit., pp. 26-27 (my translation).

57 HAHN, Ferdinand, op.cit., pp. 24-25.

58 SCHMIDT, K.L., op.cit., p. 585.

59 BORNKAMM, Günther, op.cit., pp. 92-93.

60 VERKUYL, Johannes, op.cit., pp. 145-146.

61 LADD, George E., op.cit., p. 327.
    CULLMANN, Oscar. *Christ and Time*. London: SCM Press, 1962, p. 157.

JEREMIAS, Joachim. *Jesus' Promise to the Nations*. Naperville: Alec R. Allenson Inc., 1958, p. 75

62 SCHNACKENBURG, Rudolf. *God's Rule and Kingdom*. New York: Herder & Herder, 1963, p. 220.

63 BORNKAMM, Günther, op.cit., p. 79.

64 SCHMIDT, K.L., op.cit., p. 588.

65 BARTH, Markus. *Ephesians*. Garden City, N.Y.: Doubleday/Anchor Bible, 1974, p. 209.

66 WCC. *Mission and Evangelism: An Ecumenical Affirmation*, para. 6.

67 BOFF, Leonardo, *Jesus Christ Liberator*, p. 221.
    MOLTMANN, Jürgen, op.cit., pp. 191-192.

68 ANASTASIOS (Yannoulatos), op.cit., pp. 239-240.

69 NEWBIGIN, Lesslie. *The Open Secret*, pp. 44-48.
    KUZMIC, Peter. The Church and the Kingdom of God, in *The Church in Response to Human Need*, ed. by Tom Sine, pp. 15-16.

70 MOLTMANN, Jürgen. *Theology of Hope*. New York: Harper & Row, 1967. pp. 224-225.
    BRAATEN, Carl E., op.cit., pp. 43-44.

71 PANNENBERG, Wolfhart. *Theology and the Kingdom of God*. Philadelphia: Westminster, 1969, Chapter II, "The Kingdom and the Church".

CHAPTER IV

1 PANNENBERG, Wolfhart, op.cit., p. 51.

2 CONE, James H. *God of the Oppressed*. New York: Seabury Press, 1975, pp. 76-77.
   LAZARETH, William, in Foreword to J. Miguez Bonino, *Doing Theology in a Revolutionary Situation*, p. XI.
   TORRES, Sergio, et.al., eds. Reports of five international congresses of Third World Theologians, already quoted in Chapter I, Note 48.
   ARIAS, Mortimer, op.cit.
   BRAATEN, Carl E., op.cit.
   VERKUYL, Johannes, op.cit.
   BOSCH, David, op.cit.

3 CAMPS, Arnulf, op.cit., Chapter I.

4 ROTTENBERG, Isaac, op.cit., pp. 51-54.

5 See in second part, first section, article on "The Mission and Unity
   of the Church in a Global Perspective".

6 SOBRINO, Jon. The Witness of the Church, in *The Challenge of Basic
   Christian Communities,* ed. by Sergio Torres and John Eagleson, pp. 170-180.

7 WCC. *Mission and Evangelism: An Ecumenical Affirmation,* para 7.
   BRAATEN, Carl E. Who Do We Say that He Is? The Uniqueness and Universality
   of Jesus Christ, in *Occasional Bulletin of Missionary Research*, Vol. 4,
   No. 1, January 1980. Ventnor, N.J.: OMSC, pp. 2-8.

8 COSTAS, Orlando E. *Christ Outside the Gate*, pp. 88-90.
   STYLIANOPOULOS, Theodore. A Christological Reflection, in *Jesus Christ,
   the Life of the World: An Orthodox Contribution*, ed. by Ion Bria, pp. 43-44.

9 MOLTMANN, Jürgen. *The Church in the Power of the Spirit*, pp. 53-54.

10 SONG, Choan Seng. *The Compassionate God.*

11 OSTHATHIOS, Metropolitan Geevarghese Mar. The Gospel of the Kingdom and
   the Crucified and Risen Lord, in *Your Kingdom Come - Mission Perspectives*,
   pp. 42-43.

12 BLASER, Klauspeter. *La mission: dialogues et défis*, p. 8.
   BOSCH, David, op.cit., p. 57.

13 BARTH, Markus. *Justification.* Grand Rapids: Eerdmans, 1971, p. 41.

14 See in second part, first section, article on "World Mission - A New
   Opportunity".
   MOLTMANN, Jürgen. *The Trinity and the Kingdom of God*, pp. 82-83.
   BLASER, Klauspeter, op.cit., pp. 7-8.
   CHETHIMATTAM, John. Development, Dialogue and Evangelization, in
   Toward a New Age in Mission, pp. 104-105.
   FACKRE, Gabriel. *The Christian Story.* Grand Rapids: Eerdmans, 1978,
   pp. 155-156.

Today it is generally accepted that mission has its origins in Godself.
It is not a decision of a church body, it is the loving passion of God
who sent the prophets, his Son and the Holy Spirit. The concept of *Missio
Dei* has been interpreted in a limited way to refer to the mission of the
church -- "As the Father has sent me..." -- or in a wider sense, to involve
all human aspirations toward the good and justice of the kingdom. With some
safeguards, we would like to use the expression in this latter sense. God
is active in all creation struggling to bring everything into redemption.
Attempts are made to separate grace from law, saving grace from common
grace, the right hand from the left hand of God, etc. These distinctions
could be useful and sometimes necessary, but they should not build dogmatic
barriers around God's freedom. As in the internal life of the Trinity the
pericoresis describes the interpenetration of the divine person, so there is
an interpenetration in their mission *ad extra*. The Spirit and the Word are
present and active in the creation by the Father and similarly in the
process of salvation and sanctification. We suggest in the text a
possibility for making a distinction between the ordinary -- prevenient

grace -- mission of God, and the extraordinary wrought in Jesus Christ, and now entrusted to the church. But we want to preserve the "whole counsel of God", not to isolate a single aspect of God's mission. His creative activity is an invitation to testify of his saving action in Christ and his redemptive activity. The building of shalom, peace, is a calling to proclaim the lordship of Jesus Christ and to announce the kingdom that is coming.

Missio Dei and kingdom of God are very useful theological concepts but they need to be "protected" from any attempt to make of them sectarian or universal ideologies. The centre of attention remains in God's revelation in Christ. It is from Christ's perspective that we are able to discern in nature God's creative hand, and also in him that we could have a vision of the final redemption. That means that the wider our concept of God's mission, the bigger should be our evangelistic commitment! But more of that in the text itself.

For a thorough bibliography on the *Missio Dei* debate, see Helmut Rosin, *Missio Dei*, Interuniversity Institute for Missiological and Ecumenical Research, Leiden, 1972.

15 ROTTENBERG, Isaac, op.cit., pp. 27-41.

16 BOESAK, Allan. Jesus Christ, the Life of the World, in *Gathered for Life*, ed. by David Gill, p. 226.

17 AAGAARD, Johannes. *Mission after Uppsala 1968*. University of Aarhus, Denmark, August 1970, mimeographic paper, p. 6.

18 MIGUEZ BONINO, José. Fundamental Questions in Ecclesiology, in *The Challenge of Basic Christian Communities*, ed. by Sergio Torres and John Eagleson, pp. 145-147.

> *But the global horizon and the ultimate point of reference for the Christian faith is not the church but the kingdom of God. The church is <u>relative</u> to that horizon; it must be seen in that perspective. In that sense the church is relativized.*
>
> *That sort of relativization is obvious in the Bible. It is not a "church" but a "humanity" that God creates. It is in humanity that God's image is reflected. It is to humanity that God entrusts a mission. It is with humanity that God makes a covenant of commitment; and that covenant is renewed even after sin enters the picture (Gen. 9). The central focus of Jesus' mission is the proclamation of the kingdom, whose coming is initiated in his words and deeds. The summons and mission of his disciples is framed in this perspective; and only in this perspective can we adequately frame the few references to the "church" that we find in the gospels. Finally, the New Testament expands its vision to a total fulfilment that has to do with a new "humanity" -- not a temple but a new city.*
>
> *None of that detracts from the reality of a particular election, of the creation of a "special" people. Nor does it detract from the indestructible continuity that exists between the election of Israel and what happens in the New Testament. In the latter we have the reconstruction of the "assembly", the "church", which Jesus Christ establishes and brings together, and in which he is present through*

*his Spirit. The important thing to note is that this "particular"
election is not absolute or "self-contained"; it is subordinate to
the ultimate, overall objective -- the kingdom. In that sense we
can say that the church is one of the precincts in which God carries
out the proposal to recreate humanity and the human being, to
consummate the kingdom.*

*Note that I said the church is one of the precincts. It is not the
only one because the Bible consistently bears witness to the universal operation of the Spirit in all of creation and to Jesus
Christ's universal mediation in all of history; this universal
operation and mediation is not confined within the church. And I
use the term "precinct" [ámbito] rather than "means" because the
church has its own proper dignity, a certain proper autonomy, and
even its own eschatological import. The conflict-ridden process
through which God asserts the sovereignty of divine love, justice, and
peace in the world is carried out in the church in a way that is
specific and peculiar to the church, even though it is related to
the overall horizon.*

BERKHOF, Hendrikus. *Christ the Meaning of History*. London: SCM Press,
1966, pp. 169-173.
BOFF, Leonardo. *Jesus Christ Liberator*, pp. 219-220.

19 II Vatican Council. Council Daybook, Session IV. *Constitution of the
Church in the Modern World*, Chapter III, para. 39.

*We do not know the time for the consummation of the earth and of
humanity, nor do we know how all things will be transformed. As de-
formed by sin, the shape of this world will pass away; but we are
taught that God is preparing a new dwelling place and a new earth
where justice will abide, and whose blessedness will answer and sur-
pass all the longings for peace which spring up in the human heart.
Then, with death overcome, the sons of God will be raised up in
Christ, and what was sown in weakness and corruption will be invested
with incorruptibility. Enduring with charity and its fruits, all that
creation which God made on man's account will be unchained from the
bondage of vanity.*

*Therefore, while we are warned that it profits a man nothing if he
gain the whole world and lose himself, the expectation of a new
earth must not weaken but rather stimulate our concern for cultivating
this one. For here grows the body of a new human family, a body which
even now is able to give some kind of foreshadowing of the new age.*

*Hence, while earthly progress must be carefully distinguished from
the growth of Christ's kingdom, to the extent that the former can
contribute to the better ordering of human society, it is of vital
concern to the kingdom of God.*

*For after we have obeyed the Lord, and in his Spirit nurtured on earth
the values of human dignity, brotherhood and freedom, and indeed all
the good fruits of our nature and enterprise, we will find them again,
but freed of stain, burnished and transfigured, when Christ hands over
to the Father: "a kingdom eternal and universal, a kingdom of truth
and life, of holiness and grace, of justice, love and peace." On this
earth that kingdom is already present in mystery. When the Lord returns it will be brought into full flower.*

20 What, then, does the Christian contribute? Only a knowledge? In one sense yes, but what a knowledge! The proclamation of the story of Christ, with an invitation to faith. What results from this trans- mission of that knowledge -- faith, repentance, new life -- goes beyond our capacity to plan for, or pretend. It belongs to the realm of the action of the Holy Spirit for which we can only pray, hope and give witness.

21 In general, the Bible recognizes the mission of other nations or persons in their interplay with the history of Israel. But the question of their mission, their service to the kingdom, totally unrelated to Israel, is not discussed openly. However, C.S. Song in *The Compassionate God*, gives clear Old Testament references, both in Isaiah and especially in Daniel, to prove that already in Old Testament times the vision of the prophets was wide enough to recognize the power of earthly "secular" kings as coming from the "God of heaven".

See also SONG, Choan Seng, op.cit., pp. 47-49, 68-72.

Vinay Samuel and Chris Sugden also struggle with this issue in an illuminating and pathetic way, in Tensions between Eschatology and History, in Tom Sine, ed., *The Church in Response to Human Need*. The emotions easily detectable especially in Asian theologians indicate the existential importance of this issue as they wrestle with their being Christians and Asians. Examples of the interplay -- reciprocal influence between the Christian movement and other historical forces -- train us to discern signs of God's action and human obedience in other people's histories. But again, in the practical encounter with all cultures, Christians are invited to give their testimony. We are not called to pass judgement on the "others". We thank God for them. And the best way we have to express our gratitude to God and to them is by sharing the story of God's love in Jesus Christ.

22 BOFF, Leonardo and Clodovis. *Libertad y Liberación*. Salamanca: Ed. Sígueme, 1982, pp. 33-34.
CHETHIMATTAM, John, op.cit., pp. 108-109.
It is part of the mandate of the church to lead this world back into the kingdom of God, which also means to improve it, develop and elevate it, transform it into a more human world. According to Vatican II the task of the church in the world is, on the one hand, to recognize the autonomy of the earthly affairs and the dignity of the human person, and to manifest its solidarity with the entire human family; and on the other, to see that the community of men united in Christ is led by the Holy Spirit in its journey to the kingdom of their Father. Christ's redemptive work directed towards salvation of men involves also the renewal of the temporal order.

The trinitarian basis of mission work as a movement of loving communication from the bosom of the Godhead, the infinite dynamic of the love and life of the Supreme Good demands that its waves embrace the whole man. We cannot make an artificial separation between the creating and the redeeming God, between the natural and the supernatural life of man. As Johannes Schütte says, "Redemption does not create another world, but recreates the present."

113

*Here the eschatological dimension of the church's mission is
significant. Mission is the manifestation of the eschatological
sovereignty of God among nations. Eschaton is the end, but it is
also the beginning, the manifestation of God as Master of the
whole future. Hence if Christ is the eschatological fulfilment
of the glorification of God, he must also be the fulfilment of the
missionary hopes and expectations to liberate the whole man. The
missionary command "to go" and assemble nations must be considered
the inauguration of the sovereignty of God over all men and all
creation. "The eschatological kingdom of Christ embraces and embodies the totality of creation, the whole of mankind and every man,
in the spiritual, historical and socio-economic dimension. The
final form of salvation is not merely the survival of the spirit,
the immortality of the soul, but the resurrection of the whole man,
including the resurrection of the body. In its turn the redemption
of the body implies the redemption of the whole social, economic and
political relationship of man's earthly life also."*

*In fact, the work for the liberation of peoples and for their develop-
ment is the most effective witness of the gospel which is founded in
the universal and unconditional love of God for men. Seen in this
perspective, evangelization and development penetrate each other in
a single movement for human progress and salvation embracing every
man and the whole mankind. Hence the work for human development is not
extraneous to evangelization but pertains to the gospel core.*

SONG, Choan Seng. *Third-Eye Theology*, p. 175.
*The freedom of God is the freedom to be with those who suffer in hope
and unto hope. The woman who looks down and feels the seed coming into life in her womb, the mother who fills the bowl with new rice for
her son each day, each of them encounters God in her suffering. The
seed that stirs in the woman's womb and the rice with which the mother
fills the bowl speak volumes about the hope of humanity in a world of
misery and suffering. I am sure God wants us Christians to share in
that seed of hope stirring in the womb of humanity. And perhaps he is
calling us to be a bowl of the rice of hope and life to those
struggling to be free from fear and despair. Surely this must be the
meaning of the cross, which is God suffering with us human beings
unto the hope of a new life in him.*

23 FACKRE, Gabriel, op.cit., pp. 231-232.
   MOLTMANN, Jürgen. *The Trinity and the Kingdom*, p. 157.

24 BOFF, Leonardo. *Jesus Christ Liberator*, pp. 286-288.
   COSTAS, Orlando E., op.cit., pp. 92-94.
   ROTTENBERG, Isaac, op.cit., pp. 20-22.
   WALLIS, Jim. *The Call to Conversion*. New York: Harper & Row, 1981.

25 WCC. *Mission and Evangelism: An Ecumenical Affirmation*, paras. 10-13.

26 COSTA DE BEAUREGARD, M.A. *L'Orthodoxie Hier, Demain*, p. 129.
   ARIAS, Mortimer, op.cit., pp. 48-53.
   GUTIERREZ, Gustavo. *A Theology of Liberation*, pp. 204-208.
   CASTRO, Emilio. Conversion and Social Transformation, in *Christian Social
   Ethics in a Changing World*, ed. by John C. Bennett. Geneva: WCC, 1966.

See also in second part, third section, editorial on "Conversion".

27 WCC. *Your Kingdom Come - Mission Perspectives*, Report of Section I on
    Good News to the Poor, pp. 171-178.

28 BARTH, Markus, op.cit., pp. 16-17.

29 JONES, Major J. *Christian Ethics for Black Theology: The Politics of
    Liberation*. New York: Abingdon, 1974, pp. 57-58.
    CASTRO, Emilio. Your Kingdom Come: A Missionary Perspective, in *Your
    Kingdom Come - Mission Perspectives*, pp. 31-32.

30 ANDERSON, Bernhard W., op.cit., p. 12.

31 BARTH, Karl. *Church Dogmatics*. Vol. IV, No. 3. Edinburgh: T & T Clark,
    1962, pp. 876-878.

32 PANNENBERG, Wolfhart, op.cit., pp. 75-76.

33 WALLIS, Jim, op.cit., pp. 35-36.
    See also in second part, third section, editorial on "Conversion".

34 VERKUYL, Johannes, op.cit., pp. 180-181.
    SCOTT, Waldron. *Bring Forth Justice*, chapter 11.

35 WCC. *Mission and Evangelism: An Ecumenical Affirmation*, para. 13.

    It should be obvious for the reader that I am avoiding the use of the
    words "salvation", "saved", etc. to describe the experience of conversion,
    repentance and personal faith. I think that Karl Barth is right when he
    says that biblically God calls people to a mission, a task, to be witnesses,
    and that all other manifestations around that calling are not the centre
    of attention. "The personal history of the called and its happy outcome
    never become a real theme, not even in the stories of the publican
    Zacchaeus and the Philippian Gaoler. ... It is common to all the biblical
    accounts of calling that to be called means to be given a task. ... They
    are made his witnesses...who can and must declare what they have seen
    and heard, like witnesses in a law-suit" (K. Barth, op.cit., pp. 572-576).
    As an evangelist I have difficulties in inviting people to "salvation",
    understood as something for them. I rather think that we invite
    people to Jesus, his kingdom, his cross, and all the rest, salvation
    included, comes as an "extra", even as a surprise! (Mt 6:33; 7:21; 25:37)
    But this potential surprise is not to scare people because the one who
    will judge is the one that invites today to follow him, to serve with
    him. As we enter in the Christian vocation following his calling, we know
    that in him we can hope, that our life is in his hands, that our
    salvation can be entrusted to God's love in Christ (Rom 8:38-39).

    See also *Monthly Letter on Evangelism*, Geneva: Commission on World
    Mission and Evangelism, Nos 1/2 and 8, 1981, for a discussion of
    motivations for evangelism.

36 MIGUEZ BONINO, José. *Doing Theology in a Revolutionary Situation*,
    p. 152.

37 ESQUIVEL, Julia. The Crucified Lord: A Latin American Perspective, in *Your Kingdom Come - Mission Perspectives*, pp. 59-60.

38 SOBRINO, Jon. *Monsignor Romero: Verdadero Profeta*. Managua: IHCA-CAV, 1981, p. 61.
Si llegan a cumplir las amenazas, desde ya ofrezco a Dios mi sangre por la redención y resurrección de El Salvador. Que mi sangre sea semilla de libertad y la señal de que la esperanza será pronto una realidad; sea por la liberación de mi pueblo y como un testimonio de esperanza en el futuro.

39 VERKUYL, Johannes, op.cit., pp. 176-178.

40 MOLTMANN, Jürgen. *The Church in the Power of the Spirit*, p. 190.

41 STOTT, John. *Christian Mission in the Modern World*. Downers Grove, Illinois: Intervarsity Press, 1975, pp. 22-25.
BOSCH, David, op.cit., pp. 66-70.
BARTH, Karl, op.cit., pp. 860-862.

42 CLEMENT, Olivier, quoted by Paulos Gregorios in *The Human Presence: An Orthodox View of Nature*. Geneva: WCC, 1978, p. 81.
If the spiritual destiny of man is inseparable from that of humanity (as a whole), it is also inseparable from that of the terrestrial cosmos. The sensible universe as a whole constitutes, in fact, a prolongation of our bodies. Or rather, what is our body, if it is not the form imprinted by our "living soul" on the universal "dust" which unceasingly penetrates and traverses us? There is no discontinuity between the flesh of the world and human flesh; the universe participates in human nature, as it constitutes the body of humanity. ... Man is the hypostasis (personality) of the cosmos, its conscious and personal self-expression; it is he who gives meaning to things and who has to transfigure them. For the universe, man is its hope to receive grace and to be united with God; man is also the possibility of failure and loss for the universe. Let us recall the fundamental text of St Paul in Romans 8:22. Subject to disorder and death by our fall, the creation waits also for man's becoming Son of God by grace, which would mean liberation and glory for it also. We are responsible for the world, to the very smallest twigs and plants. We are the word, the "logos" by which the world expresses itself, by which the world speaks to God: it depends on us whether it blasphemes or it prays, whether it becomes an illusion or wisdom, black magic or celebration. Only through us, can the cosmos, as the prolongation of our bodies, have access to eternity. How strange all this must sound to modern minds! That is our evil, our sin, our freedom led astray to vampirize nature; it is we who are responsible for the carcasses and the twisted trees that pollution produces, it is our refusal to love that baffles the sad eyes of so many animals. But every time a human being becomes aware of the cosmic significance of the eucharist, each time a pure being receives a humble sensation with gratitude -- whether he eats a fruit or inhales the fragrance of the earth -- a sort of joy of eternity reverberates in the marrow of things.

COSTA DE BEAUREGARD, M.A., op.cit., p. 157.
BRIA, Ion, ibid., p. 199.
ANASTASIOS (Yannoultaos), op.cit., pp. 239-240.
Metropolitan EMILIANOS of Silibria, in *The Sofia Consultation*, ed.
by T. Sabev, Geneva: WCC, 1982, p. 44.

43 MIGUEZ BONINO, José, op.cit., p. 141.
NISSIOTIS, Nikos, op.cit., pp. 151-152.

44 PANNENBERG, Wolfhart, op.cit., pp. 53-54.

45 BOFF, Leonardo and Clodovis, op.cit., p. 130.

46 SONG, Choan Seng. *The Compassionate God*, pp. 46-47.

47 BARTH, Karl, op.cit., Vol. I, No. 1, para. 2
BARTH, Karl. *La prière*. Neuchâtel: Delachaux et Niestlé, 1967, pp. 27-28.

48 BARTH, Karl. *La proclamation de l'Evangile*. Neuchâtel: Delachaux et
Niestlé, 1961, pp. 21-22, 40.
BARTH, Karl. *Church Dogmatics*, Vol. IV, No. 1, para. 58.2.

49 BOSCH, David. The Kingdom of God and the Kingdoms of this World, in
Journal of Theology for Southern Africa. University of Capetown, 1979,
No. 21, p. 11.

50 MIGUEZ BONINO, José, op.cit., pp. 141-142.
ARAYA, Victorio, op.cit., p. 219.
Russian Orthodox Church, in *The Sofia Consultation*, p. 52.
*"Jesus Christ is the life, for no other can give the life we expect,
that is the life immortal, blissful and holy. He raises us from the
dead, and restores those, who suffered death because of the eternal
curse, to what they were in the beginning. Therefore, all the beautiful and excellent things which were revealed to us will stay through
him and in him," writes St Cyril of Alexandria (12, 14, 182-183).*

*The resurrection of Christ has revealed the great significance of
the bodily element by sanctifying it and making it share in life
eternal. Moreover, the authentic and pure beauty of the world, the
joy of creativity and brotherly fellowship in love among people, all
that is transient and liable to decay here but will rise together
with the coming resurrection of our flesh and coming renewal of the
world -- all this is consolidated and made to share in life eternal
through the resurrection of the Son of God in flesh.*

51 GUTIERREZ, Gustavo, op.cit.
BARTH, Karl. *La prière*, pp. 64-70.
Faith and Science in an Unjust World. Geneva: WCC, 1980, from report
of Section 10, on Towards a New Christian Social Ethic and New Social
Policies for the Churches, Vol. 2, p. 162.
*How does the ethic of the kingdom of God relate to human decisions
and political actions?*
St Paul emphasizes that the kingdom of God is characterized by

*righteousness and peace. The kingdom of God, moreover, is not a
future possibility alone; it is a past and present fact in the
life of Jesus Christ. But it is a presence which calls for active
effort in the lives of each person and of each society; it cannot
merely be assumed. Christians are called to work in society so as
to make it more supportive of the values of the kingdom, more
expressive of the purposes of God in Christ. Human fallibility and
sin make this a perilous task for anyone, and no less for Christians;
yet we dare not refuse the invitation of our Lord to seek his kingdom.*

*Christians do not, therefore, bring in from outside history elements
which are not present within it; they try to recognize in events --
in the movements and ideas around them -- the activity of God. Because
we believe that God is working for the fulfilment of his purposes, we
try to uncover, and to give physical shape to his activity. Our
attempts to recognize where God is working have to be put continuously under the radical judgement of Christ, to whom the Bible witnesses.
This judgement must be continuous because of the human tendency to
prove what we want to prove, to fulfil our purposes, not God's. We
can say, then, that the task of the Christian mission and of Christian
moral judgement is constantly to point the world to the God who is
active within it to bring righteousness and peace. The Christian
community does this only when it is itself a community of love, which
is prepared to suffer for the sake of its Lord.*

52 PANNENBERG, Wolfhart, op.cit., pp. 80-81.

53 BARTH, Markus, op.cit., pp. 81-82.
    BOFF, Leonardo, op.cit., p. 281.

54 BARTH, Karl. *Church Dogmatics*, Vol. IV, No. 1, para. 58, pp. 152-154.
    TORRES, Sergio and EAGLESON, John, eds., op.cit., Final document,
    pp. 236-237.

55 ECHEGARAY, Hugo, op.cit., p. 155.

56 BOSCH, David. Kingdom of God and Kingdoms of this World, pp. 12-13.

57 ELLUL, Jacques. *False Presence of the Kingdom*. New York: Seabury Press,
    1972, p. 112.

58 HAHN, Ferdinand, op.cit., pp. 96-99.
    NEWBIGIN, Lesslie. *Your Kingdom Come*, pp. 41-42.
    *One final point must be made, and it is this. The more we stress the
    need that the church should develop a new openness to the world, a
    new flexibility in its structures and new styles of ministerial
    leadership to meet the changing patterns of secular life, the more
    necessary it is to stress the centrality and finality of Jesus Christ
    for everything in the life of the church, the fundamental reality of
    personal conversion to him and of confession of his name. With the
    kind of openness and flexibility which I have advocated, it may be
    difficult to say exactly where the boundaries of the church lie; this
    does not matter provided we are clear and make clear to others where*

118

the centre lies. An entity can be defined either in terms of its boundaries or in terms of its centre. The church is an entity which is properly described by its centre. It is impossible to define exactly the boundaries of the church, and the attempt to do so always ends in an unevangelical legalism. But it is always possible and necessary to define the centre. The church is its proper self, and is a sign of the kingdom, only insofar as it continually points men and women beyond itself to Jesus and invites them to personal conversion and commitment to him.

59 See in second part, first section, the editorial on the Missionary Conference of Melbourne, 1980.

CHAPTER V

1 For a thorough discussion of Jesus' titles and their evolution in the first century, see Ferdinand Hahn, op.cit. For the transfer of God's authority to the Lord Jesus, see especially pp. 103-114.

2 WCC. *Breaking Barriers*, pp. 43-44.

3 BARTH, Karl. *Church Dogmatics*, Vol. IV, No. 3, The Christian as Witness, pp. 353ff.

4 FACKRE, Gabriel, op.cit., p. 62.
   PANNENBERG, Wolfhart, op.cit., p. 81.

5 WICKREMESINGHE, Lakshman. Christianity in the Context of Other Faiths, in *Asia's Struggle for Full Humanity*, ed. by Virginia Fabella, p. 34.

6 SONG, Choan Seng. *Third-Eye Theology*, chapter 3, Love as the Possibility of Theology, especially p. 58.

7 BROWN, Colin, ed. *The New International Dictionary of New Testament Theology*, Vol. 3. Exeter, U.K.: Paternoster Press, 1978, article "Sozo", pp. 205-216.

8 ECHEGARAY, Hugo, op.cit., pp. 176-177.

9 ARIAS, Mortimer, op.cit., pp. 22-23.

10 We do not enter here into the technical question of Jesus' self-awareness and the degree of his identification with one or several prevailing images of the Messiah. For our purposes it is enough to affirm a calling, a vocation, a sense of purpose that is visible in Jesus' actions. The gospels give the origin of that calling in the baptism or in the pre-existence in God. In any case, the "holism" to every single action is provided by the person of Jesus. Each one of those actions is an expression of his love and a sign of the kingdom to come.

11 BONNARD, Pierre. *L'Evangile selon Saint Matthieu*. Geneva: Labor et Fides, 1982, pp. 219-220, 235-236.

12 COSTAS, Orlando E., op.cit., pp. 11-12.

13 See in second part, third section, The Church and its Agenda in the Mission of the Kingdom.
BARTH, Karl, op.cit., p. 576.

> *They are made his witnesses: not idle spectators merely watching and considering; not for the enjoyment of a spectacle granted to them; not for the vain increase of their knowledge of men, the world and history by this or that which they now come to know of God; not inquisitive reporters; but witnesses who can and must declare what they have seen and heard like witnesses in a law-suit. Their calling embraces not only the fact that God gives them knowledge concerning himself and the doing of his will, and that he calls them to this knowledge, but also the fact that he summons and equips them to declare what he has given them to know. In other words, their calling means both that he reveals himself in his action and also that he summons them into the witness-box as those who know. As God speaks his Word to these men in and with what he does, and as he is heard by them, he gives them the freedom, but also claims and commissions them, to confess that they are hearers of his Word within the world and humanity which has not heard it but for which his work is dumb, and in this way to make the world and humanity hear. This is their raison d'être. In vocation, then, it is a matter of God on the one side and the world on the other. It is a matter of the service of God in the form of a service to be rendered by them in and to the world. The Word of the work which God does in and on them is to be sounded out and heard in the world. What God has done and does and will do is to become a message directed to it and to be spoken in its ears. In the biblical narratives those called by God are men who are summoned, commanded and empowered to declare this message. They are responsible for addressing the message of God to his creatures. As witnesses they have to repeat what God himself has first said to them. This is the task laid upon them in their calling and to be discharged with their whole existence. This is the point of their particular existence. This makes them what they are in distinction from all others. Whatever else they may be, and especially their being, capacity and possession graciously granted as their particular experience of salvation, the ethos especially required of them, and all that they might have to undergo in the way of particular suffering -- all this depends upon and stands under the common sign of the fact that they are entrusted with this declaration and message and have to discharge this commission. They are witnesses. They are Verbi divini ministri. Hence they are called the prophets of Yahwe in the Old Testament and the disciples and apostles of Jesus Christ in the New.*

14 CASTRO, Emilio. Reflections after Melbourne, in *Your Kingdom Come – Mission Perspectives*, pp. 230-231.

*Now, how should the churches and Christians enter into the
historical struggles in the name of the kingdom of God?*

*Assuming with Romans 8 that "the world is groaning for fulfil-
ment, that God is at work", the church must dare to be present
where there are risky decisions to be taken in the ambiguities
of the world, knowing that we cannot escape these ambiguities by
retiring from the world. "In their witness to the kingdom of God
in words and deeds the churches must dare to be present at the
bleeding points of humanity and thus near those who suffer evil,
even taking the risk of being counted among the wicked. The royal
reign of God appears on earth as the kingdom of the crucified Jesus,
which places his disciples with him under the cross. Without losing
sight of the ultimate hope of the kingdom of God or giving up their
critical attitude, churches must dare to be present in the midst of
human struggles for penultimate solutions and welcome all signs of
a hopeful development" (Section II, 4). Churches must be there interceding for the problems of the world. The churches must be there
with repentance and self-criticism, recognizing their own complicity
with much of the tragedy of the world. The churches must be there to
join forces with others, knowing that God's kingdom works with
several means and instruments. The churches must be there to plant
signs of the kingdom, especially the signs of reconciliation. But
fundamentally, the churches are called to witness in the midst of
those struggles to the hope that is in Jesus Christ, to invite all
to see what is going on in the search for justice, to what went on
the cross and in the resurrection of Jesus Christ. Evangelism is affirmed in Melbourne, not as a professional programme outside of one's
participation in the struggles of the world, but precisely in the
moment in which we are cooperating with others, praying for others,
trying to plant signs of reconciliation, we are there to give reason
to the hope that is within us. We are there to "witness to the fact
that there is a common hope for humankind and for the whole of
creation in the life and death, the resurrection and the ascension
of the Son of God, and that the coming of the kingdom of God is
linked with the turning of human minds to Christ as the Lord of the
kingdom" (Section II, 5).*

*I emphasize this phrase because I think that we are overcoming the
division between social ethics on the one hand, and the gospel on
the other. Here we understand the kingdom struggling to be manifested
fully in daily history, the churches struggling to discern those signs
of the kingdom, joining forces with others instead of wanting to hold
on to the monopoly of that kingdom, but joining forces as Christians,
as churches: this means illuminating or highlighting the hidden
meaning of these human situations by pointing to the link between
them and the history of Jesus of Nazareth.*

*The concern for the struggles of the world is not simply a concern
for the social-ethical dimensions of the gospel, but a clear invitation
to announce the name of Jesus Christ in relation to the cutting issues
of human concern. The discernment of the powers and the nature of their
manifestation in history should become an invitation to exorcize them,
to control them in the name and in the power of the crucified King.*

121

15 MOLTMANN, Jürgen. *The Church in the Power of the Spirit*, p. 76.

See the agreements but also the differences in emphasis between Karl
Barth and liberation theologians. Both insist on word as well as action,
but Barth -- of course! -- giving priority to the word and the others
to action! Karl Barth, *Church Dogmatics*, Vol. IV, No. 3, pp. 860ff.
and Victorio Araya, op.cit., p. 204.
See also Carl E. Braaten, *The Flaming Center*, pp. 91-92.

16 KAPPEN, Sebastian. Orientations for an Asian Theology, in *Asia's Struggle
for Full Humanity*, ed. by Virginia Fabella, p. 120.
KRASS, Alfred C. *Evangelizing Neo-Pagan North America*. Scottdale: Herald
Press, 1982, p. 146.

17 PANNENBERG, Wolfhart, op.cit., pp. 90-93.

18 See in second part, second section, article on The Church in Latin
America and its Healing Ministry.
NEWBIGIN, Lesslie. The Future of Missions and Missionaries, in *Review
and Expositor*, Vol. 74, No. 2, 1977, p. 217.
> *The baptism which the church gives is the act by which we are in-
> corporated into that baptism of Christ with its focus on the cross.
> It is not baptism just for our own salvation. ... Rather it is our
> incorporation into the one baptism which is for the salvation of the
> world. To accept baptism, therefore, is to be committed to be with
> Christ in his ministry for all men (people).*

BRIA, Ion. Celebrating Life in the Liturgy, in *Jesus Christ, the Life
of the World*, ed. by Ion Bria, pp. 85-88.
STYLIANOPOULOS, Theodore, op.cit., pp. 51-52.

19 NEWBIGIN, Lesslie. *The Open Secret*, pp. 49-61.
ARAYA, Victorio, op.cit., pp. 207-210.

20 PANNENBERG, Wolfhart, op.cit., p. 92.
WCC. *Mission and Evangelism: An Ecumenical Affirmation*, para. 6.

21 STROMBERG, Jean, ed. *Sharing One Bread, Sharing One Mission*. Geneva:
WCC, 1983.
NEWBIGIN, Lesslie. *The Open Secret*, pp. 54-61.

22 To our notion of "representation" of the kingdom, Miguez Bonino proposes
the notion of sacrament (in *The Challenge of Basic Christian Communities*,
ed. by Sergio Torres and John Eagleson, p. 147).
> *A frequently used analogy, that of the church as the "sacrament of
> humanity", brings out both aspects well. A sacrament re-presents
> (makes present) to faith a reality that is not yet fully present to
> all. But it does not substitute for that reality or replace it. Rather
> than bottling up hope in its realization, a sacrament stimulates it.
> The new humanity of the kingdom -- where human divisions have been
> truly reconciled in authentic peace and justice -- is not yet visible;
> it is on the way towards realization. Hence we need an efficacious sign
> of the reality for which we are hoping and struggling. We need a place
> where faith can "discern" God's universal proposal. That is the point
> of the church. To confuse the sacrament with the reality, the church
> with the kingdom, would be to commit idolatry; it would be to forget*

*that the church is only a sacrament. Then we get the errors of
ecclesiastical clericalism and religious imperialism. Ecclesiastical
clericalism seeks to re-absorb the people into the church, and
religious imperialism restricts the work of God to the church. But
it is equally dangerous to overlook the specificity of the sacrament.
Then we may erroneously sacralize the notion of "the people", cut
out the eschatological perspective, and confusedly equate some
historical achievement with the new humanity of the kingdom.*

PANNENBERG, Wolfhart, op.cit., pp. 76-79, says that
*to the degree that the church follows his pointing -- Christ's
pointing toward the kingdom -- and heeds his reminder, the kingdom
of God will manifest itself through the church.*
SCOTT, Waldron. *Bring Forth Justice*, p. 217.

23   ARIAS, Mortimer, op.cit., p. 119.
      BARTH, Karl, op.cit., pp. 577, 854-856.

24   See Chapter I, the discussion on the Missionary Conference in Bangkok
      on "Salvation Today", January 1973.

25   STUHLMACHER, Peter. *The Approach, Style and Consequences of Primitive
      Christian Mission*. Colorado Springs: Young Life, 1980, Mimeographic paper.

26   ibid., pp. 14-18.

27   ESQUIVEL, Julia, op.cit., pp. 52-60.
      WCC. *Mission and Evangelism: An Ecumenical Affirmation*, para. 5, Good News
      to the Poor.

28   WCC. *A Theological Reflection on the Work of Evangelism*. Geneva: WCC, 1959,
      p. 21.
      HOLLENWEGER, Walter. *Evangelism Today*. Belfast: Christian Journals Ltd.,
      1976, pp. 42-45.
      *Likewise the eucharist of the early church explored hitherto unknown
      territory by walking forbidden paths. Not only was the forbidden made
      possible but it became the key for solving fundamental problems. It
      is thus that the barriers between slaves and free people were broken
      down in the agape meal of the early Christians (a slave could even be
      a bishop), between poor and rich, between men and women -- not
      logically nor in elaborating a social theory, but in the act of wor-
      ship. That which happened visibly in this worship (and not only that
      which was spoken) proved to be a missionary forward driving power. An
      experience of salvation was made which the world did not know. Nobody
      can think out what would happen if we Christians could really make
      visible alternatives of hope in our worship services against the grey
      background of society. Nobody can think out what would happen if our
      missionary institutions were changed into laboratories of hope. We
      could for example explore a new type of school, or hospital in which
      people were not only treated but healed. We could explore new types
      of radio programme which were popular and at the same time inspired
      new thinking. We could explore together with the people from the
      Living Theatre a new style of theatre which would open people's eyes
      to the great world theatre in which all of us have to play our role.*

123

We could explore together with the architects how to overcome the thought-killing and undialogical church architecture or the de-humanizing, expensive and meaningless individualistic design of houses. Perhaps some of us will have the courage to explore a new type of family which could cope better with the tensions of our time. In all this one would make visible alternatives to the <u>status quo</u>, a lived gospel. Thus the revolutionary freedom of the sons of God, their daring and their trust in God, speak much more forcefully than either the disembodied word or the uninterpreted, unimaginative so-called practical deeds.

Such freedom was demonstrated by the pastors and laymen, the monks and nuns, who took part as Christians in the 1974 Pop Festival on the Isle of Wight. One might be astonished that these Christians did not go as judges but as listeners among the fantastically clothed young people and that they did not point at the girl who was unashamedly showing her naked breasts, decorated with flowers, and that these Christians did not protest against the youngsters bathing in the nude. One of them, Derek Stirman, said: "When people stop feeling ashamed of their bodies they will look back and laugh at all the fuss, just as we now laugh about the bathing-machines and bloomers which our grand-parents considered essential for swimming. Some adults have labelled the youngsters "sick" for swimming in the nude, but who are the really "sick" people, the youngsters or the hordes of adults watching them through binoculars?"

The evangelists discovered among these young people not only a fantastic, sometimes deafening, but sometimes also thought-provoking music, but also a Franciscan spirit which puts many Christians to shame. "Their sense of sharing was absolute. It never occurred to them not to share everything. Their lack of dependence upon material things was impressive. Their interior happiness too. ... Some of these hippies have since become my close friends. It was they who on at least two occasions did something very good for us during the course of the festival; they brought along with them to the Communion service on the Sunday morning a whole contingent of the kind of persons that Christ was accused of mixing with -- the drop-outs and the unloved people. And they helped to find a 16-year-old girl for me, whose mother had appealed to me for help" (Robert Bowyer).

Here Christians did what appeared impossible in the eyes of the rest of society. Here they became the friends of today's "sinners and publicans". In becoming their friends they could do the unexpected and unpopular even within this pop-culture. To those who said, "We are selling drugs," they replied, "We are selling talk." And here talk was deed. Not in vain did hundreds of these youngsters come for talk. They wanted to hear more about this Jesus who is referred to in their pop-songs, but whom they had not yet met.

29 AAGAARD, Johannes. The Religious Dimension in the Mission of the Church, in *Partnership in Mission? Two Contributions.* Copenhagen: The Danish Missionary Council, September 1983, pp. 11-17.
See also the discussion in Chapters I and II.
See also Footnote 15.

30 See the discussion in Chapter II.
    See also in second part, first section, article on Evangelism, Mission,
    Liberation - Must We Choose?

31 BOFF, Leonardo and Clodovis, op.cit., pp. 152-153.

32 BRIA, Ion. *L'Orthodoxie Hier, Demain*, pp. 229-231.

33 NEWBIGIN, Lesslie. *Your Kingdom Come*, p. 28.

34 FOUCAULD, Théologue de. *L'Orthodoxie Hier, Demain*, p. 51.

35 SEGUNDO, Juan Luis. *The Liberation of Theology*, p. 33.
    *Leaving that issue aside here, I hope that it is quite clear that the
    Bible is not the discourse of a universal God to a universal man.
    Partiality is justified because we must find, and designate as the
    word of God, that part of divine revelation which today, in the light
    of our concrete historical situation, is most useful for the liberation
    to which God summons us. Other passages of that same divine revelation
    will help us tomorrow to complete and correct our present course
    towards freedom. God will keep coming back to speak to us from the
    very same Bible.*

36 BRIA, Ion, ed. *Martyria - Mission*, pp. 93ff.
    Metropolitan ANTONIE, op.cit., pp. 90ff.

37 Comment on Church-State Relations in Eastern Europe, ibid., pp. 106ff.

38 FOUCAULD, Théologue de, op.cit., pp. 53-54.

39 ibid., pp. 70-71.
    BOSCH, David, *Witness to the World*, pp. 110-114.

40 *Communauté de Grandchamp*. Lausanne: Imprimerie Centrale, 1958.
    HEIJKE, John. *An Ecumenical Light on the Renewal of Religious Community
    Life: Taizé*. Pittsburgh: Duquesne Univ. Press, 1967.

41 SHENK, Wilbert R., ed. *Exploring Church Growth*. Grand Rapids: Eerdmans,
    1983.

42 CWME/WCC. *Your Kingdom Come - Mission Perspectives*. Report of Section II.
    NEWBIGIN, Lesslie. *The Open Secret*, chapter 9.

43 COSTAS, Orlando, op.cit., pp. 43-54.
    PAREDES, Tito, On Church Growth, in *The Church in Response to Human Need*,
    ed. by Tom Sine, pp. 109-115.

44 ARIAS, Mortimer. The Experience of Mission and the Liberation of Creation,
    in Mission Congress of the U.S. Catholic Missionary Association,
    Baltimore 1983, Mimeographic paper.

45 HEUVEL, Albert v.d. *Shalom and Combat*. Geneva: WCC, 1979, especially p. 50.
    On Apartheid, Peace and Status Confessionis, in *Reformed Press Service*,
    Geneva: WARC, No. 212, March 1983.

46 ELLACURIA, Ignacio, op.cit., chapter 9 on Liturgy and Liberation.

47 GUTIERREZ, Gustavo. *La Fuerza Historica de los Pobres*. Salamanca:
    Ed. Sígueme, 1982, p. 81 (my translation).

48 KRASS, Alfred C., op.cit., p. 32
    BOFF, Leonardo, *Jesus Christ Liberator*, p. 275.

49 *Evangelism and Social Responsibility*, op.cit., pp. 24-25.

50 BOSCH, David, op.cit., p. 38.

51 ARAYA, Victorio, op.cit., pp. 142-143.
    DAYTON, Edward. Social Transformation: The Mission of God, in *The Church
    in Response to Human Need*, ed. by Tome Sine, pp. 429-430.
    COSTAS, Orlando E., op.cit., pp. 94-98. He gives his own list of
    "priorities" for the Americas today.
    BRAATEN, Carl E., op.cit., pp. 54-55.
    SCOTT, Waldron, op.cit. In p. 155, he gives this quote from Martin Luther:
        *If I profess with the loudest voice and clearest exposition every
        portion of the truth of God except precisely that little point which
        the world and the devil are at that moment attacking, I am not pro-
        fessing Christ, however boldly I may be professing Christ!*
    SIDER, Ronald. *Evangelism, Salvation and Social Justice*. Bramcote: Grove
    Books, 1977, p. 18.

52 WCC. *Mission and Evangelism: An Ecumenical Affirmation*, para. 34.
    See also GUTIERREZ, Gustavo. *A Theology of Liberation*, pp. 176-178 and
    SONG, Choan Seng. *Christian Mission in Reconstruction*, p. 118.

53 GUTIERREZ, Gustavo. *La Fuerza Historica de los Pobres*, p. 69 (my
    translation)

54 BARTH, Karl. *The Humanity of God*. Richmond: John Knox Press, 1966,
    pp. 37ff.

55 WCC. *Mission and Evangelism: An Ecumenical Affirmation*, para. 32.

56 MOLTMANN, Jürgen. *The Trinity and the Kingdom*, pp. 209-212.
    BRIA, Ion, ed. *Jesus Christ, the Life of the World*, Statement on the
    theme, p. 4.
    BOBRINSKOY, Boris. The Power of the Resurrection, ibíd., p. 105.

PART 2

Selection of Published
and Unpublished Articles

129

130

1. MISSION IN THE PERSPECTIVE OF THE KINGDOM

The articles included in this section attempt to set the missiological
discussion within the horizon of the kingdom of God. Mission begins with
God, and continues in God. The churches are invited to join forces with God
for the redemption of the whole of humanity.

The sermon which opens this collection is an attempt to show the force of
the prophetic message of Deutero Isaiah about God's movement in history and
the particular vocation of Israel, and to apply it to the situation of the
early sixties. The God of history is the God who called people to mission in
the past and calls us today. "We also know that history marches on towards a
climax -- that the crucial encounter between universal history and the special
history of our people will take place at that eschatological moment when all
nature will be transformed and God will be recognized as the King of all
nations."

The second article, "Your Kingdom Come: The Mission and Unity of the Church
in a Global Perspective", is a discussion of the relation between the mission
and the unity of the church within the creative dynamic of the kingdom of God,
the global perspective of God's universal plan. "The prayer 'Your Kingdom
Come' lifts up the vision of the plan of God for the whole universe, for the
whole cosmos. It places our personal life, the life of our congregations and
the life of the whole church of Christ at the service of a dream, a utopia,
but which is at the same time the promise of God: reconciliation with God, to
unite all things in Christ."

The third article is an editorial comment on the missionary conference held
in Melbourne in May 1980 with the theme "Your Kingdom Come". It deals with
concrete points of reference which we need if the vision of the kingdom of
God is to be credibly mediated. Christ is the King. A personal relation to him
is fundamental. The poor are the centre of concern, and that is the missionary
yardstick to apply to our missionary endeavours. Christians are sent to participate in the real historical struggles with all others and, from within the
struggles, to point towards Jesus Christ.

Fourth, "World Mission - A New Opportunity". At the close of the Bangkok
Conference on world mission on the topic "Salvation Today", we said, "We are
at the end of the era of international mission; we are entering into the new
era of world mission." This article, against the background of a rapid survey
of modern missionary history and its relationship with western colonial history,
invites the churches to participate in the new situation where mission should
be seen in a three-dimensional perspective: the fulfilment of our mission
locally, our willingness to receive help from others, and our desire to share
with others as they serve in their own missionary frontiers.

The fifth article, "Evangelism, Mission, Liberation - Must We Choose?" discusses the main thesis of the book -- the Christian freedom to engage in
mission, in a variety of ways and responding to different challenges. "The
Church believes in a living God who has accompanied humankind throughout its

history and who is at work within it. God always summons us to obedience, to militant action, to participation in his mission here and now, and as we saw in the life of Jesus Christ who had complete freedom to respond to the requirements of different situations and different people, we too are called to provide different responses to different situations."

The last chapter of this first section on "Human Rights" provides several biblical paradigms to illustrate how today the defence of human rights must be a Christian priority. "The church is sent by God into the world to liberate human beings from what hinders them from responding as free human beings to his invitation to a new life in him. The concern for human rights is the name we give today to our being sent with prophetic words to the Pharaoh who enslaves and with liberating deeds to God's people who groan under that slavery."

ON ISAIAH 55

OUR Scripture reading is that set for this Sunday in Advent. It reminds us of the Hebrew people in exile. Two or three generations have passed since a large number of families were deported to Babylon—sufficient time for the situation to be considered as normal now. There is a nostalgic and romantic remembrance of the lost homeland. Yet hardly a serious thought of a visible return. Conditions seem more or less settled forever. They can preserve their faith and their community life in this foreign land. They can even prosper financially, and indeed develop their fortunes within the very extensive economic frame of the Babylonian empire.

But such contented security is suddenly shaken. Not even Babylon has firm foundations. In an obscure province of the empire a tribe begins to agitate rebellion. To everyone's surprise, what began as an insignificant tumult gradually becomes a sweeping force. The clock of history has struck once more. The period of Persian dominance has come. Cyrus, the revolutionary, the conqueror, subdues Babylon. And now, what is to be the lot of this minority people, enslaved and displaced under Babylonian policy? Cyrus opens the gates of return. The imperial policy changes. How is this situation to be interpreted?

The prophet emerges in response to the historic occasion. The mountains shall be made low, highways shall be prepared in the desert, the hour has come when God calls for a return to Palestine, to rebuild national life, to be ready for those great future events when God will establish in Jerusalem a teaching which is for the ends of the earth. What is offered is more than mere political liberty. The prophet envisages in this freedom the opportunity to start preparing for those great eschatological events which will determine the destiny of all humanity. The vicarious vocation of the people of Israel demands the march through the desert. No phrase is lyrical enough to convey all that burns in the imagination of the prophet.

He says: 'It is too light a thing that you should be my servant to raise up the tribes of Jacob and to restore the preserved of Israel; I will give you as a light to the nations, that my salvation may reach to the end of the earth.'

Thus says the Lord, the Redeemer of Israel and his Holy One, to one deeply despised, abhorred by the nations, the servant of rulers: 'Kings shall see and arise; princes, and they shall prostrate themselves; because of the Lord, who is faithful, the Holy One of Israel, who has chosen you.'

Thus says the Lord: 'In a time of favour I have answered you, in a day of salvation I have helped you; I have kept you and given you as a covenant to the people, to establish the land, to apportion the desolate heritages; saying to the prisoners, "Come forth," to those who are in darkness, "Appear." They shall feed along the ways, on all bare heights shall be their pasture; they shall not hunger or thirst, neither scorching wind nor sun shall smite them, for he who has pity on them will lead them, and by springs of water will guide them. And I will make all my mountains a way, and my highways shall be raised up. Lo, these shall come from afar, and lo, these from the north and from the west, and these from the land of Syene.'

Sing for joy, O heavens, and exult, O earth; break forth, O mountains, into singing! For the Lord has comforted his people, and will have compassion on his afflicted. (Isa. 49.6-13).   *   *   *   *

The poetry is beautiful. The enthusiasm is contagious, but . . . perplexities are not solved with poems. There were plain facts that made it difficult for the people fully to understand what was happening. Were they not the elect nation? Did not God have a special interest in their specific history? Then what was the explanation for their having been so ill-treated by general human history? Why had they lost all national status, all political meaning, and all cultural value? Could they not say with a good conscience, 'My way is hid from the Lord, and my right is disregarded by my God' (40.27)? The only explanation that the people have received is that their fathers had sinned, and they had disobeyed the Lord. They had trusted idols and political alliances. Defeat and exile were God's judgment upon them. Foreign nations had carried out the Lord's purpose for Israel—to punish the sinner. Up to this point, even if the explanation did not please them, they were able to understand. But how were they now to believe in forgiveness? How was it possible to think that the judgment had ended? 'The time is fulfilled, and their iniquity is pardoned.' Such was the prophetic word; but how could it be made real—real with sufficient power to incite to action? How could they have the courage to accept forgiveness, when the outward sign of forgiveness, the possibility of freedom, had come not as a result of their own efforts, but through the instrumentality of pagan forces? The centre of God's concern had clearly been the discipline of his people, but now the movement of universal history had turned positive. The chosen people's liberty had come through foreign nations. What was the meaning of this? They could see that God was the Lord of the whole earth, but what was the function of the people of Israel? Was God acting independently of Israel? Was there a goodness in history, coming even from pagan nations? What then? Perhaps the end result of this line of thought was paralysing: remain in Babylon, preserve the traditions, come to terms with the world, which after all is not so oppressive, accept the facts of history, and give up all presumption of uniqueness inasmuch as it embodies a universal claim. Against this background of anxiety and problems, against this temptation to inertia, come the words of the prophet: 'My thoughts are not your thoughts, neither are your ways my ways, says the Lord. For as the heavens are higher than the earth, so are my ways higher than your ways and my thoughts than your thoughts' (55.8-9). True, there is much that cannot be understood. But the difficulty does not lie in the complexity of the historic factors. It is due to the smallness of man's conception of God.

To whom then will you liken God, or what likeness compare with him? The idol! a workman casts it, and a goldsmith overlays it with gold, and casts for it silver chains. He who is impoverished chooses for an offering wood that will not rot; he seeks out a skilful craftsman to set up an image that will not move. Have you not known? Have you not heard? Has it not been told you from the beginning? Have you not understood from the foundations of the earth? It is he who sits above the circle of the earth, and its inhabitants are like grasshoppers; who stretches out the heavens like a curtain, and spreads them like a tent to dwell in; who brings princes to nought, and makes the rulers of the earth as nothing. Scarcely are they planted, scarcely sown, scarcely has their stem taken root in the earth, when he blows upon them, and they wither, and the tempest carries them off like stubble. To whom then will you compare me, that I should be like him? says the Holy One. Lift up your eyes on high and see: who created these? He who brings out their host by number, calling them all by name; by the greatness of his might, and because he is strong in power no one is missing (Isa. 40.18-26).

We cannot encircle God within the narrow limits of our mind. His lordship is over the heavens and the earth, and his freedom challenges all possibility of our understanding. When we were thinking in terms of sin and punishment, see, he addresses us in terms of a free banquet: 'To all those who thirst, come to the waters. . . .' When we were thinking in terms of national egotism, behold, he thinks about us in terms of the fulfilment of a mission to all humanity: 'I have given him for witness to the peoples, for ruler and teacher to the nations.' When we were thinking in terms of our own provincial limi-

135

tations, behold, he was acting in terms of all the earth:

Assemble yourselves and come, draw near together, you survivors of the nations! They have no knowledge who carry about their wooden idols, and keep on praying to a god that cannot save. Declare and present your case; let them take counsel together! Who told this long ago? Who declared it of old? Was it not I, the Lord? And there is no other god besides me, a righteous God and a Saviour; there is none besides me. Turn to me and be saved, all the ends of the earth. For I am God, and there is no other. By myself I have sworn, from my mouth has gone forth in righteousness a word that shall not return: 'To me every knee ⸱ shall bow, every tongue shall swear.' Only in the Lord, it shall be said of me, are righteousness and strength; to him shall come and be ashamed, all who were incensed against him. In the Lord all the offspring of Israel shall triumph and glory (Isa. 45.20-25).

Nevertheless, in spite of this distance that separates us from God's thought and action, we have enough light to decide our next steps. Did not our fathers live thus also, fully believing that God was calling them, and obeying in the faith that all the problems and anxieties would gradually find a solution along the way? We know that God has opened through the activity of the nations doors of opportunity to liberty; we have historic proofs assuring us that the specific mission which he granted our people has not ended; we also know that history marches on towards a climax—that the crucial encounter between univeral history and the special history of our people will take place at that eschatological moment when all nature will be transformed and God will be recognized as the King of all nations. Knowing that our particular mission, that our suffering as a people, make sense when seen within the context of God's purpose for the nations, let us go out with confidence in his word:

For as the rain and the snow come down from heaven, and return not thither but water the earth, making it bring forth and sprout, giving seed to the sower and bread to the eater, so shall my word be that goes forth from my mouth; it shall not return to me empty, but it shall accomplish that which I purpose, and prosper in the thing for which I sent it. For you shall go out in joy, and be led forth in peace; the mountains and the hills before you shall break forth into singing, and all the trees of the field shall clap their hands. Instead of the thorn shall come up the cypress; instead of the brier shall come up the myrtle; and it shall be to the Lord for a memorial, for an everlasting sign which shall not be cut off (Isa. 55.10-13).

*　　　*　　　*

Here we are gathered in Mexico. We have come from all the corners of the earth to share our concerns and our visions —perhaps more of the first than the second. Since we have been gathered together by the Holy Spirit, all presumptions are out of place. We know our perplexities regarding missionary theology and action. We have come seeking the light of which we stand in immediate need. We seek the vision that will give us courage to go forth, knowing that our mission as the Church of Jesus Christ in the twentieth century has its place within the great framework of God's design for the whole human race.

The new fact of secularism meets us on every hand. Is it of God or is it of the devil? If only it were a clear phenomenon that could be classified on the basis of defined characteristics, the answer would be clearer. But it is not so—not even that help is given us! In secularism we find both good and evil aspects, similarities to and refusals of the traditional forms of our faith. What are we to say to the secular man, and how are we to say it? The anxiety of the Church in a great city, as it observes the excited coming and going of men in contrast to the polished mannerisms and human artificiality of the Sunday congregation, is a paralysing anxiety. Should we be satisfied with being the religious touch on contemporary man's secular life? Or ought we to lose all distinctive marks and involve ourselves with man in his secularity, taking the risk of the entirely unknown?

How are we to look at the resurgence of modern nationalisms? To what extent are they signs of God's working in history, awakening the peoples to their national responsibilities? To what extent are these expressions of humanity's turbulent spirit, always with a tendency to divide, pointing out our incapacity to understand? To what extent is the Holy Spirit working in this resurgence, notwithstanding the hostile attitude which some of these new nations may take towards missionary endeavour? To what extent is God's interest different from the interest of the Church which believes itself to be fulfilling God's mission?

When we were calmly thinking of the history of humanity as a progressive march towards total Christianization, several convergent movements have suddenly plunged us back into perplexity. We have already spoken of secularism. We should mention also the rising tide of ideologies which fail to see in Christianity a necessary requirement for the new humanity to which men are looking. And then there is resurgence of ancient religions, showing a vigour that we did not anticipate. What are we to think of such facts? How are we to react? How can we maintain missionary vigour and motivation in a world in which God may be working faster than we are able to perceive or appreciate?

When we see the forces that are working towards the unity of the secular world, and are aware of the impossibility of conquering our divisions, when we take note of all the good things which are being accomplished by secular agencies, and look at the limitations of our own resources, when we observe the growth of the world's population, and our inability to maintain the same increase in our missionary outreach, how can we but acknowledge our perplexities, in an attitude of humility, seeking counsel, desiring a vision, looking for the faith that our brethren may share with us?

'For as the heavens are higher than the earth, so are my ways higher than your ways. . . .' These words sound in our ears, as of old, yet perhaps with even greater force. Our problems of missionary policy, our theological difficulties, do not arise essentially from the complexities of the modern world, but from the manifold wisdom of God, which challenges all preconceptions and exposes all our securities. Every Christian generation has to fight its own battles of the faith. As yesterday, God's revelation today is revelation for the present, just for the next step. It may not be food to satisfy our whole life, but manna for today while we proceed in our pilgrimage toward the great messianic banquet.

This awareness of the distance that separates our thoughts from those of God may lead to irrationality, to despair, to inertia. Some seek to hang on to any source of dogmatic authority that will offer prefabricated answers to all our questions. Objections may be ignored as belonging, in their irrationality, to the nature of the Gospel. But to preserve a rational mind for the affairs of daily life, while dispensing with all contact between scientific thought and the affirmations of faith, to departmentalize life and to defend such departmentalization as an expression of our faithfulness, this is an escape that results in a spiritual schizophrenia which is treason to the Gospel. God is the God of all the earth, of all of life, of all the areas of life. We cannot escape the tension that comes from the encounter of faith with the world. There is no way out.

Shall we then despair? Shall we give in to panic and launch a crusade against the world? Or shall we confess the relativity of our convictions and discuss the possibility that a historic hour has struck marking the end of the Christian era? This becomes a real temptation in so far as we think more of the surrounding difficulties than of the greatness of God's resources.

Perhaps the most dangerous form in which this temptation may appear is resignation, immobility, a being satisfied to present the 'spiritual' side of culture, while refusing to permeate it totally, the limiting of ourselves to serve certain sectors of the population, while refusing fulfilment of our universal mission, to make a contribution of the teachings of Jesus, but to avoid any universal claim in his name. This is to live, and even to enjoy conditions in the world, without the agony of mission, without the passion that forces the apostle to write: 'Woe to me if I do not preach the Gospel.' But here in Mexico we do not confront these problems as beginners in the Christian life. Although the essential difference between God's thought and our thoughts makes impossible a full understanding of God's plans, yet if we have confidence that the Holy Spirit is with us, even today shall come to us the prophetic word, the light that we need for the next step.

We have facts upon which to build. There has always been a mutual inter-relationship between the world and the Church. But always also a clear consciousness of the specific mission which God has trusted to the Church. This does not mean that the purposes of God are exhausted in the Church, but certainly the revelation of his reconciliation in Jesus Christ has been the specific work given to the Church. He who calls the Church to the fulfilment of her mission is the Lord of all history. He who works in the history of the nations is the Lord of the Church. No conversation about the encounter of the Church with the world, which does not take seriously these two facts, can be a Christian conversation. We cannot proudly withdraw ourselves from the world, neither can we resign from the specific mission which has been entrusted to us here. The new universalism towards which humanity seems to be marching, does no more than point to the new context in which God has placed us, in order to give witness to his reconciling power and to his promise for all humanity. Of course we are conscious of the Church's weaknesses and its own difficulty in defining its place and mission in the world. Yet every conversation that ends in a note of pessimism, or every conversation about the world that ends on a note of condemnation, fails to be a Christian conversation, inasmuch as it does not take seriously the forgiveness of sins and the promise of God's activity.

Just as the prophet called the people to remember their

specific mission, just as he pointed out that the fulfilment of this historic mission was fundamental for the whole of humanity, just as he pointed out the source of pardon, and just as he foretold the gladness of return and the security of the messianic banquet, so we are gathered here today, hearing the same word from the same Lord of the Scriptures. The God of the world's history, who works through its movements, is the God who has brought us together here in Mexico. What a tremendous presumption! Nevertheless, and by the mercy of God, we trust that such an awareness will humbly find a surprising attestation. And just as the prophet showed the next step to be taken, or the crossing of the desert, while giving assurance of the faithfulness of the Word of God, so we today are confident of having light for the immediate tomorrow. And as the prophet discussed with his people within an eschatological perspective, within the certainty of the final banquet, and the rejoicing of all creation, even so let us live today with a similar perspective, remembering that God is taking the whole of humanity towards his appointed goal.

What are we going to look for during these two weeks? Not for definite answers to theological enigmas which the Church has always faced. Rather, we must seek illumination as to what God is doing in the world, so that we may take our place within the fulfilment of the mission he has entrusted to his Church. We seek the prophetic word and the necessary courage for action.' A history lies behind our conversations here—the history of God's faithfulness. This is nourished on personal experience, that of our repentance and our forgiveness. Fundamentally, however, our encounter is based on our confidence in the promises of God: 'My word ... that goes forth from my mouth; it shall not return to me empty, but it shall accomplish that which I purpose, and prosper in the thing for which I sent it.'

We are going to wrestle with the great Christian problems of witnessing to men near and far, to men with strong convictions and to those without any conviction, to those who already belong to a world intellectually renewed and to those who still remain in a mythological world. Our endeavour springs from this assurance, that amid our doubts and uncertainties God acts, his word does its work, his Kingdom comes.

May God grant us, quite literally, when we go out from these meetings, the fulfilment in us of Isaiah's words: 'You shall go out in joy, and be led forth in peace.'

(Key Words of the Gospel, SCM Press Ltd., London, 1964)

YOUR KINGDOM COME
THE MISSION AND UNITY OF THE CHURCH IN A GLOBAL PERSPECTIVE
==

"Your Kingdom Come" is a fundamental phrase in the prayer of Jesus. It is the first plea that refers to our human situation. Through a serious consideration of this human situation, the Commission on World Mission and Evangelism of the World Council of Churches has decided to make this phrase the center of its reflection for a long time. We are no longer living out the optimism of the Sixties. We find ourselves in situations that seem closed off. The impotence of humanity to resolve its most pressing problems calls us to look for spiritual resources which allow us to continue to struggle for a better tomorrow.

In contemplating the diverse global problems that afflict our humanity, we understand that it will be very difficult to find solutions within reach of the good will of humanity for the most important of them. The armaments race continues in full strength. Occasionally the great powers reach an agreement on the limitation of some armaments while in a parallel way they develop other more advanced technologies to evade the accepted controls in the signed agreements.

The distance between the rich countries and the poor countries continues to grow. There is full awareness of the problem, it is known that we cannot continue in this manner, but great international meetings cannot seem to establish fundamental agreements that allow change in the basic tendencies of the world economic system. Atomic equilibrium has allowed the world to enjoy a relative peace, if we mean by this the absence of global conflicts, but it has not prevented the multiplication of local conflicts that at any time might become truly universal catastrophies.

Ecological problems do not find visible solutions. We seek to overcome the energy problem by means of atomic energy, but there is still no solution to the problem of nuclear wastes! These will accumulate, awaiting technical solutions to be found in the future. The earth continues to be profaned in search of natural resources to satisfy the demands of the market, without consideration for the breakdown of natural ecological balances. The growth of the genetic sciences now makes possible the manipulation of human life in ways that could not have been dreamed of before.

Torture has ceased to be a demonstration of the brutality of a few only to become a normal, almost daily instrument of police and military interrogation. Democracy, a political system that seemed to be the bearer of all the promises and dreams of humanity, is limited in all directions. The rise of the doctrine of national security - new idolatry of the contemporary military states - places new and urgent problems upon the Christian conscience.

We could continue and the picture would be ever more dark and desperate. We realize that in the partial struggles that occur at various levels, there are glimpses of hope for a better tomorrow. Love between two young people or the love of parents for their children continue to be a vital reality in the human experience. The struggle of the peoples to create a space for human dignity continues to bear fruit here and there. But it is in the consideration of global problems that pessimism spreads and perspectives seem to be eclipsed. Facing this almost apocalyptic situation, we Christians are called upon to look for resources in the depth of our faith. In truth the apostle Paul says, "For we are not contending against flesh and blood, but against the principalities, against the powers, against the world rulers of this present darkness, against the spiritual hosts of wickedness in the heavenly places."

Good will is not lacking, nor is the understanding. What is lacking is to put into political-economic actions, in concrete actions, what is known to be good and true. But what is this, if not to repeat what the apostle Paul already said, "For I do not do the good I want, but the evil I do not want is what I do." We find ourselves in a situation of ethical slavery of humankind, the inability to escape from the vicious circle of violence and rivalry. In these circumstances, we Christians are called upon to remember that in prayer we can find spiritual resources to confront spiritual enemies, that the struggle which takes place on various levels of our world is a struggle in which God himself is committed. Because His Kingdom - the building of a tomorrow in which peace shall be a reality - struggles and works to become present in the midst of our historical realities.

"Your Kingdom Come" is the prayer of Christian desperation in facing the seriousness of the problems of the world, but it is desperation that changes into hope upon discerning in God the resources to continue the battle. The Kingdom brings us two fundamental dimensions:

1. It reminds us of the dimension of jubilee. In the Gospel of Luke, chapter 4:17-21, Jesus reads in the synagogue the passage of the prophet Isaiah that makes reference to the year of jubilee, the period in which all debts were cancelled and society in its entirety could have a new opportunity for beginning. The jubilee was the day of reconciliation, of universal pardon, of the redistribution of riches, of the establishment of new bases for a new historical period. Jesus uses it to describe the Kingdom. The jubilee was the moment in which justice operated, not as an avenger, but rather as an equalizer.

    Here we should pause in order to understand the fundamental center of the Christian Gospel. We preach the forgiveness of sins in Jesus Christ, we preach the possibility of a new beginning in life. We announce that in Christ God has forgiven, that a fundamentally new reality has been created in the history of the world. We are not condemned to live in the infernal cycle of violence, the sinful continuity has been broken, a new possibility now opens up for humankind.

    Paul, the apostle, applies this teaching of Jesus in personal terms in the Greek and Roman context and calls all persons to recognize in Jesus Christ the Kurios, the Lord, the supreme authority. He makes very little use of the image Kingdom, but the essential content implied in the term "Lord" or "King" is what is also clearly implied

142

when he proclaims the authority of Jesus to pardon and liberate. Because of this, in the same way that Jesus proclaims the free grace of God, forgiving all people, applying to them his redeeming, equalizing justice, so the apostle announces the grace of God that justifies human beings. That is to say: the grace which puts all of us on the same footing of equality, capable of beginning a new life, made new creatures by God in Jesus Christ.

The proclamation of the Kingdom not only reminds us of that fundamental truth of our faith in Christ; the possibility of forgiveness has been established, but it also speaks to us of a historical possibility, that it is possible to find at a particular moment, social mechanisms that allow us to detain the heavy load of the hates of yesterday and to build new relations for tomorrow. That in the same way a word of forgiveness is pronounced over individual sins, so a word of forgiveness can be pronounced over collective sins. The tragic inheritances of yesterday, made into structures of dependence and oppression, can be shattered and eliminated today because there is always a historical possibility of a new beginning. The year of jubilee, the establishment of the Kingdom of God, is an invitation to consider history as permanently open, to anticipate the possibility of the new, because God opens history towards newness.

    The consideration of the Kingdom of God as an object for our prayer, places before our worries and anxieties, a global goal to unite all things in Christ. (Ephesians 1:10).

We are not called to concern ourselves about our small individual world. The Gospel is not the solution to our headaches, rather the calling for a transformation of all things in Christ. It is the invitation to enter into the "kingdom", that is, in the liberating movement of God, in the establishment of new relations of a common life for all humanity. The Kingdom of God embraces in its reality all of the aspects of our life, including all of our small individual lives as well as our small community lives. In the global economy of the Kingdom of God, the global problematics of humanity are faced. This confrontation develops in the particular circumstances of our lives; in the collective circumstances of our respective communities; and in the struggle to overcome unjust international structures. There is a "continuum" in the comprehension of the Kingdom that unifies our whole life and binds us together in a spiritual battle that transcends the distances of time and the distances of geography. The traditional doctrine of the Communion of the Saints recovers all of its force in the perspective of the Kingdom. Those who fought yesterday for the Kingdom of God continue their fight in unceasing intercession before the Father, together with those of us today who lift up prayers of intercession in all different languages and in the most hidden places, in respect and gratitude for the martyrs and saints of today. Those who die confronting the military dictatorships of our world do not belong to one particular denomination; they are part of the spiritual treasure of all of the Church of Christ and as such contribute to the battle for a new day, for the "kingdom" that is coming. Those who pray in their cells, those who work in the inner-cities seeking to create community among those who are lonely, those who are found in remote corners of the globe or near the banking structures of contemporary society, in the measure in which they participate in the prayer "Your Kingdom Come", integrate themselves with the power of the Kingdom. They contribute to the whole dynamic power of the Spirit in the battle for the transformation of all things.

Much of our human experience is made up of failures. Our generation has lived with the dream of a "new day", but the realization of the "new day" is continually postponed as if waiting for a more opportune time. The apostle said in the letter to the Hebrews, "These all died in faith, not having received what was promised" (Hebrews 11:13). Like Abraham, they "looked forward to the city which has foundations, whose builder and maker is God." (Hebrews 11:10). They lived in hope, but they did not enter into the promise. In the perspective of the Kingdom all this effort of the past generations and all the suffering of love of the present generations join in a total spiritual richness that is not lost, that will be recaptured in Jesus Christ. "Therefore God is not ashamed to be called their God, for he has prepared for them a city." (Hebrews 11:16).

A few months back, Western world television painted for us the macabre pictures of a group of young people massacred on the entrance steps of the cathedral of El Salvador. Upon contemplating the sacrifice of these young people who went out to express their yearnings for liberty and paid with their lives the risk of doing so, a sensation of anger and deaf impotence took power over us. But the perspective of the Kingdom permits us to look upon that pain with all its anguish in the eschatological hope that the sacrifice is not in vain. All that has been lived and realized with love accumulates in the common treasure of the Kingdom, which one day we will harvest.

It is in this perspective that the apostle Paul can say in the first letter to the Corinthians, chapter 15:58, "Therefore, ... be steadfast, immovable, always abounding in the work of the Lord, knowing that in the Lord your labor is not in vain." The experience of death with its character of definitive closing to our historical possibilities, in the perspective of the Kingdom changes into a dimension of hope, the cross of Jesus Christ is followed by the morning of resurrection, solemn affirmation of the divine resources to take on our historical tragedies and change them into instruments of redemption, proclaiming liberation.

2. The Kingdom introduces the dimension of hope since we know who has the true power, the final power. In Matthew 28:18, Jesus Christ says, "All authority in heaven and on earth has been given to me. Go therefore and make disciples of all nations." His power is manifested in the humility of the manger of Bethlehem, in taking the towel and the basin to wash the feet of his disciples, in dying high upon the cross pronouncing a word of love before the insults of the soldiers and the people. Since we know the nature of this power, we know it is able to take those of us who are nothing on the social scale and change us into the instruments of his will; we can assume risks for the Kingdom. The vision of non-violence as a method of social change is illogical without the feeling that it is at least affirmed in a vision of the Kingdom in which that attitude corresponds to the ultimate direction of history, to the final will of God. The affirmation of the rights of the child and the mentally or physically handicapped, of the poor, of the marginal sectors of society is incomprehensible and irrational in a world that puts value on money and power of force. But such an affirmation is fundamental in the conception of the Kingdom that

values highly the power of love, of the servant capacity of its King.
We pray "Your Kingdom Come" and in our prayer goes the commitment to
live beside the disadvantaged, the exploited, assuming the inherent
risks in the confidence that history is not closed off, that a new
beginning is always possible, that a new day is dawning, which gives
direction to the human struggle.

It is the vision of the Kingdom that gives meaning to our international
solidarity. The aid that the churches in the industrialized countries
can offer to the vindicating struggles of liberty and the justice of
the oppressed peoples of the Third World nations, is justified and
understood beginning with a sentiment of solidarity in the common
battle for the anticipation of the Kingdom on earth. The Kingdom
gives the real dimension of all our actions, because each one of them,
though it be small, either adds itself to the spiritual battle in history as an aid to the action of the Holy Spirit, as down-payment for
the Kingdom, or as a hindrance, a stumbling block, an obstacle to its
full manifestation in our personal life and our social life. It is
because we believe in the coming "Kingdom" that we discover that all
action has a global dimension. We are perhaps the first privileged
generation, in that by virtue of modern means of communication we
can clearly see the interaction between human actions in all parts
of the world. We can take joy in the gifts that others have received
and in the contribution that others make to the common search for
the Kingdom. By faith, Christians have always believed the words of
Jesus: "I have other sheep that are not of this fold." We knew that
there were others - such as the personalities of the Old Testament
that appear outside of the history of Israel, considered positively
as collaborators with the plans of God for his people and for humanity.
Others have also been fighting for the purposes of God, frequently
without knowing it.

We are invited to join the movement of the Kingdom of God. Our small
rural parish, our women's group, the prayer in the home of the
elderly, the group of militant youth - and we could continue citing
diverse manifestations of church life - there are so many other ways
to join the fight of the Kingdom up to the limit of our concrete
possibilities.

How the dynamics of our congregational life would change if we could
internalize this conviction! All that we do has importance. No one
should feel left out or incapable of full participation, no one is
expendable because God calls all to join with Him in militancy for
the Kingdom. The elderly or the disabled in a wheelchair, who are
popularly considered an object for pity, becomes the protagonist in
one of the greatest spiritual battles in the expression of solidarity
with the struggles of the poor peoples; in a word, that person participates by means of prayer and thought in the total mission of God.

It is a heart-rending experience to observe those countries which,
for a variety of circumstances, are isolated from the international
missionary movement - countries which for many years had been related
to other countries and churches, but which now cannot send funds or
personnel outside their borders. Still, they have found - in intercessory prayer, in the letter of fraternal greetings, in the occasional
visit - the demonstration of solidarity at the level of their own
countries and the excitement of always participating in a worldwide

145

mission, knowing themselves to be part of a vast family in service
to the Kingdom. The mission of the Church, then, be it the small
rural parish or the great urban church, be it the small bible study
and prayer group or the grand hierarchical structure, is participation in the Kingdom as a people that know the secret of history,
that know its center and its ultimate destiny. Because we live by
the revelation of God in Jesus Christ, because there we have seen
the full manifestation of the grace that reopens history and assures
it an ultimate goal of reconciliation, we will be in the world in
the service of that Kingdom.

Our mission then under the Kingdom will undertake various actions:

First. To discern the presence of the Kingdom in contemporary
history. Looking beyond the walls of the Church we find demonstrations
of love, foretastes of liberty, expressions of solidarity, manifestations
of humanity, that we will recognize as forming part of the action of God
in all humanity. At the same time, we also see manifestations of injustice, of oppression, of hate, of division, operating in ourselves and in
the surrounding society, that are obstacles for the march of humankind
toward the "jubilee", toward an equalizing justice, toward a possibility
of reconciliation. The prayer "Your Kingdom Come" helps us to open our
eyes to the reality of the resources that are in the world operating in
the direction of the divine will. Perhaps like the prophet of old we will
see the seven thousand men who have not bowed their knees to Baal. We
will discover the forces of love and reconciliation still vitally allied
in the world. At the same time we will be alert to the factors of breakdown, the factors of sin, to the manifestations of the structures of evil,
that resist the action of the Divine Spirit and that need to be exposed,
denounced, confronted.

In second place, it is a part of the mission of the Church to identify
with and to support action in the direction of the Kingdom. In a religious
and ideologically pluralist society, we must learn to co-exist in dialogue
and cooperation one with another. We Christians do not pretend to have
a monopoly on the good, nor do we ask for first place in conducting human
affairs. We only yearn for the possibility to participate in the search
for common solutions, bringing that particular perspective that springs
forth from the biblical conception of a Kingdom where those who have no
power - the poor, the child, the elderly - should be the privileged ones.
It is from this revolutionary conception of the Kingdom, as a revolution
on all scales of human values, that we can participate in the common
efforts to construct new societies. We bring this fundamental point of
reference: the will of God to equalize, to lift up, to prefer, and to
sustain the oppressed.

Third. The mission of the Church will also consist of proclaiming
the presence of the Kingdom in the midst of history. Evangelism will
point out the relation between our human situations and the history of
God in Jesus of Nazareth, it will show how the highest human aspirations
have their logical root and their greatest promise of fulfillment in the
action that took place once and for all in the history of Jesus of
Nazareth. We must discover the possibility of proclaiming the name of
Jesus Christ in the heart of every culture. To tell his story, relating
it to the values and particular histories of each people. The preaching
of the Gospel will be possible in the measure in which we are in vital
contact with our own culture, our own people. Only from this fundamental

146

human solidarity, can we point toward the source of this solidarity, toward the goal of all human history in the person of Jesus Christ.

In solidarity with those actions which seek to overcome the present limitations of our society and move it toward the goals of greater justice, we can point to Jesus Christ and give witness to the full manifestation of the Kingdom in Jesus Christ only by standing in the midst of the struggle. Only in this way is there hope that many others will consciously join in the struggle for the Kingdom, for the realization of the New Day.

In fourth place, the mission of the Church is the recruitment for the Kingdom. The announcement of the Kingdom of God is an invitation to relate ourselves to the King. In reality this is that which is fundamentally new in the teaching of Jesus. He accepts the best teachings of the Old Testament about the Kingdom, but he presents himself as the one in whom the Kingdom is present. He is the King we are invited to recognize and to follow. The prayer "Your Kingdom Come" commits us to call upon persons to join in the service of the King. The experience of conversion is the transformation of all our concepts, of our loyalties, and consequently of all of our life. Jesus Christ invites us to walk in his company in the struggle that he carries on for his Kingdom; thus he will invite men and women to take up the cross, to follow after him, to march toward the "ends of the earth", knowing that he will be present in every disinherited and needy person. The preaching of the Gospel of the Kingdom and the invitation to Christian discipleship means a risk as much for the preacher as for the one who hears the invitation. The preacher risks his faithfulness to the King he wants to introduce: if he wants to announce the servant King, he should live as a servant. If he wishes to show the King of love, he should show it fully in his life. At the same time he assumes a tremendous responsibility because the invitation he extends to others to follow Christ is one which puts in jeopardy the very lives of those who hear the invitation. Those who dare to think on the possibility of following the King and entering the dynamics of the Kingdom know automatically that they make themselves contestants in the situation. They know that a certain risk awaits them.

We preach the news of the Kingdom and call upon all to relate themselves to the King with fear and trembling because we know the risks incurred by those who answer, "Lord, here am I, send me." The Church is placed in the world to call upon men and women to join with the building of the Kingdom and to wait for the Kingdom. Evangelism, then, is not a call to individuals to escape from the world, nor to seek refuge in the Church. To enter into the community of believers is to enter into the community of those who take part with the servant King in the building of the Kingdom in love and in sacrifice. The call to conversion, then, has fundamental importance for the whole universe. A person's decision has consequences far beyond what we can foresee!

And it is then, when the Church finds itself embarked upon the fulfillment of its mission, when it seeks to discern the presence of the Kingdom, when it attempts to add its strength to the strength of others, when it tells the Gospel story and relates that history to the concrete history of human beings, when it calls men and women to join voluntarily and decidedly in the risks of seeking the Kingdom, it is then that the Church rediscovers the dimension of its unity. Because it is the unity of the Church which permits us to have a foretaste on earth of the reality of the Kingdom that is coming. In the joint celebration of the Holy

147

Supper we anticipate in some measure the final banquet of the Kingdom. In the community and solidarity of brothers and sisters in Christ we can have a foretaste of the reconciliation of all things in Christ. In reciprocal forgiveness we begin to understand the forgiveness of our trespasses. Precisely the disunity of the Church is a contradictory factor to the promise of the Kingdom and negates the goal that the Church is called to serve.

In the second place, the unity of the Church becomes fundamental because it is the only way to authenticate in the eyes of the world the reality and power of the Kingdom we announce. How can persons come to understand the unity we have in Christ if they do not see it manifested in relations of love, in relations that overcome all our human inhibitions and that look forward to the promise for all humanity of a day in which there will be no "man nor woman, servant nor free, Greek nor Jew, but we will all be one in Christ Jesus"? The unity we seek is a real unity that surpasses the limits of a formal ecclesiastical unity. We seek the destruction of all structural barriers that impede the full manifestation of love. Obligatory segregation and apartheid legislation become a kind of "ultimate" scandal because it prevents the full expression within the Christian community of the characteristics of the Kingdom which God already wants to give us today.

To pray "Your Kingdom Come" carries us to the depth of the prayer of Gethsemane. It is not the search for suffering itself, nor is it resignation. We seek to avoid historical failures, but we will place ourselves at the disposition of the hands of God to go to the battles to which he should want to guide us in the hope that all of our failures can become his great victories.

The prayer "Your Kingdom Come" lifts up the vision of the plan of God for the whole universe, for the whole Cosmos. It places our personal life, the life of our congregations and the life of the whole Church of Christ at the service of a dream, a utopia, but which is at the same time the promise of God: reconciliation with God, to unite all things in Christ. The prayer "Your Kingdom Come" gives us a personal place in the great plan of God to create a new opportunity for all humankind, to open the year of equality among all persons. In short, to pray "Your Kingdom Come" permits us to console ourselves and mutually comfort ourselves in the unity that is already given to us and in the hope of a full unity, of the full coming of the Kingdom.

(Lecture given at the Disciples Ecumenical Consultative Council's Conference on Unity and Mission, Kingston, Jamaica, October 1979)

Theological discussions on the topics of the Melbourne conference will never do justice to the spiritual event; that was the privilege of the participants and of many people in the local churches of Melbourne. We remember the warm hospitality provided by the host churches, which included meeting participants at the airport and generously opening their homes to them before the conference started. Worshipping together in St. Patrick's cathedral and participating in the mass rally provided some of the most precious moments of the conference.

The Bible study during the conference provided an opportunity for people to share their hopes and anxieties and to encounter those of others, under the authority of Scripture. Participants coming from the most diverse theological schools and confessional families brought with them, of course, their hermeneutical *a priori*. But the Word of God was able to capture our pre-judgements and open our hearts to the message of the King and to the testimony of our brothers and sisters. How can we forget the passion with which the Korean delegates looked for news of the events taking place in their country, or the joy of the Zimbabwean delegation sharing with the churches of the world the reality of newly acquired freedom, or the anguished pain and hope of delegates from Central America? In those moments of sharing and studying, the World Council as a family of churches that confess Jesus Christ according to the Scriptures became a reality for the participants.

We did not lack frustrations. There were too many speeches during the first few days. Each of us had to overcome the limitation of his or her local situation. But in the worship around the prayer theme of Melbourne, "Your Kingdom Come", most of the frustrations, the anguish and the dreams of the participants found the right expression. To face the missionary challenges of today, the predicament of humankind, we need to go deeply into the spiritual roots of our Christian life. **So we gathered, not to make a theological study on the kingdom theme, but to pray together, looking for vision and inspiration for our personal and community mission.**

A new creation

First, the topic of the kingdom invited us to take a look at the whole of creation and to recognize links between the hopes of all people and the promise of the kingdom of God in Jesus Christ. But the conference was not embracing a general theory of history, a metaphysical affirmation of the whole of reality. **The kingdom we pray for, the one we try to understand, was the kingdom fully manifested in the person of the servant king, Jesus Christ.**

It is the kingdom that has come in his person which commands our loyalties and sends us in his name into the world. We learned to pray "Your Kingdom Come" and *Maranantha,* "Come Lord Jesus". It is only through a personal encounter with the servant king that it is possible to discern the signs, the manifestations of his kingdom in the world. Jesus came as poor among the poor, walked among the sinners, died on the cross, powerless in human eyes. But in him, despised by all men, a new power was being manifested. So Section IV, 3* reads: "**In the decisive events which followed the crucifixion, something radically new happened which seems best described as a new creation: an altogether new quality of power appeared to be let loose among humankind. Those who responded found that they shared in this power.** The inexorable bondage of cause and effect appeared to be broken and they experienced a liberation which enabled them to face their persecutors without fear, and to claim that the powers had been overthrown, disarmed, in a decisive way, even though the powers were somehow permitted to function in the meanwhile until the final consumation of history. The early Christians used many analogies to describe what they had experienced and what they believed had happened. The most striking picture is the one of a sacrificed lamb, slaughtered but yet living, sharing the throne which symbolized the heart of all power and sovereignty with the living God Himself. The principle of self-sacrificing love is thus enthroned at the centre of the reality of the universe."

The kingdom of the crucified Christ. These words remind the churches to reconsider their missionary style, strategies, priorities. One of the important realizations of the delegates in Melbourne was that the Church everywhere is increasingly called to confront the powers of the world. How do we express the power of the Lamb in terms of the power of the Church confronting the powers of the world?

A few weeks after Melbourne, several pastors were taken to jail in Australia because they were showing their solidarity with aboriginal peoples defending one of their worshipping places against the voracity of the oil companies.

This same confrontation takes place in many countries of the Third World where churches face the tensions of the doctrine of national security or in the powerful countries of the world where the craziness of militarism invites the churches to counteract with the craziness of the cross, where non-violence becomes a rejection of the growing potentialities for mass murder.

In the King Jesus Christ we discern the power of the cross as a clear challenge to all missionary organizations to come under the discipline of the powerless Christ. We have also a personal challenge, an invitation to

* Throughout this issue, the Roman numerals refer to the Section Report and the Arabic numerals indicate the paragraphs in the official edition of the Section Reports.

assume voluntary poverty, to follow Jesus the King who empties himself in order to be counted among the poor, to work among them for their salvation and liberation.

Another symbol that made an impact in the Melbourne conference was **that of Jesus crucified** *outside* **the gates of Jerusalem; Jesus walking towards the periphery of life, looking for the marginals, the down-trodden and with them and through them working for the transformation of the whole of society.** The growing numbers of independent churches, pentecostal communities, basic ecclesial communities — all working fundamentally from the bottom of society — are contemporary indications of this Christ who is at the margin, working with those who have no social powers. To announce the kingdom of God is to call people to receive Jesus Christ as King and to join with him in his movement to serve, to love all those who even today are marginal to the life of our world.

Melbourne discerned "a change in the direction of mission, arising from our understanding of Christ who is the centre which is always in movement towards the periphery. While not in any way denying the continuing significance and necessity of a mutuality of the churches between the Northern and Southern hemispheres, we believe that we can discern a development of worldwide mission in the '80s which will increasingly take place within these zones. We feel that there will be increasing traffic between the churches of Asia, Africa and Latin America among whose numbers both rich and poor are counted. This development we expect will take the form of a strong initiative from the churches of the poor and oppressed at the peripheries" (Section IV, 24).

The missionary yardstick

The second concentration point of Melbourne is the affirmation of the poor as the missiological principle par excellence. The relation to the poor inside the Church, outside the Church, nearby and far away, is the criterion to judge the authenticity and credibility of the Church's missionary engagement. The Roman Catholic Bishop's Conference in Puebla, Mexico, spoke of the preferential option of God for the poor. That is discerned in the Gospel. **Jesus established a clear link between the coming of the kingdom and the proclamation of the Good News to the poor.** The missiological principle, the missionary yardstick, is the relation of the Church to the poor. It would be very difficult to find today a theological justification for the missionary outreach of the Church without this deep concern for the poor. **"The Church of Jesus Christ is called to preach Good News to the poor, even as its Lord has done in his ministry announcing the kingdom of God. The churches can not neglect this evangelistic task. Most of the world's people are poor, and they are waiting for a witness to the Gospel that will really be Good News...** The mission which is conscious of the kingdom will be concerned for liberation, not oppression; justice, not exploitation; fullness, not deprivation;

freedom, not slavery; health, not disease; life, not death. No matter how the poor may be identified, this mission is for them" (Section I, 16). We were led at Melbourne to study the significance of the crucifixion of Jesus outside the city walls. We see this as a sign, consistent with everything else in his life, that he who is the centre is constantly in movement towards the periphery, to the margin of society, because his priorities were clear. We are invited to read the Bible anew, to see history from the perspective of the poor, with the eyes of the downtrodden. **Of course the Gospel is for all and not only for the poor. But God is a personal God who addresses himself to each one of us personally in each one of our own situations.** So Melbourne said (Section I, 4), "To the poor this challenge means the profound assurance that God is with them and for them. To the rich it means a profound repentance and renunciation. To all [both rich and poor] who yearn for justice and forgiveness, Jesus Christ offers discipleship, and the demand of service." This preferential option for the poor is not an elimination of the invitation to faith, to conversion, to discipleship. The poor are not only the recipients, the objects of God's love: they are also called to grow into faith, into community, into discipleship. The decision for Christ also belongs to them, because they are invited to be protagonists with God, to organize themselves to shape history, to become evangelists. And Melbourne saw quite clearly that the poor of the earth are those who will have the credibility to announce the Gospel of the poor Jesus Christ to the poor of the world today.

Several practical consequences follow immediately. The churches are called to repentance, because the credibility of the kingdom is at stake in the attitude of the Church towards the poor. Second, our concern for the poor should be a priority judgement in all our missionary strategies and in our missionary vocation. When we speak of the billions of "unreached" people who have not yet received the Gospel of Jesus Christ, we are talking of those against whom we Christians have sinned; those who have perhaps hardened their hearts because of the poverty of the testimony of nations that were confused with Christian nations. **If we take seriously the fact that the proclamation of the gospel of the kingdom is above all for the poor, we are faced with a clear calling to our world missionary commitment, and within that same commitment, an engagement towards justice, in order to announce the Gospel that really is Good News to the downtrodden of the earth.**

Third, to announce the Good News to the poor is to call them to become protagonists, to organize themselves to claim the promises of the kingdom. It is to call them to become evangelists. "Our study on 'Christ — crucified and risen — challenges human power' has led us to see special significance in the role of the poor... Might it not be that they have the clearest vision, the closest fellowship with the crucified Christ who suffers in them as with them? Might it not be that the poor and powerless have the most significant word for the rich and powerful: that Jesus must be sought on the periphery,

152

and followed 'outside the city'? That following him involves a commitment to the poor? **Who but the Church of the poor can preach with integrity to the poor of the world? In these ways we see the 'poor' churches of the world as the bearers of mission: world mission and evangelism may now be primarily in their hands"** (Section IV, 21). The priority of the poor also means that we need to join forces with them in their struggles for change of their destiny. And this brings us to the next concentration point of the conference.

The Church must dare to be present

The kingdom of God is related to the struggles taking place in history. Melbourne tried to see the relation of the kingdom to history, and the specific responsibility of Christians in this encounter between the kingdom and history. There is no easy optimism here. There is no affirmation at all that we are building the kingdom or that the kingdom could be confused with any social system. **No social system can be exempt from the prophetic challenge of the Church that proclaims the kingdom.** "As the kingdom in its fullness is solely the gift of God himself, any human achievement in history can only be approximate and relative to the ultimate goal — the promised new heaven and new earth in which justice abides. Yet this kingdom is the inspiration and the constant challenge in all our struggles" (Section I, 4). The kingdom is the permanent inspiration to enter into the penultimate struggles of humankind. Now, how should the churches and Christians enter into the historical struggles in the name of the kingdom of God?

Assuming with *Romans* 8 that "the world is groaning for fulfilment, that God is at work", the Church must dare to be present where there are risky decisions to be taken in the ambiguities of the world, knowing that we cannot escape these ambiguities by retiring from the world. "In their witness to the kingdom of God in words and deeds the churches must dare to be present at the bleeding points of humanity and thus near those who suffer evil, even taking the risk of being counted among the wicked. The royal reign of God appears on earth as the kingdom of the crucified Jesus, which places his disciples with him under the cross. Without losing sight of the ultimate hope of the kingdom of God or giving up their critical attitude, churches must dare to be present in the midst of human struggles for penultimate solutions and welcome all signs of a hopeful development" (Section II, 4). Churches must be there interceding for the problems of the world. The churches must be there with repentance and self-criticism, recognizing their own complicity with much of the tragedy of the world. The churches must be there to join forces with others, knowing that God's kingdom works with several means and instruments. The churches must be there to plant signs of the kingdom, especially the signs of reconciliation. **But fundamentally, the churches are called to witness in the midst of those struggles to the hope that is in Jesus Christ, to invite all to see what is going on in the search for justice, to what went on on the cross and in the resurrection of Jesus Christ.** Evangelism is affirmed in Melbourne, not as a professional programme outside of one's participation in the struggles of the world, but precisely in the moment in which we are cooperating with others, praying for others, trying to plant signs of reconciliation, we are there to give reason to the hope that is within us. We are there to *"witness to the fact that there is a common hope for humankind and for the whole of creation in the life and death, the resurrection and the ascension of the Son of God, and that the coming of the kingdom of God is linked with the turning of human minds to Christ as the Lord of the kingdom"* (Section II, 5).

I emphasize this phrase because I think that we are overcoming the division between social ethics on the one hand, and the Gospel on the other. Here we understand the kingdom struggling to be manifested fully in daily history, the churches struggling to discern those signs of the kingdom, joining forces with others instead of wanting to hold on to the monopoly of that kingdom, but joining forces as Christians, as churches: this means illuminating or highlighting the hidden meaning of these human situations by pointing to the link between them and the history of Jesus of Nazareth.

Melbourne did not explore fully the relation of Christianity to other world faiths, but it invites us to discern signs of the kingdom in the struggles of history among people who identify themselves with different ideological or religious loyalty, thus giving us a new evangelistic motivation, a new missionary passion, free from imperialistic connotation. We go as Christians who come from the revelation of the Lord Jesus Christ, who know the story of the Bible, to join forces with others, to participate with them in common struggles and, in the midst of that belonging-together, in that incarnational style, to indicate the relations between those situations and the story of God in Jesus Christ. We are not making general affirmations about general revelation, about salvific value, or this or that article of religion. **Melbourne is saying that it is in the actual participation with people in the search for solutions to common human problems that we find natural opportunities to name the Name of Jesus Christ, to render witness to his saving and liberating powers.** Christians living in minority situations or cross-cultural missionaries following their vocations to enter into other religious or ideological milieus will find here not only encouragement for their mission, but also inspiration for this style of missionary approach which corresponds both to the Gospel and to the human situation. Only God knows what really happens when Christians are able to indicate the existing link between the manifestation of goodness and love among nations of the earth and the revelation of the supreme love and goodness of God in the cross of Jesus Christ; or to point to the tragic complicity between all those forces that dehumanize human beings, inside and outside religious and ideological systems, and the forces of inhumanity that put Jesus Christ to death on the cross.

The Good News of the Kingdom includes the announcement that God has not remained without witness anywhere, but as Christians we are called to

154

point our finger like John the Baptist to the Lamb of God who takes away the sins of the world.

The fourth concentration point in Melbourne is the emphasis on the Church as a sacrament of the kingdom. Melbourne is criticized by some who say that it was not a missionary conference in the classical sense, i.e. an assemblage of people concerned mainly with foreign missions. In Melbourne, representatives of all aspects of the life of the churches were gathered, because *all those aspects* needed to be looked at, to be screened through the eyes of the missionary calling. It is no surprise, therefore, that Melbourne placed such a great emphasis on the reality of the Church as a sacrament of the kingdom, the very same Church whose sins we recognize and confess. Perhaps in a first reading of the reports, one has the same feeling I had in Melbourne, that they are too masochistic in pointing to the sins and failures of the churches. In any case, once the beautiful affirmation that the Church is the sacrament of the kingdom is made, it is good and necessary to remind ourselves of our reality: that we are rooted in this Church which has not yet reached the kingdom, but which does have the gift of the Holy Spirit to direct us to that path.

This sacramental reality of the Church, which moved us so much in Melbourne, is fully manifested in the celebration of the Eucharist. **The Eucharist is described as the pilgrim bread, missionary bread, food for a people on the march. At the centre of Church life is the Eucharist, the public declaration of thanksgiving for God's gift in Christ, and the participation of the disciples in the very life of Christ. It is a foretaste of the kingdom which proclaims the Lord's death until he comes. From that centre of the eucharistic life of the Church, the proclamation comes naturally, the unashamed announcing of the acts of God in Jesus Christ, the calling to build up a church community, a fellowship.**

The basic ecclesial communities, those grassroots churches or groups of churches that are emerging all over the world, multiply the participation of the poor in the body of Christ. They are referred to in every Section of Melbourne as paradigms of the Church of the poor, as models, that challenge the lives of our churches and invite us to reconsider all our structures to see if they are really at the service of the crucified Christ whose kingdom we announce. Churches of the poor, rooted in the Bible and the Eucharist, searching for the missionary obedience which is called for in their local situations.

Churches in Melbourne were also called to recognize the relationship between mission and unity. We can only celebrate in honesty if the Church realizes the damage done to common witness by the scandal of our divisions. **Unless the pilgrimage route leads the churches to visible unity in the one God, the one Christ, the one Holy Spirit going towards the one Kingdom, the mission entrusted to us in this world will always rightly be questioned.** So God feeds his people and they celebrate the mystery of the Eucharist in order that they may confess in word and deed that Jesus Christ is Lord to the glory of God the Father.

This community rooted in the grace of God, manifested in the liturgical celebration, is entrusted with a responsibility for the proclamation of the Gospel to the whole world.

"Authentic proclamation will be the spontaneous offering of a church which is a truly worshipping community, which is able to welcome outsiders, whose members offer their service in both church and society, and which is ready to move like a pilgrim. Such a church will not defend the privileges of a select group, but rather will affirm the God-given rights of all. It is the Lord, however, who chooses his witnesses, particularly those who proclaim the Good News from inside a situation — the poor, the suffering and the oppressed — and strengthens them through the Holy Spirit with the power of the incarnated Word" (Section III, 6).

Crossing all human frontiers

This proclamation entrusted to the Church should be fulfilled both nearby and by crossing all human frontiers. Jesus our Lord is always ahead of us and asks us to follow him in unexpected ways. God's programming of the pilgrim people will always be linked to a particular situation and to specific moments in history. It will be the joyful telling of the story of God in Jesus Christ and the illumination of all contemporary situations from that perspective. Melbourne challenges all the churches to consider themselves as the sent body of Jesus Christ in the world. The liturgical inspiration comes as challenge to activitist groups and the invitation to proclamation comes as challenge to churches centring in the liturgical celebration. These reciprocal corrections should provide inspiration for the announcement of the Gospel everywhere.

Within the life of the Church are diverse vocations. **We need to recognize among those a call to the evangelists, a call to go beyond their frontiers, to share the Gospel of Jesus Christ. But this special vocation should not become an alibi to let the majority of the congregation remain totally indifferent to the evangelistic calling of the mission of the Church. The prayer "Your Kingdom Come" belongs to all, to each one of the members of the churches; we all are challenged to make of that prayer the motivation of our lives.** We cannot pray for the kingdom to come without announcing to the world the knowledge of the King whose kingdom we hope for. We cannot pray for the coming of the kingdom without calling everybody, everywhere, to recognize this servant kingship of Jesus Christ and that belongs as a responsibility to every Christian community and to every aspect of our ministry — liturgical life, healing ministries, proclamation of the Word — all belong together as we try to announce the glories of him who has called us from darkness to his wonderful light.

156

In the few months since Melbourne, several critics have voiced their concerns about the outcome of this conference. We are very thankful for these critics and for others who will speak later. Melbourne has no pretensions of infallibility; it is not the end of the road. It is just one moment of reflection for the churches, to discern together priorities, emphases, callings, perspectives for the missionary obedience today. I will respond briefly to some of these criticisms.

First, Melbourne was a kind of mini-assembly of the World Council of Churches. There was not enough missionary emphasis or specificity. The delegates were not discussing the technical means and ways of sharing the gospel of Jesus Christ with unbelievers. What is the rationale for a missionary conference that covers also social, political, cultural, religious problems like any other big ecumenical gathering?

We need to think briefly on these critical remarks. There is here a dimension of truth that we need to pay attention to; escaping into methodological or liturgical considerations, however, is not the solution. We must face the challenges that God himself addresses to the church today. It is only possible to proclaim the name of Jesus Christ, to invite people to faith, to conversion and to participation in the fellowship of the church in terms of the clear spelling-out of the relation of this Good News in Jesus Christ to the work that is going on in daily life. The incarnation of God in Jesus Christ, his invasion of love, is fully manifested in relation to family life, children, disease, oppressors in society, inhuman structural life, and the pressures of love confronting the powers of the day. It may be that these critical remarks should be seen as a challenge as we interpret the message of Melbourne. **The evangelistic dimensions of this message, so concerned for the poor, is the challenge of the unreached; it is a rebuke to the churches who keep for themselves the Gospel that belongs to the masses of the people of the earth.** The very same concern obliges us to review all our strategies, to recognize gladly the new initiatives of the churches of the poor.

The concern for the struggles of the world is not simply a concern for the social-ethical dimensions of the Gospel, but a clear invitation to announce the name of Jesus Christ in relation to the cutting issues of human concern. The discernment of the powers and the nature of their manifestation in history should become an invitation to exorcise them, to control them in the name and in the power of the crucified king.

For CWME and for many missionary agencies the main task is how to transform a vision of Melbourne into daily decisions. And that will keep us busy in the years to come.

The second criticism centres on the christology of Melbourne. Melbourne is a clearly christo-centred conference and there is no reference to Jesus Christ there which could not be fully supported in the light of the biblical teachings and the dogmatic teachings of churches. At the same time, some will point out, the concentration on the incarnational kenosis of Christ did not pay enough attention to the atonement dimension of his death on the cross and of his resurrection. **While several passages from the documents of Melbourne make reference to the once-forever event of Jesus Christ, it is clear that much more effort should be made to relate the reality of the forgiveness of sins through the atoning death of Jesus Christ to our participation in the historical struggles of today.** By experience we know of the tremendous power that is generated by the assurance that God in Jesus Christ reconciled the world with himself, liberating us from all our pretensions and releasing us for historical actions in the ambiguities of daily history. This theological task remains before us.

A third critical remark refers to the lack of a word on cross-cultural mission, especially in relation to other religions. We have indicated above where and how it is possible to find in Melbourne clear references to this vocation. In the recognition of the poor as the unreached billions, or in the affirmation that it belongs to the task of the Church to proclaim the Gospel of Jesus Christ to every creature, in every time. But it is true that the issue didn't receive in Melbourne a specialized consideration. Even if there were professional missionaries in Melbourne, this conference on the mission of the Church was not a conference called to consider specifically the professional missionary vocation. Now that we have a theological perspective — the Gospel announced to the poor, and a vision of God's own missionary style — Jesus emptying himself, going through the cross to the margin of life, we need to engage ourselves in practical discussions with all those who receive today the calling to go to the regions beyond. Here again there is a clear challenge for the future work of CWME. Of course, and happily, Melbourne was not the end of the road or the only expression of the search for missionary obedience in the church of Jesus Christ today. Other meetings are taking place this year in Pattaya and Edinburgh which bring together sectors of the Christian church, people with a particular theological perspective or even with a particular understanding of their missionary obedience; their voices also belong within the ecumenical forum where we all contribute our experiences, our convictions, our questions, our challenges, and our praise.

(International Review of Mission, Oct. 1980/Jan. 1981)

WORLD MISSION - A NEW OPPORTUNITY

Over the past 200 years, the Christian Church has gone through
a period of tremendous geographical expansion, due largely to
the western churches that sent missionaries to every corner of
the earth. Our Lord's command, "Go forth, therefore, and make
all nations my disciples", was interpreted in its literal,
geographical sense. The pages of Christian history have been
enriched by the biographies of missionaries, martyrs, and
confessors of the faith. Missionary history can be seen as
an adventure - the expansion of faith, impelled by the sacrifice
of Christian believers. But today, that adventure is increasingly told in terms of the socio-political factors that promoted
and conditioned it.

David Livingstone opened new paths in the jungle for the sake
of the faith, but he could not prevent soldiers and traders
from following in his tracks. On other occasions, the soldiers
and traders arrived first, followed by the missionaries. The
Christian faith spread, helped by colonial penetration and
basking in the glamour of the technological and scientific
superiority enjoyed by western civilization. As a result of
missionary expansion, today the church is present all over
the world. We live in a new situation in which critical voices
are being raised within the church, judging the missionary epic
and demanding a review of the paths it has taken. Secular
societies are also raising questions about missionary expansion
and accusing it of forming part of an oppressive system that
they reject.

One aspect of the new situation is illustrated by what necessitated
the change of location of the World Council of Churches' Assembly.
Four years ago, the Indonesian Council of Churches, with the
approval of its government, invited the World Council of Churches
to celebrate its Fifth Assembly (in 1975) in Jakarta. Work went
ahead on the assumption that the assembly would be held in that
city, but in recent months various factors have been at work
creating a situation that obliged the World Council of Churches
to change the location of its meeting. Why?

Indonesia is a country with a Muslim majority, traditionally
hospitable and tolerant. However, Islam today has rediscovered
its own missionary dimension and is constantly tempted to block
Christian presence. At the same time, Indonesia is a country
that only recently shook off the yoke of a colonial power that
considered itself Christian; the Christian Church is thus
easily accused of being one of the many faces of neo-colonialism.
On the other hand, the Indonesian Christian Church, which feels
itself to be truly a part of the life-style of its nation, is
trying to contribute to the construction of a better future,
and is working for the social, political and economic
independence of Indonesia. It cannot permit religious activities
to hinder the accomplishment of a basic part of its own mission -

the construction of a multi-racial, multi-religious community
in Indonesia. Many sectors of Indonesian society are committed
to dialogue as a form of multi-religious community life.
However, an assembly that might give the impression of
Christian power or triumphalism could act as an obstacle to
dialogue among the religious communities of Indonesia.

The assembly will be transferred to another country, and the
episode has already become history. But it illustrates very
well the various factors that go to make up the new missionary
situation: the resurgence of traditional religions, the wish
to maintain dialogue and balance between different religious
communities in order to construct multi-confessional secular
states, the wish of the Christian Church to participate in the
building of a shared future for the new nations, and the distrust of the association between the missionary enterprise and
western neo-colonialism. We are now leaving the era of missionary
history in which missionaries went out from the western metropolis to dependent countries, enjoying the double advantage of
the prestige afforded them by modern technology and the economic
resources and protection of their home countries.

This is not a simple generalization about the past. We must
recognize that at the root of missionary passion lay the love,
the prayers and the faith of congregations and of individuals.
Their work led to the establishment of Christian communities
that today express their maturity in their very criticism of
the countries from which they received the gospel. We are
entering a new situation, in which sin and virtue are recognized
as existing in all parts of the world, so that missionary work
can count on no *a priori* advantages. The gospel must be seen
apart from the culture by means of which it is transmitted, and
must commend itself to the conscience of humankind on the basis
of its own appeal and its own virtue.

This new situation has provoked a variety of reactions. In some
young churches, the discovery of the complicity of the missionary
enterprise with the colonizing power has meant a break with the
ties of dependence and an affirmation of their own personality
and vocation in terms of the problems and opportunities of the
new nation. This attitude contains very positive elements that
witness to the success of the missionary enterprise since it
produced a community aware of its own situation and capable of
assuming its own responsibilities, joining the task of building
a new future for its country. But one cannot accept as totally
positive every attitude that rejects participation in mission
across national and cultural frontiers. They often hide
chauvinistic, separatist attitudes that do not express the
unity of the universal Church of Jesus Christ. How can new
churches affirm their own identity and their participation in
the new human society and at the same time a critical and
corrective militancy that maintains its responsibility to the
universal Christian community?

In the countries that have traditionally sent missionaries
abroad there has been a twofold response. The churches who
have been deeply involved in ecumenical dialogue have become
aware of the new situation. They have accepted the
responsibility demanded of the missionary enterprise in an
overall situation of neo-colonialism and sought to remove
themselves from it, in an attitude of respect for the new
national churches. At the same time, they have accepted their
socio-political responsibility to renounce links of dependence
and oppression among different countries. Thus they have
attempted to face the complexity of contemporary missiology,
but in so doing they have opened a confusing array of different
fronts. Local churches have found it difficult to locate the
focus of the missionary enterprise today. They have not been
educated to understand a situation of such complexity and
ambiguity. The result has been the withdrawal of funds and a
decrease in missionary recruitment, even if there has also been
a greater understanding and honesty in facing problems,
accompanied by paralyzing frustration.

Another important sector of the Christian Church, especially
in the United States, attempts to ignore the complexity
of the situation by making a direct link between the biblical
commandment to go and preach the gospel to the whole world and
the need to send people into other cultures with the specific
mission of proclaiming Jesus Christ. The intention is valid,
but in trying to escape from the problems with a simplistic
interpretation of the gospel and of our historical difficulties,
we lay ourselves open to the accusation of continuing the
Christian Church's participation in the cultural and economic
imperialism of the west. It is in such circumstances that
different voices begin to call for a redefinition of missionary
work in the light of this new situation.

We have been trying within the ecumenical movement to find
answers to these questions. Various phrases in our debate
have been used to indicate some guidelines: Joint Action for
Mission expressed the wish to see sending churches and receiving
churches united in a given area for better service. Mission in
Six Continents attempted to express the fact that the day was
over when countries could be divided into "Christian" and
"pagan" areas. We are now all in the same position of giving
and receiving. For post-Christian America and neo-pagan Europe
the appearance of churches in Asia, Africa and Latin America
having a clear awareness of their mission has become a source
of enrichment within the ecumenical dialogue whose consequences
have still not been fully explored.

Today we are trying to define the new possibilities for mission
in such expressions as "world mission" or, as this has been
translated in the United States, "global mission". At the close
of the Bangkok Conference on World Mission, we said, "We are
at the end of the era of international mission; we are entering

161

into the new era of world mission." This ends the period when missionary traffic was one-directional and the word "mission" referred to what happened beyond our national and cultural frontiers. We are seeking today to recover the biblical dimension of mission that permits us to see the relationship between what happens near to us and what happens in the farthest corner of the earth, as part of the total struggle of the forces of the Spirit against the forces of evil, an incorporation of the Church of Jesus Christ in the liberating mission of God in which he invites us to participate. In this sense, we are trying to face the new situation positively, not with a nostalgic lament for times past, but as a search for new possibilities.

Our entry into this new missionary era must be accompanied by an up-to-date understanding of God's mission. The Bible reveals to us God's purpose for the whole of humanity. The creation of humankind responds to the divine intention, which is love made manifest in his own threefold being. It is God who creates, seeking a relationship with his creatures. When in the exercise of their freedom human beings alienate themselves from God, he does not give up his purpose of redemption and communion. Hence the choice of a people to carry his message of hope. In Christ, God himself intervenes in a supreme effort to save humankind from their bondage to the forces of evil and to give them a new opportunity for life in harmony with their creator. The biblical revelation culminates in Christ who shows us the cosmic purpose of God.

Paul does not hesitate to say that powers and principalities must be brought down and submitted to the power of Christ. He is the crown of all creation. To him all power has been given. His ultimate goal is the reconciliation of all things with the Father. God works through his creation, through his people, through the vicarious sacrifice of his Son, through the creation of a community of faith, through the action of his Spirit, present in all the events of history.

God's mission thus seeks to overcome the total alienation of human beings - their alienation from God, from their neighbours, from themselves, from nature - to overcome all opposition, to bring everything to an ultimate harmony in which his love is recognized as sovereign. Churches and individual Christians are therefore taking part in a battle of the Spirit in which God himself is involved; local mission and trans-cultural mission are different ways of collaborating with God in the overall process of liberation. In other words, we live in an era of world mission. We cannot and must not distinguish between the service that we give to God and our neighbour in our immediate vicinity, and service given in a remote corner of the planet. The important thing is that the immediate and the distant should be integral parts of a conscious and intelligent participation in the spiritual battle, in which we join with God to struggle towards the goal of the redemption of all things in Jesus Christ.

162

The mission of the church must be seen in relation to this saving purpose of God that incorporates the fullness of the human race, the fullness of the whole of creation. The church is a people aware of the divine purposes, who sees them in action, who accompanies and proclaims them.

When all is said and done, the basic characteristic of our new situation is the presence of the church as an autochthonous reality in practically all countries of the world. Thus the recent Lausanne Congress on Evangelization (July 1974) could say:

> We rejoice that a new missionary era has dawned. The dominant role of western missions is fast disappearing. God is raising up from the younger churches a great new resource for world evangelization, and is thus demonstrating that the responsibility to evangelize belongs to the whole body of Christ. All churches should therefore be asking God and themselves what they should be doing both to reach their own area and to send missionaries to other parts of the world. A re-evaluation of our missionary responsibility and role should be continuous. Thus a growing partnership of churches will develop and the universal character of Christ's Church will be more clearly exhibited.

In this holistic interpretation of the mission of God we can see the important role of the individual prayers of the believer, inasmuch as his/her struggle for the health of a child, the fight to bring meaning and direction to the life of a teenager, the longing to save a home, participation in the struggle for justice for workers, the political struggle of a nation, or the search for more just structures at the world level are concerned - all these are part of a continuing process in which God's Spirit is seeking to make his love a signpost for all paths of life.

Thus the dichotomy between the spiritual and the material disappears; and proclamation and service, liturgy and social action, the call to repentance and changes in social structures are not independent of each other, nor are they differing contradictory realities. Rather, they are different forms of participating in the great mission to which God calls us. It is the task of the Christian Church to tell the world who is struggling, what is the goal of the struggle and, in the perspective of the Cross, to participate by accepting suffering and sacrifice where necessary to overcome human alienation and to challenge the whole community to make the changes that can lead to the hope which God promises. This understanding of mission allows us to free ourselves of paternalism. Mission does not go from "us" to "them", but comes from God for all of us. God invites all of us to participate equally in his missionary movement: "As the Father sent me, so I send you."

Bangkok says this in the following way:

> In the power of the Spirit, Christ is sent from God, the Father, into this divided world "to preach the gospel to the poor, to heal

the broken-hearted, to preach deliverance to the captives and recovering of sight to the blind, to set at liberty the oppressed, and to proclaim the year of God's favour" (Luke 4:18). Through Christ men and women are liberated and empowered with all their energies and possibilities to participate in His messianic work. Through His death on the Cross and His resurrection from the dead, hope of salvation becomes realistic and reality hopeful. He liberates from the prison of guilt. He takes the inevitability out of history. In Him the Kingdom of God and of free people is at hand. Faith in Christ releases in man creative freedom for the salvation of the world. He who separates himself from the mission of God separates himself from salvation.[1]

This vision of the mission of God gives meaning to the life of each individual. It also underlines the importance of evangelization as an invitation to participate consciously in God's universal mission. It is an understanding that permits us to come closer to the subject of the mission of the church across cultural and geographical frontiers, since it shows us the relevance of our local congregation to the total mission of God and relates what is happening in the remotest regions of the earth to our task and our immediate neighbourhood.

A few months ago, a big world congress of Christian families was held in Tanzania (June 1974). A Latin American family returning to their country wrote: "How important it is in historically closed situations to be able to say that there is hope in some part of the world." In other words, the inspiration obtained from the meeting with the Christians and people of Tanzania enabled this family to bring a message of hope to their own congregation and their own national situation, which seemed to be without hope. This seems to me to illustrate the new situation. A local congregation that is truly committed to the mission of God, discovering the places around them in which God seeks to overcome human alienation, is performing a most valuable service to the church in other parts of the world. By proclaiming the gospel through word and action, confronting the sins of racism, social discrimination, economic oppression, the exploitation of the environment, the dehumanization of humankind, and so on, the local congregation contributes to the freeing of spiritual forces for God's struggle throughout the universe. Through the mystery of prayer and through intelligent action in the community, we can contribute to the inspiration, encouragement and support of the church in all parts of the world.

Let us take the case of the North American church. Because that country occupies the first place in world attention, what the Christian Church in the United States does or does not do holds very important consequences for the mission of Christ's Church in Latin America, in Africa and in Asia. The way in which the racial problem is faced in the United States has more importance for the African churches than any number of American missionaries sent to Africa. It is active participation that contributes to God's mission in the world. Bangkok says it as follows: The local church in action should be an expression of the impulse of the whole church to further the proclamation of the Gospel of Jesus Christ to all the world so that, by responding to Him, persons and their situations may be saved.[2]

I can think of many local situations in which congregations are stuck in a repetitive, routine programme that could be transformed into a source of spiritual inspiration if only they understood that their task is not limited simply to working for their own good or that of the immediate neighbourhood, but that it is part of the fullness of the divine purpose that reaches to the ends of the earth and the ends of history. The liturgical act must not be limited to a concern for the immediate needs of the congregation, for those needs must be seen in the wider context of God's concern for all humanity. This is essential if we are to avoid escaping into generalities or succumbing to the weight of our powerlessness in face of all the problems of the world today. If the local mission of the church is seen in terms of God's universal mission, we will be able to take seriously our commitment to our immediate neighbour and will at the same time be aware of the spiritual dimension of universality that frees us from chauvinism and isolationism.

It is precisely because we can and must plan the local mission of the church in relation to the whole mission of God, that we need and must accept the help and collaboration of people from other cultures or other situations, whose experience can be a source of enrichment for our own service and witness. Through visits, correspondence, exchanges of experience and reciprocal prayer, we can create an infinite network of contacts that will enable us to bring the impulse of the universal church to our own locality. This is particularly important in countries where for political reasons the churches find it impossible to engage in any missionary service beyond their national borders. This does not mean that they are in any way prevented from participating in God's total mission; their faithfulness under the socio-political circumstances in which they find themselves is itself participation in the whole mission. At the same time, through visits, correspondence and reciprocal prayer, they can participate effectively in God's spiritual economy through the missionary task that is being carried out in other parts of the world.

A global vision of mission re-establishes the priority of prayer as a link of union and mutual support among Christians. It allows us to overcome the geographical and ideological barriers in a joint encounter in the divine wisdom. But the local congregation that assumes its immediate responsibility as part of the mission of God, receiving the help of others in the fulfilment of that mission, can and must also place the gifts, talents and opportunities that God has given it at the service of the other churches in the world. And it is essential that every congregation of the faith have that openness to the wider world which, even if it can only be shown in symbolic

action, illustrates, anticipates and is a parable of that
ultimate goal towards which God seeks to lead humanity - the
goal of interdependence, reconciliation and communion among
people.

It is only by maintaining a dialectical relationship between
the three elements that I have so far defined that we can
really move forward into the new day of missionary activity.
Active commitment to the local situation, a receptive attitude
towards the rest of the Christian community and readiness to
participate with others in their local situations will allow us
to discover new guidelines and models for action and a more
mature relationship among the churches. This will also allow
us to overcome our dependence on the dominant culture in the
country from which missionary resources come. Because, in order
to be faithful to the mission of God in a given place, a church
must have a clear awareness of its own identity. It is when the
church defines itself in relation to the gospel that it can stand
back from its own culture in order to serve it better.

The process is clearly visible in the so-called younger churches,
where the gospel arrived by the missionary's culture. Today we
can see the establishment of the gospel in the traditional
cultures of Africa, Asia and Latin America as a wish to express
the authenticity demanded by obedience to Jesus Christ in a
particular situation. This process must also take place in the
western churches, and in particular the North American churches;
they can no longer see themselves as the centre of the world
missionary operation, but rather as one of the regions in which
the mission of God is being fulfilled. They must stand back from
their culture and become a critical element within it. They must
undergo the arduous experience of identifying the cultural factors
that we unconsciously assume to form part of the gospel and the
biblical tradition which puts all our human loyalties to the test,
in order that this discovery of our identity as a church might
allow us to assume our concrete responsibilities in our own
locality.

Bangkok says this in the following way: What we must seek is rather
a mature relationship between churches. Basic to such a relationship is
mutual commitment to participate in Christ's mission in the world. A pre-
condition for this is that each church involved in the relationships should
have a clear realization of its own identity. This cannot be found in
isolation, however, for it is only in relationship with others that we discover ourselves.[3] The logical application of this vision has
consequences for our theological reflection, our church
structures, and our pastoral service. It demands serious
thought on the nature of the church within the mission of God,
the nature of the church within North American society, and on
the nature of the church in relationship to other churches. We
must restructure ourselves in such a way that we can receive, be
questioned and inspired, be enabled to participate and to

contribute. We must recognize that the frequent dichotomy
in many of our denominations between one structure for foreign
mission and another for home mission is inappropriate to the
new situation in which we are living. It is difficult for the
outside world to make a real impact on the churches of the USA
because the traditional channels of contact with other churches
have been thought out in terms of the American contribution to
those other churches and not in terms of what the American
churches can receive. When a third world person visits your
churches, you generally expect a story of need and of
inspirational service that encourages you in your wish to
contribute to what the church in his or her country is doing -
a generous impulse, to be sure. But it does not fulfil the
function basic to encounter between the churches, which is the
reciprocal contribution from outside to the local situation.
The challenge, the inspiration, the help of others is essential
for the local congregation.

But to get away from the level of abstract ideas and principles,
let me end by telling you something of how we have tried to
face this problem in Latin America. The gospel in its Protestant
form reached Latin America reflecting the glory of Anglo-Saxon
society. Liberal groups helped the first missionaries to settle
in Latin America in order to gather forces for the breaking down
of the official Catholic cultural establishment. Schools and
clinics brought an air of modernity to our people, and the early
converts adopted a life-style that imitated that of the North
American missionaries. Gospel songs were sung in translation,
the American order of service was established, and even church
buildings copied the architectural models of North America and
England. But as the church grew numerically, and Latin America
became aware of its dependence on the great centres of the west -
first England, then the United States - at the beginning of the
1960s the intellectual elites of Latin America began to see that
the fundamental problem was their countries' lack of freedom to
take their own decisions, and especially their economic dependence
on the foreign centres, essentially the United States.

Now we see our missionary history in another perspective. Our
colleges, of which we were justly proud, were suddenly revealed
as servants of the elite holding economic power in our countries.
The teaching of English, common in many parishes, was seen as
another way of linking us to the western powers. The lack of
church autonomy was a reflection of our lack of economic and
political autonomy. The desire therefore arose for independence,
to affirm our own personality, even to oppose the Anglo-Saxon
presence represented by the missionary. We went through serious
crises of conscience, because our desire to affirm our solidarity
with our people implied the adoption of a critical attitude
towards the nations from which we had received the blessing of
the gospel. We thus experienced conflicting loyalties and emotions,
which could only be resolved by affirming our own Christian

identity and responsibility in face of our immediate surroundings, but with full awareness of our participation in God's mission that went beyond the geographical limitations of our Latin American continent.

It was within this process of critical self-examination that the so-called *theology of liberation* arose on the Protestant side, which was an attempt to discern the action of God in the midst of the socio-political and economic processes of our people, and a definition of the mission of the church that placed itself at the service of the vision that it received from a reading of the Latin American *kairos*. The theology of liberation is an attempt to be responsible and authentic in our own situation, and it is from this acceptance of our own theological nature that we can turn to our brothers in North America and in other parts of the world, questioning and opening ourselves towards the questions that are put to us. It is on the basis of an awareness of our being as a church in Latin America that we can be truly able to be more faithful in our local situation and to make a contribution, no longer merely in an attitude of receptivity but also in an attitude of complete participation, to the mission of the church in all parts of the world.

Thus our congregations should have a triple missionary direction: active participation in the local situation, which for many means prison or exile; solidarity with other Latin American countries, which impels us to help each other by crossing the frontiers that divide our countries; and passionate participation in world ecumenical dialogue, trying to contribute with our criticism and witness - and trying to overcome our own chauvinism in order to remain open to the possibility of help, correction and inspiration that comes to us from other places. The example I quoted above of the Latin American family visiting Tanzania can be understood within this context.

All this shows how anything that can be done in your own country to overcome alienation can become a source of deep inspiration and help in our own situation. In Latin America, a small church is trying to remain faithful to a vision of God's mission, which demands responsibility in the light of local needs, but which is at the same time open to participation with the church of Jesus Christ in the whole world, on the other frontiers of struggle which belong to our Christian responsibility. The world mission of God is the vision that can give meaning to each person's individual vocation, to the existence of a small Christian community in the most marginal areas of our planet, to the solidarity among Christians across all human frontiers, and that can convert the church of Jesus Christ into a parable that anticipates God's great promises for all humanity.

(Address delivered at Methodist Pastors' Institute, Portland, Oregon, 1974)

Notes

1) Bangkok, Section II, part I - see IRM, April 1973, p. 199

2) Bangkok, Section III, part I, para. 2 - see IRM, April 1973, p. 217

3) Bangkok, Section III, part III, para. 5 - see IRM, April 1973, p. 221

EVANGELISM, MISSION, LIBERATION

Must we choose?

As can be seen from the many formal statements made at international meetings and from documents issued by ecclesiastical authorities, there is a growing consensus among Christians on the reciprocity and close relationship between the task of evangelism and Christian service, between proclamation of the gospel of Jesus Christ and participation in human liberation.
According to the Lausanne Covenant:

> To evangelize is to spread the good news that Jesus Christ died for our sins and was raised from the dead according to the Scriptures, and that as the reigning Lord he now offers the forgiveness of sins and the liberating gift of the Spirit to all who repent and believe. Our Christian presence in the world is indispensable to evangelism, and so is the kind of dialogue whose purpose is to listen sensitively in order to understand. But evangelism itself is the proclamation of the historical, biblical Christ as Saviour and Lord, with a view to persuading people to come to him personally and so be reconciled to God. In issuing the gospel invitation we have no liberty to conceal the cost of discipleship. Jesus still calls all who would follow him to deny themselves, take up their cross, and identify themselves with his new community. The results of evangelism include obedience to Christ, incorporation into his church and responsible service in the world." (Lausanne Covenant 4).

Or again, in Lausanne Covenant 5, we find the following statement: „Here too we express penitence both for our neglect and for having sometimes regarded evangelism and social concern as mutually exclusive ... We affirm that evangelism and socio-political involvement are both part of our Christian duty."
Orthodox theologians meeting in Bucharest in June 1974 expressed similar views in a report entitled, *The Evangelistic Witness of Orthodoxy Today*.

> The evangelistic witness is a call to salvation, which means the restoration of the relationship of God and man as understood in the Orthodox Christian teaching of theosis. This message has its source in the scriptures, which witness to redemption of mankind in Jesus Christ, yet it also includes a world-view that locates man vis-à-vis God and vis-à-vis his fellow man as individual and society, as well as his own personhood and

destiny. It includes both the God and man (vertical) relationship and the human being to fellow human being (horizontal) relationship. (*International Review of Mission*, Jan. 1975, 86.)

One could quote from many other documents such as those Bangkok, Nairobi, and the encyclical *Evangelium Nuntiandi*. All such documents acknowledge the close connection between these different dimensions of our life as Christians.

Nevertheless, questions of a theoretical and practical nature do arise about the way in which the various aspects of Christian obedience are related to one another within the whole mission assigned by God to His Church. The various theological explanations put forward differ considerably. Some refer to evangelism *and* justice, others to evangelism *in* the struggle for justice, while sometimes the issue is posed in practical terms. Should we, in planning our Church's mission, opt for participation in liberation, in development, or in the „proclamation" of the gospel? In entering this debate, we are fully aware of the importance of such questions, but at the same time they have to be seen as relative from the outset, for we give thanks to God that his liberty is greater than all our theological forms. Thus, in everyday life we may come across Christians who are committed to the same path of obedience but explain it in comparatively different theological terms. In the long run the real proof is in a life of obedience. Nevertheless, theological reflection is a vital element in Christian action and should help to strengthen and purify it. Also when we consider our missionary priorities it is essential to have criteria based on deep convictions to guide our choices.

Mission is the fundamental reality of our Christian life. We are Christians because we have been called upon by God to work with Him in the fulfilment of His purposes for humanity as a whole. Our life in this world is life in mission. Life has a purpose only to the extent that it has a missionary dimension. Moreover, life begins anew every day if it is seen as part of God's purpose which we help to fulfil, either individually or as a community or both. This dimension of mission, vicariousness, is also present in the Church's own internal life. A community worships God not for its own edification only, but as the priestly people of God praying for the good of all humankind. „As my Father sent me, I now send you". Throughout his whole life Jesus Christ showed this element of being a messenger, an envoy or ambassador for God the Father. Even in his childhood the missionary dimension showed itself. "Did you not know that I must be in my Father's house?" (Luke 2 : 49). Moreover, even as he hung on the Cross at the supreme moment of abandon Jesus was concerned for everyone around Him. "Mother, there is your son"; "Father forgive them"; "Today you shall be with me in Paradise". He also sought to explain the missionary purpose of his own death. "Why hast Thou forsaken me?" In the same way any Christian and follower of Jesus Christ in this world is invited to regard his entire life and eventual death as missionary service, a dimension of obedience and participation in the mission of God the Father. The question arises, however: in what way

171

does everything we do serve God's purpose?

One central emphasis of Christ's mission is revelation. "My task is to bear witness to the truth. For this I was born; for this I came into the world." (John, 18 : 37). "Anyone who has seen me has seen the Father," (John, 14 : 9). The life and ministry of Jesus Christ provide the supreme example of God's love invading the world. By observing the activities and listening to the words of Jesus, men were not only confronted with the specific problems besetting them but challenged to see beyond such problems to the supreme revelation of God's love manifested in Christ. Jesus did not come into the world merely to proclaim a message of revelation; He himself was that revelation. At times His activities were of a practical kind, such as healing the sick, and at others they involved highly polemical questions, such as forgiveness of sins. "Where are they?" (those who were about to condemn a woman). "Has no one condemned you? Nor do I condemn you. You may go; do not sin again." (John, 7.53 : 10-11). Throughout the Gospel Jesus is given complete freedom to deal with situations according to specific needs, demonstrating the love of God the Father through words of love, reproach, explanation or acts of healing. His whole life and ministry were devoted to announcing the Kingdom of God. In the oft-quoted passage from Luke 4 : 17-21, Jesus not only described the various facets of his ministry, but also proclaimed that the promise of the Old Testament – the dawn of the acceptable year of the Lord – was fulfilled in Him. Although each one of the activities mentioned in verse 18 could have been entirely secular, as a whole they are linked to the person of Jesus and to the essential purpose of his life, i.e., to fulfil the will of God and usher in the year of salvation.

Dr. Paul Löffler, in a background paper on evangelism presented to the Central Committee of the World Council of Churches in 1977, put it in this way:

> *Evangelism, mission, conversion and dialogue*:
> Evangelism represents the core of Christian mission in the world. Inseparable from it are all the other expressions of Christian service and solidarity which make up the totality of mission. But it is equally true that the struggles for liberation, service among the poor, identification with the oppressed, all centre in the witness to Christ who is the liberator, the servant and the sufferer. Whichever the sensitivities to be observed towards people of other faiths and convictions, whatever the modes of witness in the modern world, a living confession of Christ is the heart of the missionary calling in which we participate under God.

Thus, as with Jesus Christ, mission leaves the Church and every individual Christian completely free to choose their options; it leaves us to use our own judgement as to the words or deeds best suited to the circumstances at a given time, provided they are always aligned on Jesus Christ. "Who is this man?", his contemporaries asked on seeing his miracles. "Who are these people who have turned the world upside down?"

"Be always ready with your defence whenever you are called to account

172

for the hope that is in you." (1 Peter 3 : 15). Similarly when the announcement emphasizes the revelation, when proclamation or the symbol is a call to faith, to decision, to conversion or new birth, this call invariably has a social dimension that is inherent in it, not superimposed. In Christ we encounter God made man. "If any one says 'I love God,' and hates his brother, he is a liar;" (1 John 4 : 20). This means that mission and evangelism are intimately bound up. Mission is God's action, summoning people to participate in His purpose of peace and love; but this mission reveals and points to "the Lamb of God who takes away the sins of the world" and, in doing so, it is always at the same time an invitation to participate in the totality of God's mission. As to its *theological meaning*, "evangelism" is practically identical to "mission". When used in the sense of *evangelistic witness*, "evangelism" more specifically means the communication of Christ to those who do not consider themselves Christians. Thus, evangelism is sufficiently distinct and yet not separate from mission.

In other words, although a distinction may be drawn, the two concepts are wholly inseparable. There can be no proclamation of the Gospel without commitment to God's mission which includes justice, liberation and service. No Christian can participate in God's liberating mission or in different forms of service to the community unless his life and witness are focussed on the hidden reason for his participation, and the ultimate secret of the liberation process within himself. There can be no evangelism outside the divine mission in its totality, and no conscious participation in the mission of God without awareness of the revelation involved. The report of the Nairobi Assembly puts it as follows:

> The Gospel is good news from God, our Creator and Redeemer ... The Gospel *always* includes the announcement of God's Kingdom and love through Jesus Christ, the offer of grace and forgiveness of sins, the invitation to repentance and faith in Him, the summons to fellowship in God's Church, the command to witness to God's saving words and deeds, the responsibility to participate in the struggle for justice and human dignity, the obligation to denounce all that hinders human wholeness, and a commitment to risk life itself.

Evangelistic proclamation can and must have a point of emphasis such as the Cross, forgiveness of sins, or healing the sick. But it will be *evangel* only to the extent that it points to the wholeness of God's love breaking through in the world, and looks forward to the reign of his peace in all human relations. There are a number of things to be said in connection with this dialectical relationship between mission and evangelism.

1. In carrying out God's mission, we *cannot opt permanently* for one or other aspect of mission, whether it be liberation, development, humanization or evangelization. These are all essential and integral parts of the mission entrusted to us and cannot be set against one another without becoming simply a caricature of what they really are. Indeed, they only exist as parts, and can only be discovered or recognized separately within the framework of

their inter-relatedness. For example, as citizens we may take part along with others, who may or may not be Christians, in the struggle against under-development or against anything that threatens human freedom. Our partici-pation in this process implies a spirit of selfcriticism based on eschatological thinking. Since all human effort is ultimately subject to God's judgement, if we participate faithfully in the process of liberation, if we are disciplined participants in the struggles it involves, we bring to it a capacity for critical appraisal which we consider to be constructive and salutory for the whole process, and which questions it in various respects. Our critical approach will be credible only if it is clearly seen to be closely linked to a declaration of our faith in Jesus Christ and does not stem from any connection with competing ideologies or rival power groups. As Christians participating in a political liberation struggle, it is absolutely essential never to lose sight of our commit-ment to the Christian community as a whole and to the deepest roots of our faith. But at the same time our evangelism can be credible only when its message is seen to be valid in relation to the often cruel facts of real, everyday situations. As the South African Bishop, Manas Buthelezi puts it,

> The future of the Christian faith in this country will largely depend on how the Gospel proves itself relevant to the existential problems of the black ... The whites insofar as they incarnated their spiritual genius in the South African economic and political institutions, have sabotaged and eroded the power of Christian love. While professing to be traditional custodians and last bulwarks in Africa of all that goes under the name of Christian values, the whites have unilaterally and systematically rejected the black as someone to whom they can relate with any degree of personal intimacy in daily life and normal ecclesiastical situations ... The black theologian must therefore discover a theological framework within which to understand the will and love of God in Jesus Christ outside the limitations of white institutions. The future of evangelism in South Africa is therefore tied to the quest for a theology that grows out of black experience ...

2. *Options and priorities* to suit the circumstances *are at all times possible and sometimes* they are undoubtedly *necessary*. The Church believes in a living God who has accompanied humankind throughout its history and who is at work within it. God always summons us to obedience, to militant action, to participation in His mission here and now, and as we saw in the life of Jesus Christ who had complete freedom to respond to the requirements of different situations and different people, we too are called to provide different responses to different situations. For example, in Latin America, the call to missionary obedience and participation in the struggle against oppression has been heard by large sections of the Christian community, especially in the Catholic Church. Their response takes the form of conscienti-zation work which enables people to discover their vocation as sons of God and calls on them to organize themselves and take their own destiny in hand, or it may involve making representations to oppressive state authorities,

demanding respect for basic human rights. Some talk of a theology of liberation, others prefer to call it a theology of exile. Whatever term is chosen, it serves to underline the priorities required by the situation, at a time when the Christian community discovers that one particular aspect of the Gospel is required by the dynamics of history in order to make God's redeeming power present in that particular time and place in history.

In such theological efforts and renewal movements the Christian churches of Latin America are frequently accused of distorting the Gospel for political purposes. In point of fact, those who accuse the churches in this way are allowing their own ideological judgements to prevent them from seeing the work of their fellow Christians as a practical demonstration of their missionary obedience. Now that the Catholic Church in Latin America has convened its next Bishop's Synod to study the question of evangelism, we are discovering how such prophetic and practical obedience has generated a dynamic renewal of the whole Church and a redoubling of its missionary zeal. What once appeared to be exclusively political has clearly turned into a powerful impetus for renewal in the Church and is affecting every aspect of its work. In the situation of struggle for liberation, or in the oppressive situation of Latin America, evangelism has become vital once again; it announces the Good News of God's love for all the oppressed, calling them to conversion, to a change of perspective, summoning them to assume their role in the whole liberating mission of God.

As evangelism becomes vital once again, it provides clear options, including the reality of martyrdom. Evangelism is at all times a public matter. As it participates in struggles for liberation, the Christian community has discovered the relevance of the biblical message, the importance of a personal encounter with Christ, the value of small local communities, the reality of ecumenical cooperation, the existence of a popular religious conscience which incorporates not only syncretic elements but the promises of the Gospel, keeping them alive in the minds of the people. The forthcoming synod of Latin American bishops will be going into all these questions, not only from a theoretical point of view or in order to recover the evangelistic dimension which the Church has lost in the course of its history, but in order to learn from present experiences, to study them in greater depth and subject them all to the authority of the Scriptures. At the same time, I must mention the tragic experience of various protestant denominations, whose evangelistic work had, for many years, a dimension of liberation, making them into agents of dissent in the existing oppressive systems and opening the door to progress for the community as a whole. However, they failed to keep abreast of developments in Latin American societies in the sixties and took a step backwards, making evangelism a purely private personal and religious affair. In so doing, they found themselves in the role of endorsing and often justifying the new oppressive systems, and lost the evangelizing power that had once been their distinctive feature. The very same people who had once acted as the leaven in the evangelism process in Latin America, through whom the bible filtered through into the Catholic Church itself, failed to make the most of their new opportunity and to discern the *kairos* of God and have, unfortunately, been largely left out of what has become the finest hour of the Christian Church in Latin America. We pray that God in His mercy may grant that there still be time to repent and to recover the dimension of mission and evangelism.

I have referred to Latin America at great length for obvious reasons, but there are other equally clear-cut cases. For centuries the Orthodox churches have preserved the faith in Muslim countries, keeping it alive for future generations. In spite of legal and social pressures, hindrances to evangelism and, therefore, to any increase in church membership, these churches have not failed to fulfil the words of Jesus, "let men see your good works and glorify your Father who is in Heaven". As a result of such patient, persistent and courageous witnessing, many people have been able to see something of the glory of Jesus Christ. Generations of Christians in these countries have hoped for divine intervention to open the door to greater participation in the Gospel. For the time being they are doing what they can, in the name of the God of love, by carrying out acts of humanity and service which point towards God's future and which are possible even in such situations. I would refer also to the present situation in socialist countries, particularly those where the Orthodox churches were to some extent the focal point of everyone's life in the secular community. Such churches have now been marginalized and have no recognized place in the system. They have to struggle to maintain their identity as churches and to preserve the faith, not only for future generations but for the people to today, to give them the chance to discover that the community of faith is a reality which enriches the whole of life, even within a socialist system. Prevented by the new organization of society from carrying out their traditional forms of diaconal service, the Orthodox churches have concentrated on a humanizing liturgy, and, with the spiritual dimension and the mysticism of their liturgy they are helping to preserve a human dimension within a system based on a rationalism which overlooks fundamental elements of human nature. I would also mention the evangelistic work being done in Hong Kong to prepare the Christian Church in the China of the future.

There is a great deal of discussion at the present time on the problem of the numerical growth of the Church. This is not one of our themes for this essay. However, I would say that efforts to achieve numerical growth are indeed of fundamental importance, but only when this is seen as part of the whole mission to be fulfilled. It is because of God's love for the whole of mankind that we seek to increase the number of Christians committed with God Himself to the liberation of the whole community. All these options determined by circumstances, geographical situations and strategies must be seen as a point of entry into the whole of God's mission. The Bangkok conference puts it this way:

> These points of entry differ from situation to situation in which we work and suffer. We should know that such anticipations are not the whole of salvation, and must keep in mind the other dimensions while we work. Forgetting this denies the wholeness of salvation. Nobody can do in any particular situation everything at the same time. There are various gifts and tasks, but there is one spirit and one goal. In

this sense, it can be said, for example, that salvation is the peace of the people in Vietnam, independence in Angola, justice and reconciliation in Northern Ireland and release from the captivity of power in the North Atlantic community, or personal conversion in the release of a submerged society into hope, or of new life styles amidst corporate self-interest and lovelessness. (*Bangkok Report*, 90).

This does not mean that such a definition of salvation in a given place limits the content of the message and the reality of salvation, or the content of our mission there or for the whole world. It means that in such and such a place the message of salvation is relevant when it is linked to this or that priority or urgent need to which God calls His people. In a paper entitled "A theological Reflection on the Work of Evangelism" dating from 1959 we read:

> There is no single way to witness to Jesus Christ. The Church has borne witness in different times and places in different ways. This is important. There are occasions when dynamic action in society is called for; there are others when a word must be spoken; others when the behaviour of Christians one to another is the telling witness. On still other occasions the simple presence of a worshipping community or man is the witness. These different dimensions of witness to the one Lord are always a matter of concrete obedience. To take them in isolation from one another is to distort the Gospel. They are inextricably bound together, and together give the true dimension of evangelism. The important thing is that God's redeeming Word be proclaimed and heard.

3. The whole life of a Christian community in a given place including its international relations, provide the framework which integrates and explains the diversity of gifts and vocations. The message proclaimed is understood by those who hear it in light of the image of the community which proclaims it. Even an act which, objectively speaking, is the same everywhere, like the distribution of the Bible, for example, may become a vehicle for trans-mitting different messages, depending on the person or the community distributing the texts. Similarly, an action which in itself may seem to be entirely secular, such as feeding the hungry, may likewise become a sign of God's love if the hand that does it is visibly related to a community which considers that it worships God. Because of this, we can accept that within the Christian community there is room for personal gifts and a diversity of vocations, and that it is rather unrealistic to proclaim such slogans as 'every Methodist is an evangelist' or 'every Christian is an evangelist'. It is likewise unrealistic when, in stressing the inescapable political dimension in the life of every individual, we go a step further and demand that every Christian should be actively militant in the political affairs of his country. It is the whole Christian community which is evangelistic and which has to adopt clear positions towards liberation movements and struggles against oppression in the secular community. The conviction as to the important role

a Christian community has to play in this respect is what authenticates the vocation of individuals and different voluntary groups, but at the same time it sets clear limits to what they can do. The religious orders committed to an ideal of service to the poor, to education or medical work, or the preaching of the Word, or contemplation and prayer fulfil a very important function when they are part of the whole. If, however, they attempt to reduce the whole to what they are doing as their specific vocation, then obviously they are distorting and restricting the reality of the love of God which embraces a greater whole. Similarly, the missionary groups specializing in student work, or the problems of the ghettos in large cities, or organizing the rural communities, or preaching the Word across geographical or cultural barriers are all valid and necessary, provided they see themselves as part and servants of a whole. Years ago I put it as follows:

> The Christian community that evangelizes can only do it genuinely to the extent in which its life shows the signs of the encounter with the one whom it announces. Therefore every genuinely Christian act is part of the evangelizing process. Words or silence, the discovering of signs of the presence of Jesus Christ or the planting of those signs, worship or social action, the religious activity or the secular activity of believers, all that is done in the name of Christ. It is evangelism if it forms part of the total being of a community that is linked historically through the presence of the Bible to the Master of Nazareth and is living in an eschatological perspective. While we can organize activities that we can call specifically evangelistic and that have as a conscious goal communication with "the world", what makes them genuinely evangelistic is the form in which the existing Christian communities will become living examples of the Gospel of the God who lives for others. Evangelism only exists where there is social concern. Without it there may be propaganda, proselytism, but hardly Good News.

The liturgy of the Church therefore assumes fundamental importance since it is here that, symbolically and representatively, we find the Body of Christ praying for the whole situation of the world. It is the place and the moment when the meeting of heaven and earth is represented by the members of the Body being consecrated for vicarious service, and the world as it is being presented in prayers of intercession for its salvation.

Let me end by quoting a sentence from the Nairobi report on Section I "Confessing Christ Today", that I think sums up quite well our understanding:

> Confessing Christ *today* means that the Spirit makes us struggle with all the issues this Assembly has talked about: sin and forgiveness, power and powerlessness, exploitation and misery, the universal search for identity, the widespread loss of Christian motivation and the spiritual longings of those who have not heard Christ's name.

(Occasional Bulletin, USA, 1978)

178

HUMAN RIGHTS

In a world where torture, imprisonment, kidnappings and psychiatric confinement are becoming the accepted way for political authority to handle its opposition, the consolation of those in prison, the visitation of their families, the utterance of prophetic words, the undertaking of symbolic actions, and the proclamation of the Word are some of the ways God's love invades that world, showing his concern for all mankind, and, particularly, the oppressed.

The term "human rights" comes to us from the French Revolution and must, when used by Christians, be constantly reinterpreted to make certain that it conveys more than the philosophical presuppositions of that particular historical period. It is clear that, from a Christian perspective, this phrase refers to the dignity and freedom bestowed by the Father on his children. God does not want to live without man. The creation stated that fact, the incarnation confirmed it. And the ascension of Jesus Christ symbolized his taking to the Father our very humanity so that "our life now is hidden with Christ in God" (Col. 3 : 3). Through the eyes of faith we discover, therefore, in every violation of human rights evidence of the forces that thwart God's will for man and, in every persecuted one, we see Jesus Christ himself as the oppressed.

In this issue of the IRM we will examine the present struggle for human rights from the perspective of the mission of the church. God invites every creature to new life in him, and the church is sent into the world to struggle against everything which keeps that invitation from being presented to them and everything that hinders their freedom to respond to it. The freedom to respond to God implies more than what is normally called religious freedom, or even political freedom. The freedom to respond to God implies the liberation of man from everything that enslaves him, that deprives him of the possibility of standing as a free human being before God. Freedom from hunger, from want, from fear are aspects of that liberation. Such liberation creates community.

In theological discussions we often play with the words "text" and "context". Human rights are not the "context" of our mission but its very "text" and the heart of the freedom-bringing Gospel. "Human rights" is not just the slogan of the political activist; it sums up the Christian missionary imperative.

****

John and Peter went to the temple to pray. There, at the beautiful gate was a man who had been lame all his life. They stopped. They looked at the man and pronounced a word of healing: "In the name of Jesus Christ of Nazareth, I order you to walk" (Acts 3 : 6). As John and Peter were fulfilling their religious duties, they discovered a man in need and they met his need. They cared about that man, and, as a result, unrest and popular tumult troubled the city.

The temple as a socio-religious institution guaranteed the divine order. The priesthood was there to assure the permanence of the Covenant. Religious and civilian authorities worked together for the maintenance of law and order. But Peter and John disturbed the peace, healing without authorization and creating unrest by making people aware of a power greater than that of the civil and religious authorities. This had to stop. "Under no condition were they to speak or to teach in the name of Jesus" (Acts 4 : 18).

The parallel to many missionary situations of today is striking. Christians responding to their missionary calling are obliged to face real human problems. Impelled by God's love, they cannot remain indifferent. They recognize in the God of the Bible, in the Father of Jesus Christ, a bias towards the poor, the captive, the blind, the oppressed. They know that Jesus has come "to announce the year when the Lord will save his people" (Luke 4 : 19).

Today, as yesterday, Christians care for the poor and those crushed by totalitarian regimes. They live among them, helping them to find the kind of social organization which eliminates social paralysis and allows them to discover new opportunities in life. Among them and for them, Christians exercise their mission of prayer, proclamation, love and service, discovering as they do so the constraints imposed upon them by the structures of society or the counter-demands of authoritarian governments. Like John and Peter they are obliged to clarify their choices before the authorities: "You yourselves judge which is right in God's sight, to obey you or to obey God. For we cannot stop speaking of what we ourselves have seen and heard" (Acts 4 : 19-20). Like the apostles, their activities threaten the established order because they will not limit themselves to private, individual, religious practices. John and Peter obeyed God, fulfilling their missionary calling and the result, to their surprise,

180

was that "the people all praised God for what had happened" (Acts 4 : 21). The attempt to limit missionary freedom to religious acts of speaking *about* freedom has always been present. Today public relations officers of authoritarian governments claim that they not only grant religious freedom, but even help Christian organizations to fulfill their religious duties. They are ready to open public stadiums for their use, provide free public transportation, facilitating in every way public rallies where people are called upon to accept the status quo, to forget about the fate of the oppressed, to escape from the realities of life to a world of fantasy. But as soon as the preacher of the Gospel calls upon all authority to kneel before the Christ, conflict takes place. Whenever the Christian, following his missionary vocation, calls to repentance, to a change of priorities, to a surrender to God's higher judgement, to a manifestation of his love, the conflict situation is there. It is easy to discredit such Christians today by calling them "political trouble-makers", "ideological". But it is impossible to silence those voices that are telling in the language of today, the message of yesterday to the poor and the lame of the world: "In the name of Jesus of Nazareth, stand up and walk."

The church is sent by God into the world to liberate men from what hinders them from responding as free human beings to his invitation to a new life in him. Every liberating act has public consequences: public disorder, confrontation with authority, civil judgement follow upon it. But with it all — the miracle of the freedom to walk after a lifetime of immobility, and an act of public praise to God from the people.

****

Moses killed an Egyptian soldier to protect some Hebrew peasants. But when the emotion of the moment had subsided, Moses knew he was in trouble and ran away. The story that follows is well known. Moses reordered his life, raised a family and made his living by taking care of his father-in-law's sheep. He had escaped not only the soldiers of Pharaoh, but also the challenge that had been put before him. With a family to bring up, sheep to care for, security assured, Moses was satisfied, but God was not. Hungry children, families living in the streets, dictators with life and death power over the lives of people — we have become used to all this and go on with the business of assuring our security in the performance of our religious duties. But God hears the voice of the oppressed. "I have seen the affliction of my people who are in Egypt, and I have heard their cry because of their taskmaster. I know their sufferings and I have come down to deliver them out of the hands of the Egyptians" (Ex. 3 : 7, 8). God transmits the cry of the suffering to Moses. What he wanted to forget, what he did not want to see or hear, is brought to life in his heart by the Spirit of God.

God sent Moses yesterday; today he sends every Christian to break the chains of oppression, to make possible the worshipping of God in freedom. We are called today to discover the oppression of our own people and our own participation in the oppression of others, and hear in the cries of the people of the earth the voice of God saying: "I send you; I will be with you." We do not, of course, want to listen. But God himself listens and multiplies the cries of the oppressed of today. Moses' resistance was broken by God. "By faith, Moses when he was grown up, refused to be called a son of Pharaoh's daughter, choosing rather to share ill-treatment with the people of God than to enjoy the fleeting pleasures of sin. He considered abuse suffered for the Christ greater wealth than the treasures of Egypt" (Heb. 11 : 24-26).

Like Moses yesterday, many Christians today are finding in their struggle for the rights of others, in the response to God's calling to listen to the voice of the people, that the promise of God, "I will be with you", is a daily reality.

The church is sent by God into the world to liberate men from what hinders them from responding as free human beings to his invitation to a new life in him. The concern for human rights is the name we give today to our being sent with prophetic words to the Pharaoh who enslaves and with liberating deeds to God's people who groan under that slavery.

****

I cannot stay entirely outside of my Latin American context. For me it is impossible to discuss a theology of mission without thinking of the present situation in that continent. Because we are concerned with the eternal destiny of human beings, we are concerned with the multiplication of torture in our continent. Torture kills the human in the torturer and crushes the personality of the one tortured.

We are sent to demand the right of every individual to respond freely to God's invitation. When we struggle against inhumanity in the handling of political prisoners, we proclaim a word of judgement and forgiveness in God's name. When we press for amnesty, we announce the possibility of a God-given reconciliation. When we call people to metanoia, to conversion, to discipleship, we call them to take as their own cause that of the damned of the earth. How can others believe in a Gospel that speaks of the one who gave himself for others, seeing our complacency or fear? How can the oppressed majorities of the world today understand our Gospel which has no cross. It is the credibility of the Gospel on the lips of the church that is at stake. We cannot be Christian and remain indifferent to the struggle for basic human dignity and freedom.

It is because they are not indifferent that many in Latin America today, as the saints of yesterday, are "enlightened": ". . . after you were enlightened, you endured a hard struggle with sufferings, sometimes being publicly exposed to abuse and affliction, and sometimes being partners with those so treated. For you had compassion on the prisoners, and you joyfully accepted the plundering of your property, since you knew that you yourselves had a better possession and an abiding one" (Heb. 10 : 32-34).

Through my mind and heart a great procession of names and faces pass, pastors, priests, nuns, simple Christians, men and women of God who in Latin

America and in other parts of the world "were tortured, refusing to accept release, that they might rise again to a better life ... suffered mocking and scourging, and even chains and imprisonment. They were stoned, they were sawn in two, they were killed with the sword; they went about in skins of sheep and goats, destitute, afflicted, ill-treated — of whom the world was not worthy" (Heb. 11 : 35b-38a).

To them and the many others in God's mighty army this issue is dedicated in the hope that being "surrounded by so great a cloud of witnesses, we will lay aside every weight and sin which clings so closely, and we will run with perseverance the race that is set before us, looking to Jesus the pioneer and perfecter of our faith, who for the joy that was set before him endured the cross, despising the shame, and is seated at the right hand of the throne of God (Heb. 12 : 1, 2)."

As we look through the contents of this issue of IRM, we find the peoples of affliction — Filipinos, South Africans, Americans, Brazilians, Namibians, Guatemalans — and the Pharaohs and their henchmen. Here, too, are the prophets — the determined voice of John Perkins who leads a community liberation movement in Mississippi, USA, the pastoral voice of Bishop Kurt Scharf who dares to care about the human rights of those guilty of serious crimes, the passionate pleading of Julia Esquivel for the rights of Indian campesinos in her country, the counsel of Georges Casalis to take up intercessory prayer as a continuation and corrective to the struggle against torture, the call of José Míguez Bonino to see the biblical imperative for commitment to human rights as rooted in the very heart of the faith, and Sister Maria Ramona Mendiola who sees that finally it is the evangelizers who are evangelized when they commit themselves to this most central of Christian missionary tasks, the liberation of all men so that they may be saved and come to the knowledge of the truth.

(International Review of Mission, July 1977)

2. LATIN AMERICAN KAIROS

For many years my own ministry was confined to Latin America. It was there
that the vision of the kingdom of God, with all the inspiration and freedom
it promises, captured my faith and imagination.

The first article, "The Church in a Revolutionary Situation", is an attempt
to describe the Latin American scene and to discern God's purposes and
priorities in that situation. The prophetic, priestly and servant roles of
the church in a revolutionary context are dealt with from a holistic perspective. "The church cannot be reduced to a mere group for social struggle;
it participates in the social struggles of humanity, but from its own
particular perspective in which it seeks to raise levels of personal and
collective awareness to the height of the will of God, revealed in Jesus Christ."

The second article is "The Church in Latin America and its Healing Ministry".
"Every time the church approaches a person or a community, it expresses its
concern for the total well-being of that person." The article is a discussion
of Christian concern in health issues, and describes a series of possibilities
for participating in the struggle for health: prayer, caring local communities,
individual vocational calling, auxiliary services, theological contributions
to the setting of priorities by the secular society, and prophetic responsibility.

Through the Programme to Combat Racism, the World Council facilitated an
encounter of anthropologists in Barbados to study the situation of the Indians
in Latin America. It produced a declaration issuing an invitation to stop all
missionary work among Indians. The third article is an attempt to interpret in
a positive way the Barbados Declaration while affirming our Christian missionary
vocation. "We must examine our missionary practices in the light of the
liberating and redeeming mission of the God made known to us through Jesus
Christ. If our mission contributes to the alienation of human beings, to their
alienation from their own culture, to their reduction to a state of submission,
even though conceptually and doctrinally it could have a Christian content,
it is existentially, in fact, denying its 'missionary' character."

The fourth article is an appeal addressed to Christians and churches in Latin
America to assume their protagonist role in the liberation of the continent.
The churches must call people to militant discipleship, relate liturgical
celebrations to God's liberating purposes and harness their institutions,
like schools and hospitals, to the service of the masses of poor people. The
churches are called to develop a prophetic ministry and to challenge the
oppressive powers in the structures of Latin America. "We need sociological
analyses, political and technical planning, an ideology, a strategy, a tactic.
But how direly we need also the moral fiber, the human depth, the authentic
freedom of the militants for freedom. Here is where the dimension of faith
comes in, when we realize that we are not involved in some personal struggle,
but in God's own great struggle down the centuries to dignify human existence.
Humanization, liberation, redemption, all are part of the will of God."

The Church in a Revolutionary Situation

Let me begin by giving a few basic facts about Latin America which will provide the background for the revolutionary situation. If there is one word
which sums up the historical situation of our continent it is "dependence".
With the arrival of the Spanish and Portuguese, a process of exploitation of
the natural resources of the region began, to the benefit of the Spanish and
Portuguese metropolitan centres. The gold and silver of Peru and Bolivia and
Mexico were quickly taken away in the Spanish galleons. Trade patterns were
established for the convenience of the colonizer. Throughout the colonial
period there was no serious attempt to develop prosperous industry. Perhaps
the greatest difference between the colonization of North and South America
lies in this fact - that in the north a market and national industries were
quickly created to supply it, while in the south an attempt was made to
satisfy the demands of the market by means of trade with the European metropolis. The result was total dependence. One might have thought that with
the declaration of independence by these colonies in the first half of the
19th century, things might change. But this did not happen. On the contrary,
national elites, closely linked with trade interests, maintained the links
of dependence, by changing the destination of the exports and origin of the
imports. Throughout the 19th, and part of the 20th, century England took over
the role of colonial metropolis on which the economic fate of the Latin
American nations depended.

With the Second World War, English influence disappeared, to be replaced
progressively by that of North America. Today, the framework of dependence
can still be seen within Latin American society and in the relationships
between our nations and the rest of the world. Exports of raw materials continue - tin, copper, oil, coffee - to the industrialized centres in the north,
principally the USA. In exchange, we receive cars, TV sets, cinema films,
news, magazines.

The same framework of dependence can be seen inside the nations, where dominant groups control the larger part of the national income. The huge masses
of Latin America have no access to the basic goods of culture and fortune.
Suffice it to say here that almost 50% of the population of the continent is
illiterate. It is the alliance of the ruling elites with international trade
interests which basically explains the deterioration in culture, in the
economies and the social and human condition of most Latin American countries.

It is against this background, which I have painted only in very general
terms, that the work of the churches must be understood. Let me give a brief
historical description of the situation. The Catholic Church came to our continent with the conquistadores, in a very real sense "sanctifying" the conquest. The evangelization of pagan people was an officially declared aim of
the Spanish and Portuguese colonizers, and was symbolized by the presence of
the priest with the conquistadores. In practice, the interests of the
colonizers lay rather in the body and fortune of the native than in his
spiritual life. Nevertheless the Cross arrived with the soldiers - a strange
collaboration which has been maintained over the centuries. To its favour,
it must be noted that the Church was concerned for the humanization of the
situation of the native, easing the worst consequences of the exploitation
to which he was submitted. However, it must also be recognized that the
Church solidified and sanctified the status quo.

Protestant Churches arrived in the second half ot the 19th century, by two different routes. On the one hand was the migratory church, accompanying the Italian, Swiss or German colonist who came to seek his fortune in the fertile lands of Latin America. They understood the mission of the church as being the maintenance of the faith for future generations. The church served as a social, cultural and religious centre, but there was no feeling of belonging to a wider community. On the other hand, there came missionaries from North America, England and Scandinavia. They made an aggressive attempt at pro-selytism and evangelization, particularly towards non-practising Catholics. But very soon this Protestantism also began to constitute a sub-culture in Latin America. This sub-culture has accepted, without any serious question-ing, the cultural values which the missionary brought with him. The Gospel was received, together with a style of life, both ecclesiastical and per-sonal, which was alien to the surrounding community. The result was the creation of cultural sub-zones, real islands cut off from the cultural main-land which prevented Protestants from feeling they were a part of the total community.

This picture of Roman Catholic complicity and Protestant withdrawal, which might also be termed complicity, was brutally shaken towards the end of the 1950s by an awakening of the Christian conscience towards the problems of Latin America. What happened? A series of factors led to the termination of the traditional siesta and an awareness of its new historical possibilities. It would be difficult to outline all the different influences which produced this change in the emotional and mental panorama of our continent. First, there was the end of the war, which produced great hopes throughout the world. Second, the cinema became very popular. The poor peasant looked won-deringly at the new world which developed before his eyes. Third, there was the movement of people from the country to the towns. They sought better possibilities of life, only to find a worse situation than the one they had left behind. Even so, a man who dared to act, breaking the barriers of tradition - all the things he was used to - began to look to the future with hope.

This movement of the Latin American masses from the country to the towns is one of the most interesting phenomena, both for its social and political significance but also for its theological meaning. In social terms, there was a break between man and his milieu - a departure towards new possibili-ties. In the political field, there was the sudden appearance in the cities of a mass of people open to the emergence of the populist movements. In theological terms, migration provided a real invitation to see the masses as part of the liberating movements of history; just as the Jewish tribes marched through the desert in search of new horizons of life, so the people of Latin America move around in search of a new day. The basic problem is how to find the Moses who will lead them, help them to understand the basic meaning of their search and help them to build a truly new society. During this period, Marxist ideas circulated freely, and were heard more calmly outside the Cold War situation.

The population increase continually added to the number of young people on the employment market, as well as increasing the discontent among students. The result of all this has been an increasing awareness that the historical situation is not the result of chance nor of the will of the gods but rather responds to the behaviour of human beings who have acted in a certain way and who could have acted differently. Alongside all this, there has also been a rediscovery of the national and cultural roots of the Latin American. There is a new pride in the discovery of the Indian origins of Latin American culture, we have revalued the artistic and cultural conditions of our fore-fathers, and found a new desire to build a huge new motherland which could incorporate the whole of Latin America.

In other words, there has been a change of consciousness which has been accompanied by a change in action. The radical political and social revolution which took place in Cuba is well known. While the phenomenon cannot be considered as a model for the whole of Latin America, first because of the North American blocade and second because of the support from Russia, it nevertheless served to galvanize the Latin American masses, particularly the organized proletarian groups and the students, who saw in this little country which had been able to challenge its powerful neighbour a symbol of the possibilities open to them in Latin American history.

This awakening in Latin American history coincided with, and was influenced by, an awakening in the conscience and behaviour of the Latin American church. It could be argued that the most important political event in Latin America during the past 15 years has been the internal renewal of the churches, particularly the Roman Catholic Church. A few years ago, Governor Rockefeller travelled to Latin America on a mission for President Nixon, to study the Latin American situation and advise on foreign policy. Rockefeller mentioned the revolutionary potential within the church and recommended that it be given careful attention. This experienced statesman saw that seeds of discontent and a passion for justice were germinating within a body which traditionally had been allied to the status quo, and would soon have an effect on all aspects of Latin American society.

While an American politician could lament this fact, young people in Latin America took part in this phenomenon, and of course saw it with very different eyes. While a few years before it was normal for young people to be indifferent to religion, believing that the church could produce nothing good and nothing new, today they look to the church as an institution from which, perhaps, may come the word which stimulates liberating action.

In the Catholic Church, this process reached its culmination in the Medellin congress of 1968, where the bishops of Latin America committed their church to the liberation of the Latin American people.

Within the Protestant Church, there has been a similar increase in awareness and commitment to the Latin American situation. It is probable that the very increase in numbers of the Protestant churches prevented them from remaining in cultural isolation and forced them to define themselves in terms of the agonizing problems which face Latin Americans today. Of course, this prise de conscience of both the Protestant and Catholic churches did not take place easily, and there have been tensions and divisions on both sides. But here there is an interesting phenomenon: the divisions are no longer between Catholics and Protestants, but rather Christians in both churches take up different positions in their understanding of the revolutionary process and of Christian responsibility. There is a new type of ecumenism for them which is no longer obsessed by the various doctrinal affirmations of the confessional bodies, but which addresses itself to the common historical task that has to be undertaken to change dependence into freedom.

But if it is difficult to live through the tensions produced by change within the Christian community, how much more difficult it is to experience them in the surrounding community! Sociological studies have shown in abundant detail how Latin American dependence is accompanied by structural violence which permanently condemns great masses of the population to sub-human conditions - lack of housing, of food, of education, of employment opportunities. It is a violence established within the system and which implies the exploitation of man by man. Guerilla groups and revolutionaries have taken up the challenge of this violence in a counter-violence which aims to overcome the violence of the system. Naturally, the system defends itself by launch-

187

ing counter-attacks in the form of repression, massive military expenditures fortify the army and modern techniques of torture are used to overcome the forces of popular resistance. The result is a terrible vicious circle which seems to offer no means of escape. Overriding injustice, followed by a violent attempt to fight against injustice, followed by a new wave of repression to defend the status quo, with its consequent tragic reaffirmation of injustice.

It is in this context that we must understand the challenges which face the Christian churches in the revolutionary situation in Latin America. The church cannot be reduced to a mere group for social struggle; it participates in the social struggles of man, but from its own particular perspective in which it seeks to raise levels of personal and collective awareness to the height of the will of God, revealed in Jesus Christ. The church must therefore understand its function in terms of the Gospel and in relationship to all aspects of Latin American life. We must take as our starting point a concept of the message of salvation which encompasses the whole of human life. As the Bangkok conference on world mission said:

"The salvation which Christ brought, and in which we participate, offers a comprehensive wholeness in this divided life. We understand salvation as newness of life - the unfolding of true humanity in the fulness of God (Col. 2:9). It is salvation of the soul and the body, of the individual and society, mankind and 'the groaning creation' (Rom. 8:19). As evil works both in personal life and in exploitative social structures which humiliate humankind, so God's justice manifests itself both in the justification of the sinner and in social and political justice. As guilt is both individual and corporate so God's liberating power changes both persons and structures. We have to overcome the dichotomies in our thinking between soul and body, person and society, human kind and creation. Therefore we see the struggles for economic justice, political freedom and cultural renewal as elements in the total liberation of the world through the mission of God. This liberation is finally fulfilled when 'death is swallowed up in victory' (I Cor. 15:55). This comprehensive notion of salvation demands of the whole of the people of God a matching comprehensive approach to their participation in salvation."

In the light of this understanding of salvation, we seek to build a church capable of accompanying this liberating action of God. For this reason, too, Bangkok says:

"We are seeking the true community of Christ which works and suffers for his Kingdom. We seek the charismatic church which activates energies for salvation (I Cor. 12). We seek the church which initiates actions for liberation and supports the work of other liberating groups without calculating self-interest. We seek a church which is the catalyst of God's saving work in the world, a church which is not merely the refuge of the saved but a community serving the world in the love of Christ."

All this means that the church must fulfil its mission by assuming the traditional roles attributed to its Lord, sent to serve as the Father sent Him. Firstly, the church must be prophetic in the name of God. This implies working at the level of individual conscience, helping in the process of reflection which leads men to assume responsibility for their own destiny. Inasmuch as the church calls men to a personal decision towards God, it brings them to the conviction that they are neither objects nor masses, but individuals who look to an integral human destiny which shows itself in the construction of the earthly city and is projected towards eternity itself.

188

This process of awareness-building permits it to shake the masses from their lethargy and helps them to see themselves as builders of their own destiny. The prophetic task includes also the denouncing of situations of open injustice. In particular, one should mention the courage shown by some Brazilian bishops in denouncing the fact that while the nation is enjoying accelerated economic growth, large sectors of the population are becoming daily more wretched. There is documentary evidence of such action in practically all the Latin American countries. The church cannot attack sin in the individual unless it attacks with equal force the sin which is present in social structures allied to the rich and powerful. The church can pronounce a word of encouragement, stimulation and pardon only when it has challenged face to face the oppression which it sees around it. The awakening of the church, its rejection of any alliance with the status quo, permits it to see clearly the injustices of the situation, and to call attention to the need for change. The prophetic task is also a word of encouragement and hope, inasmuch as it points out to men that in the time of the Lord there is a new day towards which they can work, inasmuch as it encourages those who are trying in some way to interpret the signs of the times and collaborate with the saving action of God.

The second task, the priestly one, concerns the internal life of the church but also has consequences for the whole revolutionary situation. When the church's liturgy becomes an intercessory prayer for the healing of national divisions, for an end to injustice, for the encouragement of hope, we find our true political vocation - not one which involves party divisions but one which takes up the politics of God, seeking humanization, the liberation of human beings.

Even in the task of evangelization, when the church calls men to awake to their belonging to God and to become followers of Jesus Christ, it performs a valuable service to the revolution because it is providing the basis of internal spiritual structures which will permit men to commit themselves to Jesus Christ in the world. If evangelization were the assurance of a passport to eternity, it would be no more than a form of escapism from contemporary reality and therefore a betrayal of the need for change. But in so far as the call to evangelization becomes an invitation to Christian discipleship in terms of following Christ in the midst of the Latin American community, we are again faced with an act of great political significance and of humanizing power. The priestly task of the church, the submission of man's everyday life to the final purposes of God, plays a central part in the Latin American situation. We have already mentioned the importance of finding the Moses who can interpret theologically the movements of the rural masses of Latin America towards the cities so that they can understand that their longing for abundant life corresponds to those same concerns which God holds so dear. Inasmuch as men can understand that their longing for liberty is a response to divine calls their commitment is deepened, their morale is raised and their action becomes more human.

The third task is the one which has traditionally been defined as the royal role of Christ, and which has a very deep meaning: Christ as servant. The son of God came not to be served but to serve: the church must do the same, providing mediation, reconciliation and sanity in situations of tension. But it is clear that the Lord Jesus Christ was able to fulfil the task of reconciling man with God only because he took upon himself the suffering of the vanquished and rejected. It is only through our identification with the dispossessed, the wretched and oppressed that we can think of acting as mediator between oppressor and oppressed. The church cannot of course do this from a neutral position, but only through a close identification with justice and with the poor - a clear command of its Lord. When the risen Christ appeared to the disciples, it was the sign of the wounded side, hands and feet which put an

189

end to their intellectual doubts. Only the marks of a servant, fighting to protect the oppressed, struggling against injustice as if it were a wound in its own flesh, will give the church the moral authority to speak words of reconciliation. The church can only call men to reconciliation in the knowledge of its own participation in guilt and the longing to right injustice.

It is in this framework too that the vocation of many Christian movements which demand nonviolent action to obtain social change must be understood. You all will have heard about the work done by Archbishop Helder Camara of Recife, who attempts to conscientize the masses of Recife in terms of the search for justice by nonviolent means. Like him many others in Latin America and in other parts of the world are trying to call Christians to suffer rather than make others suffer and to mobilize internal resources of personal conscience as a means of struggle. This strategy has had good results in some historical situations such as in India and in the US, and it could also have good results in our situation.

Nonviolence as a Christian stance needs no defence. But it has to be authenticated, because the world looks at the church through the prism of its history and finds it at fault. The church has not consistently been on the side of the suffering; it has accepted to serve as chaplain to the victors, who gained most from the situation of injustice. Only in so far as the church rejects injustice and takes upon itself the suffering which it causes will its preaching on nonviolence be credible. Naturally this will not happen through discussion about nonviolence but rather through practical service to the neighbour in rejection of injustice.

Basically the church must be a community which bears and nourishes hope. When we find ourselves in a situation like that of Latin America, in which we feel that we are in a tunnel with no visible end, we can only continue our march because we believe in Jesus Christ and have glimpsed the final purpose of God. Consequently, we must refuse to accept the tribulations of history, the frustrations and failures, both individual and collective, as the final word. Even when our human eyes cannot see the way out of the maze, we are sure that there is a way out and that the moment will come when we will leave our exile and set out for the promised land. God in history overcame the tragedy of the Cross and transformed it into the triumph of the resurrection; the church which knows this can remind men that they must not live in terms of yesterday but must look forward to tomorrow, that they cannot simply accept today, with all its brutality, but must be continually challenged by the new day which God is building. The church which is called to live with the suffering people in the revolutionary situation, participating in their suffering, can be the prophet of individual conscience, although sometimes it cannot do the same for the collective conscience. It can act as the priest who raises up the suffering of the people when they cannot lift themselves up exultant to proclaim liberation. It can act as the servant who is there to heal the wounds of the people and extinguish the flames of hatred. It can encourage work and hope for the coming of the new day in which its prophetic task can shake all the social structures. Its priestly life will be the celebration of freedom given to us by God and its servant life will be the bearer of hope.

(Lecture given in Basel, Switzerland, January 1974)

The Church in Latin America
and its Healing Ministry

In his life, Jesus personified divine concern for the whole person. For him, the only priority was love. Many of our theological discussions about the word or action, or even evangelization being more important than the manifestation of love and concern for justice, are artificial and completely lacking in biblical foundation. There have always been attempts to separate spiritual values from other facets of human life, but this does not respond to the divine message of Jesus Christ. In the Bible, people are called to the abundance of life in Jesus Christ and the full realization of peace includes all dimensions of health and wholeness.

This call has been heard, and answered. Throughout the history of the church, there has always been a ministry of healing. Prayer and anointing of the sick were the first expressions of this concern, but very soon, the Christian community focused particular attention on those people who, traditionally, were marginalized from the life of society. Looking at the history of the church we see how the monasteries were changed into resting places for pilgrims and refuges for the sick, little by little evolving to become our modern hospitals. Religious orders whose primary concern is helping the sick are part of the Christian heritage.

We start, then, with an a priori fundamental biblical principle: the healing ministry pertains to the whole being of the church. It is not something secondary that is done when there is time. Every time the church approaches a person or a community, it expresses its concern for the total well-being of that person. The Christian faith cannot be indifferent to the problems of sickness or, even more seriously, the problems of want, hunger and all that which degrades people and alienates them from the full manifestation of their God-given faculties.

The theological affirmation is clear. But we must ask how the Christian church in Latin America has, in fact, been concerned with health and wholeness. Can we affirm that the church has always been a protector of people's health? Or we must admit that, in some cases where the welfare of the people was seriously compromised, the church was actually to blame. History tells us that the church came to America with the Spanish and Portuguese conquistadores whose dual purpose was to conquer and to evangelize. Nevertheless, within a very few years, the number of indigenous peoples who came under the influence of the Europeans rapidly decreased. The

working conditions imposed by the Europeans, the introduction
of new contagious diseases and the disruption of traditional
life styles, reduced indigenous populations until some, such
as the Caribs, actually became extinct. It is significant
that Padre Bartolomé de las Casas took up the defense of the
Indians before the Spanish court and, in a last desperate
effort to save them from extinction, suggested the introduction of black slaves from Africa who were stronger and more
resistant to the hardships imposed by the Spanish invaders.
On the one hand, the church accompanying the conquest became
the accomplice in the elimination of huge Indian populations;
on the other hand, an individual priest tried desperately to
protect a suffering people and took such drastic measures
that he also must be critized!

Little by little, religious orders, who assumed responsibility
for Europeans as well as for the peasant populations, came to
Latin America. The dual concern for education and health is
evident in all the Latin American institutions, hospitals and
clinics as well as in large educational systems. Appreciat-
ing the charitable character of much of this work, we should
nevertheless note that it did not always benefit the common
people in the more remote zones of our countries. Hospitals
and clinics gradually became concentrated in urban centres
where they served the more privileged sectors of the population. But the peasant population and the urban poor were
nevertheless able to combine their faith with their search
for health: to the shrine of the Virgin or of the local
patron saint were directed their petitions, their prayers and
their search for health. A glance at the Sanctuary of the
Virgin del Luján, the Virgin of Guadalupe, or of Santa Rosa
of Lima shows very clearly the people's dependence on the
spiritual power of these shrines for their health, both
mental and physical. Even today, these shrines play an important role, both spiritually and psychologically, by providing a place of hope for the marginalized multitudes who
find no other alternative in their desperate search for
wholeness. Through the liturgical life of the Roman Catholic
Church the common people have appeal to a higher power in
their search for health. From a Protestant point of view, we
can express profound criticism of popular religion that expresses itself through worship at such shrines and, no doubt,
many of our Catholic friends would share a good measure of
this criticism. But we must take into account that this popular attitude responds to a social situation, a felt need. We
cannot oppose it at the theoretical level if we do not offer
practical alternatives which will enable the people to live
with and face the problems symbolized by the inscriptions
found at their shrines. We can also say that the Umbanda
spiritist cult practised in the slums of large Latin American
cities is another manifestation of popular religion. This
and similar groups do not belong to the Christian religion,
but they do symbolize the search for spiritual answers to
their health needs, which society has failed to meet. In
addition the Catholic Church has expressed its concern for

health through the various religious orders that have this specific ministry.

Protestantism came to Latin America in the second half of the 19th century with North American missionaries, English workers and railroads. They were later joined by Scandinavian missionaries. Protestantism came representing modernism. In Guatemala, a liberal government welcomed the Protestants as a challenge to Catholic predominance, and as an opportunity - for the elite - to adopt a modern, or North American, life style. Even Benito Juárez affirmed that Mexico needed Protestantism because it taught the Indians to read: the Bible. Literacy was - and unfortunately still is - a real problem in Mexico. Protestantism came, then, bringing medical services that had been developed in the United States, introducing the first nurses' training and building model hospitals. In almost all of our countries, today, we find clinics, hospitals and nursery schools that were built by Protestant missionaries. Thus, Protestantism also reflects in action the concept of the integrity of the whole person that we find in the pages of the Gospel: concern for health as an integral part of the concern for people, and for their final salvation.

We must recognize that some evangelical groups have not assumed their responsibility in this area, because they feel that they have a higher calling in a spiritual ministry. But they are in the minority. As the churches have grown numerically and begun to show signs of being truly autonomous, the concern for the wholeness of human life has increasingly expressed itself in institutional forms.

Protestantism was also a pioneer in developing organizations of mutual assistance in the health area; in Brazil, Argentina and Uruguay, for instance, an insurance system was developed whereby, for a monthly payment, a member was entitled to adequate medical care. The cooperative movement in Latin America introduced this same practice and, in many countries, this system has become one of the pillars of the health care system.

Soon Protestantism became locked into a hospital syndrome; the hospital became the supreme manifestation of concern for health. There was no understanding that, given the constantly rising cost of hospitalization, health services were limited to privileged groups who could afford to pay.

Various motives, alone or together, led to the building of hospitals. Some missions wished to avoid the proselytism of religious personnel in public hospitals who insisted on confession, attendance of mass, and even extreme unction. It was assumed that, in an evangelical hospital, love and altruistic service would combine with an element of proselytism, thus creating an evangelical environment in which patients and their families could enjoy the spiritual life of their own community. There was also a desire to ensure hospital care to congregation members. This aim was especially evident in cooperative medical insurance schemes. As Latin American society has become more open ecumenically, or more pluralistic in its religious ideology, and as proselytism has disappeared, this motive has remained: a desire to participate in service to the community.

The Protestant missionaries came into contact only with the higher levels of the proletariat, the lower levels of the middle class, and, through their network of private schools, with some of the privileged sectors of society. However, being an imported system, Protestantism was not able to reach the popular masses. Only the Pentecostal movement, which separated itself from traditional Protestantism and took on autonomous forms, has drawn in large sectors of the masses. In all its activities, Pentacostalism adopted a religious life style that responded to the reality and experience of these sectors. Thus, within Pentecostalism, prayer for the sick and faith healing are of fundamental importance. In fact, it is impossible to conceive of a Pentecostal religious service without a concern for the health of those who attend and of the whole community. Within Protestantism, Pentecostalism is a popular response to the problem of sickness as is the devotion of Catholics to their shrines. Since the poor are unable to find resources to solve the health problems in their communities, Pentacostalism is their "last tribunal", since it allows them to carry their burden of illness to God. Here again, we could criticize some of the exaggerated practices of the Pentecostal movement, and the propagandistic use that is sometimes made of faith healings. But we must not be distracted from the essential fact: these manifestations respond to a real need of the Latin American people, in ways which are comprehensible to them and represent a form of reciprocal help and support.

To summarize, we would say that all branches of Christianity in Latin America are conscious of the intimate relationship between providing health care and sharing the good news of God's love. In all of these branches, the concern for health has been expressed in the classic forms of individualized, institutionalized, curative care. The failings of this kind of care has given rise, within the heart of the church, to the phenomenon of popular religiosity, which is a protest against the helplessness of the masses, a consolation and, at the same time, a tool in the search for a solution outside that which society offers.

Reflecting on their situation, so-called progressive groups within the church have discovered the intimate connection between health and the economic and sociopolitical structures of our respective countries. They have begun to understand that malnutrition, sickness and low life expectancy are the result of structural problems. Absence of national planning which gives priority to this concern has led to a lack of

essential public health services. Anachronistic production
systems have caused unemployment and poverty. Appalling living conditions are a breeding ground for all kinds of ill-
nesses and epidemics that decimate our peoples. We could
continue elaborating how health, or rather ill health, now
constitutes the most important evidence in the case against
the whole framework of society in Latin America. In recognition of this, the churches are beginning to practise a
prophetic ministry of health in activities that denounce
certain social conditions and announce a "new day" of popular
participation in establishing new structures.

But we have gone ahead of ourselves. We will try to speak
systematically of the different forms of health ministry open
to the churches in Latin America, if their aim is to help
their respective communities to intelligently assume their
responsibility in the search for health and wholeness.

We should express our thanks to the Christian Medical
Commission of the World Council of Churches for its pioneer
work in awakening the conscience of the churches to the multi-
ple possibilities in this area. The Christian Medical Commission has also clarified the concepts of wholeness and community solidarity. Its conscientization work has had reper-
cussions even outside of ecclesiastical circles.

A small book, published by the Christian Medical Commission
in English, French and Spanish, Community Health and the
Church, is worthy of our attention. In this book we read:

> "Because of the many different factors that influence
> man's health and life in an interdependent and inte-
> grated way, both as an individual and in community, a
> community health programme should also be an integrated
> effort directed towards this whole life situation.
> Factors related to food, housing, work, education and
> general living conditions are therefore important, as
> well as everything that helps man with regard to his
> identity and dignity, and give room for initiatives
> related to human development, individually and in
> community."

and

> "A concept of health which is merely that of a restored
> balance, a static 'wholeness', has no answer to the
> problem of human guilt or death nor to the anxiety and
> the threat of meaninglessness which are the projection
> upon human life of the shadow of death. Health in the
> Christian understanding is a continuous and victorious
> encounter with the powers that deny the existence and
> goodness of God..(1) It is the kind of life which has

---

(1) This does not exclude germ and molecular theories
of disease.

overcome death and the anxiety which is the shadow of
death. Whether in the desperate squalor of overpopu-
lated and underdeveloped areas or in the spiritual
wasteland of affluent societies, it is a sign of God's
victory and a summons to His service.(2)

On the one hand, while accepting the achievements of contemporary medicine in understanding the chemical and biological
causes of illness, these definitions recognize the role of
various social, political, economic and cultural factors.
And it is God Himself, the Creator, who fights to carry
creation to perfection. People, particularly Christians,
are called to participate in the creative actions of God
against death, disability or oppression. Here, the physico-
psycho-social dimensions of humanity are taken into consideration.

* * * * * *

Recognizing that we, as Christians, should commit ourselves
at various different levels, let us consider in pastoral
terms how our affirmation that health is the will of God can
lead to participation in the struggle against illness.

In no sense do we want to establish a list of obligations to
be imposed on individual churches represented at this meeting.
We are not laying down rules; we are simply describing a
reality which corresponds to our faith. Jesus Christ practised healing; therefore, the proclamation of His presence must
be a proclamation of health. The concern for health is not
something that is added to the life of the church; it is a
normal manifestation of its total ministry. With this understanding, we can begin to look at the different levels at
which this ministry can be expressed:

I We have said that the popular masses in Latin America have
   found help in their struggle for health in their shrines
   and in Pentecostal worship. This reminds us of a permanent
   Christian value: intercessory prayer, based on our profound
   conviction that prayer helps to restore the sick. It is
   possible to describe the psychological mechanisms that
   allow the organism to recover from illness, but we choose
   instead to affirm our faith in the work of the Holy Spirit
   in each individual, in response to prayer. Neither, however, can intercessory prayer be set in opposition to
   other instruments through which God also acts to heal the
   human being. We cannot exempt ourselves from the responsibility of using the resources of medical science or from
   political participation simply because we are praying for
   the sick! On the contrary, prayer should reinforce our

_____

(2) "The Healing Church", World Council of Churches, 1965,p.35

efforts to obtain the resources that work against illness.
Intercessory prayer creates a spiritual atmosphere that
supports health workers. Prayer reminds us not only that
we have profound spiritual resources within ourselves for
the struggle against today's problems, but also that, in
the final analysis, this struggle does not end even with
death itself.

The churches' liturgy should naturally incorporate the concern for health so that those who participate are motivated
to share their health, their time, and their efforts with
those whose effectiveness is temporarily or permanently
limited. Prayer invites us to unite our forces with those
of God and, with that help to struggle against the presence
of illness.

II   The second dimension of the church's healing ministry is in
     the life of the local church. Christians are called to
     gather in congregations where the majority of people know
     each other by name. Here, a dimension of reciprocal pro-
     tection exists. It provides a sense of security and a
     spirit of solidarity to its members. The early Christian
     church's experience of sharing all things, though it may
     not be found in its pure form in our present-day congrega-
     tions, is present symbolically in sacramental acts, and
     practically in reciprocal visitation, in the consoling
     embrace, in supporting one another. In activities such as
     caring for children, women's societies and Bible study
     groups, small congregations provide an environment of funda-
     mental mutual support in the area of psychic health that is
     an important component in integral health. At the same
     time, mutual understanding can help even in situations of
     physical need. The work of the Chilean churches at the
     present time, as they provide free lunches to all the con-
     gregation, expresses this potential for mutual support. To
     belong to a community that cares, that is concerned and that
     shows its solidarity, is tremendously important, especially
     in large cities because of the growing anonymity of life
     styles there. It is also, no doubt, vital in small towns
     where intimate relationships among members of the congrega-
     tion allow even greater mutual help and solidarity.

III The third level of the church's healing ministry is in the
     vocations that it awakens among its members. It is very
     important that those who work professionally to care for
     their neighbours' health have a clear motivation, inspired
     by love. Christians cannot pretend to have a monopoly of
     this virtue, nor do they always manifest it. But, on the
     basis of the experience of the love of God in Christ for
     all people, many feel motivated to take up service activi-
     ties, in particular those related to health. Historically
     there has been an intimate relation between religious and
     health vocations. Medicine is spoken of as an "apostolate"
     or a "ministry". Dedication and altruism, sustained by a

197

profound inner vision, flow naturally from the Gospel of Jesus Christ. The church should remind its youth of the possibility of social service, humanitarian and health vocations which should be undertaken in a spirit of self-denial and dedication to one's neighbour. It is equally important that the church should help those who take up these vocations in a spirit of love to discover the spirit of justice. It is not enough to manifest humanity, compassion and solidarity. We must also insist that medical services serve primarily the most needy. There is also a labour of justice and of reparation to be accomplished to ensure that the marginalized strata of our society has access to the means of health. Personal vocation, therefore, is not simply a call to service; it is also a call to a profound conscience for justice.

IV Fourthly, the church has always, still does, and always will fulfill a supporting role in providing those services that the community itself is still not capable of offering. In those places where there are no schools of nursing or medical services the churches - as organized communities with access to their own and international resources - may well offer, temporarily, those services that the community needs and cannot provide. It is necessary to take care that, in playing such a supportive role, the church does not provide an easy escape from its responsibility to the State and the other sectors of the community. The church should and can offer temporary solutions until society as a whole faces the problems of health. Thus, the hospital that was needed yesterday may not be justified tomorrow, and the clinic that we thought was unnecessary yesterday becomes necessary today when it becomes evident that public health services have deteriorated. A creative imagination is required to discern between what is appropriate in terms of what is lacking in the community, and what is competing with parallel services provided by other sectors of our community.

V The fifth aspect of the healing ministry is the participation of the church and her members in the theological discussion of health care, and in setting priorities in this area for itself and society. The constantly rising cost of medical care makes governments limit budgets and establish priorities in medical services. Here, the church should represent the voiceless, the needy and the marginalized, claiming health care for these groups even if its provision limits the standards of medical perfection which can be offered to the privileged minority.

A dialogue being carried on over the last few years within the World Health Organization, in which the Christian Medical Commission has actively participated, can offer some interesting insights on the topic of how we - the church - can participate in this idealogical dialogue.

198

At both government and international levels there is a
growing consciousness of the health priorities of the poor.
It is imperative that theoretical principles are translated
into practical guidelines to be transformed into effective
action. In this ideological dialogue, in this work of per-
suasion, the churches have an important function to fulfill,
especially in Latin America, where they still have considerable influence.

VI Finally, Christians are obliged to face the problem of
health in terms of their prophetic responsibility toward
society. Today, the churches of Latin America have taken
up the banner of human rights. They have organized to protect the exploited and have raised their voices to demand
the respect of the law for the fundamental human rights of
all the inhabitants of our countries. The right to health
constitutes an essential and central dogma that must be
presented to the public authorities. In her effort to con-
cientize the church can help to understand the fundamental
problems of society and stimulate people to participate in
the search for their own solutions. These imperatives oblige us to enter into the difficult area of politics. The
church, because she is the gathered community, is closely
related to politics since wherever the community gathers, a
factor of social concientization and social power is present.
We deceive ourselves if we want to flee from our political
responsibilities. Of course, it is not for the church to
dictate health care policies and priorities to the community.
The church must, however, call peoples' attention to the
intimate relationship between production, distribution of
wealth, popular participation, social organization, the
practicability of an effective democracy and the general
health condition of our communities.

Our health ministry is part of our total ministry, the proclamation of God's love for all peoples, the call to all
people to assume a protagonist's role in the transformation
of living conditions. Our ministry in Latin America re-
quires an abundance of comprehension of God's wishes and
promises, and the courage to proclaim them through our life
style, with our word or in our silence. Our ministry is to
continually seek ways in which our community can move
toward that health which is full humanization in Jesus
Christ.

(Lecture given at the WCC Christian Medical Commission's
Central American Regional Conference on the Churches' Role
in Health and Wholeness, Omoa, Honduras, March 1979)

SOUTH AMERICAN INDIANS

THE BARBADOS DISCUSSION

This issue of the IRM is dedicated to comments on and
articles about the controversial Declaration of Barbados
on the situation of the Indian in South America. In
January 1971, the World Council of Churches' Programme
to Combat Racism, under the auspices of the Ethnological
Institute of the University of Bern, brought together
twenty persons, most of whom were anthropologists, at the
University of the West Indies, Barbados, to study the
Indian problem in Latin America. Their declaration
appears as part of a large volume containing the prepara-
tory studies presented at the Barbados meeting which can
be ordered from the Publications Department of the World
Council of Churches.

We recognize that in many segments of the world Christian
community the Barbados Declaration as a whole, which is
inevitably unjust when applied to particular situations,
has been roundly criticized, especially where it affirms
that the greatest service which the churches can render
is to terminate all missionary activity!

Bearing all this in mind, let us consider the following:

I.   Faced with a critical judgement, we are called by Scripture not to a defensive attitude, but to conversion, self-criticism and reciprocal correction. In the Old Testament, even the armed invasions of other peoples were interpreted as the expression of God's judgement. We would lose a magnificent opportunity to study critically our missionary enterprise if we were to reject the Declaration of Barbados, protecting ourselves by hiding behind the injustice of the accusations of which it may be guilty, or the fact that it was produced without participation of representatives of Christian mission. Here we have a judgement made by a group of scientists on the Indian situation and on our missionary work. We should humbly review our basic convictions and the validity of our actions in order to learn, to correct and to reform our ways. Defensive attitudes are pharisaical. If, like the Publican we can say, 'Have pity on me, a poor sinner', we may find light and wisdom in our thinking together.

II.   The scientists who met in Barbados came to the conclusion that it was necessary to put an end to all missionary activity; they were convinced that this would be best for the Indian peoples and was necessary for the preservation of the moral integrity of the churches themselves. We are grateful that the meeting was not concerned solely with the defense of the Indian, but also with the Church's moral integrity. But from a Christian perspective, putting an end to mission is an impossibility. Mission is not an option for Christians, but their whole *raison d'être*. Church and mission ought to be almost synonymous. Doctrinally, mission resides in the very essence of the triune God who has created beings capable of entering into communion with him. Biblical mandates concerning the missionary responsibility of Christians are well known. There are two missionary actions in the world: one centripetal — the nations of the earth will come and sit down at the feast of the Lord; the other centrifugal — the messengers of the Lord will go to the ends of the earth, teaching in the name of Christ.

But if mission cannot cease, missionary activity as we know it can, and perhaps should, change. This is not to deny the fact that God reaches out to man, nor is it to deny the serving and proclaiming vocation belonging to a people which consciously calls itself Christian. It is a matter rather of questioning whether or not the forms which have historically developed and have been preserved in our missionary enterprise are in accordance with the essential and genuine Christian mission which wells up out of the being of God and seeks the redemption of all men. We must examine our missionary practices in the light of the understanding which contemporary theologians have given us of the liberating and redeeming mission of the God made known to us through Jesus Christ. If our mission contributes to the alienation of man, to his alienation from his own culture, to his reduction to a state of submission, even though conceptually and doctrinally it may have a Christian content, it is existentially, in fact, denying its 'missionary' character.

III. It is undeniable that there is an evangelistic mandate to make known to men the message of God revealed in Jesus Christ. But if the incarnation tells us anything of the Christian faith, it is that the Gospel cannot be reduced to words, to verbal expressions, to doctrinal formulas, but that it is the reality of a freedom given by God to men and the experience of the life of love which binds them in community. This reality constitutes the fundamental requirement for the transmitting and sharing of the Gospel in conceptual categories.

By participating in the liberating mission of God and thus making the fate of all men his own, the Christian makes believable his verbal explanation of the Gospel. To be at the disposal of others, to be open to all men, to go about learning from others in humility, to participate with one's neighbour in his struggle for fulfillment, battling to eliminate those factors of dependence which exclude the possibility of his becoming himself, in these human situations the Christian incarnates the Christian Gospel of universal love, of brotherhood among men, and of a God in Christ who gave his life for the redemption of all. We cannot therefore ask for the elimination of catechetical activity, but we should ask that the context of love and of total concern should be provided in such a way that the contents of Christian teaching can be understood and believed. On this we must be clear : our work of assistance to and protection of the Indian is useful, and often important. But if our Christian presence ends there, or becomes petrified there, it is no longer Christian, but alienating. If we dare not raise our voices or act with the Indian in his struggle for liberation, even though we take risks in the jungle, we will be confessing our cowardliness. The true risks are encountered in the struggle against institutionalized oppression, the worst of whose effects are manifest in relation to the Indian communities.

IV. God gives his gifts, charisma, to men and nations. We must go to the encounter with our brother looking for the particular gifts that God has given him. We must go to the encounter with the Indian populations eager to see in them the manifestations of the divine wisdom — blemished, yes, by the presence of human sin, just as our own acts, supposedly Christian, are also blemished. But unless we approach them confident in the hope that God has left no people without his witness, we will not find in ourselves that humble attitude of spirit that is necessary if we would learn from others.

The Declaration of Barbados ends with a sentence which, unfortunately, is not developed further. 'The Indian peoples, in spite of their small numerical size, clearly present alternative ways to the traditional well-trodden paths of national society'. We take as given, without discussion, the economic individualism of the system which prevails in our countries. Perhaps we ought to examine the wisdom of our own system in the light of Indian experience in communal living. We assume too readily the values of a materialist culture which finds in possession of objects its sense of security, only to discover that the more it has the more it needs, in a vicious circle of materialism. The poverty of the Indian civilizations and their communal way of meeting it can offer useful insights into possible solutions for our own problems. Traditional forms of social organization could have much to teach our societies, torn by class division, displaying enormous opulence and desperate misery. A humble approach and the recognition of talents, not as natural phenomena, but as the blessings of God capable of enriching the entire human community, are spiritual essentials for the Christian.*

---

* The Bangkok Conference on Salvation Today looked at the subject of racial and cultural identity as gifts of God and made the following helpful statements ;

   The problem of personal identity is closely related to the problem of cultural identity. 'Culture shapes the human voice that answers the voice of Christ'. Many Christians who have received the Gospel through Western agents ask the question : 'Is it really I who answers Christ ? Is it not another person instead of me ?' This points to the problem of so-called missionary alienation. Too often, in the history of Western

V. 'Let him who is without sin cast the first stone'. When we come to an Indian village we notice immediately aspects of a style of life which we would call 'uncivilized'. We need not idealize the situation; we know that many tribes are in a period of involution, having previously enjoyed a much more advanced stage of cultural development. But even in those areas where cultural values, family cohesion and social development remain, we will without doubt find signs of human sin in the exploitation of men by other men. As Christians we recognize that this ultimate alienation of man in the face of God is not eliminated simply by a change of the structures of dependence and oppression. If we wish to come to these tribes at the level of human solidarity, we must come carrying a consciousness of the sin of the white race. We cannot ignore our history of hate, of oppression, of fratricidal warfare and pharisaically judge the living conditions of our brother. In the solidarity of the sin of all humanity we take refuge with him in the pardon which God's grace offers us. We must cooperate with him in every way possible to develop the implicit values in his culture in such a way that any limitations it might have may be overcome from within. We must do for him now that which it is not yet possible for him to do for himself: denounce his situation and demand legislation to provide the legal and economic framework within which the fulness of the Indian's human value can flourish.

VI. God in Christ offers us a salvation which places us face to face with the question of construction of our own destiny: 'Let my people go'. The goal of mission is the enablement of men to build in community with others, their own social and personal destiny. The love of those who come to the Indian communities ought to show itself in collaborating with the Indian's own organizations, enabling them to struggle to fulfill their own personal and communal destiny. Ultimately,

---

missions, the culture of those who received the Gospel was either ignored or condemned. At best, it was studied as a subject of missiology. However, the problem is : how can we ourselves be fully responsible when receiving Salvation from Christ ? How can we responsibly answer the voice of Christ instead of copying foreign models of conversion — imposed, not truly accepted ?

We refuse merely to be raw materials used by other people to achieve their own salvation.

The one faith must be made to be at home in every context and yet it can never be completely identical with it. Therefore there will be a rich diversity.

Racial and cultural identity are divine gifts and human achievements to be taken up into Christian identity which is to be conformed to the image of Him.

204

no one can save another ; only Jesus Christ can be the saviour of all men and he, more than anyone, respects the human condition, calling men to make a choice for freedom, inviting them to build the future. Our missionary presence among the Indian groups of Latin America must therefore be critically examined in the light of some basic questions : Is the leadership of our work in Indian hands ? Are we seeing to it that they develop their ability to make decisions, even to the point where they can refuse our missionary efforts ? Are we at their side as equals in order to give and receive, or the opposite ? Do we have a paternalistic attitude which keeps them at a distance and, inevitably, in submission ? Problems such as commercial relations between the missions and the Indians, sentimental relationships between their children and ours, must be analyzed in the light of another, even more fundamental question : Do we, both Indians and non-Indians, know ourselves to be free men through the saving will of God, called together to be participants in the struggle for freedom of the peoples of Latin America ?

VII. We must recognize that in the mission to the Indians there is a call, a personal vocation, that is fundamental. The Declaration of Barbados refers to missionary activity in a somewhat pejorative tone when it says : 'it has a spurious quality since the missionaries seek only some form of personal salvation, material or spiritual'. While we can agree with the denunciation of those who manipulate the Indian for personal ends or who seek honour, power, or recognition in their home countries, we must say that it is unjust not to recognize the genuine vocational motivation which inspires many of those who have adopted the fate of the Latin American Indian as their own.

The Barbados report is very realistic when it associates, finally, the liberation of the Indian with the liberation of the nation and the Latin American continent. There is only one human movement towards full humanity, towards liberation, towards redemption. The movement for Indian liberation in the jungle is a part of the movement across the continent for the liberation of the proletariat of the urban areas who seek better living conditions, a greater degree of personal participation in society and more human dignity. The question looked at in this broad fashion might seem to imply that he who understands this fact wastes his time going to the jungle and dedicating his energy to the dignifying of the Indian and the building of his future. There are more urgent tasks to be accomplished in the cities, in the metropolises where the major decisions are made, affecting the Indian as well as the rest of the population. But if there are people capable of militancy in other areas who make theirs the fate of the Indian and put themselves physically at his side and spiritually identify with him, it is in response to a direct call interpreted as coming from God, and which therefore cannot be disobeyed. This call ought to be tested, of course — given the inevitable ambiguities in the process of human decision-making — in dialogue with the Christian community, the secular community and in the light of the fundamental values of God's mission. The Declaration of Barbados is an excellent warning to us to avoid the repetion of yesterday's mistakes and to discover imaginative new forms of Christian presence and mission for the carrying out the mission of God which seeks man's liberation.

No document is absolute : they are all tools. If the Declaration of Barbados is useful in awakening the conscience of Christians in Latin America to the situation of their Indian brothers, if it obliges us to reconsider our own missionary labours, if it forces us to rethink our convictions, then it has had a positive effect and we ought to be grateful for it. Whether the group which met in Barbados was right or not, the fundamental question is : What are we to do, in the fulfillment of our Christian obedience, to share the glorious liberty given to God's children with all our brothers in Latin America, and in particular with these, the most disinherited.

We must look ahead with hope and work toward the dawn of that day in which the fullness of Indian culture will receive the fullness of the Gospel in such a way that in cultural diversity there might be found new forms of praise to the Lord of all men. We must hope that that day will soon come in which the forms of service and Christian witness characteristic of our Indian brother can inspire and correct the superficial and comfortable Christianity of the Latin American cities.

(International Review of Mission, July 1973)

A CALL TO ACTION

I think all of us will agree that, in God's good time, the hour of
liberation has sounded for Latin America; the siesta is over.
Popular awareness is vibrant with the conviction that the present
situation can go on no longer; that it can change, ought to change,
and will be changed. We will all agree that the Christian community, bearer of God's promise for humanity, herald of his redeeming will, liberator, is called upon to play a role in the
liberation epic of Latin America.

The importance of that role, compared with the role that other
ideological, political, cultural and professional elements may play,
is not great at this moment. What is important for us is that the
church, the ecclesial community, both by its primary vocation of
proclaiming a gospel of freedom and by its key social position as
an institution in touch with the masses, has a special responsibility that no one else can fulfill. If the church failed to fulfill that responsibility, it would automatically become a defender
of the status quo, an enemy of the liberation of the Latin American
people.

I want to insert into my talk a certain personal tone. I will try
to answer the question: "What are we to do?" from the particular
angle of the profession to which I have dedicated myself, because
I believe that all of us who engage in this conference are in a
certain way performing a sacerdotal and pastoral task, a service
through the church community.

What does it mean for us as church people to say that we live the
joy of liberation? What does it mean for us to accept God's
invitation to the struggle for liberation in Latin America?

Certainly there can be differences in the ways we act. There ought
to be differences, an internal dialogue in the community of faith
concerning the responsible ways of living up to the command to
proclaim and to further that liberation. But where there is not
the slightest difference is in the recognition that the church's
vocation is essentially bound up with this struggle. To adopt an
attitude of neutrality is to put your money on yesterday, to
combat the very purposes of God. Because the internal differences
are sufficiently serious to threaten more than once, to paralyze
the action.

However, on the basis of the statements made and shared in our
meeting, I, as an ecclesiastic, understand my task -- our task --
as follows:

1. A call to responsible disciplehood. We Protestants in Latin
   America are famous for our evangelizing zeal or, if you prefer,
our proselytizing zeal. We are forever calling on people to be

converted, to repent, to see themselves as God sees them.
Basically, this is the church's proper and permanent task: to
stir people to a metanoia, to discipleship. In connection with
our struggle for liberation, stirring people to an acceptance
of Jesus Christ, to discipleship, means calling on them to join
the ranks of those who struggle to liberate human beings from
all their limitations, from all their enslavement. When our
evangelical preaching is synonymous with recruiting for a
liberating militancy, we are living the gospel as it ought to be
lived in the daily context of Latin America. If our preaching
convinces men and women, either through the life of the church or
through the proclaimed word, that a decision for Christ is a
decision for one's neighbour, that a decision for one's neighbour
is a decision for a lifestyle that affirms and defends our
essential liberty, we are summoning people to a militancy, a life-
style that will complicate their existence, but that will make them
workers for our continent's tomorrow.

The churches should provide to the liberation process of Latin
America men and women with an awareness of the importance that
their social militancy has for their essential relationship to God.
Only to the extent that we combine repentance with a new awareness,
discipleship with the following of Christ in the community, converting people to the Christian faith while recruiting them for
the work of redemption and liberation, shall we be truly preaching
the gospel and doing something useful in Latin America; something
that the mountain pastor can do just as well as the most sophisticated preacher in the capital city.

2. The Christian community in Latin America traditionally serves
    to link an individual's peak occasions, the rhythm of his/her
natural life, with the promises and demands of faith. Such
occasions -- birth, marriage, sickness, death, popular feasts,
even the routine of Sunday worship -- become moments through which
we try somehow to mesh people's life with God's promises and
demands. Well then, we must re-think our weekly liturgy and pastoral
work in the light of the overriding importance of liberating action
and ask ourselves how it can concentrate all the people's
activities on the liberating, emancipating effort.

Let me explain myself. We preachers often make long speeches
whipping people up to revolution, but speeches that make sense
only to small minorities who understand us, and who have the
strength and intelligence to sign up for a real militancy. But
our churches are filled with immense masses of housewives, old
men and children who cannot see any connection between their
particular problems and the emancipation of a community, its
liberation from structures of oppression. Inasmuch as the liturgy
is a way to get the whole community praying for the problems and
hopes of the people, it can make the common man and woman feel involved, a participant, even a militant, for the cause of liberation.
To the extent that we can link the birth of a baby to the need for
transforming the community so that it will be a better place for
the baby to grow up in, we will be linking the joy of its parents

to the adventure of the militancy that is expected of them. Only to the extent that when blessing a home we demonstrate that it is not just a dream house for two people but a multiplication of forces, a start on a life of mutual support in the cause of a greater and more effective militancy for one's neighbour, will we be truly sanctifying the institution of marriage. The same in our assistance to old people, to the sick, trying to show that every facet of life can be connected with a liberating action, and that no one, however humble, can say that he or she has no part to play in the adventure that awaits us in Latin America.

We preachers and church leaders are tempted to add more and more new activities to the church, tranquilizing our consciences because that way there are departments to take care of every social problem, instead of linking the entire life of the Christian community to the need for humanizing change in our communities.

3. Whether we like it or not, the Christian church in Latin
   America is an institution, and a powerful one. It is probably the one social institution that has contact with all levels of society, including the common people. It is true that secularism has come to Latin America, too, though perhaps not with the same intensity as in other continents. The common person still looks with respect at his or her bishop and priest. What happens in the life of the church is important. What emerges from the church gets headlines in the press and becomes a matter of gossip. But more, too. The church has its own channels of communication that enable it to spread information rapidly among the people. It is perhaps the only institution that can laugh at the limitations that the mass media put on the renewing ideas in Latin America. In this sense, the church as an institution has to become an effective channel of liberation. Often our impatience with the institution makes us forget its potential and look for other allies. That might seem an easy alternative, but let us not forget that the institution exists, it is a resource, a potential. And even if some quarters in the church must be avoided -- and maybe even eliminated -- there are still a number of possibilities for a constructive usage of the church's institutional channels.

What would happen if we stood up seriously to our educational task through the enormous network of private religious schools that exist in Latin America? What would happen if we really utilized the enormous communication outlets represented by the masses and religious services in Latin America to transmit information that does not reach the common person about what is going on in his or her own country, or beyond the national frontiers, but that is pertinent to forming his or her independent judgement on the situation?

We are aware that there is a serious ecclesial debate over the how and the how much of institutional participation in the social process. But we have to realize that the church's resources are sociologically potent for its fulfilment of a liberating mission and that, theologically, the ecclesiastical institutions ought to be judged precisely as instruments: to what extent do they stand at the service of God's purposes, which we define today as liberating purposes? By the very fact of the church's existence as a social institution and by its position in key areas of social life, it has a decisive importance and a paramount role to play.

In this sense, too, the incipient ecumenism in Latin America ought to be judged on whether or not it moves the church in the direction of liberation. Ecumenism understood as a body of abstract ecclesial relations, without any concrete theological content, can simply be a buttress of existing institutions, and consequently an enemy of the renewal that Latin America needs. But to the extent that ecumenical dialogue reflects the yearnings of the Latin American people, ecumenical activity will multiply the effectiveness of each single ecclesial organization, and in that sense will help us to do our job more responsibly.

4. People look to us for prophetic judgement and for inspiration.
    Prophecy can be most dramatic when it is an act -- like the prophet carrying the yoke, or the Jesuits closing their great Colegio Patria in Mexico City; gestures like that ought to be imitated throughout Latin America. As the common people see the church renouncing its associations with the status quo, they will understand better than from long speeches what it means to cut loose from yesterday and cast in one's lot with tomorrow. There comes a time, too, when the church has to speak up with its opinions, judging the prevailing situations. Obviously, the prophecy that carries most weight is the one that is most concrete. To the extent that the church dares put its head on the block by saying what it thinks of day-to-day events that stifle human initiative, to that extent it will be useful.

Sometimes we who participate in conferences end up tiring our-selves in the profusion of documents and we tend to minimize their value. Yet all of us -- those who go back to country parishes and those who return to the big national shrines -- contribute to forming an ethos, on the basis of which fundamental decisions will be taken. We bring home motivations to many individuals who may be wavering as they make conscience decisions.

Among its prophetic judgements, the church has another one: to demythologize words and situations. The church is free to approach highly controversial ideological topics with an independence that other sectors of society normally do not enjoy, so that it can dispel many semantic-social taboos along the militants' path toward free-dom. An inspirational effort is also needed: depicting the tomorrow that God promises us, in such vivid colours that humanity will be entranced by that ideal and be ready to fight for it. Here is an extramural task for Latin American theologians: to begin a dialogue with the secular forces that are exercised over the shape that the future will take, to describe, out of the wealth of biblical tradition, the basic living conditions that we believe will assure genuine freedom for humanity.

Even at the risk of being misunderstood, let me say that the
church must take a prophetic and inspirational stand regarding
groups protesting the status quo that appear as the entering
edge of freedom in Latin America. The hairline difference between
criticism of them and encouragement is certainly very difficult
to observe, and yet it is indispensable for the good of those
very groups and for the effectiveness of their service to the
cause of freedom in Latin America: let no realistic word from the
church be held back should evidence appear that they are veering
from the proper direction and therefore perhaps forsaking the
very purposes they proclaim.

5. The Christian community, we Christians who make it up, must
   not lose sight, when speaking about liberation, of the full
meaning of that word and the entire humanizing dimension it implies.
We are not merely seeking liberation from unjust politico-social
structures -- though we certainly want that -- but the honesty of
our struggle to eliminate those structures and to implant better
social norms will be to some extent guaranteed by the way we
treat our neighbour, the concrete individual we deal with in
daily life.

If woman continues to be a sexual plaything, we can hardly prate
about a humanizing and revolutionary vocation. If our personal
dealings do not evince respect for the neighbour next door, we
can hardly boast of a struggle for humanization. This may sound
very pietistic, very churchy, and even paralyzing in the sense
that it would seem to regret that we are not angels, we who embark
on revolutionary work. Neither more nor less. In the midst of all
human situations, biblical realism makes us recognize that human
sin will always be present. That same realism is what keeps us from
bandying about high-sounding revolutionary slogans without previously displaying a personal and concrete love of our immediate
neighbour. This has a basic importance, not only in our life of
personal dealings with the child, the woman, the old man, but also
fundamentally in the life of the ecclesiastical institution. How
much of our church activity continues to be infrahuman, and fails
to recognize the reality of that freedom with which Christ made us
free? As we lay down norms of conduct for individual consciences,
we will be denying Christian freedom. As fear of institutional
authority paralyzes our action, we will show the bankruptcy of
our vaunted liberation. The freedom we want for ourselves and for
our peoples ought to be a reality already in all those institutional
and interpersonal areas where we are quite able, even now, to over-
ride the structural barriers that threaten to dehumanize us. And
it will be the clash of our personal actions with the hypocrisy
of those barriers that will trigger the most varied forms of
action to eliminate them. But we load the enemy's guns when there
is a contrast in equations between our alleged thirst for the
redemption and liberation of our neighbour and our daily treatment
of him or her as a mere object.

6. The church has to accecpt the risks that go with an ambiguous
   and fluid situation. As a consequence, it cannot be hoped that

211

the various manifestations of Christian obedience will always
hew closely to the traditional canons of behaviour, and it must
recognize some freedom for experimental ways of being a church
and of living as Christians. At the same time, the groups and
communities that, in the name of their dedication, take postures
radically different from the traditional ones, must recognize as
logical that their pioneering, daring character may not be
easily accepted, defended and legitimated by the ecclesial
authority.

We have to live with risk and faith these moments that are
apparently chaotic but rich in creativity. To the extent that the
ecclesial authority dares to believe that "if it be of God, it
will prevail", and looks with hopeful expectation at the
revolutionary movements within the Christian community and the
varying styles of commitment to liberation, it will be constructive, even for the correction of what might seem excesses in the
new ecclesial forms. We will have to learn to live with tension,
in dialogue, in protest, in an internal struggle, but with a
providential faith that God is bringing good even out of our
divisions. Indeed, the internal squabbling in the church not only
catches public attention but also enables a number of fundamental
breakthroughs to achieve a certain popularity. The worst that
could happen to the Christian liberating protest movements is
that ecclesial authority might either bless them or ignore them.
The very situation of tension has to be seen as a creative one.

Then, too, the very flexibility of the situation obliges the
church to take on ministries for which it is neither prepared nor
even designed. For example, if we are talking seriously about
liberation, we will realize that political instruments are needed.
The Latin American church is unlikely to repeat the error of
Christendom, although this time it would more probably be a
Christendom of the centre or left, but somehow Christians will
have to figure out how to bring forth political forces that can
present real options of power to the political parties in each
country. Or, recognizing how universally the communication media,
which form or deform the public opinion, are tightly controlled,
a church that talks about liberation cannot avoid wondering how
to break that deforming monopoly. And what about the ministry to
subversive groups? The main-line church can hardly take on those
tasks, but experimental groups willing to grapple with this or
that particular problem could arise, helping to carry out the
vocation of the whole people of God.

I would like, too, to discuss what seems to me a basic presupposition of our conference, which I see as delicate -- and
dangerous. It may be that I am committing an enormous blunder,
since I have had to prepare these notes without having read the
position papers, much less heard the ensuing discussions. Possibly,
then, I am going to criticize what is only a suspicion of mine. I
would feel very happy if all I am going to say were completely
inapplicable because our discussions had settled the issue. I am
referring to the apparent presumption that the situation of mar-

ginalization and exclusion from power occurred practically
identically for all people of both Americas, North and South.

It is an evident fact that the developed, or consumer, society
tends to reify -- to thing-ify -- and massify people. And this
challenges the Christian conscience to come up with imaginative
ways to preclude such a mercantile utilization of people. But
it is not true that this abuse is qualitatively or quantitatively
comparable to the deprivation and marginalization, with their
attendant hunger, ignorance and poverty, that are found in
Latin America.

While I can understand that one may see parallels between the
plight of the poor in the United States and that of the under-
developed communities in the third world, I find it hard to grant
that there is a parallel between the plight of the sophisticated
strata of this latter society and the human condition in under-
developed countries. When all are rich, all are poor. If we are
all of us poor, helpless, pitiable individuals, the inevitable
result is a paralysis in action. We have to set up a list of
priorities among the enemies to be combated and the jobs to be
done.

It seems to me that on the world-wide scale the number one
priority is to combat the underdevelopment -- in the sense of
oppression, exploitation and deprivation of the minimum
conditions of a decent life -- that affects the great masses of
the third world. This is all the more urgent, since by his or
her vocation, every genuine Christian and real revolutionary
ought to utilize the struggle for the suppression of the existing
poverty to raise himself or herself to a nobler level of humanity.
But let us be careful that when we talk loftily of human participation we are not reflecting the aspirations of the social class
that we belong to and fail to understand the common person for
whom participation means access to living and working conditions
that provide him or her with at least the bare minimum.

There is a struggle for liberation in every country that will go
on till the end of the world. But there is another, more urgent,
more immediate struggle to liberate the crushed peoples of the
third world that does not allow delay.

I realize that the alliance between those who are struggling for
a cultural revolution in the developed countries and those of us
who are struggling for liberation in the underdeveloped countries
has some positive elements, effective in action and probably enriching. But at the same time I am afraid that it also errs by
equating very different situations, likening distinct vocations
and eliminating priorities. It would lead us into an intellectual
error, misreading the people's aspirations, who have a series of
priorities quite different from those that we are tempted to
establish.

I believe that then we have to say: "We deplore, dear North
American friends, the impotence and marginalization that you say

213

you are suffering. But we have a more pressing task, and to the
extent that you realize the urgency of this other task you will
begin to exercise the little power that you think you have, and
you may well see more results than you had dreamed of."

A second assumption that seems to me to preside over our
conference I consider equally dangerous. I recognize that this
assumption is not clearly formulated. I have the idea that in
view of the importance of the enemies we face, when we understand
the Pauline statement that our battle is "against powers and
principalities in the airs", we are prone to fall into a certain
fatalism. I get the impression that fate, the Greek fatality,
crops up again in our thinking. At the very moment when we affirm
the creativity and historicity of people, we are at the same time
describing the enemy in such impressive terms that our arms drop
and it seems that no one knows where to start. We must get back
a realization of the full historicity of human beings. We are not
faced with human structures that are the fruit of fatality or of
a manifest destiny. What we are facing is concrete tasks that
point in the direction of full liberation, and only if we look
on the difficulties as hurdles to overcome will we start to live
fully as human beings and exercise our freedom.

I do not know if I explain myself clearly. For example, we cannot
admit a fatalism that would recognize the existence of two great
powers in the world, which divide up spheres of influence. We
cannot admit the fatalism of immutable ruling forces in the world-
wide commercial structures. We have to insist that the totality of
the life of nations be brought under the rule of reason, of intelligence, and placed at the service of humankind. Clearly, this is
a gigantic task. But it is the inspiration, the perspective, the
vital attitude that moves us. We shall go ahead, taking on the
immediate tasks that we can cope with, and not conceding that any
de facto situation has to be as it is. Let us accept our
responsibility for creating something new in history, for only
the new befits a genuine humanity.

With these two convictions -- the priority of the third world's
development and the viability of the entire historical task that
people set for themselves -- we can formulate the question: What
are we all to do about these matters that we have discussed?
And here there is also ample scope for imagination and planning.

A lot is being done, in the area of information, in the mutual
support among those resisting oppression, in the conscientization
of secular communities. We can do much more, of course. How are
we going to control the mass media that are invading Latin
America from the United States, with an illuminating message
that will counterbalance to some extent the alienating influences
of the screen, film and television? What can we do to oppose the
massive trend toward de-nationalization of the basic Latin
American industries? What can we do to stimulate an integral
national development? To what extent can symbolic actions contribute to light, in the hearts of our people, a bright hope in
a new tomorrow?

We will have to ask ourselves whether the institutional possibilities of the churches in the United States will let them rally behind our venturesome experiments in promoting a liberating awareness and activity in Latin America. We will have to study together to what extent we can help each other in all our creative efforts in the cause of freedom. We shall have to live on the edge of -- and sometimes even cross the line of demarcation between -- the known and the unknown, the legal and the illegal, but always seeking a greater measure of fidelity to him who established the priority of humanity over the sabbath, over all our traditions.

I would like to end with an invitation to formulate our problem in terms of our personal contribution to the liberating struggle. Each one of us has to answer to God for the lights he or she has received. The great humanizing decision is the one we take regarding God himself, when we are asked through our neighbour about the genuineness of our love. In view of the seriousness of the problems of underdevelopment, of marginalization, of dependence, in view of the evidence of people's exploitation of people, and the reality of the dehumanizing structures that dominate us, this is no moment for personal opinions, or likes, or dislikes. The problem ceases to be debatable and turns into an unavoidable challenge. I may not continue to think of my profession, my work, my family, prescinding from my marginalized neighbour. My vivid awareness of the problem will lead to my personal vocation, my decision to take on a leader's role, however small it may appear in the eyes of others, but one that I may look on as uniquely mine in the divine economy. This problem has to mean for everyone a new attitude in looking at the map of the world, in dealing with one's next-door neighbour; it has to offer a new perspective for the totality of our lives, so that we can devote to it our humanizing action and energy. Unless each one of us resolves to re-examine the wisdom and profundity of our devotion to the struggle for freedom, this conference will have been only a pleasant pastime and will have no lasting result.

Like the Hebrew people, we hear the words of their leader: "Death and life stand before you." Our spiritual death if we focus on our personal security, or our life in our neighbour, in Christ -- the only life possible today, even though it involves some imminent risk of death.

Finally, it seems indispensable to me to underline the importance of faith in the liberating struggle. We need sociological analyses, political and technical planning, an ideology, a strategy, a tactic. But how direly we need also the moral fiber, the human depth, the authentic freedom of the militants for freedom. Here is where the dimension of faith comes in, when we realize that we are not involved in some personal struggle, but in God's own great struggle down the centuries to dignify human existence. Humanization, liberation, redemption, all are part of the will of God. Then, if we devote ourselves to changing the infrahuman living conditions of our peoples, if we dedicate ourselves to the cause of the liberating revolution, we do so in hope, as a responsible offering to him who gave himself up for us in Christ Jesus. In this perspective we look full of hope to tomorrow, because it is a morrow prefigured, announced and promised in the resurrection of our Lord Jesus Christ.

(Address delivered to the 1971 CICOP Conference and published by Division for Latin America, USCC, Washington D.C., USA)

3. THE CHURCH AND ITS AGENDA
IN THE MISSION OF THE KINGDOM

These articles focus on the church in the total economy of the kingdom of God.

The first, "A Saving Community", describes the church as serving the salvation that God has wrought in the history of Israel and in the life and death of Jesus Christ. To be a saving community is to be a community of hope which identifies with the poor, develops an ecumenical world missionary perspective, and responds in obedience, functioning as a catalyst for all creative human forces.

The second, "Mission and Church", deals with the implications of the integration of the International Missionary Council with the World Council of Churches. (1) Mission belongs to the entire church. (2) Cross-cultural mission should be developed in full appreciation of the local churches. (3) The issues of justice are an essential part of the proclamation of the Gospel. (4) The faithfulness of the local congregation is basic to the world mission of the church. (5) The ecumenical missionary forum today reaches far beyond the International Missionary Council constituency.

The third, "Mission in Six Continents", describes the present missionary situation, with national churches established in almost every country and churches in western Europe in numerical decline, and affirms that God is "a missionary God and that his mission...knows no human frontiers. ... In his mission we participate with our gifts and our limitations, hoping also to receive God's blessing through the work and witness of the churches of other countries. ... The missionary task will fulfil its prophetic function, its critical and reconciling function...if, while helping third world Christians to become self-reliant and masters in their own house, ... we work in our own country...to change the policies of our governments, of our industrial concern or financial establishments."

The fourth, "Evangelism in the Local Community", invites the missionary organizations and churches to learn from their own past experience in foreign mission work for the re-evangelization of Europe. As a missionary going abroad, one needs (1) to tell the story of Jesus Christ with freshness; (2) to develop groups of Christians whose faithfulness challenges the surrounding community; (3) to be attentive and listen to the needs of the community; (4) to develop and encourage the gifts that are already present in the gathered Christian community; (5) to transform our minority complex into a sense of vocation; (6) to call to radical conversion to Jesus Christ; and (7) to recognize all the frontiers to be crossed in the name of Jesus Christ -- in terms of class, profession, culture, etc.

The fifth, "Evangelism in the World", develops common perspectives for the churches' evangelistic outreach: (1) A reminder of the centrality of the local congregation in God's plan. (2) The validity and need of the actual search for cultural identity. (3) The importance of the moratorium debate. (4) Ecumenical sharing of personnel. (5) Reaching the billions of people who do not know the gospel of Jesus Christ. (6) The spiritual, prayerful dimension of evangelism.

Articles six, seven and eight focus on specific issues of the missionary agenda. "Evangelism in the Third World" discusses the strengths and limitations of North American missionaries in third world countries. The editorial on "Moratorium" introduces it as an expansion of the missionary potential of the church; in no case as an abdication of the missionary vocation. Moratorium should be understood within the concept of world mission. The editorial on "Conversion" develops a central theme of "Mission and Evangelism - An Ecumenical Affirmation": "The proclamation of the gospel includes an invitation to recognize and accept in a personal decision the saving lordship of Christ." Attention is given to critical voices that warn us of an easy use of this word. However, we cannot dodge the demand of the gospel for a clear commitment to Jesus Christ and the kingdom of God. Conversion makes every person a co-worker with God in God's kingdom. The awareness of belonging to God's kingdom makes all the difference.

A SAVING COMMUNITY

As we think about our theme, we need to keep in mind the church
of Jesus Christ as it is today, with its denominational divisions,
its hierarchical institutions, its multiplicity of colours,
languages and cultural forms. Can this community, which we know
so well, be called a *saving community* ?

The question is foreseen in the Bangkok Report:

> Without the salvation of the churches from their captivity in the
> interests of dominating classes, races and nations, there can be no
> saving church. Without liberation of the churches and Christians from
> their complicity with structural injustice and violence, there can be
> no liberating church for mankind. Every church, all Christians face
> the question whether they serve Christ and His saving work alone, or
> at the same time also the powers of inhumanity. "No man can serve two
> masters, God and Mammon" (Mt. 6:24). We must confess our misuse of
> the name of Christ by the accommodation of the churches to oppressive
> powers, by our self-interested apathy, lovelessness, and fear. We are
> seeking the true community of Christ which works and suffers for his
> Kingdom. We seek the charismatic church which activates energies for
> salvation (1 Cor. 12). We seek the church which initiates actions for
> liberation and supports the work of other liberating groups without
> calculating self-interest. We seek a church which is the catalyst of
> God's saving work in the world, a church which is not merely the refuge
> of the saved but a community serving the world in the love of Christ.[1]

Of course, the Bangkok Assembly had no dogmatic authority, and
there has been much discussion about its conclusions. But this
inspired statement indicates that our search for an image of a
saving community responds to the concerns of Christians throughout the world. I shall begin with a paradox. The Christian
community can only be a channel of salvation inasmuch as it maintains before itself the central truth of the Bible: only God saves.
The institution, the community, the Christian movement can be an
effective instrument for proclamation, distribution, discovery,
and service of the salvation that God is working, but what defines
the Christian Church as a community of salvation is its loyalty -
its voluntary bondage - to the revelation of God, in which we
recognize him as saviour.

In the Old Testament, the prophets were able to call the Hebrews'
attention to the most important episode in their history - the
liberation from captivity in Egypt. Because God's mighty hand
had wrought their salvation, they were called to constitute a
holy people, a nation of priests. Throughout the pages of the Old
Testament, in the face of all calamities, God appears as the
saviour, the one who brings health, the one who restores. He is
the one who calls the slave to freedom, the oppressed to
liberation. He liberates from hunger, from the death of sin itself.

In the New Testament, in the person of Jesus Christ, the saviour
is incarnate and at last shows his face. There is the very

incarnation into human misery, symbolized by the manger, and an identification with the moral tragedy of humankind, dying on the cross in the place of the sinner. Jesus' exodus through death towards resurrection vividly recalls the faith of the Old Testament that it is God who saves, even from death, bringing new life. He saves humankind from the burden of sin, both personal and collective, and makes possible a new creation. The Christian community today is formed around the memory of these fundamental facts. They give us a measuring stick, a criterion by which we can measure contemporary events. The tradition is at the heart and being of that community, it is only in the tradition that we discover the fullness of salvation and can consciously put ourselves at its service.

But the Christian community does not live by memories alone: It inserts their living reality in the present. Liturgical celebration joins yesterday with today. In the sacrament of holy communion we can affirm the real presence of Christ as we venerate his memory in the yesterday of the church while celebrating his coming today within the gathered community. Through the liturgy, the reading and interpretation of the word, the celebration of the sacrament, the communion of brothers, we live again in the presence of the saving God.

The saving God of the Bible does not limit himself only to those who remember him. He acts throughout the secular community in which the members of the community of faith live. Thus God acts through the movements of nomadic tribes in the desert, through political uprisings, through the "still small voice" and through the curing flood. In one way or another he is present in the secular events of our world. So Christians are not just recalling past worship, but events in the life of a people, or of a person, within the early church. Events took place within the secular history of the time. Consequently, a contemporary interpretation of faith in the saving God cannot remain closed around the liturgical act; there can be no true liturgy if it does not celebrate the great acts of God in the contemporary world.

As the community of faith, it attempts to make people aware of the presence of the saving God in contemporary experience, by a prophetic reading of secular events, seeking to discern the saving hand of the Lord that it knows in history. In the gospels, the risen Christ often comes to his followers as a stranger. When they prepare a meal for him they discover who he is. Today also, in both the tragic and hopeful events of our lives, the spirit of the Lord works to bring humanity towards the goal of peace, shalom, which he pre-figured. It is the task of the Christian community to discern this working of God, to accompany him, to help him, and to proclaim him. Jesus is with us and before us, so the community lives not only on the past or the miracle of the presence of Jesus Christ, but also in the future, looking towards tomorrow as an eschatological community anticipating the fullness of the kingdom. We have been given the Holy Spirit as the pledge, the anticipation of the final promises. The experience of new life in Jesus Christ promises eternity. We know it now only in part, but we shall know it as well as we know ourselves. Throughout the Bible we have this looking forward: tomorrow is full of the promise of the presence of God, we are a pilgrim people celebrating the past, realizing the present and anticipating the future. The manna in the desert sustains us as we remember with gratitude the exodus from Egypt. The promised land is before us as the goal of our striving.

The reunion of the Christian community is also built around the remembrance of the divine revelation, at the same time it is nourished by the perception of the action of God within and outside the community. But it looks towards the future, seeking the lines of history that point towards the goal that God has promised - the summing up of all things in Jesus Christ. Consequently, a community that seeks to be a saving community is a community that brings hope; it cannot accept any given situation as definitive. It is called from the depths of its faith to challenge the *status quo* and is constantly stimulated to overcome the present. A socio-political and economic analysis of the situation of our world easily brings despair. But neither the individual Christian nor the church can stop at a closed and pessimistic analysis of the future of peoples or individuals, because every day is a new day in which the Lord comes to meet us: Jesus Christ, the same today and for all ages.

Up to this point, we are probably all in agreement with this relatively doctrinal analysis of the common convictions that belong to the treasure of all Christians. The risks begin when we try to define the characteristics of the saving community today. Its existence is conditioned by remembrance, presence, and promise for the future; its life-style must correspond to the moment and circumstances in which God calls us to live. But when we try to describe the marks of this life-style we come up against an almost insuperable difficulty. By definition, the Christian community must be incarnate, identified, forming part of a given people. When God wishes to engage in a decisive battle for the liberation of humankind, he comes in the person of his son, to participate in the human condition from within. The manger, the line of sinners awaiting the baptism of repentance which Jesus himself joined, his life among people as one of them and his death on the cross together with two thieves, clearly dramatizes his belonging to a given people within whom he works the salvation intended not only for them but for all the peoples of the earth. God does not want to act universally but from within a specific historical identification. How much more, then, must Christian communities, seeking to serve the salvation that God offers, identify with their respective peoples, making the fate of their nations their own?

This brings us to the whole problem of cultural identity which Bangkok raised so sharply. It would seem that we can no longer

221

speak in a universal language of faith, but rather that we must describe our obedience and our life in the faith in terms that correspond to our national identity. Perhaps our first impression of that is chaos, disorder and lack of understanding. But we can only define a Christian life that takes seriously a God who saves people in specific historical situations from an understanding set within our own peoples. If we are to pronounce a saving word, to catalyse saving actions within our nations, we must assume their fate and make it our own. As much as I might try to speak a language that corresponds to the situation of a church in the rich world, my belonging, my immediate obedience, my being is linked to the Latin American situation, and I can only speak and express myself from within that situation. In limiting myself to this perspective, I will perhaps give the impression of speaking to the Christians there and not to those of us who are here. But if we hear the confessions of Jesus the first disciples gave us, we will learn what he says to our own situation by listening to the various ways of confessing him in different parts of the world. The description of the saving community that is appropriate to a country like Sweden must be the result of a dialogue in community; what we say from our situation as Latin Americans can act as a catalyst, as a challenge and a help to imagination.

A church will be a saving community if it puts itself on the side of the poor of the earth. This is not a slogan, but a basic truth. "As the Father sent me, so I send you." The Father sends him to be born in a manger, to live among the poor, having nowhere to rest his head, to die naked on a cross. The incarnation implies identification with humanity in its need. The Christian Church can have no other geographical or social location than on the side of the poor of the earth.

In Latin America this presupposes a basic choice. The church that is allied to the *status quo* and benefits from special protection is now faced with the agonizing choice: Where is its place? Where should it be if it is to fulfil its vocation? This is the heavy cross that many Christian leaders in our continent have to bear as they face the decision to commit themselves to the poor. There is, of course, much ambiguity in any human decision, even within the church. The lines that divide social groups are not as distinct as we preachers often claim. Commitment to the poor can mean conflict in relation to other poor people. But it is a decision that involves a definitive commitment. The church is called to speak a word of reconciliation, but in the manner of its Lord who could not speak of reconciliation from outside the conflict but only from within. It is only to the extent that our Lord took upon himself the fate of sinful human beings that he could proclaim the word of reconciliation. It is only to the extent that we know where the church is and what the salvation that it serves is, that a word of reconciliation can be heard and accepted, not as an easy way of avoiding conflict, but as a means of overcoming conflict in favour of justice.

Within the saving community, we commit ourselves to those to whom salvation has been promised.

The second characteristic of the community is that it is ecumenical. It lives on the remembrance of a God who acts in human history, it therefore knows the reality of a presence that breaks through all human barriers and looks towards a hope that includes all humanity. This community lives in a given place but is at the service of all people. The world missionary task is an expression of the ecumenical fact that faith belongs to the whole inhabited earth. The charismas God gives to the Christian community are for the benefit of all humankind. For a long time, the church could only fulfil this function through intercessory prayer, but inasmuch as our geographical knowledge of the earth expands and the interrelationship of people is made clearer, the missionary responsibility of each local church becomes more evident. At the same time the knowledge of the existence of other manifestations of this same community of salvation - the same church of Jesus Christ - in other latitudes, provides precious resources for our own saving task. The ecumenical nature of the Christian Church refers not so much to the overcoming of denominational limits as to the incorporation of a missionary conscience and a feeling of belonging to world mission, giving and receiving. As we belong to a community that places itself at the service of the poor, we discover that we are part of a community of loyalty to God that overcomes all our human barriers.

Third, a saving community is a free community. "Be free, then, with the freedom with which Christ freed you." Liberty is the availability of the community to the saving mission of God in the place and moment in which we find ourselves. We see clearly that sharing the knowledge of salvation given to us in the biblical story is a service to the saving mission of God. It is equally clear that we are invited to see the contemporary actions through which the spirit of God seeks to work for salvation in the everyday life of the poor to whom we commit ourselves and in the historical movements of our time. As soon as we see an invitation in this situation, or a sign in accordance with the spirit which we see in Jesus Christ, we are immediately recruited for service to the liberating purpose of God. Thus the Bangkok Assembly can speak of the various priorities given to the service of salvation, or of the different ways of entering into the saving process and serving it.

One might say that in Northern Ireland reconciliation and justice are the basic priority, while in Vietnam it is peace. In each place in which we find ourselves we must discern not only what is the immediate frontier on which we are called to serve in the name of God, but we must also try from our own privileged situation to discover the frontiers at which other brothers and sisters find themselves and join our spiritual, personal and material resources to their struggle. As our Lord Jesus Christ, so we are called today as the Church of Jesus Christ to do like-

wise. To the sick man whom they brought down to him by breaking
the roof of a house so that he could give him the word of healing,
he first gave the word of pardon; to the blind who cried out for
pity, he gave back their sight. Health and pardon are both
expressions of the total salvation that God promises to humankind and to each individual. The passionate dialogue that sometimes takes place in the church amongst those who emphasize a
dimension known as vertical and those who emphasize what has been
called the horizontal, in other words between those who emphasize
preaching and those who emphasize social service, is completely
foreign to the biblical purpose, and is theologically false. The
God of our remembrance is the God of contemporary action, the God
whose fullness of purpose we discern as a promise to the whole of
humanity. Consequently, the community of faith which proclaims
and remembers the events of yesterday discovers the contemporary
invitations and challenges of the divine spirit. It responds in
obedience and in the use of freedom.

Fourth, the saving community knows its own human limitations. In
a free and ecumenical spirit, the community works among the poor
of the earth to discern what it must do. It begins and encourages
the work of the Lord. Throughout its history, the church has again
and again taken upon itself responsibility for essential services
to humankind. When human communities have organized themselves
and assumed responsibility for specific areas of life, the church
has relinquished that particular work and concentrated on new
tasks. In other words, the church recognizes that its role is not
to be the sole agent for the totality of God's salvation. From
its understanding of the centrality of the revelation of the
saving will of God in Jesus Christ, the church becomes a catalyst,
taking on responsibilities or delegating them as part of its work
of encouragement of service.

Concerned with collaborating in the total salvation of humankind,
the saving community rejoices in everything that is a full manifestation of the divine spirit, even in its most secular forms.

The church will be a saving community, then, to the extent that
it recognizes that it cannot fulfil this task, since only God
saves. Only by serving the divine purpose can it participate in
making real the saving purpose of God. The church knows that it
has received salvation in Christ; time and time again it returns
to the sources of that memory to discover in it the basic criteria
that will govern its actions today. This is not a fixed task. The
church lives in the expectation of the surprises that come from
the discovery of God in contemporary events. The church is a
community of hope, looking towards tomorrow in anticipation of
the full salvation that God has promised. Looking towards a
world perspective, it affirms the freedom that it has received
from God and promotes the transformation of the whole human
condition. Like a grain of yeast, the church gives itself in
service, taking up its cross and anticipating the fullness of
salvation. So the role of the Christian Church, to the extent that

it assumes the condition of being a saving community, is tremendously important. It is concerned with the totality of humankind and of history. It is so important that it is essential to the recruitment of disciples for the service of the Lord.

One of the main successes of the Bangkok Conference was that it did not hesitate to speak of the growth of the church as a legitimate goal because it understood this not as the salvation of the institution but as the salvation of the whole world. Evangelization, the communication of the good news of Jesus Christ, is a natural result of the existence of the saving community; it is a concern of the Christian community by right because we have an obligation to increase the saving forces at work to benefit all humankind. Evangelization is not proselytism, because it is no longer merely concerned with increasing the number of church members or congregations, it is trying to recruit servants of humankind. Christian discipleship, which is both a conscious participation in the remembrance of the acts of God in the story of Jesus Christ, and a joining with God in the saving acts of today, is a response to the felt needs of humanity and is the way in which God makes the knowledge of his saving plan available to future generations. Remembrance can become an escape from surrounding tensions, but when it is based on the memory of Jesus Christ, the call to join the people who celebrate that story and bring it into contemporary experience is a recruitment call for the kingdom, a recruitment call for the salvation of all humankind. Evangelization is contained in Jesus' words: "If any-one will follow me, let him deny himself, take up his cross and follow me." This is the normal and essential chracteristic of a community that associates itself with the saving purpose of God. Precisely because it believes in the salvation that God is working for all humankind, the church is ready to increase the hosts of servants of the kingdom.

(Address delivered to a consultation on mission, organized by the Church of Sweden Mission, May 1974)

Note

1) Bangkok Assembly 1973, Minutes and Report of the Assembly of the Commission on World Mission and Evangelism of the World Council of Churches, December 31, 1972 and January 9-12, 1973, p. 89.

MISSION AND CHURCH

In 1961, on the occasion of the Third Assembly of the World Council of Churches in New Delhi, the integration of the International Missionary Council and the World Council of Churches took place. This action was preceded by an intense theological polemic. A few members of the IMC felt obliged to retire their membership; others felt so enthusiastic as to see in this merger the culmination of the initial ecumenical vision of Edinburgh in 1910. While something of the polemic of those days and of the ensuing years can be found in this issue of the International Review of Mission, we are not primarily interested in an historical reappraisal. We do not need to "justify" the integration nor make a defensive presentation of the World Council of Churches. Both the International Missionary Council and the World Council of Churches are only instruments in God's hands to advance the cause of the unity of the Church in the fulfilment of its mission. We want, rather, to learn from the decision and its consequences something relevant for our actual missionary obedience. Are we using the instruments we have to maximum potential, in order to help the churches in the proclamation of the Name of Jesus Christ that all may turn to him, believe and be saved? What were the values affirmed by those who decided for integration? What are the values which have emerged in this process of integration that we must encourage and preserve? Here is my tentative list:

1) Mission belongs to the entire church and cannot be delegated. Of course the churches are free, following the inspiration of the Holy Spirit, to devise the best instruments, structural organizations, that advance the fulfilment of their missionary responsibilities. We recognize that the sins of the Church have frequently provoked persons to set up parallel organizations. In a very protestant interpretation of the Bible text, "Where two or three meet in my name, I am in the midst of them", these organizations are considered to constitute a valid manifestation of the Church. But inasmuch as we are called to live in the unity of the Church for the fulfilment of our mission, inasmuch as we are sent as the whole people of God into the world, one ongoing responsibility of those who have a missionary calling, a missionary charisma, is to attempt to permeate the total life of the Church with this missionary conviction. We recognize the important role that missionary societies of a voluntary nature have played and are playing in the total mission of the Church. They should be recognized as disciplined members, instruments of the Church universal. But they should include as a fundamental dimension, a constitutive dimension, a dialectical, creative and faithful relationship to the churches both in their home countries and in whatever other countries they are working. Christians are not assuming their full mission responsibilities when they cross frontiers, at home or abroad, unless they are in relationship to the local Christian community.

Structures need to be under continual correction to be sure that they are valid expressions of the missionary spirit of the church and educational means to encourage and stimulate that spirit. It is a pitiful situation where strong foreign missionary societies exist side by side with dying local congregations. Something is wrong! Either we are escaping from our local responsibilities to find satisfaction far away, or we are not responsibly bringing something from the experience of those Christians far away to the local communities.

But we should not believe that once we have integrated the missionary organization into the structure of the Church our problems are over! In the last twenty years we have seen a gap growing between new agencies created by the churches in the West and the missionary dimension of the Church's life. Organizations for Service and Development are growing in numbers and resources, looking for relations with churches in the Third World, bringing with them a limited self-definition of their role. How could we, in God's mission, make a schizophrenic separation between announcing the name and serving the needs of our neighbour? How could we accept secular notions of development as commanding orders for Church work? The old question of the integration of mission in the life of the Church remains with us as we battle to overcome this and every reduction of the Gospel to a particular manifestation. *The Gospel of Jesus Christ is the total invasion of God's love manifested fully in the cross of Jesus Christ. The Christian community as a worshipping, proclaiming, teaching, serving reality is an indivisible unity that should be both at the root of our missionary sending and the aim of our missionary concern.*

2) We have learned to respect the local church as we engaged in cross-cultural international mission. While Edinburgh could make plans from a central place and see the whole world as a territory to be covered with the proclamation of the Gospel, today, thanks to the effort of those who followed in the steps of Edinburgh, the churches are present in almost every nation. So today, our mission is a mission in cooperation with local churches. We are not saying that because one church is planted in a given country, that country is totally closed to the missionary concerns of churches abroad. *What we are affirming is that it is essential to create a relation of cooperation, loyalty and respect with the churches that are already in those countries.* It is true that the present borders of nations do not correspond to ethnic or socio-economic realities and that the fact that there is one church in a capital city does not mean that that church is able to reach to all borders of the nation. Churches working in a given language or cultural milieu inside a country where other linguistic areas and other cultures are expressed may be in no better position than churches far away to cross cultural and linguistic barriers to bring the Gospel to those territories.

But the national boundaries exist. The political entities are real and whatever we do in one part of the nation will have consequences for Christians who are considered to be co-responsible for those actions in other parts of the nation. When missions go to work in the jungles and open the road for multinational corporations and mining exploitation, the blame is not limited to the work of those missionaries who, in the phrase of David Livingstone, "were opening the jungle for the Gospel and trade", but also reaches by association the work of the total church in that country. We are learning to consider the totality of the missionary engagement of the church in a country and not only the possible mission that "my" group could develop. Are missionaries reporting back to their constituencies stories about what *they* did or what the Christian communities to which they relate, whose ministry they want to enhance, are able to do? *We have learned that the cross-cultural missionary of today should be a more humble, a more faithful member of the Body of Christ in the whole world.*

The World Council of Churches is a fellowship of churches that support each other, searching for the unity that will facilitate or make possible the carrying on of our mission to call the whole world to faith in Jesus Christ. The inter-church aid system of the World Council has a central aim: to help local churches become the servant Body of Jesus Christ in their respective communities. We know that the time is running short during which we can help each other; we need to be wise in our helping to develop local communities of Christians fully responsible for the evangelization of their respective countries. We don't know when the moment will come when the doors of opportunity will be closed.

In the last few years, a real attempt has been made, especially by Protestant Christianity, to recapture the vision of the billions of people who have not

228

yet had the chance to know the name of Jesus Christ and to be attracted by his life. "Reaching the Unreached" has become a slogan for the prayer and concentration of many people in many congregations. This concern is as valid today as it was when Jesus sent the disciples, as the Father had sent him, into the world to proclaim the Gospel to every creature. But we need to be wise in the fulfilment of our mission. General slogans will not help us. The fact is that almost two-thirds of those unreached are living under social systems or under legislation that make it impossible for western Christians to be the main carriers of the Gospel. Let us recognize also that by far the majority of the missionaries go from western countries into other regions of the world where Christians and Christian churches are already giving testimony of Jesus Christ. It hurt our heart to hear on the Swiss radio a study of the situation in Haiti, describing the misery of that country, followed by the journalist's comment: "One way to progress economically in Haiti is to organize your own religious mission. Then you make a trip to the United States, tell the story of your success and your financial problems are over." More than three hundred different missionary groups are working in Haiti, a country where the Gospel of Jesus Christ has been announced by the Roman Catholic church for centuries and where Protestants are already more than twenty per cent of the population! How many thousands of North American missionaries are in Latin America? *Let us recognize the challenge to share the Gospel of Jesus Christ to the whole world; let us be humble about our possibilities and the way in which we help the whole church in the whole world become protagonists in this mission in which we all are called to share.*

3) The integration of the IMC and the WCC was not simply the integration of two different organizations and headquarters. It was more than that. **It meant the entrance into the life of the World Council of many churches of the Third World that were in the past related to international forums through national councils of churches and the missionary organizations.** Now they themselves came forcefully to the international arena, and they used this opportunity to air the sufferings of their countries in their relation with the powerful nations of the world. I believe that this is one way to understand the seeming lack of visibility of the concern for evangelism in the life of the World Council of Churches. Those churches coming from Asia, Africa and Latin America, who are in their daily lives fully engaged in evangelism, who are growing churches, did not come into the international arena to ask help for this particular dimension of their Christian obedience which they knew how to fulfill. They wanted to highlight the plight of their people and the responsibility which they felt was shared by Christians in the West for that plight. So Christians from South Korea, whom no one could dismiss as not being concerned with cross-cultural mission, came to the ecumenical arena to highlight the issues of human rights and social justice. Christians from South Africa, who again could not be charged with not being concerned with evangelism and even with mission in other countries in Africa, voiced their grievances about the apartheid system.

There is the same phenomenon inside the Lausanne Continuation Committee on World Evangelization. Both at the Lausanne meeting in 1974 and at the meeting in Pattaya in 1980, strong voices, especially from the Third World, were heard demanding that the wider issues of social justice and human rights should be given a strong and important consideration. Churches in the Third World cannot accept easy dichotomies or dodge the issue of our complicity with countries and structures that are the source of the problem for their countries and their churches. The issues of justice and injustice both in national and international relations are considered to be an essential part of the concern for the proclamation of the Gospel of Jesus Christ. *The very same people and the very same churches who week after week are proclaiming the saving name of Jesus Christ and inviting people to repentance and faith are coming to international assemblies in order to demand our Christian solidarity with the predicament of their people and with their attempt to show that the Gospel of Jesus Christ brings in itself the seeds of justice and the promises of a new human order.* The recent world missionary conference in Melbourne reminds us that the Gospel was announced to the poor as a sign of the messianic presence of Jesus Christ and that to them the kingdom of Heaven is promised. In highlighting this biblical truth, Melbourne was inviting the churches to look at the whole world in terms of the overwhelming facts of poverty; most of the poor of the earth are also those who are deprived of the knowledge of the Gospel of Jesus Christ.

Of course social concerns were never absent in the International Missionary Council's meetings before the integration with WCC, but the integration provided a wider forum at a particular moment of world history when the awareness of the growing disparity between north and south and the interplay of our economic, political and military systems was becoming increasingly visible.

4) The local mission, the local congregation is a fundamental part of the total world mission of the church. The separation between foreign and home mission is increasingly artificial in a world that is becoming smaller and smaller. We realize that we need to organize our service to have some relevancy, but the fundamental fact remains: *it is the totality of the life of our church that has a missionary connotation; our churches, local communities, are either missionary or antimissionary, but they cannot be neutral in the fulfilment of the Great Commission.* They help or they hinder the cause of mission. Of course this is more clearly seen in countries at the centre of world power today, because they are more in the eyes of the world. Their attitude towards racial problems or social problems in their communities, their judgement concerning the economic relations among nations, their solidarity with foreign workers, etc., is visible, is spoken of, and has consequences for the acceptance or rejection of the Christian faith that unhappily is still closely confused with the lifestyle of the northern world. The testimony rendered to Jesus Christ by churches in an affluent society, or in socialist societies, is of tremendous importance for the churches in the rest of the world. The credibility of the Gospel is at stake in our attitudes and the way in which we confront the powers in our respective societies. Churches in China have been prevented from participating in international mission during the last twenty years; however, when we discover today the reality of the faithful churches in the middle of the turmoil of that country, it is a powerful, inspirational motivation for churches and Christians everywhere.

The prayer life of our congregations cannot be limited to the concerns of the local Christian communities, but there should be continual intercession for the spreading of the Gospel all over the world. The reception we give to students, tourists, visitors knocking at the doors of our communities, is a testimony they will take back to their respective nations. A local missionary commitment, the sending of our children, our support to help other churches to spread the Word somewhere else, should all be normal manifestations of our participation in the world missionary vocation.

5) One of the most important consequences of the integration of the International Missionary Council with the World Council of Churches has been the increasing numbers and varieties of churches that participate in the missionary forum. In fact, one of the main values of this integration is seen in the growing participation of the Orthodox churches, not only in the missiological discussions, but in the world mission of the Church. If integration means that the whole Church is becoming missionary, that should be seen in the incorporation of new sectors of our traditional churches in the missionary concern. New regions, totally out of reach of the International Missionary Council constituency, are now open for our missionary questioning and missionary help. *The reality is that the actual missiological discussion reaches far beyond the traditional borders of the IMC constituency; it incorporates the Orthodox churches, Catholic churches and independent churches in the Third World.* Increasingly they bring to the discussion their respective experiences and they learn through the testimony given by others. Melbourne was perhaps an excellent microcosm of the total engagement of the Church in mission in the most diverse circumstances and in crossing the most diverse frontiers. The participants were not only representatives of the traditional constituencies of the IMC, but they represented the total participation of the Church of Jesus Christ in God's mission of love to the world. The facts of renewal in missionary concern in churches that were totally out of touch with the IMC tradition should be shown as one fundamental value that has been brought about through the integration process. CWME has become an international multicultural forum where churches of the most diverse cultural background and theological traditions

231

come together to bring forth their witness and submit themselves to reciprocal correction. Assemblies, consultations, provide a chance to highlight
some of the prevailing convictions inside a process of reciprocal sharing.
We see each other as pilgrims, as missionary people committed to the total
mission of the church.

**6) The aim of CWME remains basically the same as the aim of the Interna-
tional Missionary Council, to help the churches in the proclamation of the
Gospel of Jesus Christ in word and deed so that all may believe and be saved.**
The linkage of every human situation to the story of Jesus Christ, the proclamation of the Name, to give witness to God's actions in Jesus Christ, the
invitation to discipleship, all these belong to our main vocation and to the
central vocation of a fellowship of churches like the World Council whose
basis is "to confess Jesus Christ as God and Saviour according to the Scriptures". The topic of the coming assembly of the World Council, "Jesus
Christ, the Life of the World", will provide an excellent occasion for this
evangelistic vocation. How could we announce to the whole world that in
Jesus Christ there is life, without spreading the knowledge of that life
through all the world, without highlighting its meaning for the life of the
individual, of the family, of society, without facing in his name all the
issues threatening human life? Jesus as the "Life of the World" is an
evangelistic proclamation around which member churches of the World
Council will rally to affirm forcefully their common convictions and to get
new inspiration for their missionary task. But the missiological implications
of this topic we will discuss further in the *next* IRM issue.

(International Review of Mission, October 1981)

MISSION IN SIX CONTINENTS

We all of us have some notion of the church's responsibility in
distant lands. From our early years we have known that some of
our compatriots, our Christian sisters and brothers, have gone
off to share the gospel of Jesus Christ with people in other
continents and other countries. Most of our missionary societies
have a history of more than a hundred years of fruitful work in
the farthest corners of the earth. Throughout those years, these
societies have sought to raise the level of missionary awareness
in the churches and among Christians here in Switzerland. At the
same time they have organized the efforts to establish, then
train and support, churches in other countries. We have not the
time today, of course, to analyze the European and American
missionary work of the past in the countries of what we call
the 'third world'. We simply note the close relation between this
missionary expansion and the colonial expansion of Europe and the
United States. European traders, European soldiers, and European
missionaries arrived, sometimes all at once, sometimes in a
different chronological order. From the standpoint of the
indigenous population, however, at the receiving end, all these
arrivals formed part of one and the same cultural invasion with
its inextricable mixture of blessing and curse! It is essential
that we should analyze in depth this historical phenomenon, if
we are to avoid possible neo-colonialist dimensions and
implications in our own contemporary missionary plans. We shall
then realize that in the past this parallel work of colonialisation
and mission was almost inevitable. But, having become aware of this
connection, it would be intolerable for the churches' missionary
work to become an aid to domination in the service of foreign
influences, firms or countries. While taking cognizance of this
chronological parallelism between missionary expansion and colonial
expansion, however, we have no grounds for failing to appreciate
the work of our missionaries in the past as one which expressed
and still expresses Christian love and the longing to share our
knowledge of Jesus Christ. The colonialist expansion was an
historical epoch within which the missionaries worked and it was
almost impossible for them to divest themselves of this frame of
reference. But they made every effort to become humanizing
factors in this situation and to proclaim within it a gospel
of grace, love, equality and human freedom. Some years later,
as a result of these efforts, there emerged a sense of
liberty and national independence of which the missionary movement can now be proud!

In these recent years, our missionary work has rested on an
assumption which is perhaps no longer valid today. The motives
which derive from the depths of our faith, the basic principles
of the love of God for all human beings, the duty of Christians
to proclaim the gospel to the ends of the earth until the end of
time, of course, remain the same. These are the permanent
motivations, the same basic elements of our missionary awareness
and work. But our missionaries perhaps had other assumptions, too,
which, while they may have been valid when they began their
missionary work, are no longer so today. For example, their

basic assumptions were geographical: on the one hand there
were the 'Christian' countries, on the other hand the 'pagan'
countries; on the one hand the churches, on the other hand a
complete ignorance of the gospel.

1. The first thing we need to realize today is that, precisely
as a result of this missionary work, the Church of Jesus
Christ has become a living reality in almost every country in
the world. The churches are growing numerically, in spiritual
depth and in Christian commitment towards their people in
Africa, Asia and Latin America. In no country in these three
continents or in the Pacific islands or the Caribbean can we
speak of mission without considering the primary responsibility
of the churches in these countries, i.e. their obligation to be
a demonstration of the revealing will of God for their
respective peoples. In other words, the type of missionary we
send out today is quite different from the kind needed a few
years ago. The colleagues we send today will work with other
missionaries in a team which already knows that there are
trained leaders on the spot capable of assuming leadership in
and responsibility for the missionary task. The responsibility
of today's missionaries is a humbler one, therefore, yet at
the same time a very serious one, since it means sharing the
joy of Christian life and service with the brothers and sisters
already there.

Every contribution from outside this local situation will
necessarily take the form of support, collaboration and sharing
with the Christian communities in these countries. There are
still some parts of the world where the Christian Church is not
physically present, but the normal situation is one where we
are working with other Christian churches which are already
autonomous and whose desire it is to enter into a relationship
of equality and mutual cooperation, which is the main datum of
the new missionary situation.

2. But our traditional understanding of the church's mission is
likewise called in question today, for we can no longer claim
that our countries - those of Europe, including Switzerland, of
course - are Christian countries. It is still hard to define
exactly what we mean by a Christian country, of course. One
could examine the patterns of social life in our countries,
asking to what extent Christian values have permeated or influenced the life of our people. At a pinch, it could be said
that if we want to know more about the spiritual life of a
people, it is not the religious columns in the papers that we
should read but rather the political, economic and crime pages.
Where else are we to find pointers as to how far a given
community - in our case, Switzerland - is really under the influence of the gospel of Jesus Christ? The tragic thing is that,
on the whole, the religious news in our papers is at the same
level as the news of mundane life. Fashion, the social calendar
of the dominant classes, and the religious news are all of a

piece! That is to say, religion is something which is not big enough to change anything at all in the life of our people. To find out the degree to which our society is Christian, it is to the pages of the newspaper and the programmes on the TV or the radio which speak about the vital problems of our country that we should turn. But it is far too risky a business to assess the Christian character of a country! I would simply remind you, therefore, of the number of Christians who gather in your churches Sunday by Sunday, to make my point that we are living here not in a Christian country but on the mission field. The basic fact which impresses the foreign Christian who visits Switzerland and attends Sunday services here is to find himself or herself with a Christian minority, whereas most of the population, while perhaps paying its church taxes, for the most part remains impervious to preaching.

This means that it can no longer be considered the normal thing to send missionaries to distant countries when, at the same time, the fundamental challenge to the churches in Switzerland and in Europe generally is still the almost complete absenteeism of our people from the life of our church, the unfamiliarity of the majority of Europeans with the Bible, and the need to permeate the life of our people with the spiritual vitality of the gospel of Jesus Christ. The question we should ask ourselves is by what right we send missionaries to the third world countries to proclaim the gospel there while here in our own country, right beside us, are masses of people who are indifferent to the church's existence and with whom we have almost completely lost contact.

To what extent is Christian fidelity among us a help or a hindrance to the whole missionary task of the Church of Jesus Christ in other countries? That is the question we need to ask today. The implications are not far to seek.

3. We need to realize that fidelity to our own mission in each of our respective countries is the best missionary service we can render to the church in other parts of the world. Knowledge of your fidelity and loyalty to the gospel of Jesus Christ here in Switzerland is an inspiration to us to be faithful in Uruguay. The courageous witness of the churches in South Korea and their defence of human rights in their small Asiatic country are the best inspiration for our own fidelity in Latin America.

Some local churches - those in the socialist countries, for example - are no longer able to share in the world mission of the churches by sending missionaries or money. Yet these churches can still support the missionary work of others by their prayers and, above all, by their own fidelity to the gospel of Jesus Christ. To know that there are local churches keeping alive the flame of faith and sharing their knowledge of Jesus Christ with the younger generation in circumstances quite different from ours, in the process of shaping a new form of society which challenges traditional Christian motivations, is a witness which inspires us

235

and encourages us to fulfil our own missionary responsibility
in a different situation, a more comfortable and easygoing one
perhaps.

The churches of the United States, for example, which are very
missionary-minded and send thousands of missionaries to other
countries throughout the world, have an enormous responsibility
because, depending on the degree to which they are involved in
solving the race problem in their own country, they are a help
or a hindrance to missionary work in Africa. What the churches
here in Switzerland need to do is to identify as clearly as
possible the areas in this highly developed and industrialized
society where a missionary commitment to God is called for. On
this basis, a new model of Christian life could perhaps begin to
be developed in Switzerland, a sort of challenge, a longing and
determination to find new patterns not subservient to the
pressures of a consumer society. That would be the best service
Switzerland could render to the missionary cause. It is students
and foreign workers, holiday-makers and travellers visiting your
country who discover the numerical weakness of your churches and
are brought up with a jolt by this more than are the Swiss themselves, for they believed that they were coming to the country of
the Reformation. But it is also the case that these foreigners
encounter certain isolated Christians who are trying to live
their faith in the midst of a complex scientific and technological society and to bring their witness to Jesus Christ to
bear on all aspects of public life in Switzerland. It is this
witness which inspires us and gives us courage to return to our
respective countries and there to apply ourselves to our own
missionary task. This fidelity to the missionary task in our own
countries is the fundamental form of our participation in the
church's mission on all the continents. If we fail to accept
this missionary commitment at home, the mission abroad will be
no more than an alibi for us, a way of evading the responsibility
which lies nearest to us. Without this commitment in our own
society, mission abroad is in danger of becoming merely a desire
for prestige or adventure or some other more exotic experience.

4. Does this focus on the local mission in our missionary theory
   today mean that the time of missionary expansion or of the
international missionary task is now over? Not at all! We speak
today of world mission. This means that we know our God to be
a missionary God and that his mission, in which we share, knows
no human frontiers. We share in this mission by beginning
precisely where we are, in the society in which we live, and
on this basis, joining other Christians in working together in
all parts of the world. If it is true today that all Christians
are called to engage in the world missionary task, then this
means that we are all called not only to give but also to receive.
We have specific vocations. Our sons and daughters will set out
to work with churches in other fields of God's mission. We have
the right to send them, for in recognizing our own needs we shall
ourselves be ready, too, to receive help from the sons and

daughters of other Christians from other parts of the world
who share the same concern, the same missionary vocation.
Traditionally, we thought of mission in terms of sacrifice for
others. An intelligent giving of our life and our material
resources is always necessary, of course. At the same time,
however, we must recognize that God has endowed churches in
other parts of the world with gifts and charisms which could be
very useful for missionary service among us. There is something
almost ironical in the present situation when the churches which
are growing in numbers and in spiritual capacity are precisely
the churches of countries which are economically the poorest.
These churches are endowed with a powerful missionary concern,
the longing to share the gospel with others. But they do not
have the financial resources that we have, to enable them to
release their sons and daughters for work in the mission overseas.
We need to learn to separate the money from the person. What
matters is that the missionary task should be carried out in the
framework of collaboration between the churches in all parts of
the world. This missionary task knows no frontiers; it begins in
other countries and reaches out towards us. The mission will only
be truly universal when it becomes plain to all that we all adopt
the attitude of receiving as well as giving. Remarkable spiritual
blessings are just waiting to be received by the Swiss churches
and the Swiss community in its entirety, once they seek to draw
on the reservoir of spiritual resources which exists in the
churches of the third world especially, but also sometimes among
those who come into your midst seeking work, asking your help,
i.e. among the so-called migrant workers and expatriates who
often bring with them a depth of faith which it is quite indispensable to put to good use. Among the migrant workers and
expatriates I have met in the churches in Geneva, there are
people of radiant faith, filled with the desire to live a
profoundly Christian life, people I should love to have in my
own family and in my own parish.

In our group discussions, perhaps, we may discover specific
missionary needs which might be served by brothers and sisters
from other continents in our midst. In university circles, there
are foreigners whose close personal friendship with other students
permits a quite normal Christian witness, and the same is also
true of the places where we work, where there are many
opportunities of human contacts. But the important thing is the
spiritual question. Do we understand that the mission is that of
God himself and that we are always, all of us, those who receive
of his grace and fullness? In his mission we participate with
our gifts and our limitations, hoping also to receive God's
blessings through the work and witness of the churches of other
countries.

5. A critical review of the missionary task at once raises the
    question of the connection between international relations
and interchurch relations. I stressed earlier the close connection
between the spread of European colonialism and the missionary ex-

pansion of the European churches. What we have to realize today
is that we form part of a society with a whole series of relationships with the countries with which we are trying to establish a
spiritual relationship. The Swiss man or woman who, because of
deep personal Christian conviction and supported by the faith of
a Christian community, goes to another area of the world to cooperate with other Christians there cannot ignore the fact that
he or she belongs to a community which is in a position of
domination in relation to the culture and society of the country
in which he or she will work. Although Switzerland has never had
any colonies in the traditional sense, close relations nevertheless exist between Switzerland and the third world countries at
the financial, industrial and commercial levels. These relationships, moreover, are often forms of domination and even sometimes
of exploitation. We have to recognize that the mission abroad
takes place within a much wider framework of relationships between
different communities. The missionary task will fulfil its
prophetic function, its critical and reconciling function, to
the degree that we take this wider context seriously and try to
work on both sides of the frontier, i.e. if, while helping third
world Christians to become self-reliant and masters in their own
house, at the same time we work in our own country here in Europe
with the object of changing the policies of our governments, of
our industrial concerns or financial establishments which have a
certain influence on the life of third world countries. In other
words, our mission will be a global and total mission concerned
with the fullness of life which it is God's will to bestow on all
human beings. When we find, moreover, that relations between our
countries are relations of dependence or exploitation, this means
that we must meet a fundamental missionary challenge, shoulder a
missionary responsibility and task. I hope that in the work of
your own Federation and, very specifically, within the discussion
groups, this dimension of totality in our national responsibilities
for others will be discussed and clarified.

We come to the end of these reflections. Missionary work today
corresponds to a vision of God's mission in the whole world. We
can share in this mission in our own homes by lifting our hands
in prayer towards God. By such prayer we uphold Christians who
seek to be faithful in their own situations, whether in their
own countries or abroad. We share in the redemptive mission by
common prayer in each parish. We recognize one another as members
of the one body of Christ, who knows no frontiers and we identify
ourselves with the destiny of all the peoples of humankind. We
share in this mission of God whenever we seek to be faithful and
obedient to the commandments of love and justice in our own
lives. We share in this mission when, through the gifts we give
and through the commitment of our sons and daughters, we cooperate
with other churches in their specific missionary tasks. We share
in this mission of God whenever we willingly receive the blessings
God reserves for us through Christians from other continents
and climes. We share this liberating mission of God in the measure

that our whole life reflects a missionary concern in which our spirituality, our participation in the Christian community and in the secular community, are seen as ways in which we can demonstrate our missionary fidelity.

(Address given at the General Assembly of the Swiss Federation of Protestant Women, Basel, May 1975; translated from the French, WCC Language Service)

EVANGELISM IN THE LOCAL COMMUNITY

In one sense it is strange for us, as people concerned with
foreign mission, to use our time to discuss evangelism in the
local community. I understand this topic as referring to our
situation in western Europe, especially here in Britain, and to
the evangelistic possibilities that our local congregations have.
It is important for us, not only because we as individuals live
here in this country and belong to different local areas and
parishes, but also because our credibility in foreign countries
is at stake. If at some historical time it could have been assumed
that we belonged to Christian countries from where the gospel was
being sent to other lands, today we know that this is no longer
true. So, only inasmuch as we take seriously the command of our
Lord to preach the gospel to every creature at our side, do we
have the right to go beyond our boundaries and to share with others
in the same task. The gospel of the kingdom shall be preached in
Jerusalem, Judaea, Samaria and to the utmost corners of the earth;
but it must be preached in Jerusalem and Judaea. It must be preached
in our own city, in our own neighbourhood, and unless this happens
with the same seriousness and the same commitment that we try to
devote to our particular responsibility in foreign mission, something is entirely false. Our foreign missions will then be an
alibi, an escape from our immediate responsibility. Unfortunately
we know of many situations where it is easier to love humanity
than to love one's neighbour.

The evangelistic dimension of our church life at home is the basic
credential for an evangelistic outreach in other parts of the world.
I want to invite you to a conversation on this topic from the
particular perspective of our own expertise in foreign mission.
What did we learn from the geographical expansion of the church
to other countries that could now be useful for our missionary
and evangelistic task at home? What is the feed-back that we receive
from sister churches all over the world? When we see the thriving
numerical growth of churches in Africa or in some parts of Latin
America we should ask ourselves if this is only the result of
different sociological, political, cultural situations, or if it
has to do also with a different attitude, approach, obedience and
fidelity of the local communities concerned.

For somebody like myself, coming from Latin America to Europe and
worshipping in different local congregations, a striking difference
appears immediately. In Latin America it would be difficult to find
a Protestant church of a missionary tradition where the evangelistic
dimension is not daily present, be it in general exhortation to
evangelize or in the actual fact of people being added to the church.
Nobody can come to our churches without being reminded that the
gospel does not belong to the Christians but is entrusted to them
for the salvation of the world. In Europe we get the impression
that things are being taken for granted, that nobody wants to

spoil the peace of their neighbours and that an evangelistic conviction is not at all common property of the church members. It does not mean that we will demand the same kind of aggressive zeal as is present in our Latin American churches to be present with the same value everywhere in the world. But the passion to relate, the love to share, the obedience to the great commission should be in some way a permanent factor of Christian life. How can we help, out of our missionary experiences, our churches here in Britain to become missionary and evangelistic-minded churches? This is one essential element of what we call world vision: this belonging together and learning together.

We are discussing with several western countries the possibility of receiving visitation teams from churches in the third world in order to discuss with them our missionary commitment in our respective countries, in order to encourage the sharing of gifts, of resources, of vision. Maybe this is the real outcome of the Christian missionary enterprise: when those who have been thinking and acting in terms of giving, are confronted with the wonderful realization that those who have received are now spiritually rich and have gifts to share with them!

1. Our foreign mission cannot presuppose any knowledge of the gospel of Jesus Christ in the surrounding community. It is true that here or there some hints indicating a spiritual pre-anticipation of the gospel have been discovered, like in the case of Paul in Athens calling the attention of the people to the unknown God. But basically the missionary is the one who is supposed to tell the new story to people who are totally out of touch with the facts of the same. And once the churches are organized they are obliged to pay attention to the training of new converts and to the expansion of the communication net-work: Bible translations, literature production, later on radio broadcasts -- all these have been attempts to put before the minds of the people the facts about Jesus Christ. Today in the west we are practically in the same situation. But our strategies, tactics and most of our work assume a knowledge of Jesus Christ and of the basic facts of the gospel that are no longer there. It is true that classical literature and our traditions all speak about the interpenetration between church, gospel and culture in our history. But it is also true that the prevailing secularism and the new paganism dominating the trade, economic and entertainment social life is far more pervasive than any kind of remainder of Christian knowledge. The church, the local parish which wants to evangelize today must recognize that it should begin to teach the essential elements of the history of Jesus Christ and of the Hebrew people. Bible distribution is today more important than ever. And all kinds of means and ways should be found to convey the history of Jesus Christ. While it is true that to evangelize is more than just to tell the story, to tell the story is an essential content of all evangelism.

241

2. The missionary is the tradition which accompanies the gospel.
   Even if he did not wish it, the normal attitude of the new
   converts was an imitation of the values and style of life of
   the missionary, because they had no other possibility of
   seeing Christianity in action than to see it embodied in the
   lives of those who were the actual representatives or
   incarnation of that Christianity. This could be criticized
   because it meant the taking over of undue cultural values
   from the missionary. But this is a fact: there is no such thing
   as a pure gospel. It is always accompanied by the image projected by those who announce it. The local church should
   realize that its style of life is the illustration of what the
   gospel is all about. If our preaching is not matched by our
   obedience, then there is no chance of real evangelism. Philip
   Potter repeats that our crisis is not one of faith but of faithfulness. While this could be discussed in many ways, we all agree
   that there is a close connection between the one and the other.
   The gathered Christian community is an inhibiting factor, a
   hindrance to the proclamation of the gospel or the real argument
   for it. And this has nothing to do with the actual numbers or
   human qualities of the congregation. A group of old people with
   a vision, a group of women with a vision, or a group of young
   people with a vision could provide the challenging presentation
   of the gospel that our surrounding communities desperately need.

3. The ecumenical discussion in the sixties used the slogan: "The
   church for others." Behind this was the conviction that the
   church should be the servant people of God, looking around,
   discovering possibilities of service in the name of Jesus
   Christ. A second slogan came up during the same period: "The
   agenda is provided by the world." In fact those two slogans were
   not entirely new for the foreign missionary enterprise of the
   churches. It is true that the missionary went with his own
   convictions, with his own text of the gospel of Jesus Christ,
   but he reacted to the milieu in which he found himself out of
   the desire to serve, out of his openness to the possibilities
   and needs of the surrounding world. Medical work, educational
   work, social service, even political participation came as a
   logical reading of the needs of the people to whom the gospel
   was to be announced. The question for our communities in Europe
   is in how much they could be able to open afresh their eyes to
   discover the real needs of the surrounding communities and to
   accept the challenges of those communities. What is our worship?
   An exercise in our own piety and in selfish concern with ourselves, or a bringing before God of the aspirations, dreams,
   failures, needs of our surrounding community? In how much are
   we willing to open the windows to discover God's calling to us
   in the needs and aspirations of the surrounding community?

4. It was evident to the missionary that he was not supposed to
   be there for ever, even if the missionary history has not been
   faithful to the Pauline vision of coming for a short period and

moving ahead. But anyhow, as a general factor, the missionaries recognized immediately the need for mobilizing all the charismas in the emerging congregation and working through lay people for the total mission of the church. And this participation of the lay people has been multiplied in the efficiency of the independent and Pentecostal churches where people with a minimum of training but with a great spiritual sensitivity are being entrusted with most of the tasks of the Christian community. In Europe it is almost impossible to preach from a pulpit without having a university degree. I preached for the first time when I was 15 years old! Maybe the charismatic renewal will help us to remember the gifts that God grants to every local congregation, especially the gift of being able to discover gifts!

5. The missionaries first were alone as Christians in a non-Christian surrounding. Later on they were members of a small growing community. Even today, in most of Asia the churches are small minorities vis-à-vis the total population and in relation to other religions. The temptation to develop an inferiority complex and to feel and act as marginal to this society has been an ever-present reality. At the same time, what really surprises us in foreign mission at its best, is the way in which the contemplation of the biblical God, the God of history, has encouraged Christians to go on in their mission, trusting that notwithstanding the small numbers they were the bearers of God's revelation and those who could help the surrounding communities to interpret their own situations in the light of God's will. The missionary zeal was not only to bring new converts into the communities but also to discover God's action in the surrounding history. God has been acting through secular forces, through religious movements and by the mystery of his wisdom it is the small church as bearer of the revelation that will give meaning to the whole history and that will be challenging the whole of society. It was the knowledge and the faith that God was in action which encouraged the small churches to proceed in missionary obedience, knowing that God will take care of the future. In the present situation of the western world Christians are still within a structure that corresponds to a majority situation, but de facto they are a small minority vis-à-vis the rest of the population. The temptation is to give way to a sense of defeatism and to look around to the old people who sit in our pews and see there the image of a dead church. We need to recover the sense of vocation of being the bearers of a revelation which will illuminate the totality of our community: to dare to proclaim a word of judgment and encouragement, of condemnation and mercy, to recover a sense of the mystery of God whose power is not limited to the size of our congregations but whose love wants to use our little communities for the benefit and the salvation of others.

6. The missionary call is to a radical conversion to Jesus Christ. Today we criticize -- and with good arguments -- the unhappy history of the destruction of cultural values of so many people

243

through the conscious or unconscious work of the church's missionary expansion. We must repent about that and be willing to recover the roots in the soil of our national cultures and to express our praise of God according to our inner being. At the same time we should recognize that even this exaggeration of the missionary zeal was an attempt to preserve a clear Christian truth. There is a radical need for a new birth, a new beginning, a new relation to God that we call conversion. This calling to recognize in God such an abundant love calls for our repentance and for our acceptance of his forgiveness. This call to belong to his kingdom and to go forward to our surrounding society with the values of that kingdom, the call to begin our life afresh from God, with our neighbour, is an essential and permanent part of the Christian gospel that the foreign missionary enterprise of the church has tried to keep alive before the people of the respective countries. This need for a radical conversion to Jesus Christ is perhaps the utmost need of European Christianity. Because Christianity has been so much intertwined with the fabric of its respective cultures, the distinction between belief and un-belief, obedience and disobedience is no longer clear. We need to recover the clear calling of the Bible to a new beginning with God, to a new relation to Jesus Christ, to a belonging to a kingdom which is not synonymous with the status quo of the surrounding community. There will be no evangelism in our local communities without this calling people to enlist themselves with Jesus Christ for God in the world.

Converts in my part of the world have been obliged to pay a very high social price for becoming Christians. What is the price we are asking our western fellow citizens to pay for coming to Jesus Christ? In my part of the world conversion is an essential element for the renewal of society because it is only through internal conviction that we can go to face and endure the risks and realities of oppression which are a permanent feature of any kind of Christian obedience today. How can we recover the dimension of joyful obedience, of forgiveness as offered and accepted, of personal belonging to a kingdom and to a king? This is our basic need in every local parish and in every evangelistic attempt. We are not advocating for a recovery of the psychological marks of the 19th century experience of conversion. We are taking from the experience of the foreign missionary enterprise the freshness of a calling to a clear decision for Christ and demanding that this freshness should be alive anew in the pulpits and in the daily conversations of European Christians.

7. We must recognize that much of our foreign missionary enterprise was due to an attraction for the unknown, for the new. Even today, so many specialized groups are working in the jungles, among very small groups of people, trying to reach them with the gospel of Jesus Christ, motivated by this attraction for the frontier situation. We hear some voices complaining that

244

the shape foreign mission has taken today appears as church-to-church cooperation, as inter-church aid. We are convinced that theologically this is sound. But the attraction for the frontier situation, the going beyond, is a permanent feature, a permanent challenge, a concern of anxiety for the foreign mission organizations. We need to bring down to earth in our own local situation the same attraction, the same search for frontier situations, because close to us those situations exist. There are cities in the world where you will find Christian churches very well attended in one part of the city and practically non-existing or empty in other parts. There is a real frontier that not many people dare to cross between certain parts of a city, between social classes, between structures of society. How do we bring back the glamour of foreign territories and apply it to the glamour, to the attraction of the barren sides of our population where we are not alive as a Christian presence? There it is, the "lumpen proletariat"; those who have been an object of our charity but to whom belong the promises of the kingdom. There it is, the workers' organized world; there where the struggle for economic progress and social power is taking place and creates a block very difficult to penetrate for those who worship in our normal, customary parish life. And then the student world where so many are engaged in the frontiers of science or in the struggle for political change where a clear Christian challenge should be present. Of course we have many traditional organizations that have been created for the relation of faith and science, for the evangelization of workers or evangelization of the university world. But it seems to me that during the last few years we have been so enthusiastic about general slogans that we have lost the sense of specificity. We need to recover from the foreign missionary experience the reality of a self-imposed vocational limitation. Sometimes a frustrating limitation has provided a cutting edge for the possibility of real missionary service. How do we recover the sense of being sent into specific territories, into a specific human zone of our society?

I am going to stop here. Surely, in our conversation we shall discover many other facts of the foreign missionary enterprise which have something to teach to our new missionary situation in the western world. One obvious conclusion comes to mind.

Evangelism in our local situation has much to learn from evangelism in other situations. The genius of the foreign missionary adventure has been to give; now we need to develop the genius to receive. We belong together. There are then clear implications for our organizations. In how much are we challenged to bring forward that heritage as a richness by which we contribute to the salvation of our own society? In how much are we keeping for our specialized organizations the richness, experiences and gifts of God granted to the churches in the third world and thus being ourselves a hindrance for those blessings to reach the level of our local parishes in our own church? World mission is a real challenge to our imagination, wherever we want to join the evangelistic task.

(Address delivered to the Conference of British Missionary Societies, June 1975)

EVANGELISM IN THE WORLD

In internal Christian conversation about mission and evangelism
I think we are coming to the end of a long and frustrating
tunnel. After years of misunderstanding and much energy
consumption in internal strife, through the interplay of big
assemblies such as Bangkok, Lausanne and even the Synod of
Bishops in Rome, we are coming to a general atmosphere of common
conviction and common understanding. I do not mean that all
theological debates are over, nor that there are no nuances.
What I mean is that today there is enough agreement and enough
understanding so as to be able to concentrate most of our energy
on the actual task of evangelization, trusting each other, and
not allowing the world to see the spectacle of our internal
strife and division.

We live today with a growing concern and even enthusiasm for the
work of evangelization. Some voices have just called our attention
to the fact that this could be a very ambiguous phenomenon because
it comes or it happens at the same moment in which other religious
phenomena are also present among us. We live today in a period of
new religiosity, but religiosity as ways and means to escape from
daily frustration, from the monotony of industrial life. The
attraction of the oriental forms of worship could be an indication
of the search for something deeper. But our answer to that search
could be at the level of a religious need of humankind and in that
way betraying the total gospel of Jesus Christ. Also, this new
concern for evangelism comes at a moment when a wave of
frustration is taking hold of the majority of western communities
and of western churches in relation to humankind's ability to
solve its own problems. The oil crisis has opened the doors to
the realization of a series of crises that have shaken every
optimism in relation to the future. This general frustration is
an invitation to concentrate on our small worlds and to provide
for areas of meaning for our individual lives. Evangelism can
either be a way to escape from frustration or a way to offer
protection to our individuality in a period of general dismay.
But if we read the documents from Lausanne, Bangkok or the
Synod of Bishops and take seriously what is being said and
written today, it is clear that a new concern for evangelism
is in no way a wish to retreat into some kind of refuge in
theology or in religious systems of the past, but a desire to
go forward with God in Christ, in his redeeming and liberating
struggle.

Evangelism is a presentation of Jesus Christ as saviour and lord.
It is an offering of forgiveness and an invitation to discipleship. It is a calling of people to enter into the struggle of
the kingdom. The struggle of the sixties to bring social justice
and participation in development to the forefront of the
Christian consciousness is today incorporated into this understanding of God's mission, Christian discipleship, repentance

and conversion. There are still nuances, but there is enough
common ground to concentrate our energy upon the actual task.

Of course, we cannot cover today all the waterfronts under the
heading 'world evangelization'. So I want to open with you a
general conversation, sharing some reflections that come from
our daily work in the Commission on World Mission and
Evangelism (CWME). To participate in God's world mission and
to name his name among all the people is the prevailing concern
of all our activities. The CWME aim says it very clearly: It is

> ...to assist the Christian community in the proclamation of the
> Gospel of Jesus Christ, by word and deed, to the whole world to
> the end that all may believe in him and be saved.

1. Time and time again, we are called to recognize the importance
   and the validity of the local congregation as the main locus
for world evangelization. Of course, we strongly believe in the
crossing of frontiers, but this crossing of boundaries is only
possible and justified when it belongs to a total understanding
of mission in which we take seriously our immediate surroundings.
Fidelity here is in close relationship to the spreading of faith
all over the world. Today especially the world begins here. News
is carried all over the world, providing an image of our own
faithfulness. More than that: migrants coming from the most
diverse parts of the earth are close to us. Our pretension to
preach the gospel of love is tested in our daily manifestation of
love around us. But it is not only because of this interplay in
history that we should pay attention to what happens locally. It
is because in God's economy, in his mission, we all belong together.
We need to recover this world dimension of the local engagement
as a way of incorporating the faithfulness and experiences of
the local congregation into the total missionary outreach. I am
thinking especially of churches in certain countries where they
are deprived of the right to send people and funds abroad. They
can only participate in world mission by their own fidelity, by
the way in which they bring in prayer to God the concern of
churches all over the world. How many of our local parishes
could be renewed, challenged and inspired if they understood
themselves in their daily fidelity as full participants in God's
mission which reaches every corner of the earth! In no way should
this emphasis on the local community be seen as a competitor to
our concern for spreading the faith beyond our borders. It is the
necessary foundation, the real test of our missionary vocation.

2. Bangkok has emphasized the search for cultural identity as
   a necessary task of the Christian community today. Throughout
the world, especially in Africa and among minority communities
in America, this desire for discovering their own soul, for
having roots in their own culture, is present. What is this?
Could it be a way to consume our energy by digging into our own
cultures and by building up nationalist systems, thus closing our
eyes to the universality of the gospel, and to concentrate on
secondary tasks while forgetting the task of evangelism? In a

way it is out of a realization of the historical complicity
of the missionary outreach of the western churches with
colonialism and neo-colonialism that new churches have begun
to search for their own identity, trying to discover how much
the gospel was really related to their inner national being
and not only an imposed factor by the dominant culture. This
serious and intellectual struggle, this digging for firm roots
in national cultural soil, is precisely a necessary condition
for intelligent and faithful evangelism today. Not only, nor
primarily, to obtain cultural data that could be used in the
disseminating of Christian ideas, doctrines or Christian
knowledge, but in order to test the fidelity of our obedience
in every situation, in order to discover the fruits of the
gospel that belong to our particular country, in order to be
able to talk with our neighbours out of the depth of our common
belonging to the same people. This searching for identity comes
out of a desire for more faithful obedience and for a more
relevant communication of the gospel. Surely we need to learn
here in the west from this search in Africa, and try to discover
what is our own cultural identity and how much the gospel that
we preach and practise is tainted by our belonging to cultural
traditions that we are not challenging or recovering theologically!

3. It is in the same direction that we should understand the
whole debate on moratorium. It is a searching for the self-
reliance of those churches who are the result of foreign missionary
work. It is also a desire to liberate foreign missionary
organizations for new possibilities. Moratorium should be tested
in the light of the implications that it has for our total mission
and specifically for our evangelistic task. Is the assuming of
full responsibility for our church life a liability or an empowering factor for the spreading of the gospel? At the same time,
as the Lausanne Congress says, several circumstances, such as the
retiring of foreign personnel and foreign money, could allow for
this personnel and money to be invested in other new missionary
situations, or, as the Bangkok Conference says, this money and
personnel could be redeployed, even at the home bases of western
countries, for a re-education of the minds of the churches and
of the common people in relation to what God is doing in other
countries. But in any case, the moratorium debate cannot be a
philosophical debate or a beautiful way to express reciprocal
resentment. It must be tested as to how much it is the moratorium
that enables mission to take place, in how much it enables engagement or disengagement of the churches on the spot, and of
churches supporting others in other parts of the world to be
more efficient participants in God's mission. If we talk seriously about world evangelism, business as usual is not the correct
response. The moratorium debate provides a chance to reconsider
our priorities, to re-open our thinking on strategies, to redeploy our resources and personnel. How many mission administrators
would dare to think of what they would do if suddenly they lost
all existing commitment in given places and were entirely free
to plan anew the mission entrusted to them? The search for this
kind of freedom is an essential element in the moratorium con-

versation. But we must stress and repeat and repeat: moratorium,
self-reliance, freedom of operation, cultural identity, etc.
are never ends in themselves; at maximum they could be temporal
expressions of our desire to be faithful.

4. This dream of a new freedom in our missionary and evangelistic
   endeavours is expressed also in the programme which we call
'Ecumenical Sharing of Personnel'. It is an attempt to use all
the charismas, all the resources that God has given to his church
all over the world. It is the irony of the present situation that
the churches are growing numerically and are showing signs of the
Holy Spirit precisely in those countries which are economically
weak, and that, on the other hand, churches are struggling to
survive in those countries which are economically powerful. How
do we match gifts, those of humanpower and those of a financial
nature, for an evangelistic strategy all over the world? We know
how administrative pressure demands from us the recruitment
abroad of our own sons and daughters in our own country and
church. There is a permanent value here, vocation, personal
involvement, and personal knowledge that should not be denied.
But if our main concern is with the evangelization of the world
and not with the preservation of our own organization, we need
to be more free to redeploy financial resources to match the
growing vocations and charismas that God has given to his church
all over the world. The multiplication and diversification of
people crossing all kinds of frontiers in the name of Jesus
Christ is a priority today, and we need to recover that freedom
and to re-educate our constituency in order to understand the
joy of trusting other people as bearers of the gospel of Jesus
Christ to us and to others.

5. The Lausanne Congress has called our attention to the millions
   of people who have not yet been reached with the gospel of
Jesus Christ. When we look at those numbers seriously we discover
that the majority belong to highly sophisticated religious systems
or are living in societies of a highly developed ideological
system. Those religious systems are not far away today, they are
here with us as migrants or as missionaries. In fact, we are
living today in a pluralistic situation where missionaries of
different living faiths cross each other's way. The recent
experience of the World Council of Churches' having to change
the venue of the Vth Assembly - from Indonesia to Nairobi - is
a good illustration of the many factors involved in our
evangelistic world endeavour vis-à-vis those other religions or
ideological systems. The Orthodox Church has a long experience
of living in daily touch with these systems and keeping alive
the Christian faith. What do we learn from their experiences?
How do we prepare ourselves and our churches all over the world
for this great task? It is very clear that it will demand the
patience of love, that it is not possible to talk in numbers of
a big success, because as soon as we do this we are involved in
a kind of political struggle that will not only jeopardize
innocent lives but which will betray our very purposes. The

problem we face is perhaps one of generations. It might be possible to explore the possibility of religious orders, of the missionary societies which specialize in living side by side with people belonging to other systems, in the hope that the radiance of the Christian faith, the validity of the Christian liturgy, will finally impose themselves to the consciousness of the surrounding community. We cannot make a successful story here, but, we hope, a faithful history! We are now planning an encounter between Muslim and Christian missionaries in which they will try to understand each other and perhaps agree on some code of missionary behaviour that will allow for a real dialogue and interplay between our respective convictions. We are calling with great intent all missionary-minded people in order to avoid any temptation of syncretism or easy cultural accommodation. We have a gospel that we want to share, but we live side by side with people who believe that they have also something to pass on to us. In this vital encounter we hope, we pray, we expect God's manifestation in Jesus Christ to be a permanent reality. What we need today is not only, nor basically, intellectual research but life together. When we listen to our brothers and sisters living in such situations, we hear that this Christian presence, this Christian community, this Christian love, this Christian liturgy are the evangelistic elements that carry weight.

6. These considerations call us to recognize that evangelism happens within a spiritual realm. It has to do with worship, intercession, prayer. We are expecting a miracle; we are not planning a crusade. We are hoping that the mystery of God's revelation in Jesus Christ will happen through the Christian church, through our Christian life, and will produce the appealing, convincing spiritual argument which will bring people to Jesus Christ. He said: "I shall draw all men to myself when I am lifted up from the earth" (John 12:32).

We are trying to raise his name, his word, his life, his calling. This prayerful life will add to the urgency of our commitment because we cannot pray without being immediately summoned, recruited, involved. At the same time this prayer will produce humility. It is not our cause, it is God's cause, and it will give us a sense of God's time, which is not always our time. Today we are moving towards a new commitment of the Christian church, to the proclamation of the gospel all over the world. It is our task as ancillary servants of the church to think of how to love God with all our mind and with courage, trusting in his mercy.

Let me close by repeating something I said at the beginning, but that now appears in a different light. Foreign mission has been under fire. Even the word mission means colonialism, imperialism for many people. While we surely could defend foreign missions on their own records we must not be defensive. We should recognize

251

how much our own human sin is mixed with everything we do. Repentance means purification, new consecration. In any case, mission also is not saved by words but by grace. The command is clear: to love, to proclaim. The privilege is there - perhaps under the slogan "world mission" we could develop a vision of a new missionary situation where all Christians here and far away are called to share together.

(Address delivered to the Conference of British Missionary Societies, June 1975)

Evangelism in the Third World

What is an appropriate role for the evangelist from the West in the Third World? This question without doubt has reference to Christian action that seeks to cross cultural barriers with the good news of the gospel. Culture, as used here, refers to race, class, values, organizations, etc., without reference necessarily to geography. Cultural barriers exist within each one of our cities. However, given the title of our article and the general theme of this issue, it is evident that the emphasis is to be placed on crossing geographic frontiers which necessarily implies crossing cultural lines. But we ought not to escape so easily — nor indeed can we — the problem of intercultural relations in our own national society.

Some Prior Questions

The question which is the theme of this article may be preceded by another: What role does the middle class Anglo-Saxon play in cross-cultural evangelization in his own country? Even if the Third World geographically speaking and the Third World of poverty in the United States are not exactly the same, still they have enough in common to raise a preliminary question for anyone who would seek to assist the evangelistic effort in the Third World. In what measure and to what extent does your previous experience, in your own country, first of all, demonstrate the seriousness of your commitment to the people of the Third World; and, second, have you opened your eyes to the necessity of full participation in the transformation of the human historical destiny as a fundamental element of your evangelistic preoccupation? Said in a different way — how do the inner city ghettos of North American cities, the racial and poverty mixtures, the indigenous and Spanish-speaking minorities — how do they receive the evangelistic message from one who represents, whether you desire it or not, the dominant groups in your own society?

The fact — sociologically observable — that churches follow race and class lines points out the limitation of our traditional evangelistic methodology and today, because society as a whole and Christians within society have not succeeded in rising above the barriers of poverty and race distinctions, a new consciousness of cultural identity of minority groups is arising — groups which defend themselves against the "others," representatives of the majority. Whoever intends to serve dispossessed or oppressed groups of North American society, in the name of Christ, finds that he or she is accepted only when there are concrete proofs of identification with such groups in their total life, and that acceptance is accorded him or her in the measure to which he or she accepts those minority or dominated segments of society.

What is the role of the missionary from the West in the evangelization of the Third World? Think for a moment from the perspective of the situation within the U.S.A. *Should not every Christian who is considering helping in the evangelism of other countries first be obliged to achieve in his or her life an experience of immersion in, of identification with, of Christian participation alongside minority groups of his or her own country?*

Let us now take up some necessary preliminary considerations.

1. Every Christian is an evangelist. Faith wants to communicate itself; no one has the right to guard it as an exclusive privilege for himself. In this article we shall be thinking of an occidental. Probably we shall have in mind a North American. More specifically even a missionary, someone sent by a mission board from the United States to a country, perhaps of Latin America. But no category such as those which we have mentioned—occidental, American, missionary, etc., should be set up as a barrier against the fulfillment of the evangelistic privilege and responsibility. The appropriate role for a North American who lives in a country of the Third World is like that of every Christian in that or in any other country: to live in such a manner in the light of the gospel that his life-style raises the question as to the hidden root of his being and of his actions.

In the course of our article we shall discuss some of the difficulties which a North American citizen will find in the exercise of a professional ministry for the Church in other parts of the world. But that does not mean to question the possibility of a Christian life-style of identification, of service, which is an evangelistic affirmation and which permits making explicit an evangelistic testimony. But all that we shall say ought to be understood within the framework of this fundamental affirmation: Every Christian has the possibility of sharing the gospel with his neighbour, near or far; however, every Christian who wants to dedicate his life professionally and vocationally to the communication of the gospel to others in other countries will have to consider the various points which we shall raise in the course of this article.

2. Evangelization normally is done within the context of a local Christian community. It may be personal work, or preaching in the surrounding area, or personal encounter while at work; however, every one of these presupposes the existence of a local community that provides a frame of reference which make possible an understanding of what it means to be Christian. The same words in a message with an evangelistic intention will communicate different meanings if they are sustained by congregations with completely different attitudes of obedience.

When a missionary comes for the first time to a territory in which the Christian gospel has not been announced, he is the only projected image of what is Christian. Quite naturally the converts imitate, not only what may be called a Christian life-style, but also the culture which accompanies the missionary from which he or she cannot separate himself or herself. In these circumstances it is almost inevitable that the missionary will transmit his or her cultural values

254

along with the gospel. There still remain some situations of this type. But they are decreasing since, thanks be to God, the Church has spread to all parts of the world, and even if in some places it is not physically an actual reality, at least, through mass media, travels, etc., there exists an image of church, against which the words and life of the missionary are interpreted. Normally, a national church is constituted in order to fulfill the mission of announcing the gospel. The evangelistic contribution of a person, therefore, cannot be measured in terms of his or her own work but in terms of the total work of the church in which he or she has become integrated and to which he or she contributes. The Christian community receives the gifts of grace from God for the total fulfillment of its mission. Among these gifts is that of evangelization. A missionary organization does not assign this gift as a function to a particular person. Rather, it is for the local church, in the exercise of its spiritual discernment as given by the Spirit, to recognize the gifts and assign specific tasks. The important thing in international work is that the church expresses its solidarity with other churches helping in the total ministry, because it is the total ministry which will have evangelistic consequences.

3. The important thing in evangelism is the evangelistic proclamation, its profundity and its multiplication. The question of the role of the missionary from the West is secondary. Perhaps later we shall find in each place a particular answer to the question: how does the Western missionary participate intelligently and responsibly in the evangelistic proclamation which is suited to each particular community of Jesus Christ? But we cannot propose a general answer to the question. In some places, beyond other frontiers, we shall contribute to the total testimony of the Christian community through the lives of some of our children who specialize in the communication of the word. In other circumstances the best service we can render is intercessory prayer, sympathy, and spiritual support for the integration of a community into the surrounding culture in order that evangelistic communication may be produced in this integration. When we have made it very clear that the top priority is preparing the Church for missionary service, we shall be completely free in our missionary strategy, freed of the necessity of thinking in terms of North American personnel for a specific task in another country.

The current debate concerning a moratorium on the sending of funds or missionaries ought always to be kept within this perspective: What is the best way to serve the mission of God? We must be ready to listen to voices which, in some circumstances, tell us that for the cause of Christ the best thing that can be done is to interrupt the sending of missionaries. For example, let us note this radical affirmation of Murray Rogers:

> Partly because the Church has not heeded prophetic voices and partly because of the tremendous social, religious and economic upheaval which is taking place in the country, the image of the Church with which people are most familiar is not so much a spirit movement as

255

a power structure, wealthy and influential, exclusive and sectarian, proudly self-assertive and possessed of an arrogant theology which it is trying to foist on the people of the land by deceptive and seductive means. Its offices are centres of social and political power, symbols of prestige and high-roads to Europe and the U.S.A. or privilege and preference in India.[1]

The words of an American missionary these — not mine!

Rogers goes on to say:

More insidious by far is the effect of Foreign Missions spiritually. Modern Missions were motivated by a sublime confidence in the superiority of the 'Christian west' and with the conviction that if western Christians were 'to take Christ' to India (often thought of as 'dark' in contra-distinction to the west) then the superiority of Christian Faith and Christian morals and Christian Scriptures and of Christ himself would be obvious to the meanest intelligence. This made us — it still does! — introduce into India our church structures, our ways of worship, our architecture, our hymnody, our western theology, our western ways of prayer and loving God, taking it for granted that these, being western and 'Christian' (sic) are obviously best for men everywhere. To quote from Raymond Panikkar (the 'Hidden Christ of Hinduism' man) (sic), i.e. The Unknown Christ of Hinduism) we have 'equated the dominant form of Christianity today—a particular sociological form—with Christianity itself' and that has involved us in a 'particularism incompatible with catholicity and an anachronistic theological colonialism that is absolutely unacceptable.[2]

We may or may not be in agreement with Rogers that the solution to existing problems might be the total interruption of cooperation among men within churches of different countries, but without doubt his words and the reality to which they point are a clear invitation to reconsider our missionary practices and to ask ourselves in what way we ought to express intelligently *today* the same passion and the same love which the missionary expression of the church manifested in past times.

We shall now try to come to a more definite answer to the specific question put to us, always remembering that this answer is subordinate to a previous question: How are we to participate fully in the world evangelistic task? It is also understood that no reply, however radical it may appear to us, ought to be eliminated from the discussion.

Basic Theses

The international missionary relation cannot see itself isolated from total contact between two peoples and between two churches. The image that our nation projects and the reality of that nation's involvement in another country are the background conditions against which the missionary work will be understood. We need to be deadly serious in order to measure the total impact

256

which our country and our church have upon situations. We have to pay attention to the total conduct of the members of our churches in their relations with other countries. Imperialistic conduct in commercial relations, for example, implies the negation of the gospel which may destroy many years of patient work of love and preaching of many missionaries and national workers. The responsibility of anyone who wants to consecrate his or her life to evangelistic missionary work in a country of the Third World does not begin on arriving at the coast of that country, but begins and continues with his interest in and efforts for the totality of the relations between his country of origin and the country to which he comes and their respective churches.

Thesis No. 1: The occidental missionary, who seeks to collaborate in the evangelistic task in the Third World, ought to be concerned with the total relation of his or her country and church with the country and church in which he or she expects to pursue his or her evangelistic activity. His or her responsibility begins before arriving at his or her place of work and continues on two fronts: direct work in the new church and the continuous supplying of information to his or her friends and to churches in other countries concerning the situation and outlook of the country and church which he or she is serving.

This reference to the total context of relations is especially important at this time, in view of the divulgence by the United States Senate of the CIA's intention to use United States missionaries in its intelligence activities. This fact, widely publicized by world news agencies, hangs over all missionary work at this time, especially in the Third World. Door to door visitation, questions concerning family situation, filling out questionaires, utilizing traditional evangelistic methods, all lend themselves today to unfortunate interpretations. The missionary from the West works today under the handicap of a suspicion which falls back on himself or herself and on the whole missionary enterprise. In recent discussion with leaders of the Islamic world community, their one preoccupation was evident—they were dominated by what they considered to be a neo-colonialist conspiracy to use the churches for the domination of the under-developed countries. Consider the recent decision of the Peruvian government to cancel, after almost forty years of existence, the work of the Summer Institute of Linguistics in that country, in order to understand the magnitude of the damage done by this confusion of national interests and missionary activity.

Thesis No. 2: The missionary from the West who wants to participate in evangelistic work in the Third World should be aware of the suspicion which from the beginning rests upon the missionary enterprise and therefore should organize his or her work in such a way as to show very evidently the purity of his or her motives and his or her complete independence from the dominant attitudes and policies of his or her country of origin.

A missionary from a western country cannot escape from the fact that he or she comes from a part of the world which is economically privileged in comparison with other parts. Moreover, it is plain that there is a lamentable interrelationship between the economic abundance among some peoples of the world and the scarcity and need among others. This problem in its worldwide aspect is related to our first consideration concerning the total relations between our two countries. But at the same time it has another dimension: almost inevitably the style of the life and work of the missionary from the West reflects the standard of living to which he or she is accustomed in his or her own country and consequently brings a contrast to the local situation. While the Apostle Paul was able to come as a poor man among the poor and took up offerings from the new churches for the mother church, today the situation is completely reversed. The missionary from the West is regarded as a kind of Santa Claus or as a person who has access to the advantages of modern technology for facilitating his or her work. A radical question must be raised: Is not our wealth an obstacle to the possibility of the gospel being understood in its fullness by the poor people through gifts or the solving of their material problems? However, the underlying relation of our respective economic situations makes the "buying" of converts difficult to avoid.

Thesis No. 3: The missionary from the West who seeks to contribute to the evangelistic work in a country of the Third World ought to consider carefully his or her life-style and ought to so identify it with that of the local Christian community that the image of what is Christian may be projected by the whole community and not so much by him or her individually.

But we should not look at the situation of the missionary from the West only with reference to the country, the church, and the culture from which he or she comes. We also should look at it in relation to the new situation into which he or she integrates himself or herself. We have already said that what is important is the facilitating of the evangelistic work of the local Christian community. Now, then, a foreigner from the West brings to that community handicaps and advantages. If, as we were saying before, he or she maintains a standard of living superior to what is normal in the new community, he or she projects an image of social injustice which is an obstacle to the proclamation of the gospel. Language, cultural adaptation, etc., are other examples of such handicaps. But at the same time it should be recognized that this same foreignness of the missionary is a factor which contributes to enlarging the ecumenical horizons of the local community and thereby multiplies its capacity for work. It is he or she as person who is important rather than the fact that the number engaged in the total missionary effort is increased, and this ought to be recognized as the important contribution made by his or her presence; the increase in the total work force is far less important than the specific contribution of the foreign missionary as a reminder of the catholicity of the church.

Thesis No. 4: The missionary from the West ought to find his or her place and service with the national Christian community. He or she will seek to enrich the internal dialogue of that community with his or her own international experience, but he or she will always remember that it is appropriate for that local Christian community to increase and for him or her to decrease.

Perhaps we ought to recognize that the missionary models placed before young recruits in missionary training schools do not contribute to the creation of the spiritual and missiological perspective necessary for today. We cannot think any longer in terms of the pioneers who opened ways in other epochs and who were true leaders of the churches being born. Today the existence of the local Christian church responsible for the witness of the gospel in its own community is the fundamental element which must be taken into account. Consequently the type of missionary that is needed is one who can work on a team, who can add himself or herself to others, contributing his or her gifts and particular perspectives. When a missionary from the West arrives in a country of the Third World he or she finds normally a local church which receives him or her and often fellow missionaries who are also interested in him or her. Almost naturally his or her outlook is limited to his or her receiving church and to the interpretation of it which his or her colleagues give him or her. This situation is understandable, and it is important to the total identification of the missionary with the local church. However, unless he or she dares to become a part of the surrounding secular community, he or she will not be able to know first-hand the sentiments, expectations, hopes or criticisms which the national community raises in relation to the local church. Participation in support of social service groups, or in the schools which his or her children attend, that is to say, in all the situations which permit him or her regular human encounter with the surrounding community, will enrich his or her capacity for working within the local church. It will help him or her to achieve quickly a sense of pertinence toward the total national community. At the same time it will provide natural opportunities for Christian testimony which arise in the community work, in social life, and in responsibility shared with other persons. Rather than seeking to be a professional evangelist within a national church, the foreign missionary can live immersed in the people, knowing that God will utilize these encounters for his own blessing and for the blessing of those who relate themselves to him.

Thesis No. 5: The missionary from the West who desires to do evangelistic work in the Third World should have ample possibilities for normal contact with the secular community to which he or she relates himself or herself. He or she should participate in it, side by side with his or her good neighbours, seeking in this participation to understand them, to render service to the surrounding community and to bear a natural testimony to his or her faith.

All these conclusions try to express in detail the ways in which a missionary from the West can relate responsibly to the witness of the mission of the church in a country of the Third World. Obviously, we are not answering directly the lead question of this article—what is the role of the missionary in a Third World country? But implicitly it is answered. The foreigner from the West will arrive in a country of the Third World not with the idea of playing a particular role, but with the idea of serving as a Christian, corresponding to the

259

vocation he or she has received, integrating himself or herself in the community of the brethren. He or she does not have a particular role to play which can be defined beforehand. Yes, he or she does have a personal and community experience by which he or she incorporates himself or herself into the local community. He or she brings with him or her, too, the handicaps of his or her own foreignness, his or her linguistic limitations, that which is suitable to his or her own country which usually is rich and is ideologically, economically and culturally different from the country which receives him or her. But just as he or she is, trusting in this country, he or she confident that his or her humble service of witness can be useful in the transformation of many lives. At the same time, because he or she loves profoundly the new country and because he or she wants to help the total mission of the church in it, he or she is disposed to consider all the factors involved in the situation and to analyze together with the community the advantages or disadvantages of his or her presence in it, the place where he or she is to work, and the particular responsibility of relating his or her faithful ministry in the new country to the faithfulness which the churches that receive him or her have the right to expect and demand of their brethren in the country of his or her origin The missionary responsibility of a denomination in the West should be measured, not in terms of the number of missionaries which it sends, but in terms of the number of responsible relationships which are created with churches in other parts of the world, in a relationship of giving and receiving in which all are jointly responsible in the common missionary undertaking. It is easier to measure the success of our operation in terms of money or of personnel which cross frontiers than to measure it in terms of the faithfulness which accompanies all our activities. However difficult this criterion might be, we have to assume the difficult task of applying it. Because only in this way will we be discovering our true role in the evangelization of our own country and of other countries.

Now for a brief digression in order to discuss the problem of missionaries from the West working in areas where a local Christian church does not yet exist. Quite evidently, here the work of the missionary cannot be that of adding himself or herself to a nonexistent community! However, if we have learned anything from the transmission of models of cultural conduct through mission, and of service which mission has contributed, consciously or unconsciously, to colonial and neo-colonial expansion of western culture, it would be well to consider the feasibility of fulfilling our missionary mandate by the use of international teams by means of which dependence on one cultural model only or one country can be eliminated in some measure.

It is ironical that the Christian church grows today in those countries whose economies are dependent and that they therefore cannot have the economic means for projecting a missionary activity of an international character. Why not recognize the gifts which God has given to his Church among various peoples of the earth, and why not separate the resources from the person and participate with the resources and the vocations of all Christendom in the total missionary task? This ecumenical interchange of personnel would give to our churches a sense of full participation in the total mission throughout the world, and it would not be tied to the presence of any given person. No one then would be under the compulsion of giving reports of his or her specific work, but we all would be invited to share experiences, anticipations, and blessings received in our respective missionary efforts.

In conclusion: The missionary from the West who goes to a country in the Third World ought to prepare himself or herself with all humility to integrate himself or herself into a Christian community and a secular community in which he or she wants to be a servant of Jesus Christ. But a Christian church in the western world which desires to share the gospel in other countries of the world has only the limitation of its imagination in finding ways of cooperating in prayer and in joint work with sister churches in other regions. In this sense we would do well to study the experiences in missionary participation of churches in socialist countries which cannot send funds or personnel but, nevertheless, through programs of visits, of shared information, and of prayer, participate spiritually in the common task. By virtue of the interdependence of national and international factors, it is evident that many countries of the Third World will go on closing their doors to the possibility of missionary work whose base is in the Occident. How much more important is it, then, that we Christians learn to share resources and possibilities and that we dare to have confidence in the strength of the local Christian church as a fundamental element in the evangelization of its own people!

Historical and political circumstances may force us to change our missionary tactics. What they are not able to do is to kill the missionary vocation!

---

[1] "Missionary Service in Asia Today," (A Report on a Consultation held by the Asia Methodist Advisory Committee, Feb. 18-23, 1971), University of Malaya, Kuala Lumpur, p. 126.

[2] Ibid., p. 127.

(Review and Expositor, Southern Baptist Theological Seminary, 1977)

After a time in which emotions have run high, we have finally entered a period when rational discourse on this theme is possible. To suggest even the temporary withdrawal of missionaries and funds from particular countries was bound to provoke a strong emotional reaction, for the work of mission is an expression of the Christian churches' evangelistic passion and their readiness to serve. It is no mere appendage, a luxury to be indulged or not at will, but a natural and normal expression of their life in Christ. One must admit, however, at the same time, that mission work has often gone hand in hand with the imperialistic activities of our respective countries. But this fact, which must be analysed and its effects judged in order to purify the contemporary missionary experience, cannot negate the spirit of sacrifice and love in which men and women have dedicated their lives to the service of Jesus Christ among peoples who live beyond their own frontiers.

Whenever we debate issues which touch our basic convictions, our emotions are aroused. But when our emotions make us react to the mere sound of a word and lead us to caricature our neighbour, accusing him of being an "enemy of mission" or a "neo-colonialist", then we must admit the injustice we have done and repent these emotions. One cannot possibly judge a person's convictions on the missionary calling of the Christian Church solely by his attitude toward the question of moratorium. Both the Bangkok Conference on Salvation Today and the Lausanne Congress on World Evangelization discussed moratorium, whether the actual word was used or not. Both of these Christian conferences have raised the possibility that in particular places and under certain circumstances a withdrawal of funds and missionary personnel may well be necessary to carry out more effectively the missionary task.

Decisions on what mission methods are suitable for which particular situations, including the possible use of moratorium, remains, as it always has, with the churches engaged in mission in that country. The only contribution we can make through the IRM is to provide a forum where experiences can be shared and questions raised, where we can stimulate each other to think about the questions the call to moratorium raises and correct one another's misapprehensions. This issue of the IRM begins with an essay by a young African candidate for the Roman Catholic priesthood. Mr Mwasaru's cry from the heart is a reminder of all the problems which remain unsolved, the problems which frustrate a healthy witness to Christ by the African Church. We begin with this as a reminder of what moratorium is all about. Elsewhere in this issue our easy assumptions about the missionary significance of the New Testament are challenged in the Bible study on the Book of Acts, and the missionary vocation is looked at in the light of moratorium in a provocative article from the US. What does it mean to be a North American missionary in a time of moratorium? And in the time of Vietnam and Watergate? A Nigerian writer looks again at the old question of church and mission, this time in the light of the moratorium issue. Two articles attempt to give some indication of how health care and theological education could be carried out in a manner that does not reproduce foreign patterns nor produce perpetual dependency on foreign funds. Brief descriptions of several actual moratorium experiences, including an account of the aftermath of the well-known withdrawal of the White Fathers from Mozambique, offer some idea of what moratorium is really like, while two other writers reject the moratorium idea for cogent reasons. Responses to a questionnaire on moratorium from eleven carefully selected people, a sampling of the great variety of those concerned about the future of mission, reveal the complexity of the questions surrounding moratorium. The Documentation Section offers excerpts from documents tracing the recent history of the moratorium idea. Its earlier history is documented in the article found on pp. 210-217.

Among the many aspects of the moratorium debate, there are several that have become clear:

1. *Moratorium is no new idea.* But the use of this particular word is new — and many would argue, unfortunate. That question aside for the moment, we should note that the practice of withdrawing a foreign missionary from a given country or church has its antecedents in the New Testament itself. The Apostle Paul does not want to impose his presence on the churches which he founded. After a short time he goes on his way leaving them to express in their own way their obedience to the faith which he has made known to

them. At a recent consultation on moratorium, Dr Philip Potter, General Secretary of the WCC, reminded us that as early as 1910, at the Edinburgh Conference, there was evidence of awareness of the fundamental concerns of this debate: the problem of missionary paternalism, the identity of the new churches, and the need for them to be self-governing and self-propagating. The theme therefore is far from new; perhaps it has had the misfortune to reappear in the missiological discussion at a time of intense mistrust and great polarization. But the more we move away from our caricatures and our stereotyped responses to them, the more we discover that the word *moratorium* is an attempt to describe, in terms which make sense in our time, a style of action aimed at recreating the very relationships which have long been the goal of mission and which stand firmly in the tradition of the Church.

2. *Moratorium does not mean isolationism.* Sometimes a complete break in relations occurs because of political decisions taken by governments. Sometimes situations arise in which the rupture of relations takes place as a result of human sin, of a power struggle in a partnership. The idea of moratorium does not justify ruptures which occur because of distrust or rejection. Moratorium does not, in fact, in any way, aim at a loss of relations but rather the suspension of one particular type of relation in order to allow other possible relationships to emerge. Thus the Apostle Paul, who did not want to make the congregations he founded dependent by imposing his physical presence upon them, maintained constant contact with them through his letters, developing a relationship of great richness and honesty. It may be that after giving up a relationship of dependency, real spiritual relations can be established through which we can at last give and receive with greater authenticity. Prayers of intercession, mutual visits, personal encounters and the sharing of experiences — all these can and must be maintained while a moratorium on funds and personnel is being applied. Moratorium is not advocated in order to bring about an isolation in the Christian faith but a recovery of respective identities in order to achieve more effective missionary action at the local level and a richer and more mature relationship among partners in mission.

3. *Moratorium seeks to affirm an area of freedom, not only for the churches which receive missionary assistance but also for the sending churches and organizations.* In Bangkok it was suggested that such funds and personnel as could no longer be sent outside the boundaries of the Western world might be used in the re-education of Christians in the churches of the West and of the citizens of those countries. In the Lausanne Covenant it was noted that this freeing of funds and personnel might make it possible to "release resources for unevangelized areas". The subject of how these resources should be used must be discussed seriously. Moratorium does not mean the elimination of the missionary vocation nor the duty to provide resources for missionary work. It does mean freedom to reconsider present engagements and to see whether a continuation of what we have been doing for so long is the right style of

mission in our day. Some early reactions in Western missionary circles to the very mention of the word *moratorium* indicated a certain reluctance to grasp the possibilities it offers us to exercise freedom and imagination.

We seem to have organized ourselves in mission in such a way that we cannot stop. It is almost as if we were a great business enterprise with its own rhythm of production which cannot be interrupted without causing great calamity. The moratorium obliges us to reflect seriously on how to regain a freedom that will allow us, in obedience, to reconsider our goals, taking into consideration the present world missionary situation. Moratorium may also mean recovery of freedom for the churches which have been receiving help, freedom to ask fundamental questions such as: Do we really want foreign personnel? What sacrifices are we willing to make in our own finances in order to maintain this personnel? Do we need foreign money? To what extent is our style of pastoral work, our church administration a copy of foreign patterns, making us forever dependent financially on foreign sources? Does our way of being the church tie us in a natural way to our own people?

4. *Moratorium has to be understood within something we call, for lack of a better name, "world mission".* It is only when we begin to accept the missionary responsibility of each local church that we can speak of a moratorium on our present relationship of assistance and dependence. Only if I am committed to the accomplishment of the mission of the church in my own country have I the right to think of assisting other countries and other regions. It is the faithfulness of my commitment to Christ in my own national situation which makes my missionary concern in other parts of the world authentic. We have often said that the way in which the North American churches face the racial problem in their own country is the best missionary service they can render in foreign lands. Only as a church is committed to justice in its home country does it have the credentials for preaching a liberating Gospel in other parts of the world. At the same time, the church which chooses moratorium for the sake of its own authenticity must do so certain that in this way it is searching for a more adequate expression of its missionary responsibility and is contributing to the total service rendered by the Church to the world.

Whenever motives unrelated to our concern for announcing the Kingdom of God lie behind our call for a moratorium, we falsify the issue and use the word *moratorium* as a cover-up for other motivations and other purposes. To repeat what has been said so many times: there can never be a moratorium *of* mission; there can be — and perhaps in various places must be — a moratorium on missionary service both for the sake of those who receive and for the sake of agencies and churches which send funds and personnel.

5. *The whole debate on moratorium is already accomplishing an important missionary function: It obliges us to re-think our motivations and our relations and forces us to make use of our imaginations.* The challenge of the mora-

torium shakes our previous assumptions. We cannot go on doing business as usual. It urges us to seize the freedom to think through our mission again without the weight of our traditional, usually bilateral, relationships, so that we may then discover the real values within those relationships and go about finding ways of preserving those values without creating dependency. In short, taking up the subject of moratorium may mean the recovery of the critical freedom and the freedom of imagination so necessary for intelligent obedience to God. It may be worthwhile to note that the recent ecumenical discussion on moratorium was initiated in the course of the struggle to formulate a set of guidelines or criteria by which the churches, moving beyond the state of mere mutual recognition, might engage themselves in a pact of mutual responsibility for engagement in six continent mission. It is not surprising that the moratorium issue had to be faced by this group of people, the Interim Committee on the Ecumenical Sharing of Personnel, all of whom had been struggling to experiment with new ways of sharing ecumenically the churches' resources, human as well as financial. Once faced, the issue of moratorium was seen to raise, with greater than ever urgency, the whole gamut of ecumenical issues from ecclesiology to the unity and universality of the Church, cultural identity, the use of power, the relationship between God's people and God's mission, and not just the question of structures for mission.

Certainly, though moratorium is not a new idea, it is a new way to raise old questions, and to raise them perhaps more sharply for our day. Moratorium poses a penultimate question. The real question is not whether or not there should be a moratorium but how to be the Church of Jesus Christ, how to live up to our calling to be God's messengers. In the search for an answer to these ultimate questions, reflection on moratorium may perhaps be of help. As an aid to that reflection, let's listen to Mr Mwasaru . . .

Africanization!
We want to see the Church African!

Such are the cries that one hears every day.
Indeed, they are far too frequent.
One even begins to wonder what on earth we mean by "Africanization".

We must have African bishops!
We want African priests!
Yes, and even African sisters and brothers.
True we need them.
The African Church should be in the hands of Africans themselves.

(International Review of Mission, April 1975)

CONVERSION

"The proclamation of the Gospel includes an invitation to recognize and accept in a personal decision the saving lordship of Christ." In this very simple phrase, Mission and Evangelism — An Ecumenical Affirmation declares what should be obvious for every Christian preacher. The proclamation of the gospel is not a disinterested story-telling. We tell the story of the gospel with the public hope that decisions will follow. To open the word of God, to announce its meaning to the human community, is an exercise of hope in the action of the Holy Spirit that could provoke the miracle of a response of faith, even to our very limited testimony of Jesus Christ. Notwithstanding possible misunderstandings, of which we are going to talk later on, we need to open this consideration of the topic of conversion in the *International Review of Mission*, affirming that the Christian gospel is an offer, an invitation, a call to people to respond personally and socially to God.

Paulo Freire has taught us the importance of the process of conscientization, a process through which people come to understand their own predicament and recognize the forces that are at work in their lives and in the life of society, and as a consequence become protagonists both of their own destiny and the destiny of their community. Applying the same phraseology, we could say that conversion is the moment of conscientization, of awareness, of a personal relationship with God in Christ, an invitation to enter with him into the actual task of transforming this world according to God's will. The cross and resurrection express better than anything else the content of our new loyalty in conversion, loyalty to the crucified Christ, loyalty to the kingdom of the risen Christ. Conversion is a changing of perspective, assuming a relationship both with the historical and the living Christ as point of permanent reference. Conversion means to be incorporated into the new dimension of being a co-worker of God in his kingdom.

As a psychological fact, conversion is well known in other religions and even in political movements. Different schools of psychology could explain the mechanism which produces this particular experience. The distinctiveness of Christian conversion is not in a psychological manifestation, but in its central point of reference. Jesus Christ is perceived as the focus of integration of the personality, and God's kingdom is conceived as the centre of meaning for all human history. To be Christian is not to be a new person in him/herself, it is to be a new person in Jesus Christ; it is not a different psychology, it is a different relationship. For this reason, the Christian teaching explains that the work of the Holy Spirit is necessary to produce conversion, because it is the Holy Spirit that allows the actualization of the yesterday, the Jesus of history, and leads us today into the encounter of the living Christ in the middle of the struggles and dreams of people.

Conversion is an awareness of God's grace, God's will, God's love, God's law, a response manifesting itself in faith, repentance, obedience and community.

Having affirmed quite clearly the centrality of the expectation of conversion in the mission of the Christian church, we are now ready to listen to many voices that warn us of an overemphasis or easy use of this word. Let us be aware of the religious enthusiasts who, in the name of a radical religious experience, lead people astray! After the experience of Jim Jones, the North American preacher who brought his whole congregation to Guyana, and who shared with his congregation in a tragic collective suicide, we must be very humble in providing evidence of human conversion through the intensity of emotion experienced by one or many members of a group. Jim Jones remains the dramatic evidence of contemporary religious fanaticism, even in the name of Christ. Psychology helps us understand the control techniques of the human mind which have been developed by sectarian religions. Psycho-social studies reveal the mechanism of submission of the personality. This manipulation of mass psychology or of the individual is a well-known temptation to every charismatic Christian leader.

Other critics refer to an old phenomenon, well known from Christian mission everywhere in the world — the exploitation of a situation of weakness of the recipients of our proclamation. The phrase "rice Christians" was coined in China and referred to people who professed Christianity in order to receive the advantages granted by the churches. A similar phenomenon can be observed in Asian refugee camps where people waiting for a visa to go to the U.S. are easy prey to the call for conversion with the expectation that this will speed up the granting of the longed-for entry visa.

Muslim friends go so far as to claim that Christians should stop all diaconia services in relation to Islamic groups because they see there only a
manifestation of a proselytist drive. As Christians we reject this accusation
immediately; our desire to share the gospel with people in need is not an
attempt to abuse them, but to share with them our profound convictions.
We must be aware, however, that, seen from the perspective of secular
people or of other religions, this is proselytism and creates new stumbling-
blocks to people coming to real and living faith in Jesus Christ. How do we
respect the freedom of the person in an unfree situation? Part of the difficulty is that this modern missionary diaconia is done in the name of and
with the resources of an economically powerful church or Christian organization. How to convey in those circumstances the image of Christ, the
powerless one, who had only his life, which he surrendered for the salvation of humankind? This model, built into the central core of our faith,
should be the basic criterion presiding over our service. Do we render our
service in the spirit, after the model, of the crucified one?

In certain cases, a sociological analysis will interpret conversion as the
simple passage from the control of a religious or cultural group with a certain set of values to the control of another group with a different set of
values, but with the same mechanism to control and limit the free expansion of the person. This is particularly true in sectarian groups where the
control of the community over the behaviour of its members is such that
people accommodate to the expected behaviour without much freedom in
choosing the way in which they will respond to the living Christ, not only
inside the new Christian community to which they adhere, but especially in
relation to the present problems and needs of the secular society.

A very important point of criticism and a warning to our emphasis on conversion comes from highly explosive political situations where conversion
means a change of socio-political loyalties. It is a move from one tribe to
the other, from one political community to the enemy community; conversion then is considered a betrayal of the tribe, culture, family or nation. In
this issue of the *IRM*, this problem is described particularly in terms of
what is happening in India. Should conversion always mean the visible
belonging to the historical church, or could conversion in relation to the
living Christ be developed inside one's own cultural and religious tradition? What is pleaded for here is sensitivity to the issues raised, and not an
imposition of solutions practised in countries where a Christian background can be assumed easily onto situations where the majority of the
population sees in these practices an aggression on their cherished values.
What is there in the Christian call to conversion — i.e. to centre life around
Jesus Christ, the historical and the living one — that could make people
better citizens of their society, better members of their families? What is
essential, what is secondary? And how do we best point to Jesus Christ in
highly critical, polemical situations? A great deal of sympathy should sup-

port all those who, in India, Egypt, the Middle East, etc., try to find ways to present Jesus Christ in a manner that does not jeopardize, but, on the contrary, *preserves* the life of the community.

We need to be aware of all these criticisms and be humble in the appraisal of our evangelistic work; we need to be called back time and time again to the essentials for conversion — a living relationship with Christ, a disposition to serve the neighbour and the community, a desire to participate in the life of a worshipping community.

"Conversion happens in the midst of our historical reality and incorporates the totality of our life, because God's love is concerned with that totality. Jesus' call is an invitation to follow him joyfully, to participate in his servant body, to share with him in the struggle to overcome sin, poverty and death" (Mission and Evangelism — An Ecumenical Affirmation).

Trust in God's own *kairos* — God's own time — should help us to come to terms with our impatience, which can degenerate into an imposition on the weakest of our society. All these warnings, however, should not distract Christians from the central fact that to be Christian is to be in a personal relationship with Jesus Christ. Conversion will always be an ambiguous phenomenon because it happens in the realm of human life and historical reality. There are no final claims to be made by Christians, there are no final pretensions for us; the basic attitude is to point to Jesus Christ with the hope that, by contemplation of the crucified one, the non-pretentious, non-crusading, non-imperialistic character of our evangelism can be understood.

The word conversion — to turn around — is used especially in the Old Testament for calling the whole people, the nation, to change its ways. While there are some examples of personal conversion, generally the emphasis is on collective conversion. The sins of Israel are those that need to be repented in order to overcome the historical judgement looming on the horizon. In fact, we are social beings, we are influenced by and do ourselves exert influence on the total community. Inside the Covenant relationship between the people of Israel and God, this call to turn back — even to turn forward — was a call to fulfil God's will, to live in God's love, to respect God's law. The broken relationship of the Covenant needed to be restored by a public act of repentance of the people, accompanied by a clear manifestation of a change of loyalties in their daily life. This prophetic call to repentance and change remains the responsibility of the church vis-à-vis the total community. Like every individual, the community, too, needs moments of a new beginning, of a common awareness, of a rejection of the paths of yesterday, and the opening of a new period of hope and construction.

In nations that were permeated long ago by Christian teaching and tradition, the call to national conversion reflects a situation very similar to the

Old Testament — the church, the prophet, reminding the community of the central values of God's justice which prevailed in the attitude of the founders of the nation, values which need to be brought back to the centre of the attention and loyalty of the whole community. Whether it is in South Africa, calling white Christians to repent of their racist ways; whether it is in socialist countries, calling for an affirmation of the eternal value of the individual person — the church's vocation involves an evangelistic proclamation of repentance and change of the whole community. The church that evangelizes, inviting people to faith in Christ, will give clarity to its call if, simultaneously, it shows in its internal life the signs of the new life and publicly calls the whole community to turn to the basic demands of God's justice. In particular today, a church that is not concerned with the gap between rich and poor among the nations, the question of nuclear peace, racial equality and a community of love and respect between man and woman, a church that is silent vis-à-vis these and other challenges of our present human situation, will have much difficulty in being credible when it announces the gospel of the kingdom of God, inviting people to repent and to enter into the service of that kingdom.

In this period, when the mass media play such an important role, this prophetic, collective call to conversion provides the overall context in which the individual call will be understood as having concrete historical meaning. As our Lord Jesus Christ cried over Jerusalem, as the prophets cried over the sins of Israel, so Christians are called to cry over the sins of their respective nations with the same passion and to be always in the proclamation of the "year of the Lord", the year of grace where repentance and a new beginning are possible. While, due to the pluralistic character of contemporary society, much of this calling to collective or national conversion must necessarily be phrased in very secular terms, the voice of the church, however, should be clear in identifying the roots of its concern for the changes in the ways and the behaviour of the total community — "so says the Lord". It is because there is a vision of the kingdom and an understanding of God's will manifested in Jesus Christ, that churches are under the moral and spiritual obligation to call the total community to change their ways and to comply with God's will.

The experience of conversion uncovers the sad reality of human sin. In the parable of the Prodigal Son (Luke 15), the actual moment of conversion occurs when the father embraces the returning son and he cannot finish the discourse he prepared. He surrenders with the recognition, "I am not worthy to be called your son." After Jesus' conversation with Zacchaeus, the latter confesses, "If I have defrauded anyone of anything, I restore it fourfold" (Luke 19). The breaking of the Covenant in the Old Testament was the fundamental manifestation of the human tragedy in the perspective of the prophets. The self-centredness of our life, the closing in on ourselves, has destroyed our relationship with God and the relationship with our neighbours. The language of the New Testament, which describes conversion as passing from death to life, from darkness to light, cannot be understood from outside the experience of conversion. In fact, many people who, socially, are "decent" citizens, are talking about this passing from death to life. It is, in the Christian interpretation of the situation, the action and presence of the Holy Spirit working in each one of us ennabling the recognition of our sin and then empowering the acceptance of forgiveness and the beginning of a new lifestyle. In the actual encounter with God's grace, the awareness of sin is awakened. It is also the Holy Spirit who produces repentance, the profound realization of the wrong done, commitment, and the search for sanctification. The Holy Spirit inspires Christians to overcome the past, entering into historical projects of justice and reconciliation. Sin is the human presupposition of the conversion experience, recognized *a posteriori* by those who experience conversion. Grace is God's presupposition, awakening the sense of guilt, but simultaneously granting forgiveness and the power to try again. To announce the Holy Spirit at work is not to introduce a magical dimension to our human situation. The Spirit also works through historical agents — the love of a friend, the face of a child, the social turnover of the whole community, etc. Through chosen historical methodology, the Spirit reaches every human life with this call to conversion, with this empowerment for conversion. Conversion is the word that indicates both the seriousness of the concern and the hope with which the Christian faith looks at the human predicament. If something as radical as conversion is needed, it is nothing less than the direct action of the Holy Spirit that is presupposed. It indicates the seriousness of our human sin; at the same time, it points toward the unlimited grace of God who works time and time again to renew the Covenant and the relationship of love.

"Conversion as a dynamic and ongoing process 'involves a turning *from* and a turning *to*. It always demands reconciliation, a new relationship both with God and with others. It involves leaving our old security behind (Matt. 16:24) and putting ourselves at risk in a life of faith.' It is 'conversion *from* a life characterized by sin, separation from God, submission to evil and the unfulfilled potential of God's image, *to* a new life characterized by the forgiveness of sins, obedience to the commands of God, renewed fellowship with God in Trinity, growth in the restoration of the divine image and the realization... of the love of Christ...'" (Mission and Evangelism — An Ecumenical Affirmation).

"While the basic experience of conversion is the same, the awareness of an encounter with God revealed in Christ, the concrete occasion of this experience and the actual shape of the same differs in terms of our personal situation. The calling is to specific changes, to renounce evidences of the domination of sin in our lives and to accept responsibilities in terms of God's love for our neighbour. John the Baptist said very specifically to the soldiers what they should do; Jesus did not hesitate to indicate to the young ruler that his wealth was the obstacle to his discipleship" (Mission and Evangelism — An Ecumenical Affirmation).

Conversion brings with it concrete demands for change and action. In his book on conversion,*Jim Wallis describes beautifully what this means especially for the North American reader. We could speak of the fruits of conversion — "By their fruits you shall know them" —, but only if the fruits are seen as integral parts of the plant and not simply as consequences thereof. In the realm of the Spirit, a plant without fruits is a contradiction in itself! The cost of discipleship — taking upon oneself the cross — is an essential part of the proclamation of the gospel. Not that we announce a new law, but, yes, that we indicate that the fellowship offered by Christ — his baptism — implies a struggle with him for the kingdom and its justice in the very concrete circumstances of daily life.

Conversion always implies the question of the Apostle Paul, "Lord, what do you want me to do?" And the evangelist should not be hesitant to indicate what in his/her knowledge is implied in a concrete manifestation of the living Christ, calling us to join him in the struggles of the world and in the struggles of his kingdom. We need special help today to understand the structural realities which impinge upon our neighbours beyond our personal possibilities of helping them. Love of my neighbour, assuming his/her situation, which is basic to the experience of conversion, should find ways of expressing itself not simply in a face-to-face relationship, but also through the intermediary structures of reciprocal support in society. As Jesus and John were pointing to very concrete attitudes expected from their listeners, so Christians today should be able to point to very concrete territories where the living Christ is waiting for them to join him. The preacher cannot stay aloof in a supposedly neutral religious territory, calling people to religious allegiance to Jesus Christ. Conversion could be a religious phenomenon happening in a religious meeting, but it always brings along concrete historical content. Or, on the contrary, conversion could be a very secular historical event happening in the middle of the struggle for justice, but it should always have a concrete religious reference to Jesus Christ, his life, ministry, death and resurrection. What is fundamental is to give specific historical content to the notion of "turning around", "new birth", etc., by pointing to the world which is eagerly waiting for the "manifestations of the children of God". A "conversion" which is closed in upon itself in the sense of personal, internal bliss, is a denial of real conversion to him who gave his life for the salvation of the world.

The fundamental human value of the experience of conversion is its personalizing character. When the Apostle Paul says to his readers in the first chapter of the *First Letter to the Corinthians:* "For consider your call, brethren; not many of you were wise according to wordly standards, not

*Wallis, Jim. The Call to Conversion. New York: Harper & Row, 1981.

many were powerful, not many were of noble birth..." (I Cor. 1 : 26), he is pointing towards a wonderful reality: Those who are nothing in the eyes of the world are called by God and empowered not only to respond to him, but also to work with him for his kingdom.

As the ecumenical affirmation on mission and evangelism says: "The proclamation of the Gospel includes an invitation to recognize and accept in a personal decision the saving lordship of Christ. It is the announcement of a personal encounter, mediated by the Holy Spirit, with the living Christ, receiving his forgiveness and making a personal acceptance of the call to discipleship and a life of service. God addresses himself specifically to each of his children, as well as to the whole human race. Each person is entitled to hear the Good News. Many social forces today press for conformity and passivity. Masses of poor people have been deprived of their right to decide about their lives and the life of their society. While anonymity and marginalization seem to reduce the possibilities for personal decisions to a minimum, God as Father knows each one of his children and calls each of them to make a fundamental personal act of allegiance to him and his kingdom in the fellowship of his people."

God is a living God, active in human history. From there, God calls and invites us to change the course of our life and, with him, to attempt to change the course of the life of the whole community. Conversion makes every person a protagonist in God's kingdom. The importance of the awareness of a personal relationship with God in Christ is visible in crisis situations of the world today, where Christians are called to give account of the hope that is in them under the pressure of horrendous human suffering. There, when the word "resistance" has a deeper meaning, the awareness of the presence of the risen Christ, the awareness of belonging to God's kingdom, makes all the difference. Even death, then, becomes the path towards resurrection.

"The experience of conversion gives meaning to people in all stages of life, endurance to resist oppression, and assurance that even death has no final power over human life because God in Christ has already taken our life with him, a life that is 'hidden with Christ in God' (Col. 3 : 3)" (Mission and Evangelism — An Ecumenical Affirmation).

(International Review of Mission, July 1983)

4. MISSION YESTERDAY — TODAY — TOMORROW

This section looks to the future in the light of our past and our present.

"CWME 1910 -- 1980 - 2000" focuses on the work of the Commission on World Mission and Evangelism, whose central task is to remind the churches of their responsibility to cross all cultural borders, all geographical distances, all human barriers, in order to help everyone to link their lives to God's story in Jesus of Nazareth. Looking toward the year 2000, some facts emerge: (1) The growth of population and, notwithstanding church growth, the diminishing proportion of people who belong to the Christian church. However, it is possible to dream that the church will be present in almost every human group (tribes, ethnic groups, etc.). (2) The growth of the church will be concentrated in the third world while the economic resources will remain in the western countries and in some socialist states. (3) There will be a new awareness of the political role of religion. (4) There will be a growing number of local conflicts and wars. (5) A serious challenge will be posed by the growth of the communication technology.

The second article, "An Agenda for Today", raises three fundamental issues: (1) The search for cultural identity, the emphasis on regional theologies and on self-reliance. How can the search for cultural identity be a service to the kingdom of God? How do we preserve lines of communication that will help us to learn from one another? (2) Salvation and social justice. This is not a secular struggle. We do not fight against historical human forces, but against powers and principalities. (3) The renewal of the church. We need to bridge the gap between the ongoing life of a given parish and the vision of a world struggle in which Christians are called to participate. Evangelization should be understood as an invitation to a spiritual, i.e. global, holistic, all-embracing struggle.

The third, "Mission and Evangelism after Nairobi", describes urgent tasks: (1) Mobilization of the whole church and of each church for the work of mission. (2) The permanent vocation of the churches to cross frontiers of faith and unbelief. (3) The need to develop an ecumenical discipline, a set of common convictions that will guide our reciprocal relations and ongoing cooperation.

The fourth is an attempt at describing the missiological implications of the Vancouver Assembly theme, "Jesus Christ, the Life of the World". The editorial highlights (a) the hopeful character of the proclamation of Jesus as the life of the world; (b) the search for the manifestation of the life of Christ both within and outside officially recognized boundaries of the Christian faith; (c) the need to be clear that it is the life manifested in Christ and not life in general that we are announcing.

The fifth, "Third World Christianity", indicates some secular trends, looks at the responses made by the churches and suggests theological options for the future of third world churches. (1) The churches have responded to the shaking of their traditional societies with an evangelistic emphasis that has

resulted in substantial numerical growth. This must now lead to a new
responsibility in the socio-political and cultural dimension of the life
of their nations. Theological education will have to cope with the growing
demand for trained leadership. (2) The search for cultural identity, both
of nations and of churches, is crucial. To respond to this need, churches
may have to develop tent-making ministries and experiments in worship,
prayer, mystical practices, etc. How to accommodate these new experiences
within the Christian biblical tradition will be a test of ecumenism.
(3) Secularization will continue to dominate in the west and the third
world churches will be able to make prophetic and theological contributions
to the awakening and the renewal of the churches in the west. Also, due to
the political relations between countries, churches in the third world
will be able to help churches in socialist countries in their own missionary
outreach.

The sixth, "World Mission in the Eighties", affirms: "World mission is to
see every single local act related to a struggle that God is carrying on in
the whole world, and seeing the big items in the struggle of the world as
related to my prayer life, my community life, my family commitment." Today
there are three vital dimensions in the mission of the church: (1) "To tell
the old, old story." Without the history of Jesus Christ, our specific
Christian contribution to the human community is lost. (2) "Suffered under
Pontius Pilate." The ministry of the church has always been public. The
churches are writing some of the most striking pages of church history in
the public arena. (3) Jesus said that "there are other sheep of mine" (John
10:16). We have the charge to evangelize the whole world, but we cannot be
blind to the manifestation of the Spirit of God in other human groups, in
other people's experiences. "By being together with people whose starting
point is different from ours, we will have a new and fresh chance to share
with them the old, old story."

"The evangelization of the world in this generation" - under
the spell of the slogan coined by John R. Mott, twelve hundred
delegates came together in Edinburgh in 1910. They represented
North Atlantic missionary organizations. Only very few came
from other regions of the world, so the conference as a whole
shared an optimistic outlook and the ideological perspective
of the Victorian era. Their concern was valid: how to share
with all humankind the knowledge of the gospel of Jesus Christ.
Having discovered the world through missionaries and colonizers,
and belonging to countries whose commercial and political
interests spread all over the world, they wanted to share with
the same nations the richness of Christian experience, the
tradition of a cult of love, the knowledge of the saving message
of Jesus Christ. The Victorian era provided the assurance that
with energy and work all the conditions were given to cross
every frontier and to reach all people in the name of the gospel.
The assurance of this historical period allowed them to believe
that the whole question was one of methodology of communication.
The gospel was known; the problem was to cross the frontiers to
deliver it to other peoples. For this reason, the conference defined its own limitations, stating that no question of doctrine
or of church order would be discussed. That was the final
guarantee provided, especially to the Anglican high church leaders,
in order to make their participation possible. Latin American
delegates and representatives of missionary agencies working in
Latin America were not accepted at this meeting. Latin America
was considered to be Roman Catholic territory, that is to say,
Christian territory.

Looking back, we could criticize some of these pre-suppositions,
challenge their reading of reality and perhaps, with good
theological reasons, we could even pass a negative judgement
on their endeavour. But looking at things in an historical
perspective, we are able to recognize the value of the encounter.
It was the first time that Protestants from different countries
came together to share information, to strategize together, and
eventually to consider remaining together. While the question of
unity was only touched upon lightly, the experience of being
together convinced all participants of the need to have some
permanent organization. In this way, a continuation committee
for the work of the Edinburgh Conference was formed, which later
developed into the International Missionary Council, and eventually
into the Commission on World Mission and Evangelism of the World
Council of Churches.

Seventy years have gone by and, of course, many things have
changed, both in the world and in the church. The Victorian era
belongs to the pages of history. The harmony provided by the
colonial empire has been totally destroyed. The tragic experience

of two world wars and the certainty that there is no permanent
peace in the world has dawned in the minds and hearts of
Christians everywhere in the world. The reality of the variety
of cultures to which we belong and the impossibility of strategizing
for the whole world from a central place has also called us to
be more cautious and slow in our pretensions.

The reality of the growing de-christianization of western Europe
has eliminated all possible pretensions we might have entertained
of being in a position to bring the gospel from one part of the
world to another as an attitude taken for granted. The growing
understanding of our belonging to our nations brings with it
different consequences. First of all, we recognize that we belong
to different sides in the struggle for justice - that has become
the paramount task of humankind today. The traditional sending
churches are located in the traditional imperial centres and the
so-called missionary churches, or younger churches, are located
in third world countries heavily dependent on the economy and
the military power of the metropolis. This has enlarged the area
of our concern. It is not easy to deliver the gospel 'out there';
it is necessary to open the gospel *right here* in order to manifest
its power, which challenges and judges all areas of our life.
Because we realize that there is a growing dependence among the
nations, because the relationship between dominion and dependence
is now clear in our minds, we see all our assumptions challenged
and all our easy strategizing disappear from the horizon. It is
very interesting to see that in reaction to the manifold discussions going on in the ecumenical movement, our evangelical
friends attempted in Lausanne in 1974 to call for something
similar to Edinburgh - a fresh attempt to look at the world with
the conviction that the gospel was clearly known and could be
expressed all over the world without much hesitation. The actual
debate in Lausanne proved that the question is not such an easy
one. The recovering of the gospel was demanded, with a strong
denunciation of the civil religions of the western world, the
amalgam, the mixture of the cultural values of powerful
societies with the good news of the gospel. This challenge is
one that the churches everywhere are facing today, and one that
does not allow for any easy solutions.

Next year, another group of friends will call together missionary
societies that do not recognize salvific value in any other
religion and are bound to a stated definition of the authority
of the Scriptures in order to discuss again the implementation
of the Edinburgh mandate to cross all frontiers with the gospel
of Jesus Christ. The mandate remains the same and is valid as a
biblical mandate. It came from our Lord himself: "Go to all the
world and preach the gospel to every nation." That is very clear.
The difficulty is that this living gospel of our Lord Jesus
Christ must be discovered anew in the actual struggles of humankind. Opening the Bible in the midst of the struggles of the poor
of the earth, we discover visions of the gospel that had escaped
our attention and consideration when we were far from these
realities. Looking at the division between our nations, and

278

being aware of the collective guilt of our respective countries, we understand quite clearly that the gospel of Jesus Christ must first be hammered out in a living discussion about our own responsibilities before we have the right to announce it to or to share it with the rest of the world. This does not mean that the passion for the communication of the gospel is reduced today, and it does not at all mean that Christians, ashamed of themselves, are supposed to hide their conviction that the gospel is God's good word for every creature. But it means that in the actual passion for the proclamation of the gospel, we must pay careful attention to the total engagement of the churches wherever they are located. We cannot justify the foreign missionary activities of our churches unless we assume together with that activity the responsibility for challenging our own society in terms of its irresponsible behaviour vis-à-vis other nations. The passion to communicate the gospel today demands from us an attempt to authenticate the gospel so that it is credible everywhere.

The way in which we behave in relation to the race problem will give credibility to the gospel preached by white people, or by yellow or black people in areas different from their own. It is our attitude in relation to the prevailing injustice of the economic world system today that will give credibility to our proclamation of a gospel that indicates God's bias for the poor. It is our actual involvement in God's liberation struggle trying to show a new day for humankind that will give credibility to our preaching of repentance, conversion and affirmation of eternal life. The passion of Edinburgh was the right one: to convey the gospel to every creature. But today, with the growing knowledge about one another, with the growth in social human science, with the growth of reciprocal challenges, we know that we need to engage in a permanent discussion about the content of the gospel and about the way in which we are coherent in its proclamation out there with our living of the gospel right here.

"Mission to six continents" is not simply a slogan describing the geographical fact that those lands traditionally called Christian have become today mission lands in their own right. The emptiness of the churches in Europe is a provocation and an invitation, a cry for help to all churches everywhere. But the slogan "mission to six continents" means much more than that. It means that we need to develop a holistic attitude encompassing the whole world as our responsibility. Every local congregation should be aware of the important role that its ministry plays in the total economy of the kingdom of God. It is my local service, rendered as a contribution to the spiritual forces that are struggling against principalities and powers, spiritual forces everywhere, that contributes to the missionary outreach of the church beyond our borders.

And the missionaries who cross frontiers, and the younger churches in every corner of the world, should see their own mission in the same way. Our responsibility and privilege does not stop at the geographical borders of our parish. They extend beyond in that we belong to the church universal, to a servant people sent into the world to render witness to the gospel of Jesus Christ.

But it is not only the Victorian harmony that has disappeared; radical changes have taken place inside the church. Or more precisely, the fact of the ecumenical movement has brought into the missionary picture of the church a new reality that commands our attention. As we said before, Edinburgh was a meeting of the Protestant missionary forces in the western world; today the ecumenical conversations involve churches from all continents and from all confessional traditions. At the Melbourne Conference in 1980, 20% of the participants represented Orthodox churches and a sizeable number of Roman Catholic fraternal delegates and ob-servers were representing their religious missionary orders and the Secretariat for Christian Unity. The theme, "Your Kingdom Come", was the rallying point for a real encounter of all theological tendencies and all traditions inside the Christian community. This, of course, re-opens the question of the content of the gospel; the traditional Protestant version cannot be taken for granted!

However, the Orthodox and Catholic contributions are present not only in the theological search for a better understanding of the gospel we preach; they are also a challenge to our methodological approaches. Protestants in the 19th century were part of an exciting expansion of the world and quite naturally developed similar techniques of approach to people of other convictions and other faiths -- a kind of crusade to rally everybody around our convictions centred, of course, on the person of Jesus Christ. The tradition of the Orthodox churches invites us to consider liturgical celebrations and the lifestyle of the Christian community as the normal approach to our missionary endeavour. There is in the Bible a centrifugal dimension of the mission. We are "sent" into the world to proclaim the gospel to every creature. There is also a centripetal dimension; an invitation to everyone to "come" to the messianic banquet that is ready for us in Jesus Christ.

So a discussion of mission today brings new dimensions, new experiences, new perspectives that make that discussion more complicated, but, of course, much richer. The gifts that God has granted to all families of Christianity are today harnessed to-gether for the task of the proclamation of the gospel. The Joint Working Group of the Secretariat for Christian Unity of the Holy See and the World Council of Churches has produced a new document, "Common Witness", that calls the churches to be aware of the many instances of common witness in the world today. An initial document, written in 1970, called attention to "Common Witness and Proselytism"; ten years later, we could concentrate on the growing beautiful reality of common witness and call the churches to capitalize on this new possibility. If Edinburgh was optimistic in looking to the evangelization of the world, counting only with Protestant forces, we have today much more reason for such optimism, counting on the coalition forces of all the main Christian families.

Another new factor should be taken into consideration. We have today not only the encounter of different traditions, we have also the reality of the church present and belonging to different cultures throughout the world. The great success of the modern missionary movement that had Edinburgh as one of its main expressions, has been the establishment and growth of local churches who have become autonomous and are growing along the road to self-reliance. Bangkok insisted on the right and the duty of every church to develop its own cultural identity. Today the ecumenical arena is the meeting place of different theological manifestations of the gospel of Jesus Christ. The recent study of the Commission on Faith and Order, "Giving Account of the Hope that is in us", is a good illustration of the new situation.

Everywhere churches and Christian groups are responding to the challenges and demands of the contexts, of the cultures where they are working and living. Their confession of Jesus Christ comes in different words, with different music, in different colours, and with different emphases. It is the same old gospel, but now being opened in the midst of new, challenging and exciting situations. Again, this is our opportunity. We count today, for the missionary outreach of the church, on this reality of the church already planted in every country. And we have these attempts to incarnate the gospel in the manifold cultures of the world as avenues that penetrate with the message of Jesus Christ far better than through any other methodology. So our situation is also different in terms of the reality of our churches.

But the situation of the world is also different, because other forces are awakening and are challenging the missionary outreach of the church. While Edinburgh could look at the world with the confidence that with due planning the world may come to know Jesus Christ, today we know the reality of other centres of missionary faith, both religious and secular, that are also interested in "conquering" the world and are spreading their teachings to millions of people all over the world. In the last few years we have seen the renewal of Islam and the union of Islam and oil monies to promote a new kind of missionary outreach. We must also be aware of the ongoing invitation of secular faiths and secular humanism to the consciousness of humankind today. The dialogue with other religions and ideologies is not a luxury that we Christians afford in a condescending frame of mind. In fact, dialogue is the only Christian attitude that corresponds to our relations with our neighbours. We must recognize also that dialogue is the only possible attitude for reciprocal respect and cooperation in nation-building with people who represent other persuasions and who are equally convinced that their persuasions correspond to the best that could be offered to humankind. A pluralistic world, a pluralistic church, is perhaps the best summary of our present

281

situation. But happily the ecumenical movement provides instruments to help the churches cope with the challenges of today. Not a single church today would be able to fight alone on all fronts, to struggle individually with the manifold challenges to the Christian faith. An overall look at the agenda of the World Council of Churches indicates the many challenges facing the churches today, all of them an integral part of our missionary response.

After the integration of the International Missionary Council (IMC) with the World Council of Churches in 1961, the Commission on World Mission and Evangelism inherited the concentration point of the IMC. We are to be a continual reminder to the ecumenical movement and to the churches of the centrality of the communication of the gospel to the whole world as a Christian privilege and responsibility. We are to be the reminder to the churches and to other branches of the ecumenical movement of the sending status of Christians in the world. But the expression of this sending status and the ways through which the gospel is communicated today are not limited to the particular efforts of the Commission on World Mission and Evangelism. Colleagues in "Church and Society" are confronting the challenge of modern sciences and contemporary technologies in the ethical sense of who controls them and how they serve the welfare of the majority of poor people in the world, and also in the question of meaning. What does it mean to believe in Jesus Christ in a scientific world? How do we enter into discussion with scientifically-minded people concerning the meaning of life, ethical values at stake, and the reality of God's overall providence?

This is an evangelistic and missionary task clearly defined. Our colleagues in the Programme to Combat Racism are struggling with this particular manifestation of human sin as a missionary struggle against all that is alien to God's will in the world. They witness to fundamental Christian beliefs and so pave the way for the credibility of the gospel of Jesus Christ. It is because churches in the west are taking stands that dissociate themselves from traditional sins of the western world and making their own claims in the name of Jesus Christ that the gospel is taking on new credibility and new strength. The Commission on the Churches' Participation in Development works for the total participation of people in the development of their nations. But here again the question of what values should be central to the authors of any particular development plans belongs to the very heart of the gospel of Jesus Christ. We are facing not a secular, horizontal problem, but a manifestation of the very centre of our conviction that God loves the world and sent his son to live in the midst of all human problems, expressing clearly the total concern of God for all aspects of human life.

The message of the love of God for humankind in Jesus Christ demands from the church a total missionary engagement. Any church alone will not be able to struggle on all those fronts; it is logical that here or there particular emphases should receive special attention, provided that we see ourselves as belonging to the whole people of God entrusted with the task of proclaiming the gospel of Jesus Christ to every creature. The central task of the Commission on World Mission and Evangelism is to remind the churches of their responsibility to cross all cultural borders, all geographical distances, all human barriers, in order to help everyone to link their lives to God's story in Jesus of Nazareth. But we remind the churches that this crossing of borders, this proclamation of Jesus Christ, this invitation to discipleship is always an invitation to the liberating struggle of God that encompasses responsibility and care for all aspects of human life. The proclamation of the gospel of Jesus Christ can never be dissociated from the invitation to participate with Christ in the struggle for the salvation of the world. To call people to faith means to call them to obedience. To proclaim the grace of God is to remind us that the grace calls us to respond in love and in self-sacrifice. At the same time, the Commission on World Mission and Evangelism is under the obligation to make present to all those Christians who are fully engaged in the liberation struggle at different levels, who are handling very secular disciplines, that in the midst of those struggles they are ambassadors of Jesus Christ and that they should see themselves as part of the royal priesthood committed to intercede before the king for the destiny of humankind, for the salvation of all creatures. So the work of the Commission on World Mission and Evangelism today continues the work entrusted by the Continuation Committee in Edinburgh.

CWME is a forum where ideas, theological perspectives and experiences can be compared and challenged. We are to encourage specific research on concrete problems to help churches who are faced with these problems in their respective situations. We are to be a centre of cooperation that would enable churches to help each other in particular circumstances, especially as new missionary opportunities develop. And we are to look towards the horizon, to face all those particular issues that call for attention and response from the churches today. So CWME tries to keep an eye on what is going on in China, fully ready to be of assistance to the churches in China for the development of mission there, with the wisdom, expertise and help of the church universal. But we can also learn from the experiences of the church there as part of the testimony of churches everywhere. We are also engaged in discussion and analysis on behalf of local churches facing new religious ideological situations and limitations to religious freedom that seems to be a growing factor in the world today. This deserves our closest attention. Equally, we follow the many aspects of the justice struggle in the world today that is so close to the traditional missionary approach, so intimately part of the gospel message, so full of consequence for our mission everywhere.

The Commission on World Mission and Evangelism works in a relational style, trying to keep in touch with many local situations where some-thing can be learned to be shared with people in other situations and where the expertise and the help of other churches can be of importance. Perhaps the work of the Urban Rural Mission groups is the best focal point of the work of CWME, supporting local groups who are crossing particular frontiers in the inner cities or in the rural areas, proclaiming a gospel that calls people to organize in order to challenge the reality and to struggle for a more human quality of life. It is deeply rooted in the gospel, it is biblical work, but it is linked to local situations in such a way as to make real the incarnation of the gospel of Jesus Christ.

But you have invited me to talk not only about Edinburgh 1910 and CWME 1980. You also would like to dream about the year 2000, and obviously that is much more difficult. The delicate nature of the equilibrium in our world and the changes that are yet ahead of us, oblige us to be very cautious about futurology. It is far better to think in eschatological terms, because there, at least, we are sure that according to his promise the Lord of the church and the Lord of the world will be with us in the year 2000. Notwithstanding the many difficulties facing us in the future, he will provide the assistance of the Holy Spirit to cope with them. Even at the risk of being superficial and very selective in my readings, let me share with you some of my visions for the year 2000.

First, it is obvious that the population of the world will experience a fantastic growth, in spite of the attempts at population control. The world population will have doubled at least towards the end of the century. When we recognize that this will mean that the majority of the world's population will be under the age of 20, we see immediately the innumerable challenges, opportunities and problems for the churches. At the same time I think that I am not a pessimist if I foresee that the Christian church will be a growing minority in the year 2000. While we will be growing numerically, we will not be able to keep pace with the growth of the world population. And in that sense, our numerical importance will decrease proportionally.

Another factor to consider is the possibility that the year 2000 will see the church planted as a reality inside every local tribe, every local human group. The combination between the minority status of the Christian church in the world and the fact of having reached a particular goal will bring again into discussion the whole question of church growth and the vicarious role to be played by the church. New forms of dialectical discussion need to be discovered between this calling to the priesthood for the whole world and at the same time the clear exhortation of the gospel to share the knowledge of Jesus Christ with every person.

Second, the growth of the church will take place mostly in the third world. It is possible that North America will keep its present numbers but Europe obviously will need to face the reality of a de-Christianization that is not yet present in official statistics even if it is a visible fact.

Due in great part to the inertia of the global situation, however, the economic power and the centres of world communication will still be located in the western hemisphere or in some socialist metropolis. In terms of the missionary church, we need to face this disparity of realities: the spiritual and numerical strength in one part of the world, the technological, economic and structural possibilities in other parts of it. This debate, which is a reality right now, will grow to situations of great tension. It will be a manifestation in the life of the church of the growing tension between the nations. A search for missionary structures that will be realistic enough to recognize this fact and at the same time will promote the joining of missionary forces is a mammoth task for the missionary strategists of the year 2000. If they develop means and ways of cooperation, they will become symbols for the secular communities, pointers to the possibility of overcoming the growing dichotomy and tension between the industrialized countries and the rest of the world.

Third, there will be a new awareness of the political role of religions. The new understanding will be especially real among the governments and power centres of the world. The experiences of Iran are obliging many people to review recent history and their understanding of the religious factor in the political struggles. The fact that in different countries today restrictive religious laws are being proposed is an indication of the growing awareness of the political role that religion plays. This is not a theological problem within the interior walls of the churches, but a question of how the churches should participate in politics. The politicians of today recognize this factor much faster than the theologians themselves. This awareness will have consequences in all directions. Moratoria will be imposed in many countries, so we have a few years yet to strengthen the local churches before they are obliged to carry on by themselves inside increasingly hostile surroundings. On the contrary, the churches in other countries will play a growing role in the total ecumenical discussions. The socialist governments will increasingly understand the permanent nature of this religious phenomenon and will provide a wider margin of operation for the churches inside the countries, especially in international relations. This new situation will oblige the ecumenical movement not only to a permanent theological reflection on socio-political ethics, but also to enter into difficult negotiations with different states and religious bodies in order to create a place for the normal carrying on of our missionary convictions.

Fourth, the lack of agreement at the international level concerning the property of the sea floor and the property of outer space indicates the growing number of conflicts that are waiting on the horizon of humanity. The shortage of raw materials will provoke a series of localized conflicts that will bring much stress and oppression to those populations. While the horror of the nuclear balance may preserve humanity from a major war, this will be obtained at the price of sacrificing the rights of poor people and small countries in terms of different hegemonical areas of influence. This growing situation of hegemony and local conflict will demand imagination on the part of the churches to understand

285

situations that will be more and more loaded with ideological rationalizations and which will put our Christian international solidarity to the test. The present discussions about the Programme to Combat Racism will be remembered with nostalgia in terms of the conflicts that are awaiting us on the horizon of the year 2000! So we must be ready also for a phenomenal growth in the relief needs of the world.

Fifth, there will be a tremendous growth in technology, especially in the technology of communication. This will introduce a new series of problems to the churches. First, how to proclaim the gospel of Jesus Christ in a technologically-oriented society where people are used to receiving all kinds of messages through mass media. Can the personal encounter with Jesus Christ, the word of God become alive over and above the mediation of the technological tools? Second, the fundamental questions of justice: who controls this technology? To the service of which groups is it being directed? How do poor countries gain access to a technology that is so expensive? How to avoid the concentration of power in the hands of those who already have this power? The issues of justice and evangelization will stand together in facing all dimensions of the revolution in the information field.

Six, because of the global nature of the world, of the technological advances, of the tremendous pressure exerted upon simple people by the mass of available information, more and more small groups will be constituted as escape valves from this pressure, as islands of meaning, as the possibility for human existence. The present movement of ecclesial basic communities will grow in strength and in vitality. The ecumenical movement at a world level will be obliged to live in the tension between their relations and loyalty to church hierarchies and church structures, and the permanent and growing demands of small groups who are carrying out the mission of the church in concrete situations, assuring room for fuller humanity. They demand also to be recognized as ecclesial communities in the wider family of the church universal. I think that once we have a chance to enter into full knowledge of and relation with the experience of Christians in China in the difficult years they have lived through, we will find here more evidence of the value and potential of these small communities.

Looking to the future then, what is the role of the World Council of Churches? What is the specific role of the Commission on World Mission and Evangelism? Obviously and basically we should be an antenna ready to listen to what is going on in all corners of the earth. Every church should be able to look to the World Council of Churches as a meeting place, as a familiar ear, as a network of relations where their individuality, their belonging to a culture, their particular problems and challenges are being listened to and recognized. At the same time, the ecumenical movement should continue to be the place where experiences are shared and through which reciprocal help is channelled, where it will always be possible to concentrate strength and support to particular situations of danger or opportunity for the mission of the church.

286

The ecumenical movement should be a ferment for renewal, aiming at the moment when the proclamation of the name of Jesus Christ and the missionary status of Christians is a normal factor in every local congregation and a reality across all frontiers. The ecumenical movement will remain a forum where ideas are being tested, where theological discussions take place, where the different culturally-based gospels challenge each other to enrich and help all of us. There is awareness at a universal level of the impossibility of humankind to solve the problems that are looming on the horizon: armament, the economic gap, the ecological crisis, etc. But this mood of the coming apocalypse should not be the prevailing feeling as we face our mission during the next decades. Looking at many parts of the world, we see people who are dreaming of and struggling for a new day, who are beginning to see changes in their situation that open up new possibilities of human life, and we see churches which are growing and rejoicing in the fact that many people are coming to know Jesus Christ. While an apocalyptic mood seems to be the prevailing attitude of a majority of people, in many parts of the world local enthusiasm is the main feature of life. Endurance seems to be the virtue that we need to develop everywhere. For CWME it is important to keep alive the evangelistic missionary dimension of the church's vocation, to keep reminding ourselves and others that the gospel has been entrusted to the church to be shared and communicated. The gospel that is not shared with others is a gospel that has already disappeared from the church. We need to preserve a holistic approach, to seek the evangelization of the masses of the people in terms of justice: the unreached are largely the poor of the earth, against whom many are sinning; they deserve to know the gospel in terms of the justice of God for them and for us. We need to keep close to local groups because from them comes the concrete incarnation, the concrete challenge and the test of truth for all our theories, speculations and discussions. It is through the involvement of Christians in local areas that we receive the correction and inspiration that we need to think and plan for the missionary church throughout the world. Fundamentally, we need to remember that Edinburgh tried to be faithful to the salvific revelation of God in Jesus Christ in terms that belonged to the particular culture of that time. Today we are able to criticize the hidden values of that culture. But the important thing is not to criticize the past, but to take up the same torch, the same vocation and to risk ourselves into the obedience that is today's, knowing *a priori* that the coming generations will criticize us. But we offer humbly and full of hope the fruits of our hands to the Lord of the Harvest who will be able to overcome all our shortcomings and provide blessing to our daily work.

(Address delivered to the Netherlands Missionary Council, 1979)

AN AGENDA FOR TODAY

We want to take a look back at Bangkok and from there appraise the present
missionary situation. Bangkok was our last Assembly, and before we go to an
Assembly of the whole World Council of Churches, it would be good for us to
renew in ourselves some of the visions that we had in Bangkok. We will then be
better equipped for a more faithful participation in the new ecumenical exercise,
while at the same time we will be reminded of our ongoing concerns.

This search for inspiration in the findings of Bangkok for the task of the
churches today, two years after the fact, may paradoxically be a fruitful way
of looking forward. The Salvation Today study has produced passionate responses
in many quarters of the Church for the obvious reason that it was trying to
touch the very heart of the Gospel. As a Russian Orthodox theologian said:
"If you speak of salvation, you are speaking of the very centre of the Church's
life. We must listen and question." And this is precisely what we will do
here: listen to what came out of Bangkok, listen to the churches' response
and then consider how we may make a more earnest attempt to be faithful servants
of the Church of Jesus Christ in the future.

Section I: Culture and Identity

> "The universality of the Christian faith does not contradict its
> particularity. Christ has to be responded to in a particular situation.
> Many people try to give universal validity to their own particular
> response instead of acknowledging that the diversity of responses to
> Christ is essential precisely because they are related to particular
> situations and are thus relevant and complementary."
>   (Bangkok Report, p. 74)

Bangkok tells us that our Christian identity which is a universal factor will
only be realized as we become particular individuals within a given culture.
It is my self, with my identity, with my culture, with my belonging to my
people, which is taken over in Christ. And from Christ it is sent back to the
culture to confirm it, to challenge it, to renew it.

But this search for Christ in my culture or with Christ in my culture, is an
existential cry. How can I be black and be Christian? Or, how can I be white
and still believe that there is hope for me? If, as the Bangkok Report says:

> "Racial and cultural identity are divine gifts and human achievements
> to be taken up into Christian identity which is to be conformed to
> the image of Him,"   (p. 73)

the actual affirmation of those gifts puts me into conflict with myself, with
my neighbour, then very often the affirmation of this concept is precisely the
cause of our alienation from the whole of mankind. This is the new factor in
the missionary situation and in the ecumenical/theological reflection: Christ
is at home everywhere in the world. The newly elected Bishop of Winchester,
our friend John V. Taylor, said that the difficulty for the European Churches
in understanding what is going on in the ecumenical movement is due to the fact
that so many churches have emerged all over the world which bring to the ecumenical debate their own agendas and their own priorities, and it is the affirmation of their identity, of their cultural values and their respective missionary priorities that complicates but enriches the ecumenical panorama. The real
challenge before us is how to recognize each other as partners in a wider discussion where all contribute from their particular visions and all question
each other reciprocally, while all in their respective places and in reciprocal
confrontation try to express their deeper loyalty to Jesus Christ.

The recent Congress on World Evangelization, held in Lausanne, Switzerland, in
July 1974, took this problem of cultural belonging seriously:

> "Christ's evangelists must humbly seek to empty themselves of all
> but their personal authenticity in order to become the servants
> of others, and churches must seek to transform and enrich culture,
> all for the glory of God."

In the recent Synod of Bishops in Rome on the Evangelization of the Modern
World the issue was clearly presented, especially by several African Bishops,
who demanded recognition for varying identities and noted the emergence of
new theological perspectives. This new vision has provoked in Rome the same
unrest as has Bangkok in other capitals of Europe. Perhaps we live in a
painful but healthy tension between the various sectors of the Christian Church,

as each looks for a more obedient expression of its convictions in Christ. This may help us to understand the call for moratorium, which is both an affirmation of the selfhood of the Church and a plea for a chance to develop self-reliance. So the message is clear - cultural identity, regional theologies, self-reliance, a new ecumenical atmosphere. But of course, problems remain. Questions are raised, challenges are before us:

1. Is the emphasis on self-reliance and the plea for national cultural identity a service rendered to the mission of God or is it a hindrance to that mission? Are we looking for this self-reliance as a final goal in our missionary endeavours or are we trying to equip ourselves, our churches, our communities for a better, more responsible participation in God's mission? Affirmation of selfhood and self-reliance could very easily become demonic if they became idols or are made tools in the service of oppressive ideologies. The situation in Chad for example deserves our earnest attention. The first challenge then is to keep the concern for self-reliance, selfhood, cultural identity, contextualized theological expression under the discipline of the kingdom, under the passion for mission, under the sovereignty of our Lord.

2. The second problem we face is the relation between the past and the future in the search for cultural identity. The affirmation of our national identity and our racial background is necessary as we search for historical roots, as is an appraisal of the history of our people and a new sense of belonging to a long tradition. But this can also easily degenerate into folklorism, and an attempt to stop history. The search for cultural identity can also be looked upon entirely in terms of the future we hope to build. We cannot find our identity until we gain our freedom, until we can be free nations; historical agents must build their own destiny. To caricature, we could say that Africa is teaching us to step into the past to look for fertile soil for the Gospel to take root, and Latin America rejects the past and affirms the new future to be built and reflects theologically upon these facts. How do we bring these two currents together to correct and enrich each other? To what degree can a sense of belonging to the past not paralyse us but inspire us for the building of the future? And how can our Manichean rejection of the present be replaced by an assessment of the possibilities in our history for the building up of a real human identity? Cross-cultural theological dialogue is absolutely necessary at this moment in order to learn from and help each other.

3. Bangkok has taught us to look for a contextual church, a contextual theology: the shaping of our very being by the encounter of Christ with our culture. This basic affirmation of cultural identity by Bangkok is challenging some of our Orthodox friends who feel obliged to defend the identity of the Church expressed in their continuing tradition as a permanent factor in any human situation. When we challenge Orthodox churches in socialist countries with the question "What has changed in your church life as a result of the change in the surrounding society?", they look at us with some surprise. How could anything essential and basic change in the life of the Church which has a dynamics of her own, centred in the liturgy and the sacraments? And again comes the question: how far is the continuity of the Church a missionary help, a missionary handicap? It is true that the history of the Orthodox Churches indicates that those churches have shaped the total culture of their respective countries. But with the emergence of systems of global ideology, will they be able to perform the

same role? How much does historical continuity help or hinder the missionary engagement of the Church? What do we learn from the century-long faithfulness of churches in traditionally hostile surroundings for our more activist Protestant tradition? How much does the search for a relevant Christian life in our nations take into consideration the lasting values of church tradition? Of course, for many churches of the Third World the question of the content of that church tradition, is a very serious one. Denominational identities are so closely related to western history that they cannot pretend to represent the tradition of the Church. At the same time it is only through those westernized church forms that the real tradition has come to these countries. The question then is a theological, ecclesiological and pastoral one.

4. In the new ecumenical situation we are called to imagine new patterns of relation that will allow for a process of reciprocal learning and reciprocal correction. Up to now the criteria for judging particular Christian expressions have been provided by the western theological systems. The moment has now come for all of us to submit ourselves to the discipline of the Scripture and to so steep ourselves in the wisdom of the early creeds that we may find both the necessary roots and the necessary freedom. This, of course, is not just an intellectual exercise: it is also an administrative one. How do we develop new patterns for encounter, for setting priorities, of cooperation? How do we help the western churches to recognize themselves as provincial churches of the World Church so they will take the reverse flow seriously? Will the change in traditional patterns of missionary outreach into third world countries on the part of many European and American Churches help them to multiply their missionary efficiency in their own countries.

5. Finally, the search for identity poses very clearly the problem of the identity of traditional missionary sending agencies. In this world of ours, when the question of moratorium is discussed and counter-relations are being established, what is the role of the sending agencies? Should they continue to exist? Have they lost their initiative? Should they take any? Can they establish priorities when those priorities will interfere with others? What is their particular vocation? Should they only respond to the receiving churches? Can they operate in both directions? I suppose that this is a particularly acute problem for the Roman Catholic religious orders, organized to serve in given countries, who suddenly find that the result of their work is the emergence of the national church. What does it mean for the traditional organizations and their self-understanding? How do we help each other to develop structures of mission which will serve the best interests of the World Church today?

Section II: Salvation and Social Justice

The Bangkok Assembly Report begins by recognizing that its concern is a limited one:

> "Our concentration upon the social, economic and political implications of the Gospel does not in any way deny the personal and eternal dimensions of salvation. Rather we would emphasize that the personal, social individual and corporate aspects of salvation are so inter-related that they are inseparable."
>
> (p. 87)

291

We should not try to understand Section II without reference to Section I.
Salvation is whole. Nor should we try to understand it without Section III:
Churches Renewed in Mission. After Bangkok we were reminded that it should
also not be isolated from the clear Christian conviction about eternal life in
God. It could be said that here and there the Bangkok documents pointed out to what
this traditional and firmly rooted Christian belief affirms, but it must be recognized that this Christian affirmation was not especially highlighted in Bangkok.
We surely cannot understand our participation in the history of mankind, in the
search for social justice as a manifestation of that salvation that God has
promised us without relating it to the eternal life which is promised to us and
that neither life nor death can take away from us. That hope and the existence
of a Christian community are the two essentials for our militant participation
in society. In fact, if we look at it historically, Bangkok is a radical break
from our theological dichotomies. Social justice, personal salvation, cultural
affirmation, church growth, are all seen as integral parts of God's saving acts.
Far from being a horizontal emphasis, this is an attempt to read everything in
history and human life in the light of God's missionary intention.

1. In the final theological discussion of this Section the problem of means
   and criteria of saving work is discussed. A few lines indicate realisti-
   cally the need for economic power, political power, cultural influence, etc.
   We went so far as to discuss very briefly the problem of the use of liberating violence against oppressive violence. All these historical means of
   action do not, however, exhaust the possibilities at the Christian's disposal nor mention the principal instrumentality that the Christian has to
   use. We are learning again that our fight is not against historical human
   forces, but against powers and principalities. As Jesus said to his disciples, there are situations which cannot be released from bondage without
   fasting and prayer. If Bangkok has meant something, it has meant the full
   recovery of the struggle for human liberation in all dimensions as part of
   God's own struggle for the total redemption of mankind. And that struggle
   goes on as basically a spiritual one. We have been reminded of this truth
   through the Orthodox participation in our discussions; the Orthodox Consultation in Bucharest reminded us of the centrality of the prayer life of
   the Church, the liturgical service, the Eucharist, and the spiritual participation in mankind's struggles. We need the endurance of faith to participate fully and under every circumstance. We need that depth of hope that
   comes from resting in God's everlasting will.

2. Second, the need to see this struggle for salvation in general terms and
   in relation to the many powerful factors which are at work has provided us
   sometimes with too easy a way out of the daily life of our Christian
   parishes into an idealistic realm of ideas without making a concrete commitment. We speak in large terms about liberation and attempt to think
   about great actions in socio-political and economic spheres, but fail to
   realize the immediate relationship which that world struggle has to the
   worshipping community in a given locality. Without concrete attachment to
   a worshipping community we are lost in the ocean of the ideological, political struggle and we lose the sense of immediacy, of human proportions.
   Much of what is called today "crisis of vocation in the ministry" or "crisis
   of faith among young people" comes out of the impossibility of crossing the
   gap between the steady ongoing life of a given parish and the vision of a
   world struggle in which Christians are to participate. We believe that

our next area of concentration in theological education should be in pastoral theology, trying to relate the theological understanding of world realities to the ongoing life of the Christian community. Up to now, in our zeal for action we have coped with new challenges by adding specialized agencies or departments to our church life, escaping in that way from the painful and serious need to renew the Church, to challenge the existing body to face new missionary responsibilities.

The study on the missionary structure of the congregation was aimed precisely at challenging this ongoing parish life, but there will be no changes in it unless we take it seriously and submit ourselves to the discipline of loving it and belonging to it. When we speak about world mission, this question should come in very personal terms to every worshipper in every community: How do I join in God's struggle for liberation from here? How do I see our simple, humble parish life as part of the total mission of God? How do we have the sense of reality, the immediacy, and at the same time the joy of participating with many others in God's liberating struggle?

3. Through many action groups in urban-industrial or in rural-agricultural mission we are related to concrete engagements in the organization of people in the struggle for their own liberation. Can we affirm the existence of the Church where there is no indication of participation in the struggle of the poor? Of course many questions remain: Who are the poor? What is the ideology that will support their action groups,etc? But, while recognizing this and many other difficulties, it is clear that in humanity's present predica- ment - and we are beginning to understand that millions of people are suffer- ing - we cannot escape from the missionary responsibility to participate in their struggle for a more human life. It is God's promise to them and to us. At the same time we cannot go into this struggle unconscious of our being Christians, because it is out of this very commitment to Jesus Christ that we derive our consciousness of belonging to and participating with the poor of the earth. But the evangelistic question remains. Can we deprive the poor of the earth of the joy of consciously knowing Jesus Christ? We know that Jesus is for them, is with them, is one of them. But we know that there is a joy, a new experience of life, a new consciousness of our forgiveness and our eternal life when we come to know Jesus Christ in a personal way. How can we struggle for justice with the mass of poor people in the world and withhold from them the right to be the Church of Jesus Christ on earth? We have to live with the tension of our Christian participation within the arena of the socio-politico-economic struggle for the kingdom with a clear consciousness that to rally in churches, to be converted to Jesus Christ is in itself a blessing that we would like to share with all mankind.

How do we challenge the churches to take seriously the reality of the masses of poor people who struggle or need to be helped to struggle for their own human dignity? How do we forget ourselves, our own identity, so as to become involved with them in their struggle? At the same time, how do we show that our surrender of ourselves is precisely the clearest possible affirmation of faith in Him who, being like God, did not want to remain such but emptied himself to become man's servant. Very clearly the question of the emergence of faith is very much related to the question of fidelity of the Christian community!

4. This participation of Christians in the struggle for social justice brings, naturally enough, serious consequences. The experience of limitation of freedom, lack of respect for human rights, jail and torture, are everywhere present in our world. Christians who struggle for liberation face the reality of the cross. The old question of the relation between church and state and the problem of religious freedom comes back to us with new vigour. They present themselves not only in the imprisonment of Christians in some socialist countries for their zeal in sharing the Scriptures without respecting the law, but also in the threat of jail when Christians, out of their commitment to Jesus Christ, try to share the predicament of the masses of poor people and help to organize them to demand their own rights. We have been closely connected with the oppressive situations in different countries of the world. This is becoming more and more an essential part of our ministry. How do we provide pastoral services in an oppressive situation? How do we bring the resources of the Church Universal to the aid of those engaged in a particular struggle within a given nation? How do we support each other in prayer and action?

Section III: Churches Renewed in Mission

This is perhaps the least quoted part of the Bangkok Report. This, I think, is totally unfair. It indicates where the passions of the Christian Churches today are! Perhaps some take what is said in this Section for granted; perhaps others could not believe that this kind of calling to evangelism and church growth could come out of World Council of Churches circles! But without this Section we would lose the sense of the wholeness of the Bangkok theological approach. It is impossible to speak of cultural identity in a Christian perspective, or of a Christian participation in the struggle for social justice without considering our responsibility to call people to Jesus Christ and to join with them in Christian communities where the discipline of prayer and Bible reading will help us to grow to maturity and full participation in the search for identity and justice in our respective nations. Bangkok said:

> "The local church in action should be an expression of the impulse of the whole church to further the proclamation of the Gospel of Jesus Christ to all the world so that, by responding to him, persons and their situations may be saved."

> "Such proclamation is likely to be incredible without the visual aid of Christians who are being saved in regard to their relations both with each other and within their wider human communities. Salvation works to change persons, local congregations and their relations with each other in one place, and at the same time to bring healing and liberation to the community in which these congregations are placed."

(pp. 99-100)

An historical consciousness, a sense of a clear relation to the history of the Hebrew people and to the life and teaching of Jesus Christ, is the best safeguard against the demonic pretentions in every human culture.

The calling of people to come to Jesus Christ is not a calling to them to come out of the world but a sending back into the world in the name of Jesus Christ. The churches should be centres of training and discipleship for liberation. A few weeks ago we participated in the Synod of the Evangelical Church in West Germany. During the discussions on mission two clear questions were put: Do we believe that people should be called to believe in Jesus Christ? Do we believe that people should be called to organize themselves in Christian communities? We were shocked by the very raising of these two questions within a Christian assembly. Of course we want people to become Christians. Of course we want Christian churches to multiply all over the world provided that becoming Christian is not just joining a cultural category but signifies a deep metanoia, a conversion that impels our service to Jesus Christ from within our respective communities, insofar as Christian communities are centres of discipleship training and missionary consciousness. Orthodox theologians remind us that we need to discover again the worshipping community because it is there that the depth of faith and the calling to discipleship and the growing together in Jesus Christ should become a reality. Again we are reminded in this Section of the essential spiritual struggle in which we are engaged. We are called to depend on God and with Him to participate in our cultural and historical task.

1. We must discuss especially with the western churches the whole problem of faith and the crisis of faith in the western world. We should not idealize the past period of history when churches were full of people, nor should we forget that the masses of western Europe go their own way, making their own decisions, establishing their own values without reference to any Christian perspective. We shall try to call on the new churches in the rest of the world to help the churches in Europe to discover and to face the challenge. We shall also need to discuss with European Churches in how much former missionary personnel, coming back to Europe after years of service, can be re-deployed and their experience used in the growing missionary fields of western Europe.

2. We need learn from the emerging trends in the life of the churches, and learn to challenge them. I refer especially to the charismatic movement. How much is this a renewal of fidelity, and how much an escape from the demand for concrete engagement with Christ in the world? Is it merely a middle class western phenomenon or is it a manifestation of the Spirit of God calling the churches to renewal? What do we learn from the new religious communities' revival of apparently old-fashioned religious language and their appeal to the outcasts of a sophisticated society? What can we learn from them? How can we help them in their missionary engagement?

3. The International Congress on World Evangelization in Lausanne coined the slogan of "Reaching the Unreached." In dramatic ways our attention was called to the mathematical fact of the 2,700,000,000 persons who do not have or have not had a chance to know about Jesus Christ. While we can very easily criticize the superficiality of this slogan, the hidden assumption that there is yet a part of the world called "Christian" and a part of the world called "pagan", as well as the ambiguous imperialistic connotations of the word "reaching" - still, the challenge is there. The Christian community has a message that does not belong to it. It is to be shared. We are under the commandment to love our neighbours, and we cannot love them without sharing the most precious gift - the knowledge of God in Jesus Christ. The challenge is real, and the Church Universal must organize her-

self to face it. Much of what we have been trying to do in helping the churches to help each other and to become churches of Christ in a concrete situation is precisely working for the fulfilment of this task. It is our being renewed that will make credible our Gospel; it is our collaboration that will indicate that really we do possess a Gospel of unity and reconciliation. It is our belonging to our respective cultures that will enable us to be messengers of the Kingdom in that particular culture. More than that; we are sent into the world to be a light to the nations, and while it is clear that we want to reach every single person with the chance to know Jesus Christ, it should also be clear that it is our duty as the Christian Church to be a symbol and a vicarious manifestation of that reconciliation which God wants with all mankind, and that as much importance should be given to the actual shaping of an obedient Christian community as to the extension of the Christian Gospel to other people and other nations. And if we want to speak seriously about the "unreached", we must recognize where they are and organize ourselves accordingly for meeting them with the Gospel.

Basically we are speaking of those who live under the great religious systems of mankind and under the powerful ideological systems of today. The experience of the WCC Assembly in Indonesia should be a reminder to us of all the complications of the present situation. There we have a Church with a clear evangelistic calling and at the same time a clear desire to be faithful to the mission that God calls them in helping to build up the nation. They cannot be responsible Christian citizens if they do not learn how to cooperate with people of other faiths in the building-up of the secular community. They will not feel fully Christian if they surrender the duty and the privilege of sharing the knowledge of God in Jesus Christ with all fellow citizens. They want to belong to the Church Universal. But the sharing of resources provided by the western churches is seen by other religious communities as a threat to cherished values in their culture. How can the Indonesian churches keep a holistic approach? How can they live in such a way that the honesty of their participation in the building up of the nation will be the best apologetic instrument? How should they be renewed in such a way that their very being Christians will be an invitation to their neighbours? This is perhaps a parable of the situation we all face. Our fidelity in a given place should not be seen as a betrayal of mission but as one of the best ways to participate in mission! Our living in dialogue with people of other faiths and ideologies is the only way to be Christians and to have some hope that the Gospel of love is not only heard but also understood. Our disciplined preparation for discipleship will be the best indication of the seriousness with which we take this calling. It is not basically a problem of techniques, it is a problem of being in mission, fully committed to God and to love to our neighbours.

But how do we help the churches to prepare themselves for this missionary task that will be the work of generations? How can we develop expectation and endurance? How do we challenge the success syndrome of the western churches? How do we learn from the religious orders of the Roman Catholic Church? What do we learn from the first steps in the modern missionary enterprise? Our commitment to the evangelization of the world should be stated clearly time and time again. It should be a clear evangelistic commitment; not a crusade to conquer the world, but a sharing in the cross of Jesus Christ, showing ourselves to the world, ready to serve wherever we are called with the hope that through our humble instrumentality and that of others raised by God all over the world, many will come to the joyous knowledge of Jesus Christ as Lord and Saviour.

(Address presented to the World Council of Churches' Commission on World Mission and Evangelism at its meeting in Figucira da Foz, Portugal, February 1975; published in Occasional Bulletin from the Missionary Research Library, Vol. XXV, No. 4, May-June 1975)

MISSION AND EVANGELISM AFTER NAIROBI

Nairobi reaffirmed the missionary calling of the whole WCC.
When the new constitution of the WCC was approved, the Assembly
restated the aims of the WCC as follows:

a) to call the churches to the goal of visible unity in one faith
   and in one eucharistic fellowship expressed in worship and in
   common life in Christ, and to advance towards that unity in order
   that the world may believe;

b) to facilitate the common witness of the churches in each place
   and in all places;

c) to support the churches in their world-wide missionary and
   evangelistic task;

d) to express the common concern of the churches in the service of
   human need, the breaking down of barriers between people, and the
   promotion of one human family in justice and peace;

e) to foster the renewal of the churches in unity, worship, mission
   and service;

f) to establish and maintain relations with national councils and
   regional conferences of churches, world confessional bodies and
   other ecumenical organizations;

g) to carry on the work of the world movements for Faith and Order
   and Life and Work and of the International Missionary Council and
   the World Council on Christian Education.[1]

It is worth noting that the Assembly retained para. c) from the
old constitution. Nairobi called the churches

"to confess and proclaim Jesus Christ", and appeals to the WCC to
make "the proclamation of the Gospel in all its wholeness the highest
priority" and emphasizes "the need for a renewal of the dimensions
of witness and evangelism in all programmes of the WCC through
proclamation of the Word and active engagement".[2]

The Assembly did not stop short at issuing an enthusiastic
invitation, it also urged us to see our task in a global and
integrated way. Evangelism, it said, must be holistic, not only
in content, but also in approach and methodology. As the Nairobi
report says:

The gospel always includes: the announcement of God's Kingdom and love
through Jesus Christ, the offer of grace and forgiveness of sins, the
invitation to repentance and faith and fellowship in Him, the summons
to fellowship in God's Church, the command to witness to God's saving
words and deeds, the responsibility to participate in the struggle for
justice and human dignity, the obligation to denounce all that hinders
human wholeness, and a commitment to risk life itself.[3]

At its first meeting the Core Group of the Commission on World
Mission and Evangelism examined the decisions taken at Nairobi
and tried to draw the conclusions for our future work.

The contemporary world within which Christian communities live and witness
faces us with unprecedented and complex challenges - and opportunities as
well.

- The potential (some say the probability) of global annihilation due
  to nuclear war or ecological disaster looms over humanity as on over-
  arching threat to life itself on this planet.

- Scientific developments, while opening up new ethical dilemmas and
  dangers, also provide for many the hope of a new society freed from
  poverty and want. Scientists are increasingly uncertain about their
  ultimate goals and are open in a new way for encounters with people
  of faith. Thus the relation of faith and science takes on a new
  evangelistic dimension.

- Repressive regimes systematically curtail or destroy even modest
  visions of liberation in country after country, so that imprisonment,
  torture, exile or death are increasingly predictable for many who struggle
  for human dignity.

- Vast new experiments in societal and communitarian arrangements, leavened
  with hope yet ambiguous and complex (notably in the People's Republic of
  China), develop new models worth understanding more fully even as their
  implications for all of us are still quite unclear.

- New constellations of human communities emerge, calling ancient values
  into question and forging strange new alliances, creating forums of
  uncertainty wherein the tentative and the untried must replace the known
  and the secure.

- Increasing signs of a new hunger for spiritual realities appear in a
  wide variety of situations. People, both within and without the churches,
  believers and non-believers, as they seek to realize an expression in
  community life of their vision of a more human way of life are searching
  for spiritual foundations.

We thank God that even in such a world His power avails, His purposes
stand, His call to faithfulness remains. We also thank God that across the
earth there is a vast network of Christian communities, large or small,
that try to respond to God's call to discipleship and try as well to reach
out across boundaries of every sort to share by word and deed a witness to
God's love and a ministry of evangelistic mission. Across the world mission
is not a problem as much as it is a reality. CWME sees its task as one of
support, encouragement and participation with these persons and communities
that press the claims of the Gospel upon the world in sensitive obedience
to the Lord of all, particularly in a style that involves the poor and their
self-determining communities.4)

From the global point of view, the disagreements and divisions
among Christians over their understanding of the church's
mission and evangelism seem minimal. Relatively speaking, it
has been easier to bandy words of dispute, division and mutual
criticism in an internal church debate than to go out into the
world with a truly missionary approach.

The international debates which took place in Bangkok, Lausanne,
Rome and Nairobi have shown clearly that we Christians share a

common calling to mission, we owe a common duty to the world.
At the same time, however, they have pointed in all honesty
to the gravity of the problems and the magnitude of the
challenges we are facing as well as the effort of imagination
they require on our part.

Looking to the immediate future, it seems to me that the urgent
priorities of the missionary task can be summarized under three
headings:

1. <u>Mobilization of the whole church and of each church for the</u>
   <u>work of mission</u>

The expansion of missionary work in modern times began with the
formation of groups with a missionary vocation inside the church,
in many cases working without much sympathy or understanding
from church authorities. This dynamic aspect of our history
should not be forgotten. There will always be a place for people
with a special calling and for groups responding to a particular
vision or vocation. But over the years we have learned something
we should never have forgotten, namely, that mission is one of
the basic marks of the church: "As my Father sent me, so I send
you." Mission is not a luxurious addition to the normal life of
a congregation, but a description of its status, its being, its
very life.

So, on the one hand, through the national churches which have
developed out of missionary work, and on the other, through the
debate going on within the western churches, we have come to
recognize that the whole church must be engaged in mission.
This has led to the integration of church and mission of which
the Missionswerk is one example, and also to the merging of
the International Missionary Council with the World Council of
Churches. But such examples, whether national or international,
are only the first steps in the task. Fears have repeatedly
been expressed in missionary circles that integration like
this could spell the death of the missionary spirit and fervour,
stifled by church bureaucracy. Many of the young national
councils, on the other hand, fear lest they be regarded as the
concern of certain sectors of the western churches with a
special interest in foreign mission and hence not accepted into
full fellowship with the churches as such. Integration of church
and mission corresponds to the understanding of the church as a
missionary entity, but it needs constantly to be translated into practice in day to day reality.

Another line of reflection has taught us that mission covers
the six continents. We formulated it like this in order to
stress that nobody can use commitment in far away places as
a pretext for shirking responsibility at local level while, at
the same time, we have to support one another in a world-wide
evangelistic task which cannot stop short at any human frontiers.
By way of example, we have the transition taking place at

present in the Theological Education Fund: from being a fund specifically concerned with mission in third world countries it has now become a Programme of Theological Education intent on calling the churches to faithfulness in preparing people for ministry in all parts of the world. This is to avoid foreign mission becoming the hobby of a few while the preaching of the gospel in our own community remains the exclusive preserve of another part of church structures. The great task that lies ahead of us is the renewal of the whole church so that its faithfulness in practical things is part of the universal church's faithfulness in all things.

There is another line of ecumenical debate which can, I think, help us in this situation. We believe in a missionary God. The church shares in the *missio dei* . The God who sent his Son, also sends his church through the Son, in the power of the Holy Spirit. In God all our individual actions acquire a universal, even cosmic significance. In the divine economy our prayers for one another make it possible to transcend the barriers of time and place. Our faithfulness in our local place is valuable in two ways: it manifests the presence of the kingdom wherever we gather together and at the same time it joins our witness, our efforts, our spiritual energy to the work God is doing with us and with others. So a church in a socialist country which cannot send missionaries or funds beyond its own borders is nonetheless not prevented from being part of the universal mission of the church through its liturgical life and witness. Its concentration on prayer contributes to God's total struggle to establish his kingdom. This seems to me to be a theological line which it is important for us to explore: the mission of God summoning us to join with him in the struggle to create a new heaven and a new earth. In this vision, giving and receiving, local or international outreach, facing up to the urgent problems of justice among peoples, and the proclamation of the message of eternal salvation are all components which, in the divine economy, combine to make up mission in its wholeness. This is perhaps the first generation which can visualize this total interdependence thanks to the mass communication media. However, the interdependence we can measure today in terms of mutual influence is nothing in comparison to our total interdependence as Christians in the communion of the Triune God.

This insight has prompted us to undertake a new study on "The Missionary Structure of the Congregation". We hope through this to discover new models, situations which speak to other situations, to learn from one another and to find ways of injecting new vigour into parish life. There will certainly be some problems of method to study but the problem cannot be solved at that level alone. What we are seeking is a deeply spiritual and genuinely ecumenical experience. This is part of the reason for our emphasis on the programme of education for mission. This will undoubtedly be a wide and fruitful field of cooperation in the years ahead. Nairobi rightly emphasized the importance of the local congregation as the *locus* of

301

mission. We want to make sure this emphasis is not distorted by neglect of the task at world level for which we are all responsible.

2. The present frontiers

Our second main area of concern in mission is a logical extension of what goes before. Local congregations and national churches are set in a specific context, trying to live out the gospel and communicate it in a particular situation. The World Congress on Evangelization in Lausanne in 1974 reminded us of the millions of human beings who do not yet know the gospel of Jesus Christ.

The important thing for us is to take up this challenge in specific terms. Where do Christians come in contact with people who do not share their Christian faith? Obviously, they meet them in their normal daily relations, in their respective communities. The best international ecumenical service we can render is to relate to churches and groups living on the frontiers of Christian mission so that we can learn with them in a mutually enriching process of reflection and action. Let me just mention a few examples. While they certainly cannot claim to be exhaustive, they will serve to indicate a direction to follow and a method of doing ecumenical service in which the Missionswerk no doubt has an important part to play.

a) Perhaps the most serious problem in the contemporary world is the systematic violation of human rights. It does not require a detailed knowledge of the situation to be able to paint a picture of a world where the evidence of such violations is only too obvious. Whether in the local or the universal context, given the interdependence in which we live, we are all of us faced with the growing inhumanity in the world. This is the situation we come up against, the situation that confronts us as we seek to fulfil our mission. We can neither educate people for mission nor reflect on mission today without taking specific account of this situation. Even theological education which adheres to its traditional curriculum cannot shut out the reality of oppressor and oppressed, fear and hope.

From time to time there is some discussion of the contrast between the content of the gospel and its context. But clearly, when it comes to the abuse of human rights we are dealing not with the context but with the very heart of the gospel (Mt. 25). The churches have a good record in the field of health care and food aid but they have devoted much less attention to the prisoner, the persecuted and the victims of torture. They too are included in the parable of the last judgement. At a still deeper level we might say that, though there may be human beings who believe they can live without God, there is not a God who wants to live without them.

Churches in many countries are facing up to this situation and its implications for their missionary obedience. Liturgy, service, community life, evangelism and catechetical training are being rethought and lived out in ways appropriate to the particular context in which the church lives. The struggle for the sake of the gospel in Korea, South Africa, Latin America, etc. represents a challenge to us which puts our theological debates to shame. But in these circumstances 'foreign' mission, the international ecumenical dimension, assumes new importance.

b) In our work we regard as particularly important the reflection on mission coming to us from churches living in new kinds of societies. Some African countries, for example, are experimenting with new social forms, be they partially imported forms of socialism or forms of community life going back to traditional roots. What does it mean to live out the Christian faith in these situations? How can the Christian churches through their action communicate the good news of Christ's gospel in these circumstances? We in the western world are bound to admit that we have tended to assume that the countries of eastern Europe and the churches there are particularly in need of our prayers, without giving a thought to the faithfulness of their witness and the richness of their study and reflection. Studies on the church's mission in a socialist society, on evangelism in the church's liturgical life, the church's presence in new industrial cities, etc. will be a valuable source of inspiration for the church throughout the world. The exchange of visits and experiences, prayers of inter- cession are forms of giving and receiving, of living in the communion of saints as we fulfil our mission. We are not primarily concerned to re-establish the missionary enterprise in China but we are genuinely concerned that the people of China should be able to share in the riches of Christ's gospel. Our concern for the millions who have not yet been reached by the gospel can only be given real substance through a practical study carried out if possible with our brothers and sisters in China.

c) Working along the same lines, we have recently held a consultation with representatives of the Muslim faith. This is not a question of dialogue for its own sake ending in mutual tolerance or indifference. It is a discussion in which we talk honestly about our missionary convictions looking for ways to put them into practice openly. Considerable confusion and debate has sprung up around the subject of dialogue with other faiths. Eventually there will have to be some clarification of the problem at the conceptual level. Meanwhile, however, for Christians in many parts of the world dialogue with people of other faiths is not a theoretical problem but a reality of everyday life. Given the growing population movements, especially within Europe, with the arrival here of workers from Muslim countries we are all of us in a situation of dialogue with our neighbours of other living faiths. We do not fulfil our missionary calling simply by giving tokens of love and service, even though

they are an essential part of it. We want to bear witness to
our faith in Christ; we want everyone to have the joy of
knowing him as their saviour and lord but we cannot behave as
though nothing had happened. There is a long history of
colonialism, a situation of economic inferiority, the interplay
of religious, political and economic forces, all of which
conditions our evangelistic approach. Christian theologians
in various parts of the world are beginning to examine possible
new approaches to the phenomenon of human religiosity. We have
heard about the 'anonymous Christians', we have heard baptism
discussed as a constructive or destructive element in human
community, we have heard about the search for a 'christocentric
syncretism', to use M.M. Thomas' phrase. We may find expressions
of this kind surprising or even disturbing but they do indicate
the beginning of a dialogue on mission in which we must all
participate and in which nothing will be taboo. How, in this
pluralistic world, with all our Christian history but with the
freshness of our missionary convictions, can we set about
proclaiming the name of Christ and calling people to Christian
discipleship?

Frontiers of many other kinds could be mentioned - the academic
world, the scientific community, new towns, inner city ghettoes,
the growing importance of rural communities. But whether we talk
in terms of geographical frontiers or areas of human life we
shall always find Christian people there who are committed to
mission, who are seeking answers and are keen to do so in an
ecumenical dialogue which also includes the concerns and
experience of their brothers and sisters from other cultures and
traditions. To my mind, this kind of relationship, in which we
share in the practical problems of the people who are on the
frontiers of mission, is essential to an understanding of world
mission. This will require a double effort of imagination,
especially from western Christians, so that they can:

(a) understand the new avenues of search and experience being
    explored by Christians in the third world as they fulfil
    their mission, and
(b) discern the real challenges in the changing situation of
    Europe, the true frontiers where intelligent witness is
    required of us.

3. The ecumenical dimension

That the task of evangelism in the world is the task of the whole
church is a received truth and a common conviction. We are not
concerned with the expansion of a particular denomination but with
the proclamation of God's kingdom. God be praised, we have gone a
long way towards overcoming our confessional barriers and developing greater cooperation between and across the different confessions
in recent years. The fact that the Roman Catholic Church is a member
of some regional organizations such as the Caribbean Conference of

Churches or the Pacific Conference of Churches is a sign of the
progress that has been made in this respect. At the present time
we are also beginning to glimpse some opportunities for active
cooperation between Protestant and Orthodox communities in the
field of mission. Yet we still have a long way to go. The bulk
of inter-church aid still goes through denominational channels.
We have to take a serious look at the commitments we have inherited from our national or confessional history and ask ourselves whether they still reflect the right priorities for mission
today. As we try to do away with old bilateral relationships which
perpetuate ties of dependency, we have to be careful not to allow
new forms of bilateral relations surreptituously to take the place
of the old with the same kind of dependency. By this I mean our
national ecumenical structures which serve a specific purpose
such as mission, development, etc. which may be tempted to
'settle on' a particular clientele which gradually begins to
show all the signs of dependency. Structurally speaking, there
is no easy solution to the problem because an international
bottle-neck funnelling all church relations is not a feasible or
acceptable prospect either. On the contrary, our job is to
stimulate fellowship and mutual aid from one church to another,
but to do so in the framework of an ecumenical discipline which
will be a constant source of new energies for action as new
frontiers are discovered.

In recent years the debate on the so-called moratorium has
generated considerable feeling:

> The practical implications of the moratorium need to be seriously
> studied moving beyond the academic debate. This could be best done on
> national as well as regional levels and in the perspective of develop-
> ing true partnership in relations. It should also be examined as to how
> the various approaches to and consequences of the moratorium help the
> churches to move beyond a temporary suspension of funds and personnel
> to a more deeply committed mutual relationship.[5]

We must constantly remind ourselves that the fundamental task to
which we are called is mission and evangelism and that consequently our structures will survive or disappear and our relationships
change as they serve or do not serve this fundamental purpose.
Here in Germany years of work have gone into the structural
changes that led to the formation of the Missionswerk. Perhaps
this is not the best psychological moment to raise the problem
of the structures of world mission! Yet commitment to mission
means always being ready and willing to enter into new commitments.
We have to pay attention to new missionary patterns which are
trying to include churches in different parts of the world in
discussions and decision-making on an equal footing. We have to
make sure that the flow of aid is multi-directional and that as
far as possible it involves the whole of our churches' life.
You are certainly familiar with the Evangelical Community for
Apostolic Action which groups together about twenty-five
churches in Europe, Africa and Asia with a common missionary

vocation. This year will see the beginning of two new experiments: in London the Council for World Mission will be formed, incorporating the English Presbyterian and Congregational Churches and a group of churches in different parts of the world. And in Australia the union of a number of churches has provided the opportunity to re-examine their missionary structures and give a new focus to their relations with churches in the Pacific region.

If we constantly study these patterns, and also the experience of the Roman Catholic Church, it should help us gradually to move towards more flexible, sensible and responsible structures. The important thing is that the whole church should feel responsible so that the response to requests for aid from sister churches can be nation-wide. At the same time we must have the freedom and the humility to acknowledge our own need of the aid they can give us. In this area of concern for the ecumenical dimension of mission, too, a number of practical tasks lie ahead of us: the ecumenical exchange of personnel, encouragement of local ecumenism, theological cross-fertilization, etc. But we must remember, and this is fundamental, that our relationships are not confined to the strictly ecclesiastical level or what might be called 'official' Christian activities.

It is the total life of our respective countries which has an impact on the total life of other countries, and vice versa. The people who have an impact on or in other countries and so influence and condition the whole mission of the Church of Jesus Christ are the members of our churches as they work at their different jobs. Ecumenism in mission must, therefore, be understood as the faithfulness of Christians in all areas of life in all our respective countries and in all our relationships.

In a vision of world mission ecumenical awareness is essential.

Let me finish by reminding you of the call from Nairobi:

> We need to recover the sense of urgency. Questions about theological definitions there may be. Problems of precise implementation will arise. But neither theoretical nor practical differences must be allowed to dampen the fires of evangelism.
>
> Confessing Christ must be done *today*. "Behold, now is the acceptable time; behold, now is the day of salvation" (2 Cor. 6:2). It cannot wait for a time that is comfortable for us. We must be prepared to proclaim the gospel when human beings need to hear it. But in our zeal to spread the good news, we must guard against fanaticism which disrupts the hearing of the gospel and breaks the community of God. The world requires, and God demands, that we recognize the urgency to proclaim the saving word of God - today. God's acceptable time demands that we respond in all haste. "And how terrible it would be for me if I did not preach the gospel!" (1 Cor. 9:16).[6]

The Commission on World Mission and Evangelism and the Missionswerk will, I am sure, move forward together on this path of
obedience.

(Address delivered at the Assembly of the Evangelisches
Missionswerk [Protestant Association for World Mission],
Hamburg, Federal Republic of Germany, January 1977; trans-
lated from the Spanish, Language Service, WCC)

Notes

1) Constitution of the World Council of Churches, III. Functions and
   Purposes.

2) Breaking Barriers, Nairobi 1975. Report of Section I: Confessing Christ
   Today; Hearing on Unit I; Report of the Programme Guidelines Committee.

3) ibid. Report of Section I: Confessing Christ Today, para. 57, p. 52.

4) Report of the Core Group of the Commission on World Mission and
   Evangelism, Geneva, June 1976, pp. 3-4.

5) ibid. p. 11.

6) Breaking Barriers, paras. 69-70, pp. 54-55.

JESUS CHRIST - THE LIFE OF THE WORLD

The main theme of the 1983 Assembly of the World Council of Churches will be "Jesus Christ — the Life of the World". This *IRM* issue, as well as some future issues, highlights the evangelistic significance of this topic. The WCC and the delegates of its member churches who will be present at this important event will be obliged to say clearly and loudly to the world why they believe that Jesus Christ is the very life of the world. It might be easier to say this loudly than clearly! The very fact of having a big gathering that calls for the attention of the mass media will facilitate the spreading of the central theme of this Assembly to a very wide constituency. But the important thing is not that people should be aware that there is something called the Assembly of the World Council of Churches, but that they should be challenged afresh to the discipleship incorporated in the words "Jesus Christ — the Life of the World".

To those outside the Christian family, the theme sounds somewhat imperialistic and pretentious. Who are these Christians to claim for themselves the secret of life? Who is this Jesus, unrelated to some of the most important religious traditions of humankind, to pretend to be the bearer of life? Does not an explicit claim on the part of Christians imply a judgement of others? To those inside the Christian family, this theme is an affirmation of hope. It is for us a testimony to the life-giving reality of Jesus Christ, and an invitation to explore together with people of other faiths or convictions the potential meaning of this Christian affirmation for all areas of human life. It is a testimony that invites exploration.

The Assembly of the World Council of Churches, with thousands of participants coming from every corner of the earth, will be obliged to spell out the affirmation that Jesus Christ is the life of the world in the face of the threats and promises of the present human situation.

— When we see the escalation of the arms race, we are obliged to explain in what sense Jesus Christ is the guarantor of life for the future of our planet, theatened many times over by the already-existing arsenal of lethal weapons.

— When we observe the present debate — and not only debate, but practice — of technological manipulation of life, fostered by the development of scientific disciplines, we don't know whether to tremble because of the threat or to wonder about the promise for the future quality of life. But both those who are working on this frontier and those who will suffer or be blessed by the results of this work need clear guidelines to see how these endeavours relate to some fundamental affirmations about the quality of human life.

— When we realize that more than one-third of the world's people are undernourished, and that hunger is a growing reality and an ominous threat in extensive regions of our planet, we must ask what it means to affirm Jesus Christ as the life of the world to a human community that is not able to provide even minimal sustenance for all its members.

— When we see people dreaming of a new day and struggling for liberation — even with all the ambiguities associated with the use of violence — we are challenged, as a world gathering, to explain the meaning of the affirmation "Jesus Christ — the Life of the World" as judgement on the present situation and as inspiration to those who search for a new quality of life.

— When we see countless young people who are victims of drugs or esoteric cults — and others accommodating themselves to a monotonous routine or escaping through the violence of riots — we realize there is a lack of faith in the potentialities of life. What does it mean to affirm Jesus as the life of the world to those who are forced to submit to the dehumanizing pressures of the industrial production system?

— When we observe movements of peoples bringing together persons of entirely different religious systems, we realize we are living in a situation of increasing encounter and very often, unhappily, of religious confrontation. Some of the ancient religions are experiencing revival. What does it mean to announce Jesus Christ to people who have found meaning for their life in their respective religions? How do we recognize our common vocation to work together to preserve human life upon the earth, given our differing traditions, differing sets of symbols, differing profound loyalties?

The Assembly will address itself to the fundamental linking of our Christian convictions and the immense global issues confronting humankind

309

today. An Assembly that dares to proclaim Jesus Christ as the life of the world, however, must also be very clear in its invitation to faith in that Christ. The Assembly preparation process is the occasion to introduce into the life of every Christian community the basic question: if we believe that Jesus is the life of the world, what does this mean for our neighbourhood, for our city, for our nation?

The Assembly as such, and each one of us in our own circumstances, will work from certain basic convictions. First, "Jesus Christ — the Life of the World" is a basic affirmation about the purpose of creation and its sustaining process. We are realistic enough — and the Bible even more so — to recognize the powerful presence of sin, evil and death in the world. Just the retelling of the Gospel of Jesus Christ will be a fundamental illustration of this painful reality. But the Gospel says clearly that the light shone in the darkness and the darkness did not prevail, that even death could not prevail. The resurrection of Jesus Christ is the final triumph of life over death. Christians are called by this affirmation to an attitude of hope in every situation. This is not an escape from the tensions of the world; it assumes that every situation is a new beginning, and that God is able to use even our own death in accordance with his wise purposes. Those who proclaim the Gospel of Jesus Christ should always be full of hope. We are not prophets of doom. We are watchers for the morning that is coming, because we know the quality of life present in Jesus Christ; we know that finally that is the life that will overcome. The evangelistic message is a message full of hope.

Secondly, we need to search for the manifestation of the life of Christ both inside and outside officially recognized boundaries of the Christian faith. This is not to affirm natural theology. Christians, who in the revelation of the Gospel and in the communion of the church have discovered the reality of Jesus as the life of the world, should be equipped and challenged to discern signs and potential signs of his presence everywhere in the world, to be surprised by the manifestations of the presence of the Christ. This demands from us, first, humility in not pretending that we control the person of Christ, and second, discipline in the submitting of ourselves to the control of the story of Jesus Christ as told in the New Testament, avoiding the criteria of easy human optimism or easy human wisdom. But to make credible our affirmation, we must deepen our knowledge of other human disciplines and human situations. We cannot spell out the meaning of our biblical faith for those who work in the highly complex territory of modern science without making the humble attempt to understand the values at stake in their attempts to broaden scientific knowledge. And we cannot responsibly proclaim Jesus as the life of the world to people of other religious convictions unless we try to understand the dynamics of their own faith and the fruits of that faith that have contributed or are contributing to the total treasure of human culture.

What we have been learning in the WCC programme on Dialogue with People of Living Faiths and Ideologies should be of substantial help when we attempt to proclaim Jesus as the life of the world within the diverse realms of modern science, traditional religions, societal structures or cultural convictions. Dialogue is absolutely necessary to be able to link the story of Jesus Christ to the present predicament of a concrete human being. Dialogue is absolutely necessary to be able to criticize in love and to receive the criticism of those who not only hear our words but see our lives.

Thirdly, we are not talking about life in general. We are talking about the life manifested in the Gospel story in Jesus of Nazareth. There is nothing in this affirmation that will take us in a pantheistic direction. It is an attempt to see the relationship of all life to the quality of life revealed in Jesus of Nazareth, and a call to look toward that life and to recognize its fruition in him. Calling people to look toward Jesus Christ could be labelled a religious pretention; but this impression will be corrected when it is understood that the only affirmation of life Jesus himself made was the surrendering of his own life. By being ready to give up his life, he was able to give life.

Finally, it is to him that we want to point. This is our personal testimony. Of course this will demand from us a lifestyle that corresponds to the one manifested in Jesus Christ. It will demand a consideration of our missionary methodologies. Recently in France I heard a young man talking about his experience working with one missionary organization in Africa. "I was a truck driver. We had trucks, jeeps, planes, even a helicopter. Something was wrong. We were totally out of touch with reality. The intentions were right, but the overwhelming presence of our richness and our technology made it almost impossible to testify to the life that was manifested in the poor carpenter of Nazareth. People felt invited to participate in the goods of the West, not in the life of Jesus of Nazareth."

As we struggle with the richness of "Jesus Christ — the Life of the World" and its potential for new missionary input in the life of our churches, we invite people in every context to enrich our understanding of the evangelistic meaning of the theme. A number of theological questions have already been recognized. How does Jesus Christ as the source of life relate to the creational life of humankind, and how does our understanding of this relation affect the ways in which we approach people of other faiths or no faith? How does the affirmation that Jesus Christ is the source of life for the world relate to the promises of life to those who respond to the Christ by faith? What are the consequences of the Melbourne conference and the implications of the Assembly theme with respect to the proclamation of the Gospel to the poor and to the missionary lifestyle of the churches and congregations? How is this missionary lifestyle shaped by the understanding that life is found in self-surrendering, self-emptying, for the sake of the kingdom?

We continue our pilgrimage to the source of our faith in the life of Jesus Christ, with the hope that we will receive inspiration, encouragement and challenge for our missionary task today. We invite readers to participate fully in this pilgrimage, sending us their questions, their experiences, and the fruits of their own reflection.

(International Review of Mission, January 1982)

THIRD WORLD CHRISTIANITY

To attempt futurology is always a risky matter! Especially when we talk about the future of the Christian Church, we can not consider it a series of known facts to be projected into the future, for we must consider also the freedom of man and of God. Our predictions should be humbly made and subject to permanent revision.

To speak of "third world Christianity" demands a common understanding of the expression "third world." "Third world" applies basically to those countries that have gone through the process of colonization and are struggling today to become self-reliant, fighting against neo-colonialist forms of domination and dependence. "Third world churches" are churches which are working in countries whose economics are peripheral to the main centers of industrial and financial power of today's world, countries which in consequence are submitted to all kinds of foreign cultural and political influences.

At the same time, in almost every "third world country," there is a growing desire to become self-reliant and to discover national identity. International conferences are bringing together the industrialized nations, the socialist nations and the countries of the third world, in an attempt radically to change the rules of the economic relations between nations. The success of these meetings is still very limited. But precisely this failure in finding solutions for the problems of mankind today makes more acute the context of resentment, frustration, hope and rebellion against which the churches of the third world are working and will be working more and more in the coming years.

Inside this general framework of the third world, we must recognize different local situations as having certain specificity. It is clear that the action and emphasis of the churches in countries of a predominantly Muslim population will be different from the action and emphasis of other churches working against a background of animist religions. Similarly, the ministry of the church will be different in situations where the growing aspirations of the masses are confronted with martial law, or with a one-party system, or with a revolutionary approach, or even with a Western type of democracy.

At the same time, however, we must keep in mind the fact that the churches are not only institutions working within a given context, but also living bodies of people who confess Jesus Christ. There is an internal dynamic in each church, affected by the reading of the Bible, for example, and worship. The nature of the church itself should be taken into consideration in any contemplation of the future of third world Christianity.

What I will try to do in this brief article is select a few secular trends, consider what seems to be the corresponding response to them in the churches, and look for theological options which both secular trends and church responses seem to suggest as a future shape of the third world churches. In summary fashion I will try to suggest the kind of ministry such trends are demanding. Not everything that I say will apply to every part of the third world. But I will limit myself to three very general trends which, I believe, correspond to most situations.

1. The last 50 years have brought about a total shaking of traditional types of society. The opening up of remote regions to the influence of Western civilization has thoroughly upset traditional customs, values, and religious concepts. In every country of the third world large movements of people from the rural areas to the cities have taken place. Technology, industrialization, urbanization, etc., have produced masses of up-

rooted people whose traditional set of values and community life have been practically destroyed.

After the Second World War, in most of these countries, the search for independence has also shaken the traditional acceptance of authority and has prepared people for a new future. The natural result of all these changes has been a growing mass of up-rooted people who are searching for meaning, for new centers of community life and for a new sense of belonging.

The local Christian churches have responded to the vacuum created by the disappearance of the traditional society by multiplying their evangelistic outreach. They have offered a spiritual experience in Jesus Christ as an integrating center, and life in community in the Christian fellowship. Thus we see today a fabulous numerical growth of Christian churches in most of the countries of the third world, especially in Africa, Korea and Indonesia.

This trend in growth will continue in the next few years, obliging the churches to face new dimensions of mission and Christian responsibility. While Christians were a small minority they could be marginal to society and avoid facing national issues. Today, society has discovered the existence of the church as a powerful center of people's loyalty and as an important factor therefore in political life. The church is challenged to define and to act its mission in terms of the secular community.

H. R. Weber[2] explains that the relation of the church to the surrounding culture passes first through a period of separation and isolation, in which the whole culture is rejected as sinful in order that the new converts can affirm themselves in the new set of values around Jesus Christ. But with time and numerical growth, a certain moment arrives when the churches must begin to face the wider issues of society and try to participate in different ways. This sequence could be illustrated by the situation of the small Christian Church in Paul's time and the successive situation of the church in the second and third centuries. Christians came to be obliged to

---

[2]See, for example, his two essays in *The Layman in Christian History*, edd. S. C. Neill and H. R. Weber (Philadelphia: The Westminster Press, 1963).

face the Roman Empire, to participate, and finally to see their faith become the official religion of the state!

The simple fact is, large churches cannot escape socio-political cultural responsibilities! This is visible today, e.g., in Korea where on one side the state is trying to woo the church to get some religious sanction for the actual economic and power politics of the regime. At the same time, on the other side, key leaders of the churches confront and challenge the Government on the issue of human rights. We can see a similar situation in Indonesia, with very delicate political problems produced by the growth of the church and the interpretation of that growth by the surrounding Muslim majority. In Africa, too, churches are coming closer to centers of political power; black church leaders, for example, are very active in the liberation movement.

The International Congress on Evangelization, which met in Lausanne in 1974,[3] is a good illustration of the coming new reality. The main concern of the Congress was to discuss ways and means to reach unreached millions with the Gospel of Jesus Christ. Leaders of third world churches demanded however that consideration should be given to the socio-cultural-economic-political background factors involved in every evangelistic situation. More and more the Gospel is being tested by the churches of the third world as a message calling men to *metanoia*, to conversion in *all* areas of their lives — social, political, cultural, personal, etc. I anticipate a growing politization of third world Christianity — one that will bring its own challenges, possibilities and dangers.

Because of the numerical growth of these churches, two things will be needed: more ministers, and more theologians! The ministers must be able to help the new converts to grow into the maturity of a Christian life. And the theologians must be able to help the Christian community to face the new challenges and possibilities of serving their communities in the perspective of the Gospel.

Theological education by extension would begin to answer the first need, and in some way, the second, by enlarging the

---

[3]See the "Official Reference Volume" of the International Congress on World Evangelization, edited by J. D. Douglas, and entitled *Let The Earth Hear His Voice* (Minneapolis: World Wide Publications, 1975).

number of people able to participate in a community search for common answers to common problems. A good illustration of this new situation was given to me by the Baptist director of a Baptist Seminary in Haiti. He said: "We are not training pastors, we are training 'bishops,' because each one of these students will be in charge of 15-20 congregations where local leaders will be doing the actual pastoral work!"

2. In most countries of the third world there is a growing search for national cultural identity. Especially in Africa is this illustrated, by the change of name of both nations and individuals. This is of course a definite attempt to affirm or to recover traditional cultural values.

Most of the churches came to these countries representing in some way a foreign Western culture. The churches were built according to the missionary model and pretty soon developed a sub-culture of their own. Now, however, they are taking into their hands their own destiny. They want to root themselves in the national soil. They want to participate fully in the cultural expressions of their respective nations. This trend will continue, encouraged by the growth of independent churches which have not been the result of the direct work of missionaries of the West but are the normal fruit of the Spirit in people whose world view is that of the surrounding national culture.

Two other considerations must be mentioned in regard to the churches in this new situation: (a) While most of the third world countries are economically poor, and the majority of their populations are deprived, Christianity, through help provided by churches in the West, has enjoyed, in general, a better position and so has projected an image of economic advantage. Beautiful church buildings can be seen in many cities — the result of the abundance of foreign money!

Because the church wants to participate fully in the surrounding community, however, more and more the financial responsibility for their own life and mission must be in their own hands. That means changes in status and values in the middle class level of many third world ministers. More and more tent-making ministers and a minority of highly trained theologians will be the needed combination for the growing churches. Of course, we cannot foresee what will be the final outcome. Perhaps there will be a development of an elite who will preside through their own expertise over the masses of church people. Or perhaps there will be the development of a charismatic community where all contribute with their own particular gifts!

(b) The desire to relate to traditional cultures and the passion to penetrate those cultures with the Gospel is leading many churches to new attempts in the fields of worship, prayer, mystical practices, etc. We must be ready for an increase of these experiments, which very often will appear strange to Western eyes. The desire to participate in nation-building will lead to all kinds of discussion and cooperation with nationalist movements, with different kinds of Marxism and ideological positions. Of course, the danger of new types of syncretism appear on the horizon. At the same time however, new expressions of the Christian faith will develop in liturgical life, in the life-style of the congregations, and in theological formulations. These will challenge and enrich the Church Universal. The ministry in this new situation will need strong biblical foundations if it is to participate responsibly in the search for a new Christian cultural identity in the new nations.

3. Looking from the third world to the West, Christians can easily see a process of secularization, even of secularism, dominating the societies of Western Europe and North America. Religion seems to be taken for granted. There is a lack of passion for and commitment to discipleship. Technology, leisure, the consumer society, etc. provide at least a partial explanation for this situation. The churches in the third world, without these particular problems, see both the problems and a means of involvement in *world* mission by a contribution to the traditional "sending" countries, through challenging this cultural syncretism of the West. One of the important contributions of the Lausanne Congress on World Evangelization was precisely the challenge set before the church leaders of the West by brothers of the third world concerning the actual development of a kind of civil religion in Western countries. This civil religion, they held, eliminates the cutting edge of the Gospel proclamation of repentance and forgiveness in Jesus Christ.

This prophetic, theological contribution is one of the most important services that the churches of the West will be receiving in the near future from churches in the third world. Along with it will come the witness of a new, fresh experience of life in Jesus Christ. The very novelty of the Christian life coming from churches that are alive and struggling to be faithful will help Christians in the West to discover themselves as living on a missionary frontier and as called to the renewal there of their own commitment to Jesus Christ.

I further think the churches in the third world will find possibilities for mutual help in mission with churches in Socialist countries, opportunities that for obvious reasons of political confrontation are closed to churches in the Western world. New lines of communication, new ways and means of reciprocal support will be found.

This missionary awareness of the churches in the third world, this growing participation in world mission will mean however that the whole Christian church will recognize that there are no more central places from which truth comes to the rest of the world. Such a realization will be a particular challenge to the structure of the Roman Catholic Church, but surely also to hidden or open assumptions in most Western churches. The experiences and theological reflections of the churches of the third world will provoke the Western imagination and, in that way, enrich the Church Universal.

Towards the year 2000, Christianity in the third world will become the major segment of Christianity in the whole world! The third world churches will be facing fully the challenges posed to the church through history by numerical growth and participation in nation-building. They will also be reflecting on their place in cultural situations. They will be materially as poor as their countries will be, but spiritually alert and ready to participate fully in world mission.

When I think of the ministry of the church in the twenty-first century, I dream of a recovery of the charismatic teamwork of the early church as it is reflected in the New Testament. For only in the inter-play and cooperation of their different gifts will all the churches be able to face fully the challenge and the promise of the future.

(Southeastern Studies, Wake Forest, North Carolina, USA, 1977)

WORLD MISSION IN THE EIGHTIES

To discuss world mission in the eighties is a provocative task.

A first difficulty is due to the fact that futurology is always a risky exercise, especially in these days of acceleration of history. In the 60s we went through a period of expectation, in terms of liberation in Latin America. Today we live with the horrid reality of an overall predominant oppression. Who could have foreseen it, who would have wanted to prepare the churches for this particular new situation, when we were so busy facing daily realities and trying to organize life so as to correspond to our dreams? So, we will not try "futurology". We will try to equip ourselves to be faithful today and tomorrow.

A second difficulty comes from the expression: "world" mission of the Church. In former times this was more or less easy to understand as referring to the international dimension or the foreign dimension of our mission. But since Bangkok we have been talking about world mission with an entirely different meaning. World mission is the totality of our missionary involvement wherever we are. God's mission covers the whole world and anything done in a local situation has a consequence in God's economy for the whole of His purpose, for the whole of His world. More on that: in Bangkok also, the thoughts about cultural identity came to fruition. Today we recognize that any "world" dimension should be the interplay between different particularities. In every place we contribute to or handicap "world" mission in as much as faith becomes incarnated through us in a given culture. We have been thrown back to our local mission in order to be really in world mission.

We could escape these difficulties by selecting world problems and then see our mission in relation to them. It would be possible to speak about trends in pollution, multinational companies, power blocks, disarmament, international

economics, etc. In this way, our "world" mission will be understood as
actions in relation to overall world problems. These dimensions rightly belong to our concerns and are very much related to the mission of the Church
everywhere. But when we concentrate our attention on them, they tend to become the opera ad extra: what we do as a special programme, without challenging
the existing parish life or even my personal life style. But if by "world"
mission we understand God's mission in the world, then we are called to more
than facing general problems. It will mean living out in the perspective of
God's mission: "As the Father sent me, so I send you". The small or big manifestations of Christian love here and there are our participation in God's
world mission. World mission then is to see every single local act related
to a struggle that God is carrying on in the whole world, and seeing the big
items in the struggle of the world as related to my prayer life, my community
life, my family commitment.

With this understanding we could look forward and point out some elements or
perspectives that will surely be present in our mission in the 80s, because
they belong to the very heart of our Christian convictions, and because we
have enough indications today of the importance that these perspectives will
take in the near future:

1. "Tell me the old, old story". It is as simple as that. Visiting Russian
   Churches, I put some questions about the education of children in the light
   of the well-known limitation imposed on the Church to provide Christian
   education. The answer was an indulgent smile: "Did you see who are the
   worshippers? The majority are people well over 60. Mothers and fathers go
   out to work. Who remains with the children at home? Grandfathers and
   grandmothers. We are not worried about the future generations and Christian
   faith, as long as we can count with the living faith of these worshippers
   who in their homes are transmitting the Orthodox faith". This answer may
   be simple and perhaps naïve in the light of modern mass communication
   means. But at the same time it registers an experience of churches in
   different parts of the world. During centuries, in the middle of surrounding Muslim cultures, small ancient churches have been able to preserve
   faith for tomorrow through the liturgical and spiritual life of the Church.
   Like Paul, we are called to say: "I handed on to you the facts which have
   been imparted to me" (I. Cor. 15:3). The world will need to know that "the
   Son of man has come to give up his life as a ransom for many"; that the

price has been paid and that we are no longer slaves but that liberation is a fact; that we are called to live up to the intention of God's action in Christ for us. Without this story we could still have excellent humanitarian motivations, but our specific "Christian" contribution will be lost and the whole human process will be poorer.

This "old, old story" provides insights for the human projection, critical dimensions in the search for a new day and supportive power to those who are engaged in the struggle for it. Perhaps this could be one positive way to understand conservative trends in many churches today, a concern for a faith with content, with a clear relation to the historical facts of Jesus Christ. In every missionary education programme the constant reference to the sources and the development of a capacity to communicate the hidden revelation of God in Christ, will always be fundamental.

But it is not so simple! If the question were only to transmit the facts of a story, then we could entrust that task to specialists in the art of communication! In our example of socialist or Muslim countries, it is easy to see the liturgical life of the Church and the family life of Christians as fundamental elements in the transmission not only of knowledge but of an experience that provides a sacramental interpretation of all life. The word of the liturgy of the Bible, the old story, sounds as total novelty in the middle of a surrounding community that ignores it or considers it practically as obsolete.

But an imitation of that attitude in an entirely different surrounding could be simply an escape out of reality or one way not to communicate the story, because not many will be interested to listen to it. What does it mean to tell the old story here in your country, where statistics show that millions have been converted three or four times, and where TV and radio are full of the most dilute versions of christianity? How can the "old, old story" have any chance of being listened to afresh? Have we not vaccinated our children against religion? A few months ago the question was raised whether there is still any chance for Western missionaries in Third World countries. The assumption was that the total projection of these countries or of these churches and also the different life styles provided by different economic situations, were a denial of the "story" that the missionaries would like to tell. In other words, we need to suspect our telling of the story when the same comes very close to affirming or repeating the predominant values of one society, and when that story does not mean cross and resurrection for those who tell it and for those who will accept it. Due to this over-simplification of the telling of the story, we are tempted today to call for a moratorium on words and keep silence. Could not the Christian generation of the 80s be the one that will keep silence in order to allow the generation of the 90s to get a new chance of putting meaning into words? The temptation is very real and tactically it is - here and there - convenient, necessary, even obligatory, to be silent. But as an overall strategy it is both suicidal and impossible. We communicate with our fellow beings through the totality of our life that includes words; we share events, meaning, realities that cannot be contained in words but which are expressed through words as sacramental instruments pointing to a higher reality. But it is obvious that today proclamation, the telling of the story, needs a particular context of concern, of commitment, in order that the reality of the story becomes alive once again - or even to get a hearing possibility for it.

To go back to the question about Western missionary presence: a few weeks ago seven white missionaries were killed in Rhodesia. All kind of suppositions are possible concerning the question: "who were the murderers"? But the Christian witness was given by the Superior of this religious order, indicating that, independently of who did the actual killing, this was the consequence of an inhuman situation, and that the sacrifice of those priests and nuns should be seen as a contribution to the liberation of the people of Zimbawe. It is at this moment that the story of cross and resurrection becomes alive again and calls new attention. As Gerhard Hoffmann says: "Mission, evangelism, happens whenever and wherever it becomes clear, however partially, to others through us that our, their situation is hooked up with the story of Christ, throwing us together. To evangelize is to point out the link between our stories and Christ's story."

Also, "at the basis of the quest for 'identity' as it was raised by the Third-World churches, there was a very simple spiritual question: what is our particular (African, Asian, etc.) story/history with Jesus Christ - after having received Him by mediation through a strange and foreign story/ history (the one of the Western missionary movement) and even through a

hostile story/history (in as far as it was mediated through the imperialistic
Western countries)? From there the question came back to the churches of
the West, and the thrust of this question came through very clearly at the
Bangkok Conference: not the 'contents' of 'Western theology' was criticized,
but its (hidden or open) claim to be 'universal'. There was again the
challenge: we want to hear your particular story with Christ - not reflections
on the story of Christ in general!"

The challenge of mission in the 80s is precisely to live our own story with
Christ and be able to point from it to the once and for all story of Jesus
of Nazareth.

Next week will take place in Washington a series of religious manifestations
against torture. Marches, symbolic actions in front of banks, embassies,
government buildings, will relate the events of Holy Week in the Gospels
to the actual realities of daily life.

The cross as sharing in the suffering and guilt of mankind, as vicarious
sacrifice, and the resurrection as promise of forgiveness and new beginning
are being openly proclaimed. The old story is there. But also the new
reality: "Lo, I make all things new".

2. "Suffered under Pontius Pilate". I looked back to this little phrase of
    the creed, when I began to put together data to prepare for this conver-
    sation, because if anything is already evident today and is growing bigger
    and bigger in relation to the future, it is the fact that the ministry of
    the Church is and will be a public ministry. Churches everywhere are
    facing trials, temptations, oppressions. Whatever they do or refuse to
    do, they are exposed publicly. It is true, as Paul said, that we have been
    made "a show to the world". Very often the question has been raised: why
    does Pontius Pilate appear in the Creed, on what merits? It is there to
    prove that the events of Jesus Christ were not unrelated to the main trends
    of history. Although he was born in an unknown little town and killed as an
    ordinary criminal, his story could not remain unknown. Later on it was
    said: "The men who have made trouble all over the world have now come
    here" (Acts 17:6). How futile seems today our whole discussion about
    individual or social Gospel! How naïve is our question about the possible

participation of the Church in political life! The Gospel has always
been a public event. When we try to preserve the Gospel from public issues,
what in fact we are doing is using religion to defend a given attitude
which most of the time supports the actual situation, protects the status
quo. How could we keep our love in secret? How could we worship a Lord
and accept the pretensions of powerful authorities of today? How could
we know of the freedom in Christ and accept tyranny? Looking at the world
today, in the midst of so many turmoils and despairs, we cannot avoid a
sense of fear and exultation. The Church of Jesus Christ is coming to
live up to the highness of the first pages of church history.

When South African Christian schools begin to be integrated, challenging
the existing lway; when the Bishops in Uganda are willing to face death
in order to challenge the inhumanity of the situation; when the Bishops
in Brazil raise their voices of denunciation, protest and pastoral warning
on behalf of the Indians, the despised ones of the population; when the
churches in Chile mount a programme to protect political refugees and do
not surrender to the activity of the political police; when Christians
in Korea are facing judgement with the attitude of Martin Luther: "here I
stand, I cannot act against my consciousness", - what do we have if not a
tremendous manifestation of a spiritual power in action?

Of course there are also shameful spots of cowardice in church life, and of
course there are other groups, non-Christians, who also raise up to the
demands of humanity. We do not want to be romantic or exclusive in our
appraisal of the Church, but just recognize that some of the most beautiful pages in church history are being written today - with fear and trembling,
but with trust in the power of the resurrection - in today's public arena.
If we look to the 80s, we must realize that more than ever this will be
the moment for a public witness of the Christian community. We will be more
exposed than ever to public attention and in consequence to public persecution. Let me tell you a little about my own country, and how I see
our mission in the 80s: Uruguay is a country from which one out of 5 inhabitants has left; one out of fifty has been in jail; one out of sixty
has been tortured, and one out of 500 is still in jail! It is evident that
in this situation we cannot see our mission in the 80s without reference
to the word "reconciliation". The main task of the national community
will be to overcome the dimension of hate present in the actual situation.

Those who know the dimension of forgiveness present in the cross of Jesus Christ will be called to play an essential role in building a new human community. But will not the word "reconciliation" be too cheap a term to forget and forgive the actual realities? Are we going to pronounce such a dear word of our tradition and be exposed to the logical rebuke that reconciliation also means surrendering? It is only inasmuch as we are involved today in the struggle of the people to overcome oppression, torture and inhumanity, that we may be able to earn some right to present not only the word but also an attitude of reconciliation. It is only by taking upon ourselves the suffering of the situation, that we can have some possibility of building a new day. It is very evident that the Church in Uruguay cannot pronounce a word that invites people to repentance, faith, commitment, discipleship, community, without referring all those words to the actual repressive situation, to the struggle for a new day and to the hope that in a non-distant future we shall be able to pronounce the word reconciliation.

But then, my friends, your mission in this country will also be a public mission. Maybe the meaning of "suffering under Pontius Pilate" is appearing on your horizon. I shall not try to describe for you what could be the public issues on which you might be called to render witness "under Pontius Pilate", but perhaps I can point to some elements that will oblige your public witness inasmuch as you belong to the Church who confesses Jesus Christ everywhere in the world. Through your relationship with churches who are becoming public witnesses in other parts of the world, and due to the power of your country, you will be called to express your solidarity and in that way show yourself to the world. Today, when churches in Southern Africa are being exposed to Pontius Pilate because of the denunciation of the apartheid system through direct actions in the schools, where will be your supporting, public action? You know the World Council of Churches Programme to Combat Racism. This has meant solidarity with churches and people in their struggle for justice and liberation, but at the same time exposing ourselves to all kind of misunderstanding and worse than that, to all kind of interested attacks. A few weeks ago, Christian newspapers in England were invited by powerful financial to publish an advertisement saying: "On such and such a day, the WCC has killed 7 Jesuit missionaries". But this is nothing compared to what

326

would happen to your churches here in terms of reputation, divisions, cutting of funds, etc., once you really mean solidarity in this struggle and stress it by denouncing the complicity factors in your own society. Let me state clearly - to avoid any political misunderstanding - that I am referring to what could happen to you in the 80s!

I also think in terms of the Korean struggle. Your government admits quite clearly that there are human right violations but that factors like national security should be considered in assessing the amount of help to be given to that particular country. I shall not discuss the right or even the duty of a government to make that kind of balancing considerations, but where is the Church's stand? Are we also limited to that type of balance statement? Or, while recognizing the right of the governments to make their own decisions, are we making ours, and speak and act clearly in order to manifest our solidarity with the Christians in Korea who are struggling for democratic freedom? And of course the examples could be multiplied and take more general frontiers like those that have to do with the search for a new international economic order, and so on. In any case, when churches will be spelling out in dramatic actions, not only the voice of common wisdom, but in particular the voice of the foolishness of the cross, the suffering under Pontius Pilate will become reality.

Education for mission in the 80s should highlight the public character of the Christian mission today everywhere in the world, and help people to discover the public dimensions of our faith statements and the public reality of our Christian commitment.

3. "But there are other sheep of mine" (John 10:16). Traditionally we speak of the United States of America as a pluralistic society. To a certain degree this is true. You have many different Christian denominations, you have many racial groups; you have expressions of almost every possible religious or ideological current existing in the world today. But the new feature of the 80s will be that the ideological and religious pluralism of the world will be a reality experienced in every nation, at every level. With the world becoming smaller and smaller, with ideas travelling faster than planes, and with the constant movement of people from country to country, we are being exposed to all kinds of "Weltanschauung"

and final convictions. Also, when we look at the whole world and discover our solidarity with churches who are surrounded by powerful cultural and religious movements, this necessarily conditions all our mission. If we want to relate in a supporting, intelligent way to their endeavour, we must come to grips theologically with the reality of this outer world of religions and ideologies that exist, not with the purpose of being a hunting ground for Christian proselytism, but having their own system of values, their own self-justification and also their own expectations in relation to christianity. We will be obliged to live and work side by side with people of other faiths and ideologies. Our mission should be thought of in terms of a relation to this new reality.

Since the Apostel Paul called the unknown God of the Greek, the God of Jesus Christ, missionaries have been trying to discover in every religious manifestation of mankind, something of the Father whom we know in Jesus Christ. While all religions, including christianity, could be the worst perversion of man in his attempt to manipulate God, it is also evident that we cannot discard all religious manifestations as belonging to the devil. On the contrary, we live and work together, digging out the best of our respective traditions for the building up of a common society. Of course, unfortunately, there are still many conflicts between different sectors of society or even between nations that use religion as an ideological device for hiding the real roots of those conflicts, based mainly on economic reasons.

God has not remained without witness in every people, and in the light of the biblical revelation we could take a look at different cultural traditions and discover there values that are signs of the action of the Spirit of God that are expecting to be matched by a revelation of God in Jesus Christ. Also through secular forces God works to shape history. And we will be called to cooperate humbly with them. It is impossible to make universal judgements, but everywhere we will experience the fact that God calls us to complete obedience, in love. And there we find ourselves side by side with people of quite different ideological convictions.

A few years ago, a Latin American, Rubem Alvez, defended the ecclesiological reality of secular groups, challenging the traditional Lutheran/Calvinist teaching on the marks of the Church as Word and Sacraments. He said that

328

the fruits of the Spirit were also a mark of the Church, and that wherever you find love, charity, justice, etc., you are discovering marks, signs of the hidden Church.   This affirmation should not obscure but enlighten our evangelistic responsibility.   It is not a way to escape the duty and privilege of participating in the Gospel of Jesus Christ with all mankind, but it is the factual recognition that God is at work and that the Christian attempt to share the good news of God in Jesus Christ will have a natural linkage or relation to this manifestation of God in other religious or secular systems.

This would mean that our educational materials should highlight the Christlike values manifested in different ideological or religious systems, and encourage Christians to participate fully in daily life with people of those convictions, with the hope that together we could do better things for God, but also with the assurance that in this process the communication of Jesus Christ will come in a natural way.   As Father George from India says:

> "My problem is one of communicating Christ to the masses and the educated people of India in the way that the forefathers did - as St. Basil did, as St. Athanasius did.   To make the communication effective, I must sympathize with the hearer and have dialogue with him and tell him, 'Christ is the one who gave you whatever life you have; you have not got it from anywhere else."

An encounter with the world of religions and with ideological groups in this positive way will open up missionary possibilities of which we do not dream as yet.   By giving away our prejudice and trusting God's action everywhere, we will discover new potentialities for shaping up a more just society.   By being together with people whose starting point is different from ours, we will have a new and fresh chance to share with them the old, old story.   In one sense they provide the public in front of which we are telling the story of our life,   in another sense they are co-protagonists with us in the actual spelling out in the world of God's will for all mankind.   Of course, this is a very risky adventure, but ours is the first generation in which we can really realize the pluralistic nature of human existence.

This is a post-dinner conversation - so I better stop here.   Fundamentally, the challenge before all our educational attempts is the following: How do we help to develop a radar-like personality, a theological sensitivity, an awareness of God's movements in us and in the world, that will give us the ability to discover the place and the moment in which God calls our obedience. If you like to put it in a more biblical language: the aim for education for mission is to bring all Christians and all Christian communities to the spiritual attitude of Saul on the road to Damascus, when he was only able to say: "Lord, what do you want me to do"?

(Lecture given at the 75th anniversary of the Commission for Education for Mission of the NCCCUSA, 1977)

BIBLIOGRAPHY

AACC. *The Struggle Continues: Official Report of the Third Assembly of the AACC, Lusaka, Zambia, 12-24 May, 1974.* Nairobi: AACC, 1975.

AACC. *Fourth Assembly Meeting, 2-12 August, 1981.* Nairobi: AACC, 1981.

Acción Popular Ecuménica. Año 2, No. 2. Buenos Aires: August 1974

ADLER, Elisabeth. *A Small Beginning.* Geneva: WCC, 1974.

ALLEN, Roland. *Missionary Methods: St. Paul's or Ours?* Grand Rapids: Eerdmans, 1962.

ALLMEN, Daniel von. *L'Evangile de Jésus-Christ.* Yaoundé: Editions CLE, 1972.

ALVES, Rubem Azevedo. *A Theology of Human Hope.* New York: Corpus Books, 1969.

ALVES, Rubem Azevedo. *Poesía - Profecía - Magia.* Rio de Janeiro: CEDI, 1983.

ANDERSON, Bernhard W. *The Living World of the Old Testament.* London: Longman Group Ltd., 1975.

ANDERSON, Gerald H. and STRANSKY, Thomas F., eds. *Mission Trends No. 1: Crucial Issues in Mission Today.* New York: Paulist Press and Grand Rapids: Eerdmans, 1974.

ANDERSON, Gerald H. *Mission Trends No. 2: Evangelization.* Paulist & Eerdmans, 1975.

ANDERSON, Gerald H. *Mission Trends No. 3: Third World Theologies.* Paulist & Eerdmans, 1976.

ANDERSON, Gerald H., ed. *Asian Voices in Christian Theology.* Maryknoll, N.Y.: Orbis, 1976.

ANDERSON, Gerald H., *Mission Trends No. 4: Liberation Theologies.* Paulist & Eerdmans, 1979.

ANDERSON, Gerald H. *Kingdom of God. Witnessing to the Kingdom. Melbourne and Beyond.* Maryknoll, N.Y.: Orbis, 1982

Apocalíptica. Ciências da religião. São Paulo: Edição do Instituto Metodista de Ensino Superior, 1983.

ARAYA, Victorio. *El Dios de los pobres.* San José, Costa Rica: DEI, 1983.

ARIAS, Mortimer and Esther. *The Cry of my People.* New York: Friendship Press, 1980.

ARIAS, Mortimer. *Announcing the Reign of God. Evangelization and the Subversive Memory of Jesus.* Fortress Press, 1984.

ARMSTRONG, Bishop James. *Evangelism from the Underside.* Maryknoll, N.Y.: Orbis, 1982.

ASIAIN, Justo. *Inseguridad, riesgo y paz en la vida y el mensaje de Jesús.*
Buenos Aires: Ed. Carlos Lohlé, 1980.

ASSMANN, Hugo. *Theology for a Nomad Church.* Maryknoll, N.Y.: Orbis,
1976.

A Toi la règne. Etudes bibliques pour les Eglises. Geneva: Alliance Réformée
Mondiale, 1982.

AVILA, Rafael. *Teología, Evangelización y Liberación.* Bogotá: Ed. Paulinas,
Indo-American Press Service, 1973.

BARCLAY, William. *Turning to God: A Study of Conversion in the Book of
Acts and Today.* Grand Rapids: Baker, 1964.

BARREIRO, Alvaro. *The Basic Ecclesial Communities.* Maryknoll, N.Y.: Orbis, 1982.

BARTH, Karl. *La proclamation de l'Evangile.* Neuchâtel: Delachaux et Niestlé,
1961.

BARTH, Karl. *Church Dogmatics.* Vol. IV, Book 3. Translated by G.W. Bromley.
Edinburgh: T & T Clark, 1962.

BARTH, Karl. *La prière.* Neuchâtel: Delachaux et Niestlé, 1967.

BARTH, Markus. *The Broken Wall.* Valley Forge: Judson Press, 1959.

BARTH, Markus. *Justification.* Grand Rapids: Eerdmans, 1971.

BASSHAM, Rodger C. *Mission Theology: 1948-1975. Years of Worldwide Creative
Tension - Ecumenical, Evangelical and Roman Catholic.* Pasadena,
California: William Carey Library, 1979.

BERDYAEV, Nicholas. *The End of Our Time.* New York: Sheed & Ward Inc., 1933.

BERDYAEV, Nicholas. *The Fate of Man in the Modern World.* New York: Morehouse
Publishing Co., 1935.

BERGQUIST, James A. and MANICKAM, P. Kambar. *The Crisis of Dependency in
Third World Ministries. A Critique of Inherited Missionary Forms in
India.* Madras: CLS, 1974.

BERKHOF, H. *Christ and the Powers.* Scottdale, Pa.: Herald Press, 1962.

BEYERHAUS, P. and HALLENCREUTZ, C. *The Church Crossing Frontiers.* Lund:
Glaerup, 1969.

BEYERHAUS, Peter. *Humanisierung.* Bad Salzuflen: MBK Verlag, 1970.

BEYERHAUS, Peter. *Missions: Which Way?* Grand Rapids: Zondervan, 1971.

332

BEYERHAUS, Peter. *Allen Völkern zum Zeugnis. Biblisch-theologische Besinnung zum Wesen der Mission.* Wuppertal: Theologischer Verlag Rolf Brockhaus, 1972.

BEYERHAUS, Peter. *Bangkok 1973: The Beginning or End of World Mission?* Grand Rapids: Zondervan, 1974.

BEYERHAUS, Peter, in KÜNNETH, W. and BEYERHAUS, P., eds. *Reich Gottes oder Weltgemeinschaft.* Bad Liebenzell, 1975.

Biblical Perspective on Mission. Joint World Mission Conference. Heigh Leigh, September 1983.

BIGO, Pierre. *The Church and the Third World Revolution.* Maryknoll, N.Y.: Orbis, 1977.

BLASER, Klauspeter. *Wenn Gott schwarz wäre....* Zürich: Theologischer Verlag and Freiburg: Imba Verlag, 1972.

BLASER, Klauspeter. *Gottes Heil in heutiger Wirklichkeit.* Frankfurt/Main: Verlag Otto Lembeck, 1978.

BLASER, Klauspeter. *La mission: dialogues et défis.* Geneva: Labor et Fides, 1983.

BLAUW, Johannes. *The Missionary Nature of the Church.* New York: McGraw-Hill, 1962.

BLOSSER, Don. Jesus at Nazareth: Jubilee and the Missionary Message (Luke 4: 16-30), *Mission Focus*, Vol. VI, No. 5 (May), 5-8.

BOESAK, Allan. *The Finger of God: Sermons on Faith and Socio-Political Responsibility.* Maryknoll, N.Y.: Orbis, 1982.

BOFF, Leonardo. *Jesus Christ Liberator - A Critical Christology for Our Time.* Maryknoll, N.Y.: Orbis, 1978.

BOFF, Leonardo. *Way of the Cross - Way of Justice.* Maryknoll, N.Y.: Orbis, 1980.

BOFF, Leonardo. *El rostro materno de Dios.* Madrid: Ed. Paulinas, 1980.

BOFF, Leonardo and Clodovis. *Libertad y Liberación.* Salamanca: Ed. Sígueme, 1982.

BORNKAMM, Günther. *Jesus of Nazareth.* New York: Harper & Row, 1960.

BOSCH, David. The Kingdom of God and the Kingdoms of this World, in *Journal of Theology for Southern Africa*, 1979.

BOSCH, David. *Witness to the World. The Christian Mission in Theological Perspective.* Atlanta: John Knox Press, 1980.

BOYD, Robin H.S. *India and the Latin Captivity of the Church: The Cultural Context of the Gospel.* London and New York: Cambridge University Press, 1974.

BRAATEN, Carl E. *Eschatology and Ethics - Essays on the Theology and Ethics of the Kingdom of God*. Minneapolis: Augsburg, 1974.

BRAATEN, Carl E. *The Flaming Center*. Philadelphia: Fortress Press, 1977.

BRIA, Ion. *Autre visage de l'Orthodoxie. Eglise de Roumanie*. Geneva: Ed. du Centre Orthodoxe, 1981.

BRIA, Ion, ed. *Jesus Christ, the Life of the World*. Geneva: WCC, 1982.

BRIGHT, John. *The Kingdom of God*. Nashville: Abindgon Press, 1953.

BROWN, R. *Mary in the New Testament*. Philadelphia: Fortress Press, 1978.

BROWN, Robert McAfee. *Theology in a New Key*. Philadelphia: Westminster, 1978.

BROWN, Robert McAfee. *Makers of Contemporary Theology*. Atlanta: John Knox Press, 1981.

BUBER, Martin. *Kingship of God*. Engl.trans. New York: Harper & Row, 1967.

BÜHLMANN, Walbert. *The Search for God: An Encounter with the People and Religions of Asia*. Maryknoll, N.Y.: Orbis, 1980.

BURCHARD, Christoph. Jesus für die Welt - über das Verhältnis von Reich Gottes und Mission, in *Fides Pro Mundi Vita: Festschrift für Hans-Werner Gensichen zum 65. Geburtstag*, hrsg. von Theo Sundermeier. Gütersloh: Verlagshaus Gerd Mohn, 1980.

CAMPS, Arnulf. *Partners in Dialogue: Christianity and Other World Religions*. Maryknoll, N.Y.: Orbis, 1983.

CELAM. Latin American Episcopal Council; Second General Conference of Latin American Bishops, Medellín 1968. *The Church in the Present-Day Transformation of Latin America in the Light of the Council*. 2 Vols. Bogotá: CELAM, 1970.

CELAM. *Puebla: Evangelization at Present and in the Future of Latin America*. Conclusions, III Gen.Conf.L.A.Bishops. Washington D.C.: National Conference of Catholic Bishops, 1979.

Christian Conference of Asia Fifth Assembly, 6-12 June, 1973, Singapore. Bangkok: CCA, 1973.

COFFELE, Gianfranco. *Johannes Christian Hoekendijk. Da Teologia Missione ad una Teologia Missionaria*. Rome: Università Gregoriana Editrice, 1976.

COMBLIN, Joseph. *Teología de la misión (The Meaning of Mission)*. Maryknoll, N.Y.: Orbis, 1977.

CONE, Cecil. *The Identity Crisis in Black Theology*. Nashville: AMEC, 1975.

334

Contacts. Revue française de l'Orthodoxie. XIX Année, No. 57, 1er Trimestre, Paris, 1967.

Contacts. Revue française de l'Orthodoxie. XXVI Année, No. 85, 1er Trimestre, Paris, 1974.

Contacts. Revue française de l'Orthodoxie. XXVII Année, No. 92, 4ème Trimestre, Paris, 1975.

COSTA DE BEAUREGARD, M.A., BRIA, Ion and FOUCAULD, Théologue de. *L'Orthodoxie Hier, Demain.* Paris: Buchet/Chastel, 1979.

COSTAS, Orlando E. *Theology of the Crossroads in Contemporary Latin America: Missiology in Mainline Protestantism.* Amsterdam: Editions Rodopi, 1969-1974.

COSTAS, Orlando E., ed. *Hacia una Teología de la Evangelización.* Buenos Aires: La Aurora, 1973 (Spanish). Introduction by O.E. Costas and chapters VIII by Juan Stam and IX-XI by O.E. Costas. Also chapter VII by Ricardo Foulkes B.

COSTAS, Orlando E. *The Church and Its Mission: A Shattering Critique from the Third World.* Wheaton, Illinois: Tyndale House, 1974.

COSTAS, Orlando E. *The New Face of Evangelicalism: A Symposium on the Lausanne Covenant,* ed. by René Padilla. London: Hodder & Stoughton and Downers Grove, Illinois: Intervarsity Press, 1976.

COSTAS, Orlando E., JACOBS, Donald B., et.al. Conversion and Culture, in *Gospel in Context,* Vol. 1, No. 3, 1978, pp. 4-40.

COSTAS, Orlando E. *Integrity of Mission.* San Francisco: Harper, 1979. Spanish Edition: *Compromiso y Misión.* Miami: Caribe, 1979.

COSTAS, Orlando E. *Christ Outside the Gate.* Maryknoll, N.Y.: Orbis, 1982.

COSTELLO, Gerald M. *Mission to Latin America: The Successes and Failures of Twentieth Century Crusade.* Maryknoll, N.Y.: Orbis, 1979.

CRAGG, Kenneth. *The Christian and Other Religions.* London/Oxford: Mowbrays, 1977.

Cruz y Resurrección. Iglesia Nueva, Mexico: Centro de Reflexión Teológica, 1978.

Cuadernos de Teología. Quehacer teológico en el ISEDET. Vol. VI, No. 2, Buenos Aires, 1983.

CWME/WCC. *Your Kingdom Come - Mission Perspectives.* Report on the World Conference on Mission and Evangelism, Geneva: WCC, 1980.

Das Missionarische Wort. Juli-August 1971, Jahrgang 24, Berlin: Christlicher Zeitschriftenverlag.

DAYTON, Donald W. *Discovering an Evangelical Heritage*. New York: Harper & Row, 1976.

DAYTON, Edward R. *That Everyone May Hear*. Monrovia: Missions Advanced Research and Communication Center, 1979.

DOUGLAS, J.D., ed. *Let the Earth Hear His Voice*. (On the Lausanne Congress, for consultation) Minneapolis: World Wide Publications, 1975.

DUNN, Edmond J. *Missionary Theology*. Lanham: University Press of America Inc., 1980.

DUNN, James D.G. *Unity and Diversity in the New Testament - An Inquiry into the Character of Earliest Christianity*. Philadelphia: Westminster, 1977.

DUQUE, José, ed. *La Tradición Protestante en la Teología Latinoamericana*. San José, Costa Rica: DEI, 1983.

DUSSEL, Enrique. *History and the Theology of Liberation*. Maryknoll, N.Y.: Orbis, 1976.

ECHEGARAY, Hugo. *La Práctica de Jesús*. Salamanca: Ed. Sígueme, 1982.

ELLACURIA, Ignacio. *Freedom Made Flesh. The Mission of Christ and His Church*. Maryknoll, N.Y.: Orbis, 1976.

ELLIOTT, Charles. *Patterns of Poverty in the Third World*. New York: Praeger, 1975.

ELLUL, Jacques. *False Presence of the Kingdom*. New York: Seabury Press, 1963.

ESCOBAR, Samuel and DRIVER, John. *Christian Mission and Social Justice*. Scottdale, Pennsylvania: Herald Press, 1978.

Evangelical Review of Theology. Vol. 5, No. 1, April 1981. World Evangelical Fellowship.

Evangelisches Missionswerk, Informationen Nr. 21. Hamburg, 18 February, 1981.

Evangelism and Social Responsibility. Exeter, U.K.: Paternoster Press Ltd., 1982.

Evangelization in the Modern World. Evangelii Nuntiandi, 8 December, 1975, Washington, D.C.: U.S. Catholic Conference, 1976.

FABELLA, Virginia, ed. *Asia's Struggle for Full Humanity*. Maryknoll, N.Y.: Orbis, 1980.

FACKRE, Gabriel. *Do and Tell: Engagement Evangelism in the 1970s*. Grand Rapids: Eerdmans, 1973.

FACKRE, Gabriel. *Word in Deed: Theological Themes on Evangelism*. Grand Rapids: Eerdmans, 1975.

FACKRE, Cabriel. *The Christian Story*. Grand Rapids: Eerdmans, 1978.

FERRE, Nels F.S. *The Atonement and Mission*. London Missionary Society, 1960.

FERRE, Nels F.S. *The Finality of Faith, and Christianity among the World Religions*. New York: Harper & Row, 1963.

Fides Pro Mundi Vita. Gütersloh: Verlagshaus Gerd Mohn, 1980.

FLANAGAN, Padraig, ed. *A New Missionary Era*. Maryknoll, N.Y.: Orbis, 1982.

FORD, Leighton. *Good News is for Sharing*. Elgin, Ill.: D.C. Cook, 1977.

FREIRE, Paulo. *Pedagogy of the Oppressed*. New York: Herder & Herder, 1970.

GALILEO, Segundo. *El Sentido del Pobre*. Bogotá: Sudamerican, 1978.

GALILEO, Segundo. *Religiosidad Popular y Pastoral*. Madrid: Cristiandad, 1979.

GENSICHEN, H.-W. *Glaube für die Welt*. Gütersloh: Verlagshaus Gerd Mohn, 1971.

GENSICHEN, H.-W. Evangelium und Kultur. Neue Variationen über ein altes Thema, in *ZMiss*, 1978, pp. 197-214.

GILL, David, ed. *Gathered for Life*. Geneva: WCC, 1983

GLASSER, Arthur. *Contemporary Theologies of Mission*. Grand Rapids: Baker Book, 1983.

GLAZIK, Josef. *Mission - der stets grössere Auftrag*. Aachen: Mission Aktuell Verlag, 1979.

GONZALEZ-RUIZ, José María. *The New Creation: Marxist and Christian*. Maryknoll, N.Y.: Orbis, 1976.

337

GOTTWALD, Norman K. *The Tribes of Jahwe*. Maryknoll, N.Y.: Orbis, 1979.

GREEN, Michael. *Evangelism in the Early Church*. Grand Rapids: Eerdmans, 1975.

GREEN, Michael. *First Things Last: Whatever Happened to Evangelism?* Nashville: Discipleship Resources, 1979. (Also published with the title: *Evangelism Then and Now*).

GREGORIOS, Paulos. *The Human Presence*. Geneva: WCC, 1978.

GUTIERREZ, Gustavo. *A Theology of Liberation*. Maryknoll, N.Y.: Orbis, 1971.

GUTIERREZ, Gustavo. *Freedom and Salvation: A Political Problem. Liberation and Change*. Atlanta: John Knox Press.

GUTIERREZ, Gustavo. *Análisis Teológico de las líneas pastorales de la Iglesia en América Latina*. (Part 2, photocopies)

GUTIERREZ, Gustavo. *Beber en su propio pozo*. Lima: CEO, 1983.

GUTIERREZ, Gustavo. *The Power of the Poor in History*. Maryknoll, N.Y.: Orbis, 1983.

HAHN, Ferdinand. *Mission in the New Testament*. Trans. F. Clarke. Naperville, Ill.: A.R. Alleson, 1965.

HAHN, Ferdinand. *The Titles of Jesus in Christology*. London: Lutterworth Library, 1969.

HAHN, Ferdinand. Der Sendungsauftrag des Auferstandenen: Matthäus 28,16-20, in *Fides Pro Mundi Vita*. Gütersloh: Verlagshaus Gerd Mohn, 1980.

HAMID, Idris. *Out of the Depths*. Trinidad: St. Andrew's Theological College, 1977.

HANKS, Tomas. *Opresión, Pobreza y Liberación. Reflexiones Bíblicas*. Colección CELEP. San José, Costa Rica: Ed. Caribe, 1982.

HARING, Bernard. *Evangelization Today*. Notre Dame, Indiana: Fides, 1974.

HASTINGS, Adrian. *A History of African Christianity*. Cambridge: Cambridge University Press, 1979.

HENRY, Carl F.H. and MOONEYHAM, W. Stanley, eds. *One Race, One Gospel, One Task*. World Congress of Evangelism, Berlin, 1966. 2 Vols. Minneapolis: World Wide Publications, 1967.

HENRY, Carl F.H. *Evangelicals in Search of Identity*. Waco: Word, 1976.

HEUVEL, Albert v.d. *Shalom and Combat*. Geneva: WCC, 1979.

HICK, John, ed. *Truth and Dialogue. The Relationship between World Religions*. London: Sheldon Press, 1974.

HOEKSTRA, Harvey T. *The World Council of Churches and the Demise of Evangelism.* Wheaton, Illinois: Tyndale House, 1979.

HOLLENWEGER, Walter J. *Evangelism Today. Good News or Bone of Contention.* Belfast: Christian Journals, 1976.

HOWARD, David. *The Great Commission for Today.* Downers Grove, Illinois: Intervarsity Press, 1976.

HUNTER, George. *The Contagious Congregation.* Nashville: Abingdon Press, 1979.

Idéologies de libération et message du salut. (off-print) Strasbourg, France: Cerdic Publications, 1973.

Incarnational Evangelism. Lester Comee and Darrell Guides, eds. Colorado Springs: Young Life International, 1981.

ISEDET. *Los Pobres.* Buenos Aires: La Aurora, 1978.

JOHNSON, David Enderton, gen.ed. *Uppsala to Nairobi: 1968-1975.* Report of the Central Committee to the Fifth Assembly of the World Council of Churches. New York: Friendship Press and London: SPCK, 1975.

JOHNSTON, Arthur P. *World Evangelism and the Word of God.* Minneapolis: Bethany Fellowship, 1974.

JOHNSTON, Arthur P. *The Battle for World Evangelism.* Wheaton, Illinois: Tyndale House, 1978.

KATO, Byang. *Theological Pitfalls in Africa.* Kisumu, Kenya: Evangelical Publishing House, 1975.

KEE, Alestair, ed. *A Reader in Political Theology.* Philadelphia: Westminster, 1975.

KIRK, Andrew. *Theology Encounters Revolution.* Downers Grove, Illinois: Intervarsity Press, 1980.

KIRSCH, Paul J. *We Christians and Jews.* Philadelphia: Fortress Press, 1975.

KITTEL, G., ed. *Theological Dictionary of the New Testament.* Grand Rapids: Eerdmans, 1964 (1933). Articles on kingdom, etc. (G.v.Rad, K.G. Kuhn and K.L. Schmidt).

KOYAMA, Kosuke. *Waterbuffalo Theology.* Maryknoll, N.Y.: Orbis, 1974.

KOYAMA, Kosuke. *No Handle on the Cross.* Maryknoll, N.Y.: Orbis, 1977.

KRAFT, Charles. *Christianity in Culture*. Maryknoll, N.Y.: Orbis, 1980.

KRAFT, Charles. *Communication Theory for Christian Witness*. Nashville: Abingdon Press, 1983.

KRASS, Alfred. *Five Lanterns at Sundown*. Grand Rapids: Eerdmans, 1978.

KÜNG, Hans. *The Church*. New York: Sheed & Ward, 1967.

KÜNG, Hans. *On Being Christian*. Garden City, N.Y.: Doubleday, 1976.

LADD, G.E. *Jesus and the Kingdom. The Eschatology of Biblical Realism*. London: SPCK, 1966.

LAUSANNE COMMITTEE FOR WORLD EVANGELIZATION.
The Pasadena Consultation - Homogeneous Unit Principle. Lausanne Occasional Papers, No. 1. Wheaton, Illinois: Lausanne Committee for World Evangelization, 1978a.

The Willowbank Report - Gospel and Culture. Lausanne Occasional Papers, No. 2. Wheaton, Illinois: Lausanne Committee for World Evangelization, 1978b.

The Lausanne Covenant - An Exposition and Commentary by John Stott. Lausanne Occasional Papers, No. 3. Wheaton, Illinois, Lausanne Committee for World Evangelization, 1978c.

The Glen Eyrie Report - Muslim Evangelization. Lausanne Occasional Papers, No. 4. Wheaton, Illinois: Lausanne Committee for World Evangelization, 1978d.

Christian Witness to Refugees. Lausanne Occasional Papers, No. 5. Wheaton, Illinois: Lausanne Committee for World Evangelization, 1980a.

Christian Witness to the Chinese People. Lausanne Occasional Papers, No. 6. Wheaton, Illinois: Lausanne Committee for World Evangelization, 1980b.

Christian Witness to the Jewish People. Lausanne Occasional Papers, No. 7. Wheaton, Illinois: Lausanne Committee for World Evangelization, 1980c.

Christian Witness to Secularized People. Lausanne Occasional Papers, No. 8. Wheaton, Illinois: Lausanne Committee for World Evangelization, 1980d.

Christian Witness to Large Cities. Lausanne Occasional Papers, No. 9. Wheaton, Illinois: Lausanne Committee for World Evangelization, 1980e.

Christian Witness to Nominal Christians among Roman Catholics. Lausanne Occasional Papers, No. 10. Wheaton, Illinois: Lausanne Committee for World Evangelization, 1980f.

Christian Witness to New Religious Movements. Lausanne Occasional Papers, No. 11. Wheaton, Illinois: Lausanne Committee for World Evangelization, 1980g.

Christian Witness to Marxists. Lausanne Occasional Papers, No. 12. Wheaton, Illinois: Lausanne Committee for World Evangelization, 1980h.

The Thailand Statement 1980. *International Bulletin of Missionary Research 5*. No. 1 (January), 29-31, 1981a.

LAUSANNE COMMITTEE FOR WORLD EVANGELIZATION (cont'd)
How Shall They Hear? Proceedings and Report from the Consultation on World Evangelization, Pattaya, Thailand, 1980. Minneapolis: World Wide Publications, 1981b.

LAZARETH, William H., ed. *The Lord of Life*. Geneva: WCC, 1983.

LEFEVER, Ernest W. *Amsterdam to Nairobi: The World Council of Churches and the Third World*. Washington, D.C.: Ethics and Public Policy Center, Georgetown University, 1979.

Letter to the Churches. Wheaton, Illinois: World Evangelical Fellowship, June 1983.

MARGULL, Hans Jochen. *Hope in Action: The Church's Task in the World*. Trans. by Eugene Peters. Philadelphia: Muhlenberg Press, 1962.

MARGULL, Hans Jochen and FREYTAG, Justus. *Keine Einbahnstrassen*. Stuttgart: Evang. Missionsverlag, 1973.

Materialdienst der Ökumenischen Centrale. No. 2. Frankfurt/Main, February 1980.

MBITI, John. *New Testament Eschatology in an African Background*. A study of the encounter between New Testament theology and African traditional concepts. London: Oxford University Press, 1971.

McGAVRAN, Donald A., ed. *The Conciliar-Evangelical Debate: The Crucial Documents 1964-1976*. Pasadena, California: William Carey Library, 1977.

MESSER, Donald E. *Christian Ethics and Political Action*. Valley Forge: Judson Press, 1984.

MESTERS, Carlos. *Eden: Golden Age or Road to Action*. Maryknoll, N.Y.: Orbis, 1974.

MIGUEZ BONINO, José. *Doing Theology in a Revolutionary Situation*. Philadelphia: Fortress Press, 1975.

MIGUEZ BONINO, José. *Christians and Marxists: The Mutual Challenge to Revolution*. Grand Rapids: Eerdmans, 1976.

MIGUEZ BONINO, José. *Revolutionary Theology Comes of Age*. London: SPCK, 1975.

MINEAR, Paul S. *The Kingdom and the Power*. Philadelphia: Westminster, 1950.

MINEAR, Paul S. Vocation of the Church: Some Exegetical Clues. *Missiology*, Vol. 5, 1977, pp 13-37.

MIRANDA, José P. *Communism in the Bible*. Maryknoll, N.Y.: Orbis, 1981.

MIRANDA, José P. *El Ser y el Mesías*. Salamanca: Ed. Sígueme, 1973.

MIRANDA, José P. *Marx and the Bible. A Critique of the Philosophy of Oppression*. London: SCM, 1977. (Trans. by J. Eagleson. *Marx y la Biblia. Crítica a la Filosofía de Opresión*. Salamanca: Ed. Sígueme, 1971)

Missio Dei. H.H. Rosin. Leiden: Interuniversity Institute for Missiological and Ecumenical Research, 1972.

MOLTMANN, Jürgen. *Theology of Hope ... a Christian Eschatology*. New York: Harper & Row, 1967.

MOLTMANN, Jürgen. *The Crucified God: The Cross of Christ as the Foundation and Criticism of Christian Theology*. Trans. by R.A. Wilson and John Bowden. New York: Harper & Row, 1974.

MOLTMANN, Jürgen. *The Church in the Power of the Spirit - A Contribution to Messianic Ecclesiology*. London: SCM, 1975.

MOLTMANN, Jürgen. *The Trinity and the Kingdom - The Doctrine of God*. San Francisco: Harper & Row, 1981.

Monthly Letter on Evangelism. Geneva: WCC, Commission on World Mission and Evangelism, July 1974.

MOUW, Richard J. *Called to Holy Worldliness*. Philadelphia: Fortress Press, 1980.

MÜLLER-FAHRENHOLZ, Geiko. *Heilsgeschichte zwischen Ideologie und Prophetie*. Freiburg: Herder, 1974.

NACPIL, Emerito. *The Human and the Holy: Asian Perspectives in Christian Theology*. Maryknoll, N.Y.: Orbis, 1980.

NEILL, Stephen. *Salvation Tomorrow: The Originality of Jesus Christ and the World's Religions*. New York: Abingdon, 1976.

NEWBIGIN, Lesslie. *One Body, One Gospel, One World: The Christian Mission Today*. London: IMC, 1958.

NEWBIGIN, Lesslie. *A Faith for This One World?* New York: Harper & Brothers, 1961.

NEWBIGIN, Lesslie. *Trinitarian Faith and Today's Mission*. Richmond, Virginia: John Knox Press, 1964.

NEWBIGIN, Lesslie. *The Finality of Christ*. London: SCM, 1969.

NEWBIGIN, Lesslie. *The Open Secret. Sketches for a Missionary Theology*. London: SPCK and Grand Rapids: Eerdmans, 1978.

NEWBIGIN, Lesslie. Cross-currents in Ecumenical and Evangelical Understandings of Mission, *International Bulletin of Missionary Research*, Vol. 6, No. 4. Overseas Ministries Study Center, Ventnor, N.J., October 1982.

NEWBIGIN, Lesslie. *The Other Side of 1984*. Geneva: WCC, 1983.

342

NIDA, Eugene A. and REYBURN, William. *Meaning Across Cultures*. Maryknoll, N.Y.: Orbis, 1981.

NIEBUHR, H.R. *Christ and Culture*. New York: Harper & Row, 1956.

NIEBUHR, H.R. *The Kingdom of God in America*. New York: Harper & Row, 1959.

NILES, D. Preman and THOMAS, T.K., eds. *Witnessing to the Kingdom*. Singapore: Christian Conference of Asia, 1979.

Occasional Essays. Year X, No. 1. Costa Rica: CELEP, June 1983.

Orthodox Contributions to Nairobi. Geneva: WCC, 1975.

ORTIZ, Juan Carlos. *Call to Discipleship*. South Plainfield, N.J.: Bridge Publishers, 1975.

OSTHATHIOS, Geevarghese Mar. *Theology of a Classless Society*. Maryknoll, N.Y.: Orbis, 1980.

PADILLA, C. René. *El Reino de Dios y América Latina*. Buenos Aires: Casa Bautista, 1975.

PADILLA, C. René. *The New Face of Evangelicalism*. Downers Grove, Illinois: Intervarsity Press, 1976.

PANIKKAR, Raymond. *The Trinity and the Religious Experience of Man*. Maryknoll, N.Y.: Orbis, 1973.

PANNENBERG, Wolfhart. *Theology and the Kingdom of God*. Philadelphia: Westminster, 1977. (Spanish: Salamanca: Ed. Sigueme, 1974)

PATON, David M., ed. *Breaking Barriers: Nairobi 1975*. London: SPCK and Grand Rapids: Eerdmans, 1976.

PAUL VI. *Evangelii Nuntiandi: An Exhortation on the Evangelization of the World Today*. Separate edition, *On Evangelization in the Modern World*. Washington: U.S. Catholic Conference, n/d. Also in periodical publications, *The Catholic Mind* and *The Pope Speaks* (Vol. XXI, No. 1, January 1976).

PIXLEY, George V. *God's Kingdom. A Guide for Biblical Study*. Maryknoll, N.Y.: Orbis, 1981. (Trans. from Spanish, *Reino de Dios*, 1977)

POBEE, John, ed. *Religion in a Pluralistic Society*. Leiden: E.J. Brill, 1976.

POBEE, John. *Toward an African Theology*. Nashville: Abingdon Press, 1979.

343

POTTER, Philip. *Life in all its Fullness*. Geneva: WCC, 1981.

Pro Mundi Vita Bulletin. No. 85, Brussels, Belgium, April 1981.

QUEBEDEAUX, Richard. *The Young Evangelicals: Revolution in Orthodoxy*. New York: Harper & Row, 1974.

Reino de Deus. Rio de Janeiro: CEI Suplemento 6, December 1973.

Resource Sharing System. Progress Reports, Decisions and Recommendations in the period July 1982–August 1983. Geneva: WCC.

ROSSEL, Jacques. *Mission in a Dynamic Society*. London: SCM, 1968.

ROTTENBERG, Isaac C. *The Promise and the Presence - Toward a Theology of the Kingdom of God*. Grand Rapids: Eerdmans, 1980.

RUNYON, Theodore, ed. *Sanctification and Liberation*. Nashville: Abingdon Press, 1981.

RUSSELL, Letty M. *Human Liberation in a Feminist Perspective*. Philadelphia: Westminster, 1974.

SABEV, Todor, ed. *The Sofia Consultation*. Geneva: WCC, 1982.

SAMARTHA, S.J., ed. *Living Faiths and the Ecumenical Movement*. Geneva: WCC, 1971.

SAMARTHA, S.J. and TAYLOR, J.B., eds. *Christian-Muslim Dialogue*. Geneva: WCC, 1973.

SAMARTHA, S.J., ed. *Living Faiths and Ultimate Goals. A Continuing Dialogue*. Geneva: WCC, 1974.

SAMARTHA, S.J. *The Hindu Response to the Unbound Christ*. Madras: CLS, 1974.

SAMUEL, Vinay and SUGDEN, Chris. *Evangelism and the Poor*. Bangalore: Asian Trading Corporation, 1982.

SAMUEL, Vinay and SUGDEN, Chris, eds. *Sharing Jesus in the Two Thirds World*. Bangalore: Partnership in Mission, 1983.

SANTA ANA, Julio de. *Good News to the Poor*. Maryknoll, N.Y.: Orbis, 1977.

SCHEFFBUCH, Rolf. *Zur Sache: Weltmission*. Neuhausen/Stuttgart: Hänssler Verlag, 1974.

344

SCHERER, James A. *A Global Living Here and Now*. New York: Friendship Press, 1974.

SCHNACKENBURG, R. *Reino y Reinado de Dios - Estudio Bíblico Teológico*. Madrid: Fax, 1970.

SCOTT, Waldron. *Karl Barth's Theology of Mission*. Downers Grove, Illinois: Intervarsity Press, 1978.

SCOTT, Waldron. *Serving our Generation*. Colorado Springs: World Evangelical Fellowship, 1980.

SCOTT, Waldron. *Bring Forth Justice*. Grand Rapids: Eerdmans, 1980.

SEDOS. *Mission in Dialogue*. Proceedings from SEDOS meeting in Rome, 1982. Maryknoll, N.Y.: Orbis, 1982.

SEGUNDO, Juan Luis. *Acción Pastoral. Los Motivos Ocultos*. Buenos Aires: Búsqueda, 1972.

SEGUNDO, Juan Luis. *The Community Called Church*. Maryknoll, N.Y.: Orbis, 1973.

SEGUNDO, Juan Luis. *Our Idea of God*. Maryknoll, N.Y.: Orbis, 1973.

SEGUNDO, Juan Luis. *A Theology for Artisans of a New Humanity*. 5 Vols. Maryknoll, N.Y.: Orbis, 1974.

SEGUNDO, Juan Luis. *The Liberation of Theology*. Maryknoll, N.Y.: Orbis, 1976.

SEGUNDO, Juan Luis. *The Hidden Motives of Pastoral Action: Latin American Reflections*. Maryknoll, N.Y.: Orbis, 1978.

SENIOR, Donald C.P. and STUHLMUELLER, Carroll C.P. *The Biblical Foundations for Mission*. Maryknoll, N.Y.: Orbis, 1983.

SIDER, Ronald J. *Evangelism, Salvation and Social Justice*. Bramcote: Grove Books, 1977.

SIDER, Ronald J. *Rich Christians in an Age of Hunger: A Biblical Study*. Downers Grove, Illinois: Intervarsity Press, 1977.

SILVA HENRIQUEZ, Raul. *La Misión Social del Cristiano. Conflicto de Clases o Solidaridad Cristiana*. Santiago de Chile: Ed. Paulinas, 1973.

SMET, Robert. *Essai sur la pensée de Raymond Panikkar*. Louvain-la-Neuve: Centre d'histoire des religions, coll. Cerfaux-Lefort, 1981.

SNYDER, Howard A. *The Problem of Wine Skins: Church Structure in a Technological Age*. Downers Grove, Illinois: Intervarsity Press, 1976.

SOBRINO, Jon. *Christology at the Crossroads*. Maryknoll, N.Y.: Orbis, 1976.

SOBRINO, Jon. *Resurrección de la verdadera Iglesia*. Santander: Sol Terrae, 1981.

SONG, Choan Seng. *Christian Mission in Reconstruction - An Asian Analysis*. Maryknoll, N.Y.: Orbis, 1977.

SONG, Choan Seng. *Third-Eye Theology*. Maryknoll, N.Y.: Orbis, 1979.

SONG, Choan Seng. *The Tears of Lady Meng*. Geneva: WCC, 1980.

SONG, Choan Seng. *The Compassionate God*. Maryknoll, N.Y.: Orbis, 1982.

STENDAHL, Krister. *Paul among Jews and Gentiles*. Philadelphia: Fortress Press, 1976.

STOTT, John R.W. *Christian Mission in the Modern World*. London: Falcon, 1975

STOTT, John R.W. *The Lausanne Covenant: An Exposition and Commentary*. Minneapolis: World Wide Publications, 1975.

STOTT, John R.W. and COOTE, Robert, eds. *Gospel and Culture*. Pasadena, California: William Carey Library, 1979.

STRAELEN, Henry van. *Ouverture à l'autre: laquelle?* Paris: Beauchesne, 1982.

SUENENS, Leon Joseph. *A New Pentecost?* London: Darton, Longman & Todd, 1975.

TAMEZ, Elsa. *La Biblia de los Oprimidos*. San José, Costa Rica: DEI, 1979.

TAYLOR, John V. *The Go Between God. The Holy Spirit and the Christian Mission*. Philadelphia: Fortress Press, 1973.

Teología desde el Tercer Mundo. San José, Costa Rica: DEI, 1982.

THILS, Gustave. *Pivotal Positions on Evangelization and Salvation.* Louvain: International Centre for Studies in Religious Education, 1975.

THOMAS, M.M. *Salvation and Humanization*. Madras: CLS, 1970.

THOMAS, M.M. *Man and the Universe of Faiths. Inter-Religious Dialogue Series No. 7*. Madras: CLS, 1975.

Together. A Journal of World Vision International. No. 1, Monrovia, Oct.- Dec. 1983. (The Kingdom is Our Goal. William A. Dyrness.)

TORRES, Sergio and EAGLESON, John, eds. *Theology in the Americas*. Maryknoll, N.Y.: Orbis, 1976.

TORRES, Sergio and FABELLA, Virginia, eds. *The Emergent Gospel: Theology from the Underside of History*. Maryknoll, N.Y.: Orbis, 1978.

346

TORRES, Sergio and APPIAH-KUBI, Kofi, eds. *African Theology en Route*. Maryknoll, N.Y: Orbis, 1979.

TORRES, Sergio and EAGLESON, John, eds. *The Challenge of Basic Christian Communities*. Maryknoll, N.Y.: Orbis, 1981.

Toward a New Age in Mission. Editorial Committee, International Congress on Mission/TCO. Manila, 2-7 December, 1979.

TSETSIS, Georges. *Orthodox Thought*. Geneva: WCC, 1983.

Theological Students Fellowship Bulletin, Vol. 6, No. 4, March-April 1983. Madison: Intervarsity Christian Fellowship.

TUTU, Desmond M.B. *Versöhnung ist unteilbar. Interpretationen biblischer Texte zur Schwarzen Theologie*. Wuppertal: P. Hammer Verlag, 1977.

TUTU, Desmond M.B. *Hope and Suffering*. Cape Town: Blackshaws Ltd., 1983.

U.S. Catholic Missionary Association, Baltimore 1983. Mission Congress 1983. Mimeographic.

VERKUYL, Johannes. *Contemporary Missiology: An Introduction*. Trans. by Dale Cooper. Grand Rapids: Eerdmans, 1978.

VERSTRAELEN, F.J. *An African Church in Transition: From Missionary Dependence to Mutuality in Mission*. Leiden: Interuniversity Institute for Missiological and Ecumenical Research, 1975.

VICEDOM, G.F. *The Challenge of the World Religions*. Philadelphia: Fortress Press, 1963.

VICEDOM, G.F. *The Mission of God*. Trans. by Gilbert A. Thiele and Dennis Hilgendors. St. Louis: Concordia, 1965.

Vida y Pensamiento. Vol. 1, No. 1. San José: Seminario Bíblico, 1981.

VISSER'T HOOFT, W.A. *Memoirs*. London: SCM and Philadelphia: Westminster, 1963.

WAGNER, C. Peter. *Our Kind of People. The Ethical Dimension of Church Growth in America*. Atlanta: John Knox Press, 1979.

WALKER, Alan. *The New Evangelism*. Nashville: Abingdon Press, 1975.

WALLIS, Jim. *Agenda for Biblical People*. New York: Harper & Row, 1976.

WALLIS, Jim. *The Call to Conversion*. New York: Harper & Row, 1981.

WARREN, Max A.C. *Crowded Canvas: Some Experience of a Lifetime*. London: Hodder & Stoughton, 1974.

WARREN, Max A.C. *I Believe in the Great Commission*. Grand Rapids: Eerdmans, 1976.

WINTER, Ralph and HOWTHORNE, Stephen. *Perspectives on the World Christian Movement: A Reader*. Pasadena, California: William Carey Library, 1981.

WCC. *From Mexico City to Bangkok*. Report of the Commission on World Mission and Evangelism, 1963-1972. Geneva: WCC, 1972.

WCC. *Tell Out, Tell Out My Glory*. Risk Vol. 9, No. 3, Geneva: WCC, 1973.

WCC. *Bangkok Assembly 1973*. Minutes and Report of the Assembly of the Commission on World Mission and Evangelism of the World Council of Churches, December 31, 1972 and January 9-12, 1973. Geneva: WCC, 1973.

WCC. *Jesus Christ Frees and Unites*. Section dossiers for the Fifth Assembly of the WCC. Geneva: WCC, n.d.

WCC. *Dialogue in Community*. Statement and Reports of a Theological Consultation, Chiang Mai, Thailand, April 1977. Geneva: WCC, 1977.

WCC. *The Christian Community in Mission...in a near and global context*. A European Seminar on Education for Mission, Aarhus, Denmark, May 1977. Geneva: WCC, 1978.

WCC. Mission and Evangelism: An Ecumenical Affirmation. *International Review of Mission*, October 1982.

WCC. *Sharing One Bread, Sharing One Mission - The Eucharist as Missionary Event*. Geneva: WCC, 1983.

WCC. *Gathered for Life*. Official Report, VI Assembly, Vancouver, Canada, 24 July-10 August, 1983. Ed. by David Gill. Grand Rapids: Eerdmans and Geneva: WCC, 1983.

YODER, John Howard. *The Politics of Jesus*. Grand Rapids: Eerdmans, 1972.